McDOUGAL LITTELL

# World
# Geography

Namche Bazaar, Nepal

Leaning tower, Pisa, Italy

Masai warriors, Kenya

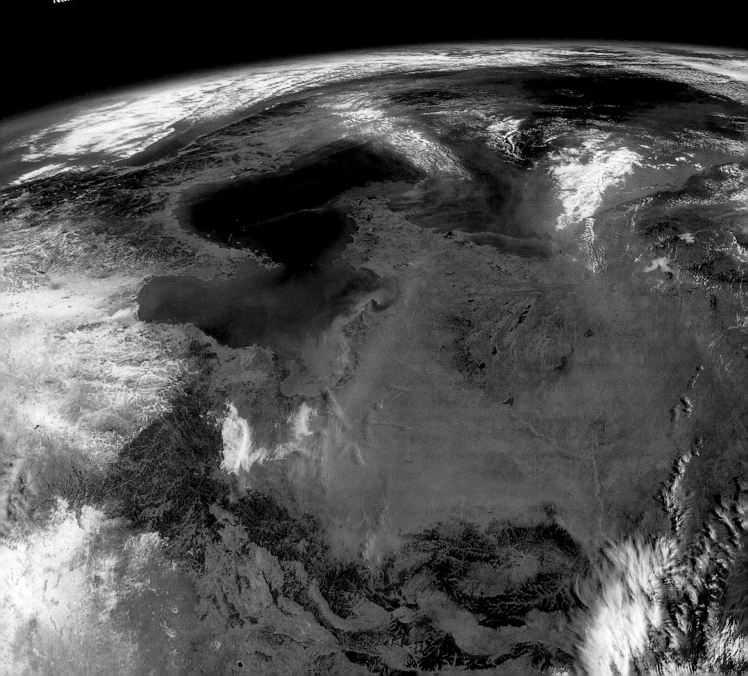

Volcano, Honolulu, Hawaii

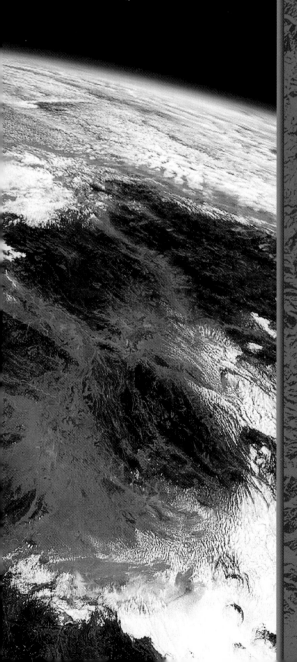

# World Geography

Daniel D. Arreola

Marci Smith Deal

James F. Petersen

Rickie Sanders

McDougal Littell

Evanston, Illinois • Boston • Dallas

Maps on pages A1–A25, 64, 102–115, 131, 179, 190–199, 206, 248, 262–271, 281, 322, 336–343, 357, 391, 402–413, 419, 464, 478–485, 494, 528, 542–549, 559, 596, 610–617, 624, 664, 678–687, 693, 733 © Rand McNally & Company. All rights reserved.

Acknowledgments begin on page R66.

ISBN 0-618-08721-4

Printed in the United States of America

2 3 4 5 6 7 8 9 – QVK – 07 06 05 04 03 02

**Daniel D. Arreola** is Professor of Geography and an affiliate faculty member of the Center for Latin American Studies at Arizona State University. He has taught world regional geography for more than a decade at universities in Arizona and Texas. Dr. Arreola has published extensively on topics relating to the cultural geography of the Mexican-American borderlands. He is co-author of *The Mexican Border Cities: Landscape Anatomy and Place Personality* and author of *Tejano South Texas: A Mexican American Cultural Province.*

**Marci Smith Deal** is the K-12 Social Studies Curriculum Coordinator for Hurst-Euless-Bedford Independent School District in Texas. She received the 2000 Distinguished Geographer Award for the State of Texas, and was one of the honorees of the 2001 National Council for Geographic Education Distinguished Teacher Award. She has served as president for the Texas Council for Social Studies Supervisors and as vice-president for the Texas Council for Social Studies. She currently serves as a teacher consultant for National Geographic Society.

**James F. Petersen** is Professor of Geography at Southwest Texas State University. He served as president of the National Council for Geographic Education in 2000. As a charter member of the National Geographic Society's Alliance, Dr. Petersen has directed summer institutes and national conferences for teachers and educational organizations. He is the author of many articles on geographic education, as well as media/book reviews, textbooks, and curricular materials.

**Rickie Sanders** is Professor and Chair of Geography/Urban Studies at Temple University. She recently served on the team that directed the National Science Foundation/National Council for Geographic Education's "Finding A Way" project, which produced learning modules for integrating gender into geography classrooms. Dr. Sanders has received numerous awards for teaching, including the NCGE Distinguished Teaching Award and the Temple University Distinguished Teaching Award. She has numerous publications and is co-author of *Growing Up in America: An Atlas of Youth in the U.S.A.*

# Consultants and Reviewers

## Content Consultants

**C. Cindy Fan**
Department of Geography
UCLA
Los Angeles, California

**Howard Johnson**
Department of Physical and Earth
    Sciences
Jacksonville State University
Jacksonville, Alabama

**Cheryl Johnson-Odim**
Liberal Education Division
Columbia College
Chicago, Illinois

**Charles Kovacik**
Department of Geography
University of South Carolina
Columbia, South Carolina

**Barbara McDade**
Department of Geography
University of Florida
Gainesville, Florida

**Inés Miyares**
Department of Geography
Hunter College
New York City, New York

**Joseph Stoltman**
Department of Geography
Western Michigan University
Kalamazoo, Michigan

**Donald Zeigler**
Department of Political Science and
    Geography
Old Dominion University
Norfolk, Virginia

## Multicultural Advisory Board

**Betty Dean**
Social Studies Consultant
Pearland, Texas

**C. Cindy Fan**
Department of Geography
UCLA
Los Angeles, California

**Cheryl Johnson-Odim**
Liberal Education Division
Columbia College
Chicago, Illinois

**Barbara McDade**
Department of Geography
University of Florida
Gainesville, Florida

**Inés Miyares**
Department of Geography
Hunter College
New York City, New York

**Pat Payne**
Office of Multicultural Education
Indianapolis Public Schools
Indianapolis, Indiana

**Betto Ramirez**
Region One Education Service
    Center
Edinburg, Texas

**Jon Reyhner**
Department of Education
Northern Arizona University
Flagstaff, Arizona

## Teacher Consultants
*The following educators reviewed manuscript or wrote classroom activities.*

**Deborah Althouse**
Thomas J. Anderson High School
Southgate, Michigan

**Jamie Berlin**
South High School
Sheboygan, Wisconsin

**Heather Berry**
Hazelwood East High School
St. Louis, Missouri

**Jewel Berryman**
Kashmere High School
Houston, Texas

**Deborah Bittner**
Sandra Day O'Connor High School
Helotes, Texas

**Dora Bradley**
Lakewood Middle School
North Little Rock, Arkansas

**Denise Butler**
Hillcrest High School
Dallas, Texas

**Deborah Canales**
Austin High School
Houston, Texas

**Fred Cibik**
Brown Deer High School
Brown Deer, Wisconsin

**Jim Curtis**
Antioch High School
Antioch, Illinois

**Sam Eigel**
Cody High School
Detroit, Michigan

**Jan Ellersieck**
Ft. Zummalt South High School
St. Peters, Missouri

**Thomas Figurski**
Thomas J. Anderson High School
Southgate, Michigan

**Karen Fletcher**
Haltom High School
Haltom City, Texas

**Kathy Gilbert**
Mukwonago High School
Mukwonago, Wisconsin

**Manuel Gomez**
McAllen Memorial High School
McAllen, Texas

**Richard Goodwin**
Yvonne A. Ewell Township Center
Dallas, Texas

**Craig Grace**
Lanier High School
West Austin, Texas

**David Haas**
Waukegan High School
Waukegan, Illinois

**Britin Hanson**
Granite Hills High School
El Cajon, California

**William Hoffman**
Capistrano Valley High School
Mission Viejo, California

**Alan Hunt**
Coronado High School
El Paso, Texas

**Amy Kiehl**
Milwaukee Trade & Technical High
    School
Milwaukee, Wisconsin

**Cliff Kinder**
Bowie High School
Arlington, Texas

**Korri Kinney**
Meridian High School
Meridian, Idaho

**Sherry Kusenberger**
MacArthur High School
San Antonio, Texas

**Rick Looze**
Ft. Atkinson High School
Ft. Atkinson, Wisconsin

**Jerome Love**
Beaumont High School
St. Louis, Missouri

**Kara Lukens**
Dakota High School
Macomb, Michigan

**Matt Lyons**
Hastings Ninth Grade Center
Houston, Texas

**Gene Mahurin**
Western Hills High School
Ft. Worth, Texas

**Joy McKee**
Lamar High School
Arlington, Texas

**Patricia Medina**
Ray High School
Corpus Christi, Texas

**Tim Murray**
Plano Senior High School
Plano, Texas

**Joseph Naumann**
McCluer North High School
Florissant, Missouri

**Phillip Owens**
Ball High School
Galveston, Texas

**Robert Parker**
St. Margaret's High School
San Juan Capistrano, California

**Cathy Probst**
Nathan Hale High School
West Allis, Wisconsin

**Dan Richardson**
East Troy High School
East Troy, Illinois

**Robert Schutt**
Detroit High School for the Fine and
    Performing Arts
Detroit, Michigan

**Martha B. Sharma**
National Cathedral School
Washington, D.C.

**Brenda Smith**
Social Studies Instructional
    Supervisor
Colorado Springs School District #11
Colorado Springs, Colorado

**Jody Smothers-Marcello**
Sitka School District
Sitka, Alaska

**Linda Tillis**
South Oak Cliff High School
Dallas, Texas

**Mark Van Hecke**
Anchor Bay High School
New Baltimore, Michigan

**Glenn Watt**
Grayslake High School
Grayslake, Illinois

**Alice White**
Bryan Adams High School
Dallas, Texas

**Sarah White**
Dakota High School
Macomb, Michigan

**Tom Wissink**
Oshkosh West High School
Oshkosh, Wisconsin

**Anne Woods**
Orchard Farms High School
St. Charles, Missouri

**Tom Wurst**
Langham Creek High School
Houston, Texas

Volcano in
Costa Rica (p. 2)

Nanjing Road,
Shanghai, China
(p. 81)

For more information on the basics of geography . . .

CLASSZONE.COM

# The United States and Canada

**Mesa Verde National Park, Colorado** (p. 135)

**Parliament guards, Ottawa, Ontario** (p. 158)

For more information on the United States and Canada . . .

CLASSZONE.COM

# Unit 3 · Latin America

**Chacobo Indians on the Amazon River, Bolivia** (p. 186)

**São Paulo, Brazil** (p. 251)

**For more information on Latin America . . .**

CLASSZONE.COM

# Europe

Unit 4

The Eiffel Tower,
Paris, France
(p. 259)

The Wetterhorn,
Switzerland
(p. 310)

**For more information on Europe . . .**

CLASSZONE.COM

# Russia and the Republics

For more information on Russia and the Republics . . .

**Frozen Lake
Baikal, Russia**
(p. 350)

**St. Basil's
Cathedral,
Moscow,
Russia**
(p. 362)

# Africa Unit 6

For more information on Africa . . .

CLASSZONE.COM

**Mount Kilimanjaro, Tanzania** (p. 399)

**Masai Girl, Kenya** (p. 434)

**Sahara Desert, North Africa** (p. 420)

xiii

# Unit 7

## Southwest Asia

For more information on Southwest Asia . . .

CLASSZONE.COM

**Oasis on caravan route from Yemen to Palestine** (p. 475)

**Kurdish family, Turkey** (p. 476)

# South Asia

Unit **8**

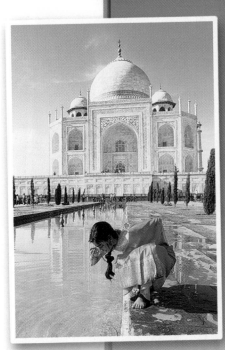

**Taj Mahal,
Agra, India**
(p. 538)

**Tea Plantation,
Sri Lanka**
(p. 586)

**For more information on South Asia . . .**

CLASSZONE.COM

# Unit 9  East Asia

For more information on East Asia . . .

CLASSZONE.COM

Mount Fuji,
Japan (p. 607)

Potala Palace,
Tibet (p. 619)

Crowded urban street,
Hong Kong (p. 668)

# Southeast Asia, Oceania, and Antarctica

Ice Cliffs,
Antarctica
(p. 674)

Fishing on
Cook Island
(p. 714)

Uluru, or Ayers Rock,
Australia (p. 729)

**For more information on Southeast Asia, Oceania, and Antarctica . . .**

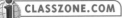 CLASSZONE.COM

# Features

## Disasters!

## RAND McNALLY Map and Graph Skills

## growing up in

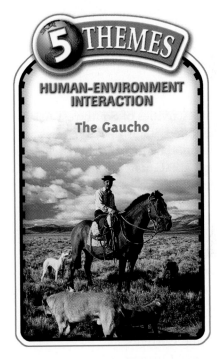

## 5 THEMES

### HUMAN-ENVIRONMENT INTERACTION

### The Gaucho

## Geography TODAY

# Maps

# Unit 4

# Unit 5

# Unit 6

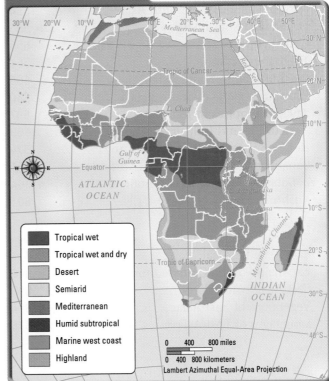

**Climates of Africa**

# Maps

# Graphs, Charts, and Tables

## GRAPHS

## CHARTS AND TABLES

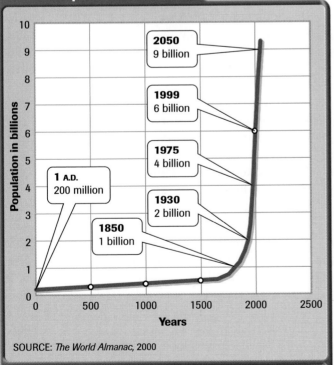

**World Population Growth**

- **2050** 9 billion
- **1999** 6 billion
- **1975** 4 billion
- **1 A.D.** 200 million
- **1930** 2 billion
- **1850** 1 billion

Population in billions (y-axis: 0–10); Years (x-axis: 0–2500)

SOURCE: *The World Almanac*, 2000

**SKILLBUILDER: Interpreting Graphs**

❶ **ANALYZING DATA** How long did it take for the population to reach one billion?

❷ **MAKING GENERALIZATIONS** How have the intervals between increases changed?

# Infographics and Time Lines

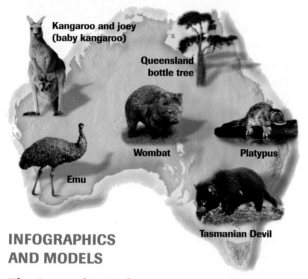

Kangaroo and joey (baby kangaroo)

Queensland bottle tree

Wombat

Platypus

Emu

Tasmanian Devil

## INFOGRAPHICS AND MODELS

## TIME LINES

# Primary Sources

"*My goodness, if I'd known how badly you wanted democracy I'd have given it to you ages ago.*"

# Primary Sources/Videos

**Primary Sources *continued***

## Unit 7



## Unit 8



## Unit 9



## Unit 10



## The Voyageur Experience in World Geography Videos

# Strategies for Taking Standardized Tests

This section of the textbook helps you develop and practice the skills you need to study geography and to take standardized tests. Part 1, **Strategies for Studying Geography**, takes you through the features of the textbook and offers suggestions on how to use these features to improve your reading and study skills.

Part 2, **Test-Taking Strategies and Practice,** offers specific strategies for tackling many of the items you'll find on a standardized test. It gives tips for answering multiple-choice, constructed-response, extended-response, and document-based questions. In addition, it offers guidelines for analyzing primary and secondary sources, political cartoons, maps, charts, graphs, including population pyramids, and time lines. Each strategy is followed by a set of questions you can use for practice.

## CONTENTS

# Part 1: Strategies for Studying Geography

Reading is the central skill in the effective study of geography or any other subject. You can improve your reading skills by using helpful techniques and by practicing. The better your reading skills are, the more you will remember what you read. Below you will find several strategies that involve built-in features of *World Geography*. Careful use of these strategies will help you learn and understand geography more effectively.

## Preview Chapters Before You Read

Each chapter begins with a one-page introduction. Study this introductory material to help you get ready to read.

**1** Read the chapter and section titles. These provide a brief outline of what will be covered in the chapter.

**2** Study the chapter-opening photograph. It often illustrates a major theme of the chapter. Regional human geography chapters open with a map rather than a photograph. Examine the map to get an idea of the location and size of the region discussed in the chapter.

**3** Read the **GeoFocus** question and activity. These items will help focus your reading of the chapter.

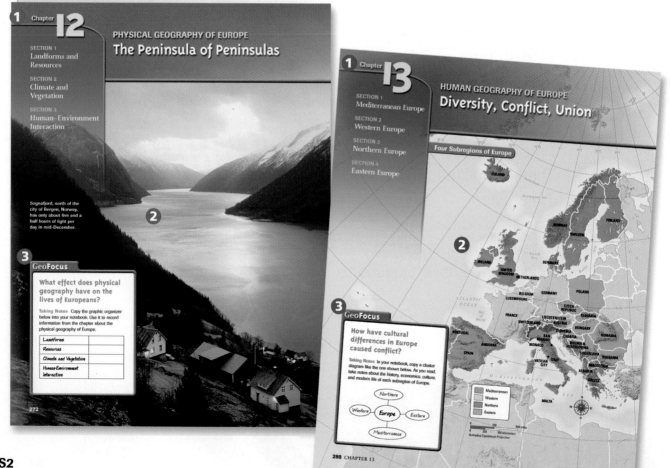

# Preview Sections Before You Read

Each chapter consists of three, four, or five sections. Depending on the chapter, these sections focus on particular aspects of physical or human geography. Use the section openers to help you prepare to read.

**1** Study the points under the **Main Ideas** heading. These identify the major topics discussed in the section.

**2** Preview the **Places & Terms** list. It will give you an idea of the locations and concepts you will read about in the section.

**3** Read the **Connect to the Issues** feature. This feature connects the section content to one of the major geographic issues covered in each unit of *World Geography*.

**4** Skim through the section and look at the maps and illustrations. They will give you a quick visual overview of the section content.

**5** Notice the structure of the section. **Blue** heads label the major topics covered in the section; **green** subheads signal smaller topics within these major topics. Together, these heads provide you with a quick outline of the section.

---

## Landforms and Resources

**A HUMAN PERSPECTIVE** Elephants in Europe? In 218 B.C., Hannibal, a general from Carthage in North Africa, attacked the Roman Empire, which was at war with Carthage. He moved 38 war elephants and an estimated 60,000 troops across the Mediterranean Sea to Spain. To reach Italy, his armies had to cross the Pyrenees Mountains, the Rhone River, and the Alps. Hannibal used rafts to float the elephants across the Rhone. In the Alps, steep paths and slick ice caused men and animals to fall to their deaths. Despite this, Hannibal arrived in Italy with 26,000 men and a few elephants, and he defeated Rome in many battles. His crossing of the Alps was a triumph over geographic barriers.

### Peninsulas and Islands

On a map you will see that Europe is a large peninsula stretching to the west of Asia. Europe itself has many smaller peninsulas, so it is sometimes called a "peninsula of peninsulas." Because of these peninsulas, most locations in Europe are no more than 300 miles from an ocean or sea. As you can imagine, the European way of life involves using these bodies of water for both business and pleasure.

**NORTHERN PENINSULAS** In northern Europe is the Scandinavian Peninsula. Occupied by the nations of Norway and Sweden, it is bounded by the Norwegian Sea, the North Sea, and the Baltic Sea. More than almost any other place in Europe, this peninsula shows the results of the movement of glaciers during the Ice Age. The glaciers scoured away the rich topsoil and left only thin, rocky soil that is hard to farm.

In Norway, glaciers also carved out **fjords** (fyawrdz), which are steep U-shaped valleys that connect to the sea and that filled with seawater after the glaciers melted. Fjords provide excellent harbors for fishing boats. The fjords are often separated by narrow peninsulas.

The Jutland Peninsula is directly across the North Sea from Scandinavia. Jutland forms the largest part of Denmark and a small part of Germany. This peninsula is an extension of a broad

### Main Ideas
- Europe is composed of many peninsulas and islands.
- Europe's landforms also include large plains and mountain ranges.

### Places & Terms
fjord    *Massif Central*
uplands    peat
*Meseta*

### CONNECT TO THE ISSUES
**UNIFICATION** Resources helped Western Europe develop industry before other regions. The European Union began in Western Europe.

**Major European Peninsulas**

SCANDINAVIAN PENINSULA
ATLANTIC OCEAN
JUTLAND PENINSULA
ALPS
IBERIAN PENINSULA
ITALIAN PENINSULA
BALKAN PENINSULA

**SKILLBUILDER: Interpreting Maps**
① **LOCATION** Where are Europe's major peninsulas located in relation to each other?
② **REGION** Why might each peninsula be considered a region?

*Landforms and Resources* **273**

---

plain that reaches across northern Europe. Its gently rolling hills and swampy low-lying areas are very different from the rocky land of the Scandinavian Peninsula.

**SOUTHERN PENINSULAS** The southern part of Europe contains three major peninsulas:

- The Iberian Peninsula is home to Spain and Portugal. The Pyrenees Mountains block off this peninsula from the rest of Europe.
- The Italian Peninsula is home to Italy. It is shaped like a boot, extends into the Mediterranean Sea, and has 4,700 miles of coastline.
- The Balkan Peninsula is bordered by the Adriatic, Mediterranean, and Aegean Seas. It is mountainous, so transportation is difficult.

**ISLANDS** Another striking feature of Europe is its islands. The larger islands are Great Britain, Ireland, Iceland, and Greenland. Although far from mainland Europe, Iceland and Greenland were settled by Scandinavians and have maintained cultural ties with the mainland. Over the centuries, many different groups have occupied the smaller Mediterranean Sea islands of Corsica, Sardinia, Sicily, and Crete. All of Europe's islands have depended upon trade. ▷

**Geographic Thinking**
**Seeing Patterns**
◁ What geographic advantages do islands have that help to promote trade?

### Mountains and Uplands

The mountains and uplands of Europe may be viewed as walls because they separate groups of people. They make it difficult for people, goods, and ideas to move easily from one place to another. These landforms also affect climate. For example, the chilly north winds rarely blow over the Alps into Italy, which has a mild climate as a result.

**MOUNTAIN CHAINS** The most famous mountain chain in Europe is the Alps. On a map you can see that the Alps arc across France, Italy, Germany, Switzerland, Austria, and the northern Balkan Peninsula. They cut Italy off from the rest of Europe. Similarly, the Pyrenees restrict movement from France to Spain and Portugal. Both ranges provide opportunities for skiing, hiking, and other outdoor activities.

Running like a spine down Italy, the Apennine Mountains divide the Italian Peninsula between east and west. The Balkan Mountains block

**HUMAN-ENVIRONMENT INTERACTION**
The Wetterhorn in the Swiss Alps stands 12,142 feet above the city in the valley below. **How do the mountains affect the lives of the people in the valley?**

**S3**

# Use Active Reading Strategies as You Read

**Now you are ready to read the chapter. Read one section at a time, from beginning to end.**

**1** Ask and answer questions as you read. Look for the **Geographic Thinking** and **Connect to the Issues** questions in the margin. Answering these questions will show whether you understand what you have just read.

**2** Try to visualize the places, events, activities, and people you read about. Studying the pictures and any illustrated features will help you do this.

**3** Read to build your vocabulary. Look for the **boldfaced, underlined** terms in the text and note their meaning.

**4** Study the **Background** notes in the margin for additional information on the section content.

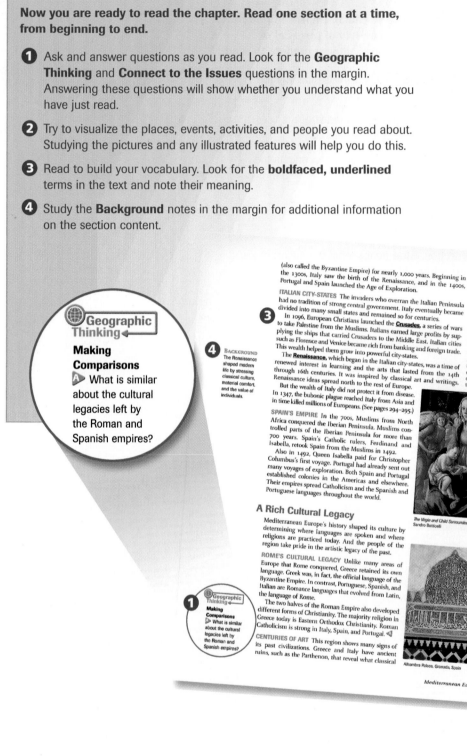

(also called the Byzantine Empire) for nearly 1,000 years. Beginning in the 1300s, Italy saw the birth of the Renaissance, and in the 1400s, Portugal and Spain launched the Age of Exploration.

**ITALIAN CITY-STATES** The invaders who overran the Italian Peninsula had no tradition of strong central government. Italy eventually became divided into many small states and remained so for centuries.

In 1096, European Christians launched the <u>**Crusades,**</u> a series of wars to take Palestine from the Muslims. Italians earned large profits by supplying the ships that carried Crusaders to the Middle East. Italian cities such as Florence and Venice became rich from banking and foreign trade. This wealth helped them grow into powerful city-states.

The <u>**Renaissance,**</u> which began in the Italian city-states, was a time of renewed interest in learning and the arts that lasted from the 14th through 16th centuries. It was inspired by classical art and writings. Renaissance ideas spread north to the rest of Europe.

But the wealth of Italy did not protect it from disease. In 1347, the bubonic plague reached Italy from Asia and in time killed millions of Europeans. (See pages 294–295.)

**SPAIN'S EMPIRE** In the 700s, Muslims from North Africa conquered the Iberian Peninsula. Muslims controlled parts of the Iberian Peninsula for more than 700 years. Spain's Catholic rulers, Ferdinand and Isabella, retook Spain from the Muslims in 1492.

Also in 1492, Queen Isabella paid for Christopher Columbus's first voyage. Portugal had already sent out many voyages of exploration. Both Spain and Portugal established colonies in the Americas and elsewhere. Their empires spread Catholicism and the Spanish and Portuguese languages throughout the world.

**REGION** Italian Renaissance paintings often show the Virgin Mary and baby Jesus. Muslim art, like the Spanish wall design below (*bottom*), often uses calligraphy to praise God.

*The Virgin and Child Surrounded by Five Angels,* Sandro Botticelli

## A Rich Cultural Legacy

Mediterranean Europe's history shaped its culture by determining where languages are spoken and where religions are practiced today. And the people of the region take pride in the artistic legacy of the past.

**ROME'S CULTURAL LEGACY** Unlike many areas of Europe that Rome conquered, Greece retained its own language. Greek was, in fact, the official language of the Byzantine Empire. In contrast, Portuguese, Spanish, and Italian are Romance languages that evolved from Latin, the language of Rome.

The two halves of the Roman Empire also developed different forms of Christianity. The majority religion in Greece today is Eastern Orthodox Christianity. Roman Catholicism is strong in Italy, Spain, and Portugal.

**CENTURIES OF ART** This region shows many signs of its past civilizations. Greece and Italy have ancient ruins, such as the Parthenon, that reveal what classical

*Alhambra Palace, Granada, Spain*

*Mediterranean Europe* 291

---

**BACKGROUND**
The Renaissance shaped modern life by stressing classical culture, material comfort, and the value of individuals.

**Geographic Thinking**

**Making Comparisons**

**A** What is similar about the cultural legacies left by the Roman and Spanish empires?

# Review and Summarize What You Have Read

**When you finish reading a section, review and summarize what you have read. If necessary, go back and reread information that was not clear the first time through.**

**1** Reread the blue heads and green subheads for a quick summary of the major points covered in the section.

**2** Study any charts, graphs, or maps. These visual materials usually provide a condensed version of information in the section.

**3** Review the visuals—photographs, charts, graphs, maps, and time lines—and any illustrated features, and note how they relate to the section content.

**4** Complete all the questions in the **Section Assessment.** They will help you think critically about what you have just read.

---

returned to ethnic loyalties. That was especially true in Yugoslavia, a nation consisting of six republics. In the early 1990s, four of the six Yugoslav republics voted to become separate states. Serbia objected, leading to civil war. (See Chapter 14 for details.) In contrast, Czechoslovakia peacefully split into the Czech Republic and Slovakia.

## **1** Developing the Economy

Because of its fertile plains, Eastern Europe has traditionally been a farming region. After 1948, the Soviet Union promoted industry there.

**1** INDUSTRY Under communism, the government owned all factories and told them what to produce. This system was inefficient because industries had little motive to please customers or to cut costs. Often, there were shortages of goods. Eastern European nations traded with the Soviet Union and each other, so they didn't keep up with the technology of other nations. As a result, they had difficulty selling goods to nations outside Eastern Europe. And their outdated factories created heavy pollution.

After 1989, most of Eastern Europe began to move toward a **market economy**, in which industries make the goods consumers want to buy. Many factories in Eastern Europe became privately owned instead of state owned. The changes caused problems, such as inflation, the closing of factories, and unemployment. Since then, however, many factories have cut their costs and improved production. As a result, the Czech Republic, Hungary, and Poland have all grown economically. ◁

**CONNECT TO THE ISSUES**
**UNIFICATION**
▷ Do you think the nations of Eastern Europe will want to join the European Union? Why or why not?

LINGERING PROBLEMS Some Eastern European nations have had trouble making economic progress—for many different reasons.
- Albania's economic growth is slowed by old equipment, a lack of raw materials, and a shortage of educated workers.
- Few of Romania's citizens have money to invest in business. In addition, the Romanian government still owns some industries. Foreigners don't want to invest their money in those industries.
- The civil wars of the 1990s damaged Yugoslavia and its former republics of Bosnia and Herzegovina and Croatia. Equipment and buildings were destroyed; workers were killed or left the country.

In general, it will take years for Eastern Europe to overcome the damage caused, in part, by decades of Communist control.

*East*

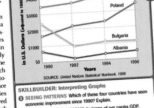

**Per Capita GDP in Eastern Europe**

Hungary
Poland
Bulgaria
Albania

in U.S. Dollars (adjusted to 1990 prices)
$5000
$4000
$3000
$2000
$1000
$0
1990   1992   1994   1996
**Years**

SOURCE: *United Nations Statistical Yearbook, 1996*

**SKILLBUILDER: Interpreting Graphs**
**1 SEEING PATTERNS** Which of these four countries have seen economic improvement since 1990? Explain.
**2 DRAWING CONCLUSIONS** In terms of per capita GDP, which country has the best standard of living? Explain.

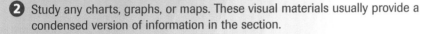

**3**

**PLACE** Crossing the Vltava River in Prague is the famous 650-year-old Charles Bridge. The bridge is now reserved for pedestrians. **Why do you think cars are banned from this bridge?**

Eastern European minority groups have often faced discrimination. Throughout history, Jews have suffered from **anti-Semitism**, which is discrimination against Jewish people. Another minority that experiences prejudice is the Romany, or Gypsy, people who are scattered across Eastern Europe. Traditionally, the Romany have moved from place to place. Because of this, other groups often look down on them.

DEMOCRACY To obtain true democracy, Eastern Europeans need to overcome old hatreds and work together. They also need to accept democratic ideals such as the rule of law—which means that government officials must obey the law. The dictators that ruled Eastern Europe in the past did not do so. But in recent years, Eastern Europeans have often held their leaders accountable. For example, in 2000, the Yugoslav people forced a dictator to accept election results that turned him out of office. You will read about this event in Chapter 14, along with other major issues of European life today.

**4**

## **Assessment**

**1 Places & Terms**
Identify these terms and explain their importance in the region.
- cultural crossroads
- balkanization
- satellite nation
- market economy
- folk art
- anti-Semitism

**2 Taking Notes**
REGION Review the notes you took for this section.

History → Eastern Europe → Culture
Economics → Eastern Europe → Modern Life

- What country dominated Eastern Europe after World War II?
- What problems did the move toward a market economy cause?

**3 Main Ideas**
**a.** Why is Eastern Europe considered a cultural crossroads?
**b.** What role did the Soviet Union play in the rise and fall of communism in Eastern Europe?
**c.** What are some important ways that Eastern Europe is different from Western Europe?

**4 Geographic Thinking**
**Making Inferences** The Balkan region has been called the "powder keg of Europe." Why do you think it earned that name? **Think** about:
- the wars in 1912 and 1913
- World War I

**S** See Skillbuilder Handbook, page R4.

**GeoActivity**

**EXPLORING LOCAL GEOGRAPHY** Like Eastern Europe, most places in the United States have been controlled by various cultural groups or nations over time. Research the history of your area and create a **time line**, like the one on pages 310–311, listing changes in control.

*Eastern Europe* **315**

# Part 2: Test-Taking Strategies and Practice

Improve your test-taking skills by practicing the strategies discussed in this section. Read the tips on the left-hand page. Then apply them to the practice items on the right-hand page.

## Multiple Choice

A multiple-choice question consists of a stem and a set of choices. The stem is usually in the form of a question or an incomplete sentence. One of the choices correctly answers the question or completes the sentence.

**1** Read the stem carefully and try to answer the question or complete the sentence without looking at the choices.

**2** Pay close attention to key words in the stem. They may direct you toward the correct answer.

**3** Read each choice with the stem. Don't jump to conclusions about the correct answer until you've read all the choices.

**4** Think carefully about questions that include *All of the above* among the choices.

**5** After reading all of the choices, eliminate any that you know are incorrect.

**6** Use modifiers to help narrow your choices further.

**7** Look for the best answer among the remaining choices.

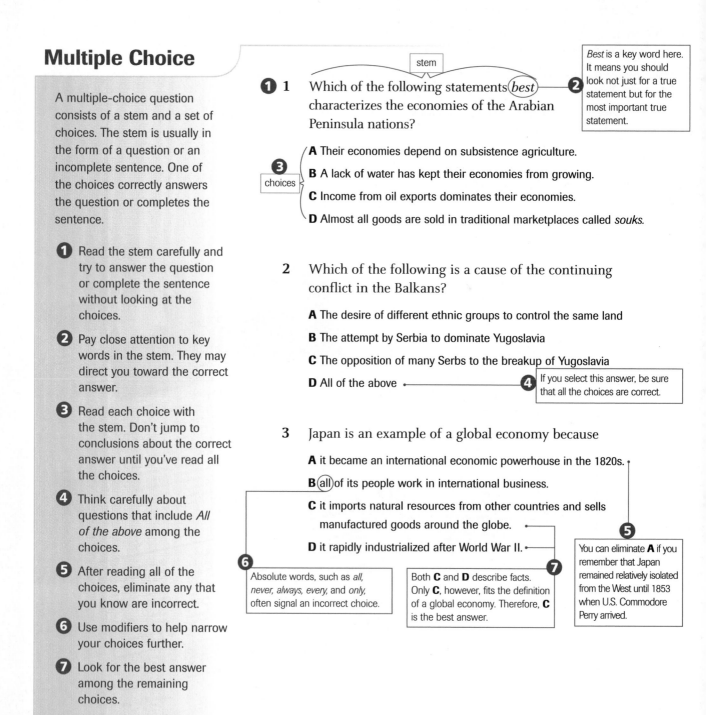

stem

**1** 1  Which of the following statements *best* characterizes the economies of the Arabian Peninsula nations?

*Best* is a key word here. It means you should look not just for a true statement but for the most important true statement.

choices

**A** Their economies depend on subsistence agriculture.

**B** A lack of water has kept their economies from growing.

**C** Income from oil exports dominates their economies.

**D** Almost all goods are sold in traditional marketplaces called *souks.*

2  Which of the following is a cause of the continuing conflict in the Balkans?

**A** The desire of different ethnic groups to control the same land

**B** The attempt by Serbia to dominate Yugoslavia

**C** The opposition of many Serbs to the breakup of Yugoslavia

**D** All of the above

If you select this answer, be sure that all the choices are correct.

3  Japan is an example of a global economy because

**A** it became an international economic powerhouse in the 1820s.

**B** *all* of its people work in international business.

**C** it imports natural resources from other countries and sells manufactured goods around the globe.

**D** it rapidly industrialized after World War II.

Absolute words, such as *all, never, always, every,* and *only,* often signal an incorrect choice.

Both **C** and **D** describe facts. Only **C**, however, fits the definition of a global economy. Therefore, **C** is the best answer.

You can eliminate **A** if you remember that Japan remained relatively isolated from the West until 1853 when U.S. Commodore Perry arrived.

**answers:** 1 (C), 2 (D), 3 (C)

For more test practice online . . .

**TEST PRACTICE**
CLASSZONE.COM

**Directions:** Read the following questions and choose the *best* answer from the four choices.

1  Which of the following was a result of the migration of Europeans to North America?

   **A** Native Americans were displaced.

   **B** The United States became a "nation of immigrants."

   **C** Plants, animals, and diseases moved between the Eastern and Western hemispheres.

   **D** All of the above

2  Which of the following is *not* an effect of the rapid destruction of rain forests in Latin America and other parts of the world?

   **A** The temperature of the atmosphere is rising.

   **B** Plants and animals are becoming extinct.

   **C** More oxygen is building up in the atmosphere.

   **D** The earth's biodiversity is being reduced.

3  After the Soviet Union collapsed in 1991 and Russia changed from a command economy to a market economy, economic control over the production of goods and services began to shift from

   **A** the central government to private businesses.

   **B** local workers to workers from abroad.

   **C** the legislature to the banks.

   **D** regional governments to the national government.

4  The Bantu migrations in Africa resulted in

   **A** the spread of Bantu languages and culture.

   **B** the end of the international slave trade.

   **C** the colonization of Africa by numerous European nations.

   **D** an AIDS epidemic in Africa.

# Primary Sources

Primary sources are materials produced by people who traveled to the places they describe or who took part in or witnessed the events they portray. Letters, diaries, speeches, newspaper and magazine articles, travelogues, and autobiographies are all primary sources. So, too, are legal documents, such as wills, deeds, and financial records.

**1** Look at the source line and identify the author. Consider what qualifies the author to write about the places or events discussed in the passage.

**2** Skim the document to form an idea of what it is about.

**3** Note special punctuation. Ellipses indicate that words or sentences have been removed from the original passage.

**4** Carefully read the passage and distinguish between facts and the author's opinions. (Note that the author's use of a metaphor, *like layers in a slice of cake*, conveys a clear image of the land to the reader who cannot see Hadar in person.)

**5** Consider for whom the author was writing. The intended audience may influence what and how an author writes.

**6** Before rereading the passage, skim the questions to identify the information you need to find.

*In 1974, the oldest and most well-preserved skeleton of an erect-walking human ancestor was found in Ethiopia. Paleoanthropologist Donald Johanson, who named the skeleton Lucy, describes the geography of the remote Afar desert region where Lucy was found. The region is rich with geological and paleontological information. Eventually, Johanson and his colleagues discovered the bones of at least 13 ancient individuals, now known as the First Family, in this desert area.*

**2** At Hadar, which is a wasteland of bare rock, gravel and sand, the fossils that one finds are almost all exposed on the surface of the **3** ground. Hadar is (. . .) an ancient lake bed now dry and filled with sediments that record the history of past geological events. You can trace volcanic-ash falls there, deposits of mud and silt washed down from distant mountains, episodes of volcanic dust, more mud, and so on. Those events reveal themselves like layers in a slice of **4** cake in the gullies of new young rivers that recently have cut through the lake bed here and there. It seldom rains at Hadar, but when it does it comes in an overpowering gush—six months' worth overnight. The soil, which is bare of vegetation, cannot hold all that water. It roars down the gullies, cutting back their sides and bringing more fossils into view.

**1** —Donald Johanson, *Lucy: The Beginnings of Humankind*

**1** Johanson's description is very detailed because he took several field expeditions to Hadar looking for fossils.

**5** Although the author is a scientist, he wrote this book for a general audience to explain the work and the excitement of finding fossils.

**1** Now a wasteland of bare rock, gravel, and sand, Hadar was once a

**A** volcano.

**B** mountain chain.

**C** lake bed.

**D** river.

**6**

**2** The author most likely describes Hadar and its geological history for which of the following reasons?

**A** Because knowing about the area's geological past might help to locate and identify fossils

**B** To illustrate how the area's current climate and geography reveal its past geological events

**C** To explain why fossils are found on the surface of the ground at Hadar

**D** All of the above

**answers:** 1 (C), 2 (D)

**Directions:** Read the following excerpt from a letter written by the Spanish conquistador Hernán Cortés in which he describes the Aztec capital city. Use the passage and your knowledge of world geography to answer the questions.

### The Aztec Capital: The Great City of Tenochtitlán in Mexico

The great city of Tenochtitlán is built in the midst of this salt lake, and it is two leagues from the heart of the city to any point on the mainland. Four causeways lead to it, all made by hand and some twelve feet wide. The city itself is as large as Seville or Córdova. The principal streets are very broad and straight, the majority of them being of beaten earth, but a few and at least half the smaller thoroughfares are waterways along which they pass in their canoes. Moreover, even the principal streets have openings at regular distances so that the water can freely pass from one to another, and these openings which are very broad are spanned by great bridges of huge beams, very stoutly put together, so firm indeed that over many of them ten horsemen can ride at once.

—Hernán Cortés, in a letter to the King of Spain

Excerpt from "The Second Letter of Hernán Cortés," from *Five Letters of Hernán Cortés,* 1519–1526, translated by J. Bayard Morris (New York: W. W. Norton and Company, Inc.). Norton Paperback Edition published in 1969, reissued in 1991. Reprinted by permission of W. W. Norton and Company, Inc.

**1** Which of the following statements *best* describes the location of Tenochtitlán?

**A** It was built on a peninsula, and all of its roads were waterways.

**B** It was built next to a lake, which the people crossed over by ferry boats.

**C** It was built on an island connected to the mainland by four hand-built causeways.

**D** It was built on the mainland with several bridges connecting it to an island in the nearby salt lake.

**2** The letter contains the information that the Aztec citizens and the Spanish conquistadors traveled around the city by

**A** canoe and horse.

**B** canoe only.

**C** foot only.

**D** wagons and foot.

**3** Which of the following statements reveals that Cortés admires the city of Tenochtitlán and its builders?

**A** "The city itself is as large as Seville or Córdova."

**B** "These openings . . . are spanned by great bridges of huge beams, very stoutly put together."

**C** "The principal streets are very broad and straight."

**D** All of the above

**4** Eventually, Cortés and the Spanish destroyed most of Tenochtitlán. On its ruins, they built what became the present-day city of

**A** Seville.

**B** Baja.

**C** Mexico City.

**D** Tijuana.

# Secondary Sources

Secondary sources are descriptions of places, people, cultures, and events. Usually, secondary sources are made by people who are not directly involved in the event or living in the place being described or discussed. The most common types of written secondary sources are textbooks, reference books, some magazine and newspaper articles, and biographies. A secondary source often combines information from several primary sources.

**1** Read the title to preview the content of the passage.

**2** Look at the source line to learn more about the document and its origin. (The spelling of the word *organized* indicates that the magazine is probably from Great Britain.)

**3** Look for topic sentences. Ask yourself what the main idea is.

**4** As you read, use context clues to guess at the meaning of difficult or unfamiliar words. (You can use the description of crime in the rest of the passage to understand that the word *pervasiveness* most likely means "being everywhere" or "existing throughout.")

**5** Read actively by asking and answering questions about the passage.

**6** Before rereading the passage, skim the questions to identify the information you need to find.

You might ask: What makes organized crime in Russia different from organized crime in other countries? Are crime and corruption in all levels of society new to Russian culture? **5**

**1** Organized Crime in Russia

**3** This highlights the key feature of Russian criminality: its **4** pervasiveness. "Organised crime usually deals with [minor] economic issues . . . [but] in Russia it's the mainstream," notes Toby Latta of Control Risks, a London security [firm]. Russian criminality reaches the highest levels of government—is, indeed, often indistinguishable from it. And it affects the humblest activity. Buy a jar of coffee? More likely than not, you are feeding organised crime: according to a grumbling Nestlé, most coffee sold in Russia has evaded full import duties. Give money to a beggar? He will have paid the local mafia for his spot on the street. Build a factory? You will pay one lot of bureaucrats to get it going, another to keep it running. In Russia, organised crime and corruption are everywhere. **3**

The last sentence restates the main idea.

**2** Excerpt from "Russian Organised Crime," from *The Economist*, August 28, 1999. Copyright © 1998 The Economist. Reprinted by permission.

**1** What is the main idea of this passage?

**A** The Russian economy is in a depression.

**B** The Russian government is ineffective.

**C** Organized crime operates in all areas of the Russian economy.

**D** Russia is on the verge of collapse.

**6**

**2** Which of the following conclusions can you draw from this passage?

**A** Anyone who wants to start a business in Russia may have to pay the mafia first.

**B** The Russian government loses money because some import taxes are not paid.

**C** The Russian mafia operates within the government.

**D** All of the above

**answers:** 1 (C), 2 (D)

**Directions:** Use the passage about Mohandas K. Gandhi's work for social reform in India and your knowledge of world geography to answer the questions below.

### Gandhi's Work in the 1920s

Gandhi's understanding of economic relations was shot through with emphasis originating in Hindu tradition, such as the duty of the wealthy to extend charity. . . . But in the 1920s he was forced to confront very precisely some of the aspects of India's social order which were rooted in Hindu tradition. . . .

His primary social concern at this time was the problem of untouchability, the rejection of a whole group of the poorest and most menial in society as a result of Hindu ideas of hierarchy. . . . Now, as he travelled widely, he saw in harsh practice the power of this social division, and the poverty and degradation it caused. . . .

Personal example was one of Gandhi's strategies to end untouchability. He mixed freely with [the "untouchables"], as everybody knew; he ate with them. . . . But Gandhi did not expect everyone to go this far. For most caste Hindus the obligation was to treat the untouchables as a caste *within* Hindu society, affording them citizens' right. They should be allowed to use wells, roads and public transport, attend schools and enter temples, though conventions prohibiting marriage or meals with them would remain.

—Judith M. Brown, *Gandhi: Prisoner of Hope*

**1** In Hindu tradition, there are four main classes in the social hierarchy known as the caste system. You can tell from the passage that the "untouchables" are

**A** the highest social group.

**B** the lowest social group.

**C** priests and scholars.

**D** merchants, traders, and farmers.

**2** As the passage explains, Gandhi broke with Hindu tradition by

**A** trying to convert the poorest people to Islam.

**B** extending charity to the poorest people.

**C** spending time with the poorest people.

**D** rejecting the poorest people.

**3** According to the author, which of the following ideas did Gandhi promote?

**A** Citizens' rights for members of the lowest caste

**B** Intermarriage among members of low and high castes

**C** Abolishing the caste system altogether

**D** Scholarships for members of the lowest caste

**4** You can infer from the last paragraph that low caste Indians in the 1920s were *not* usually allowed to

**A** use public wells.

**B** ride on public buses.

**C** attend schools.

**D** All of the above

# Political Cartoons

Political cartoons are drawings made to express a point of view on political issues of the day. Cartoonists use words, symbols, and such artistic styles as caricature—exaggerating a person's physical features—to get their message across.

**1** Identify the subject of the cartoon. Titles, captions, and labels are often clues to the subject matter. (The subject here is Chechnya's fight for independence from Russia.)

**2** Identify the main characters in the cartoon. (The main character is Russian President Vladimir Putin.)

**3** Note the symbols—ideas and images that stand for something else—used in the cartoon. (The bear is an often-used symbol of Russia.)

**4** Study labels and other written information in the cartoon.

**5** Analyze the point of view. How cartoonists use caricature often shows how they feel.

**6** Interpret the cartoonist's message.

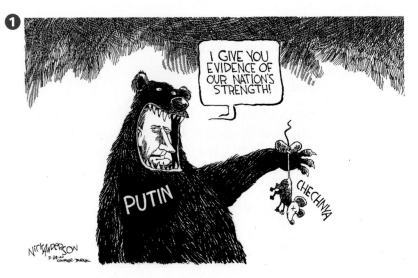

**5** Putin represents the Russian government and army. The exaggeration of Putin's nose makes him appear ridiculous.

**3** Drawing Chechnya as a mouse exaggerates the difference in size of Chechnya compared to Russia.

**1** Chechnya is portrayed as a mouse because

**A** it is so much smaller and less powerful than Russia.

**B** the region has no natural resources.

**C** its rebel leaders lack courage and the will to fight.

**D** the region produces so much cheese.

**2** Which of the following statements best represents the cartoonist's point of view?

**A** Russia should maintain firm control of Chechnya.

**B** Chechnya is not important to Russia.

**C** Russia is a military powerhouse and should be feared by other countries.

**D** Russia used more military might than necessary in fighting the rebellion in Chechnya.

**answers:** 1 (A), 2 (D)

For more test practice online . . .

**TEST PRACTICE**
CLASSZONE.COM

**Directions:** Use the political cartoon and your knowledge of geography to answer the questions below.

YOU'LL NEVER GUESS WHAT THIS USED TO BE, SON...

BERLIN MALL

©1989 THE PITTSBURGH PRESS
UNITED FEATURE SYNDICATE

ROB ROGERS
*Courtesy Pittsburgh Press*

Copyright © 1989 Rob Rogers/The Pittsburgh
Press/United Feature Syndicate

**1** The cartoonist has drawn the "Berlin Mall," to refer to the

**A** main shopping district in the center of Berlin.

**B** seat of city government in East Germany.

**C** Berlin Wall, which divided the city of Berlin into democratic and communist sections.

**D** World War II division of Germany.

**2** What does the "Berlin Mall" most likely stand for in the cartoon?

**A** the European Union

**B** Western capitalism

**C** Eastern philosophy

**D** Soviet communism

**3** The cartoonist is implying that

**A** free-market countries and corporations looked for new markets in Berlin.

**B** the people of former communist countries in Europe were eager to buy products not previously available to them.

**C** the fall of the Berlin Wall changed economics and politics in Europe.

**D** All of the above

**4** The father's statement to his son implies that this Berlin site

**A** was recently built on the site of an old market.

**B** is very different from what it used to be.

**C** is the only shopping area located in Berlin.

**D** All of the above.

# Charts

Charts present information in a visual form. Geography textbooks use several types of charts, including tables, flow charts, Venn diagrams, and infographics. The type of chart most commonly found in standardized tests is the table, which organizes information in columns and rows for easy viewing.

**①** Read the title to identify the broad subject of the chart.

**②** Read the column and row headings and any other labels. The headings and labels will provide more details on the subject of the chart.

**③** Compare and contrast the information from column to column and row to row.

**④** Try to draw conclusions from the information in the chart. Ask yourself: What trends or patterns does the chart show?

**⑤** Read the questions and then study the chart again.

**①** **Adult Literacy Rates in South Asia by Gender, 1995**

| **②** **Country** | **Male** | **Female** | **Total** |
|---|---|---|---|
| Bangladesh | 49% | 26% | 38% |
| Bhutan | 56% | 28% | 42% |
| India | 66% | 38% | 52% |
| Maldives | 93% | 93% | 93% |
| Nepal | 41% | 14% | 28% |
| Sri Lanka | 93% | 87% | 90% |
| Pakistan | 50% | 24% | 38% |

**④** Based on the data in this chart, you might conclude that males in most of these countries receive more education than females.

**③** Compare and contrast the literacy rates of males and females in each country.

**Sources**: World Health Organization; CIA, *The World Fact Book 2000*

**1** What is the general pattern in the literacy rates for males and females of this region?

**A** The rates for males and females are similar.

**B** The rates for males are generally much higher than those for females.

**C** The rates for females are generally much higher than those for males.

**D** The rates for both sexes are extremely low in all the countries.

**⑤**

**2** One observation that you can make about the literacy rate in these countries is that the

**A** higher the female literacy rate is, the higher the total literacy rate is.

**B** higher the literacy rate, the less interest females have in reading and writing.

**C** literacy rate in mountainous countries is higher than the rate in island countries.

**D** lower the total literacy rate is, the higher the female literacy rate is.

**answers:** 1 (B), 2 (A)

**Directions:** Use the chart and your knowledge of world geography to answer the questions below.

## Comparison of European, American, and Japanese Workers' Hours

| Country | Scheduled Weekly Hours | Number of Annual Days Off/Holidays | Annual Hours Worked |
|---|---|---|---|
| Germany | 39 | 42 | 1,708 |
| Netherlands | 40 | 43.5 | 1,740 |
| Austria | 39.3 | 38 | 1,751 |
| France | 39 | 34 | 1,771 |
| Italy | 40 | 39 | 1,776 |
| United Kingdom | 39 | 33 | 1,778 |
| Sweden | 40 | 37 | 1,792 |
| United States | 40 | 22 | 1,912 |
| Portugal | 45 | 36 | 2,025 |
| Japan | 44 | 23.5 | 2,116 |

**Source:** "Comparison of European, American, and Japanese Workers' Hours," from *Hammond New Century World Atlas.* Copyright © 2000 by Hammond World Atlas Corporation. All rights reserved. Reprinted by permission.

**1** People are scheduled to work the most hours annually in

**A** the United States.

**B** Portugal.

**C** Germany.

**D** Japan.

**2** If Germany has a five-day work week, the Germans' time off equals how many work weeks?

**A** More than 2 work weeks

**B** More than 4 work weeks

**C** More than 6 work weeks

**D** More than 8 work weeks

**3** People have the least number of holidays and days off work in

**A** the United States.

**B** Portugal.

**C** the United Kingdom.

**D** Japan.

**4** Compared to the Americans and Japanese, Europeans work

**A** fewer hours per week.

**B** fewer days per year.

**C** more hours per week.

**D** more days per year.

# Population Pyramids

A population pyramid is a type of graph that shows the gender and age distribution of a population. It is useful in showing patterns in these and other categories, such as ethnicity. The size of one age group compared to another may have important economic, social, and political consequences. For example, if the number of working-age adults in a country is small, the labor pool might be small.

**1** Read the title to identify the population that the graph represents.

**2** Study the age groups labeled along the vertical axis in the center of the pyramid. Each horizontal bar represents the size of an age-and-gender group. Note that the intervals between the numbers along the base of the pyramid identify the size of each age-gender group.

**3** Compare the sizes of the gender groups and note any patterns. Then compare the sizes of the age groups and note any patterns.

**4** Draw conclusions and make generalizations based on the patterns you see.

**5** Read the questions carefully and then refer to the graph again to answer them.

**1** Population Pyramid for Bolivia, 2000

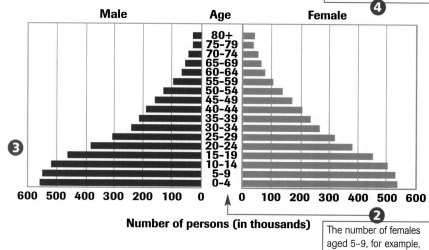

**4** A generalization you might make here is that the population is not evenly distributed. The very young age groups greatly outnumber the older age groups.

**2** The number of females aged 5–9, for example, is about 530,000.

**Source:** U.S. Census Bureau, International Data Base

**1** Most Bolivians are

  **A** between the ages of 35 and 39.

  **B** below the age of 40.

  **C** between the ages of 45 and 49.

  **D** older than 59.

**2** Which statement *best* characterizes the gender distribution of Bolivia's population?

  **A** Males greatly outnumber females.

  **B** Females greatly outnumber males.

  **C** The population has about an equal number of males and females.

  **D** Females outnumber males in the youngest age groups.

**answers:** 1 (B), 2 (C)

**Directions:** Use the graph and your knowledge of world geography to answer the questions below.

### Population Pyramid for France, 2000

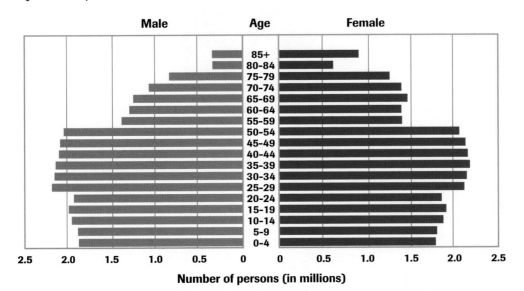

Number of persons (in millions)

**Source:** U.S. Census Bureau, International Data Base

**1** The largest age group in France is composed of people

**A** from 10 to 24 years of age.

**B** under 10 years of age.

**C** from 25 to 54 years of age.

**D** 55 years of age and over.

**2** Which statement *best* characterizes the population distribution between the genders in France?

**A** Males outnumber females in all age groups.

**B** Females outnumber males in all age groups.

**C** The genders are roughly equal except in the youngest age group.

**D** As the population ages, it changes from slightly more males to more females.

**3** Which statement accurately reflects the information in this graph?

**A** French women live longer than French men.

**B** French men live longer than French women.

**C** Very few French people live past the age of 54.

**D** There are fewer French teenagers than any other age group.

**4** Which of the following conclusions can you draw from this graph?

**A** Large families are common in France.

**B** France has a high infant mortality rate.

**C** There was a "baby boom" in France after 1945.

**D** France has a labor shortage.

# Pie Graphs

A pie, or circle, graph shows relationships among the parts of a whole. These parts look like slices of a pie. The size of each slice is proportional to the percentage of the whole that it represents.

**1** Read the title and identify the broad subject of the pie graph.

**2** Look at the legend to see what each of the slices of the pie represents.

**3** Read the source line and note the origin of the data shown in the pie graph.

**4** Compare the slices of the pie, and try to make generalizations and draw conclusions from your comparisons.

**5** Read the questions carefully and review difficult terms.

**6** Think carefully about questions that have *not* in the stem.

**7** Eliminate choices that you know are wrong.

**1** Typical Growing Season Work Day for 10-Year-Old Girl in Rural Nepal

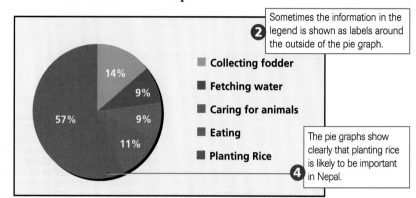

**2** Sometimes the information in the legend is shown as labels around the outside of the pie graph.

Collecting fodder
Fetching water
Caring for animals
Eating
Planting Rice

**4** The pie graphs show clearly that planting rice is likely to be important in Nepal.

**3** **Source:** Adapted from "A working day in the life of a 10-year old girl in Nepal," from *Listening to Smaller Voices* by Victoria Johnson, Joanna Hill, and Edda Ivan-Smith. Copyright © 1995 by ActionAid Nepal. Reprinted by permission.

**1** A typical 10-year-old girl in rural Nepal spends the greatest percentage of her time

**A** planting rice.

**B** eating.

**C** collecting fodder.   **5** The word *fodder* refers to feed for livestock. It is usually coarsely chopped straw or hay.

**D** fetching water.

**6**

**2** Which of the following is *not* a conclusion you can draw from the information in this pie graph?

**A** Young girls spend no time raising animals in rural Nepal.

**B** During the growing season, children in rural Nepal do farm chores most of the day.

**C** Rice is an important part of the diet in Nepal.

**D** Children in Nepal do not attend school during the growing season.

**7** You can eliminate **B** because the pie graph shows they do spend most of their day doing farm chores.

**answers:** 1 (A), 2 (A)

**Directions:** Use the pie graphs and your knowledge of world geography to answer the questions below.

### Trends in World Urbanization, 1900 and 2015

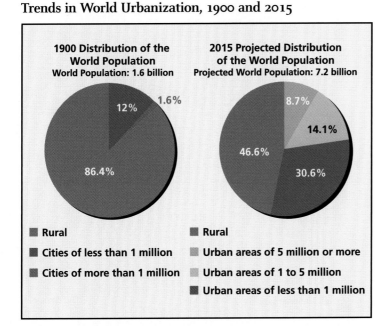

**1900 Distribution of the World Population**
World Population: 1.6 billion

1.6%
12%
86.4%

■ Rural
■ Cities of less than 1 million
■ Cities of more than 1 million

**2015 Projected Distribution of the World Population**
Projected World Population: 7.2 billion

8.7%
14.1%
46.6%
30.6%

■ Rural
■ Urban areas of 5 million or more
■ Urban areas of 1 to 5 million
■ Urban areas of less than 1 million

**Source:** "Trends in World Urbanization," from *Introduction to Geography,* Sixth Edition by Arthur Getis, Judith Getis, and Jerome D. Fellman. Copyright © 1998 by McGraw-Hill Companies, Inc. Reprinted by permission.

**1** In 1900, most people of the world lived in

**A** cities of more than one million people.

**B** cities of less than one million people.

**C** suburban areas.

**D** rural areas.

**2** Which of the following statements *best* describes the projected change in the distribution of people in 2015?

**A** The same number of people will live in urban as live in rural areas.

**B** The largest percentage of people will live in urban areas of over one million people.

**C** More people will live in urban than in rural areas.

**D** Forty percent of people will live in urban areas of all sizes.

**3** The percentage of people living in rural areas in 2015, as compared to the percentage in 1900, is projected to decline by approximately

**A** 10 percentage points.

**B** 20 percentage points.

**C** 40 percentage points.

**D** 60 percentage points.

**4** The current rise in the number of cities and the lifestyle changes that result from it are called

**A** land-use patterns.

**B** urbanization.

**C** industrialization.

**D** suburbanization.

# Political Maps

Political maps show features on the earth's surface that are created by humans. Included on a political map may be the location of cities, states, provinces, territories, or countries. There also may be some physical features, such as rivers, seas, oceans, and lakes. You can use these features to show an area's shape and size and where it is located on the earth's surface. You can also look at its location in relation to other areas, and how all of these physical facts might affect a place in ways such as its economy or population.

**1** Read the title to determine the subject and purpose of the map.

**2** Review the map labels, which reveal specific features that further illustrate the subject and purpose of the map.

**3** Study the legend to find the meaning of the symbols used on the map.

**4** Look at the lines of latitude and longitude. This grid makes locating places easier.

**5** Use the compass rose to determine directions on the map.

**6** Use the scale to measure the actual distances between places shown on the map.

**7** Read the questions and then carefully study the map to determine the answers.

**1** Kenya: Political

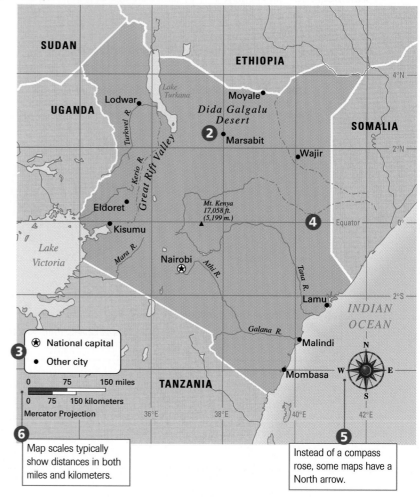

Map scales typically show distances in both miles and kilometers.

Instead of a compass rose, some maps have a North arrow.

**1** About how far is Mombasa from the capital of Kenya?

A About 100 miles

B About 200 miles

C About 300 miles

D About 400 miles

**2** The country that borders Kenya on the south is

A Somalia.

B Tanzania.

C Ethiopia.

D Uganda.

**answers:** 1 (C), 2 (B)

**Directions:** Use the map and your knowledge of world geography to answer the questions below.

**Mexico: Political**

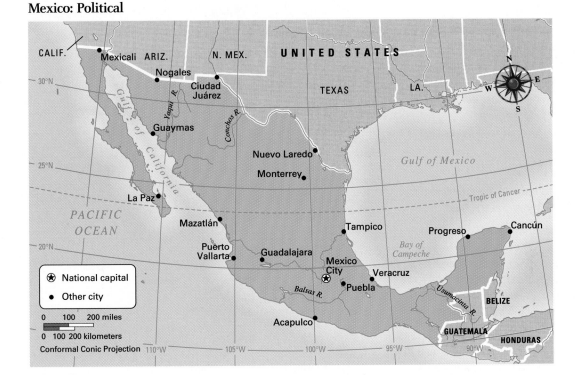

1   Which statement *best* describes the location of the capital of Mexico?

   **A** It is located on the Gulf of Mexico.

   **B** It is located on the Pacific Ocean.

   **C** It is located near the U.S.-Mexico border.

   **D** It is centrally located within the country.

2   Which of the following countries does *not* share a border with Mexico?

   **A** Honduras

   **B** Belize

   **C** Guatemala

   **D** The United States

3   Mexico is bordered on the north by

   **A** Louisiana and Texas.

   **B** California, Arizona, New Mexico, and Texas.

   **C** Arizona, New Mexico, and Texas.

   **D** only Texas.

4   The popular resort cities of Acapulco, Puerto Vallarta, and Cancún all have in common their location

   **A** on the Pacific Ocean.

   **B** on a coast.

   **C** north of the Tropic of Cancer.

   **D** in the interior of the country.

# Physical Maps

Physical maps show the landforms and bodies of water in a specific area. They use color, shading, or contour lines to indicate elevation or altitude, which is also called relief. Many maps combine features of both physical and political maps—that is, they show physical characteristics as well as political boundaries.

**1** Read the title to determine the area shown on the map.

**2** Study the legend to find the meaning of the colors used on the map. Typically, different colors are used to indicate levels of elevation. Match the legend colors to places on the map.

**3** Review the labels on the map to see what physical features are shown.

**4** Look at the lines of latitude and longitude. You can use this grid to identify the location of physical features.

**5** Use the compass rose to determine directions on the map.

**6** Use the scale to measure the actual distances between places shown on the map.

**7** Read the questions and then carefully study the map to determine the answers.

**1** Australia: Physical

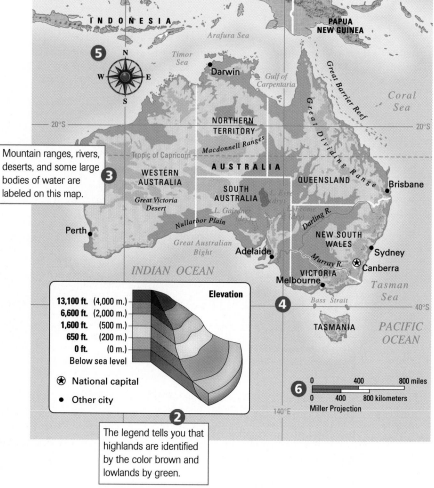

Mountain ranges, rivers, deserts, and some large bodies of water are labeled on this map.

The legend tells you that highlands are identified by the color brown and lowlands by green.

**1** South Australia, Victoria, and New South Wales contain mostly

**A** mountains.

**B** plateaus.

**C** lowlands.

**D** deserts.

**2** Where is the Great Barrier Reef located?

**A** Along the Nullarbor Plain

**B** In the Great Australian Bight

**C** In the Coral Sea

**D** Near the Great Victoria Desert

answers: 1 (C), 2 (C)

**Directions:** Use the map and your knowledge of world geography to answer the questions below.

### Egypt: Physical

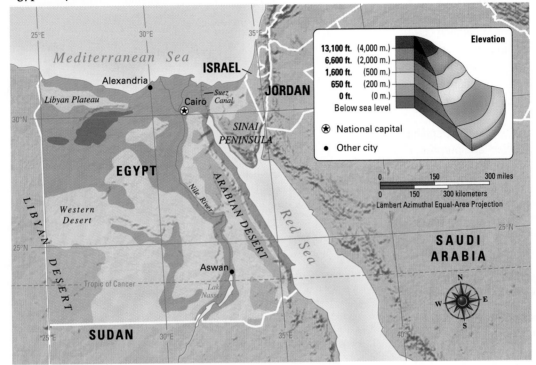

1  The location of Egypt's capital is approximately

**A** 30°N 31°E.

**B** 30°S 31°W.

**C** 25°N 33°E.

**D** 25°S 33°W.

2  The physical feature that dominates Egypt's landscape is

**A** mountains.

**B** deserts.

**C** mesas.

**D** lakes.

3  Which of the following statements *best* characterizes the Nile River?

**A** It is the longest river in Egypt.

**B** It extends the full length of the country.

**C** It is one of the few rivers in Egypt.

**D** All of the above

4  Which of the following conclusions can you draw from this map?

**A** Egypt has a well-distributed water supply.

**B** Agriculture is important in Egypt's southwest area.

**C** Much of Egypt has a dry climate.

**D** All of Egypt is sparsely populated.

# Thematic Maps

A thematic map, or special-purpose map, focuses on a particular topic. The location of state parks, a country's natural resources, the vegetation of a region, voting patterns, migration routes, and economic activities are all topics you might see illustrated on a thematic map.

**1** Read the title to determine the subject and purpose of the map.

**2** Examine the labels on the map to find more detailed information on the map's subject and purpose.

**3** Study the legend to find the meaning of the symbols and colors used on the map.

**4** Look at the symbols and colors on the map, and try to identify patterns.

**5** Read the questions and then carefully study the map to determine the answers.

**1** Ethnic Diversity in the Former Yugoslavia

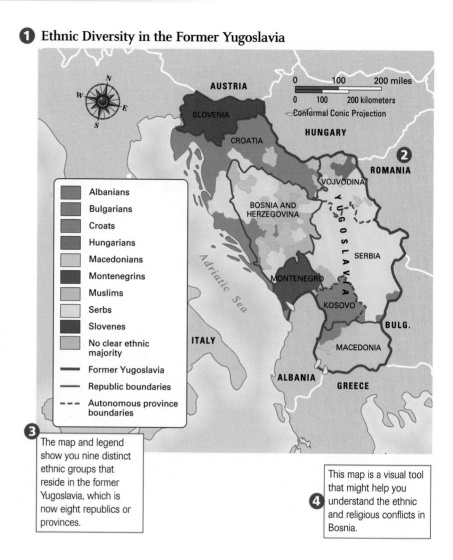

**3** The map and legend show you nine distinct ethnic groups that reside in the former Yugoslavia, which is now eight republics or provinces.

**4** This map is a visual tool that might help you understand the ethnic and religious conflicts in Bosnia.

**1** According to the map, which of the following ethnic groups live in Bosnia and Herzegovina?

A Croats, Macedonians, and Slovenes

B Serbs, Albanians, and Hungarians

C Bulgarians, Italians, and Albanians

D Croats, Serbs, and Muslims

**2** The former Yugoslavia did *not* include

A Kosovo.

B Slovenia.

C Romania.

D Croatia.

answers: 1 (D), 2 (C)

**Directions:** Use the map and your knowledge of world geography to answer the questions below.

## The Mongolian *Dzud* and Livestock Deaths

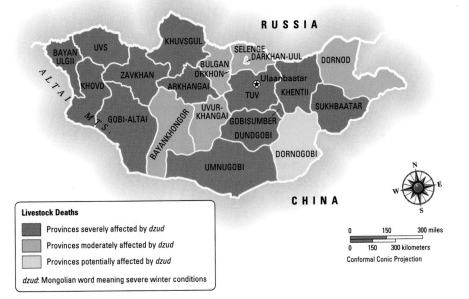

**Livestock Deaths**

- Provinces severely affected by *dzud*
- Provinces moderately affected by *dzud*
- Provinces potentially affected by *dzud*

*dzud*: Mongolian word meaning severe winter conditions

0    150    300 miles
0    150    300 kilometers
Conformal Conic Projection

**Source:** United Nations

**1** How many provinces in Mongolia were severely affected by *dzud,* the winter weather conditions?

 **A** Over half

 **B** One third

 **C** All of them

 **D** None of them

**2** Which of the following province's livestock losses were only potentially affected by *dzud*?

 **A** Zavkhan

 **B** Dornod

 **C** Dornogobi

 **D** Uvur-Khangai

**3** One of the reasons a record of livestock deaths is important to Mongolia is that

 **A** there are not many livestock in the country.

 **B** raising livestock is the basis of the Mongolian economy.

 **C** the livestock deaths are unusual because the climate tends to be moderate.

 **D** the country is shifting from a managed-style economy to a free-market economy.

**4** This map is most likely of the *greatest* use to

 **A** the Mongolian government and international relief agencies.

 **B** mapmakers and elementary schools.

 **C** the Chinese and the Russian governments.

 **D** Mongolian religious organizations.

# Time Lines

A time line is a type of chart that lists events in the order in which they occurred. In other words, time lines are a visual method of showing what happened when.

**1** Read the title to discover the subject of the time line.

**2** Identify the time period covered by the time line by noting the earliest and latest dates shown.

**3** Read the events and their dates in sequence. Notice the intervals between events.

**4** Use your knowledge of history to develop a fuller picture of the events listed in the time line. For example, place the events in a broader context by considering what was happening elsewhere in the world.

**5** Use the information you have gathered from these strategies to answer the questions.

**1** Dates of Independence for Selected African Countries

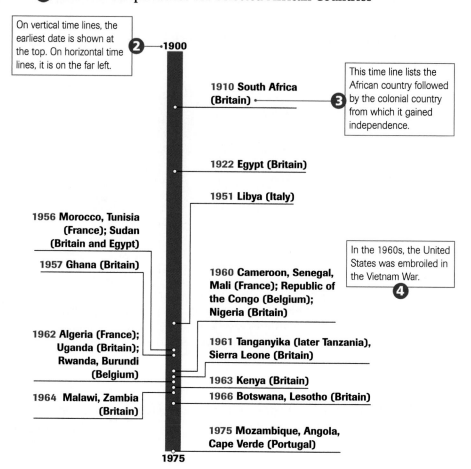

On vertical time lines, the earliest date is shown at the top. On horizontal time lines, it is on the far left.

**2** •1900

1910 **South Africa (Britain)** •

This time line lists the African country followed by the colonial country from which it gained independence. **3**

1922 **Egypt (Britain)**

1951 **Libya (Italy)**

1956 **Morocco, Tunisia (France); Sudan (Britain and Egypt)**

1957 **Ghana (Britain)**

In the 1960s, the United States was embroiled in the Vietnam War. **4**

1960 **Cameroon, Senegal, Mali (France); Republic of the Congo (Belgium); Nigeria (Britain)**

1962 **Algeria (France); Uganda (Britain); Rwanda, Burundi (Belgium)**

1961 **Tanganyika (later Tanzania), Sierra Leone (Britain)**

1963 **Kenya (Britain)**

1964 **Malawi, Zambia (Britain)**

1966 **Botswana, Lesotho (Britain)**

1975 **Mozambique, Angola, Cape Verde (Portugal)**

1975

**1** Which of the following colonial powers is *not* shown on the time line as freeing one of its colonies in 1960?

**A** France

**5**

**B** Belgium

**C** Britain

**D** Portugal

**2** You can infer from the information on the time line that French is most likely an important second language in

**A** Egypt.

**B** Morocco.

**C** Sierra Leone.

**D** Angola.

**answers:** 1 (D), 2 (B)

For more test practice online . . .

**TEST PRACTICE**
CLASSZONE.COM

**Directions:** Use the time line and your knowledge of world geography to answer the questions below.

## Milestones in World Communication

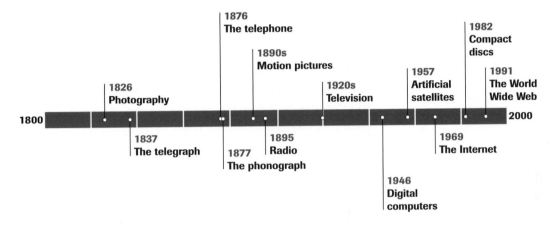

1 Two inventions of the 1800s that made long-distance communication possible were

A motion pictures and compact discs.

B television and the Internet.

C the telegraph and the telephone.

D the phonograph and artificial satellites.

2 About how many years after the introduction of photography were motion pictures invented?

A 34 years

B 64 years

C 94 years

D 124 years

3 The Internet followed the introduction of the digital computer by about

A 1 decade.

B 2 decades.

C 3 decades.

D 4 decades.

4 A design company has offices in Tokyo, Madrid, and Los Angeles. Which medium would the designers most likely use to share visual and written information almost instantly?

A Telegraph

B Television

C Compact discs

D The World Wide Web

# Constructed Response

Constructed-response questions focus on various kinds of documents, including short passages, excerpts, cartoons, charts, graphs, maps, posters, and photographs. Each document is usually accompanied by a series of questions. These questions call for short answers that, for the most part, can be found directly in the document. Some answers, however, require knowledge of the subject addressed in the document.

**1** Read the title of the document to discover the subject addressed in the questions.

**2** Study and analyze the document. Take notes on what you see or read.

**3** Read the questions and then examine the document again to locate the answers.

**4** Carefully write your answers. Unless the directions say otherwise, your answers need not be complete sentences.

**1** Size of Counties in the United States

Grounded in 19th-century ways of life, small-town America reproduced itself across a continent. Examine the counties on a map of the United States, and you will find these basic units of American self-government remarkably uniform in size across the country's eastern half. That is no coincidence; they were commonly drawn just big enough for any farmer in his horse-drawn wagon to reach the county seat and return home in a day—about a 20-mile round-trip. Out West, when the open spaces finally became too great and counties were laid off to larger scale, people devised novel ways to cope with distance; the German settlers in the Texas Hill Country built midget "Sunday houses" in town so that the necessary day-trip to church could be lengthened into two.

—Griffin Smith, Jr., "Small-Town America"

This document is an excerpt from a magazine article.

**2** Excerpt from "Small-Town America" by Griffin Smith, Jr., from *From the Field: A Collection of Writings from National Geographic*, edited by Charles McCarry. Copyright © 1997 by National Geographic Society. All rights reserved. Reprinted by permission of National Geographic Society.

**3** **1** According to the author, the size of counties in the eastern half of the United States is based upon what?

**4** *the distance that a farmer in a horse-drawn wagon could cover in making a round-trip to the county seat in one day*

**2** Why did the German settlers in the Texas Hill Country build midget "Sunday houses"?

*Because the counties out West were larger, the trip to town took two days, so to attend church, they built small houses to stay in overnight.*

**3** What 20th-century developments in transportation in the United States changed the way Americans coped with the distances described by the author?

*the development of the automobile and a national highway system*

**Directions:** Use the satellite image below and your knowledge of world geography to answer the following questions. Your answers need not be complete sentences.

### Satellite Image: Glacier in Patagonia, Chile, May 2, 2000

Satellite image: NASA/GSFC/MITI/ERSDAC/JAROS, and U.S./Japan ASTER Science Team

**Image acquired 440 miles above Earth's surface by NASA *Terra* spacecraft over the North Patagonia Ice Sheet near latitude 47°S, longitude 73°W, covering an area of 36 by 30 kilometers.**

**The satellite image is relayed to scientists who are studying most of the world's 16,000 glaciers. By comparing these new, more detailed images with older ones, scientists have found that the glaciers in Patagonia are melting. Some have receded as much as one mile in the past 13 years. Here, vegetation is shown in red and the glacier in white. The semicircular gray area around the spoon-like end of the glacier is a terminal moraine, which shows that the glacier was once larger than it is now.**

**1** What does the satellite image taken over Patagonia, Chile, show clearly?

**2** What is the significance of the semicircular terminal moraine shown on the image?

**3** How might satellite images help geographers and climatologists study global changes in climate?

# Extended Response

Extended-response questions, like constructed-response questions, usually focus on one type of document. However, they are more complex and require more time to complete than typical short-answer constructed-response questions. Some extended-response questions ask you to present information from the document in a different form. Others ask you to write an essay or report or some other extended piece of writing. Sometimes you are required to apply your knowledge of geography to information contained in the document.

**1** Read the title of the document to get an idea of the subject.

**2** Study and analyze the document.

**3** Carefully read each extended-response question.

**4** If the question calls for a drawing, such as a diagram, graph, or chart, make a rough sketch on scrap paper first. Then make a final copy of your drawing on the answer sheet.

**5** If the question requires an essay, jot down your ideas in outline form. Use this outline to write your answer.

**1** Causes of Death in Developed and Developing Countries, 1993

**2**

| Cause | Developed countries (percentage of deaths) | Developing countries (percentage of deaths) |
|---|---|---|
| Infections and parasites | 1.2 | 41.5 |
| Respiratory diseases | 7.8 | 5.0 |
| Cancers | 21.6 | 8.9 |
| Circulatory diseases | 46.7 | 10.7 |
| Childbirth | 0 | 1.3 |
| Infant mortality | 0.7 | 7.9 |
| Injury | 7.5 | 7.9 |
| Other causes | 14.5 | 16.8 |

**Source:** "Causes of Death, 1993," from *Oxford Atlas of World History,* edited by Patrick K. O'Brien. Copyright © 1999 by Oxford University Press. All rights reserved. Reprinted by permission of Oxford University Press.

**3 1** Use the information in the chart to create a bar graph showing the causes of death in developed and developing countries.

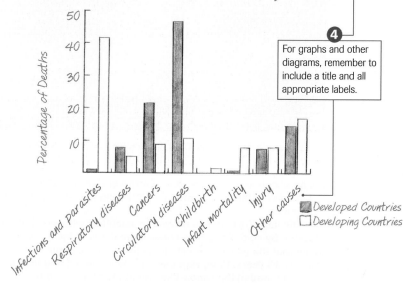

answer: Causes of Death in Developed and Developing Countries, 1993

**4** For graphs and other diagrams, remember to include a title and all appropriate labels.

**3 2** Write a short essay summarizing what the chart and graph show about the major causes of death in developed and developing countries. Give a possible explanation for the data.

**5** **Essay Rubric** The best essays will point out that infections and parasites claim the most lives in developing countries, whereas circulatory diseases and cancers are the main killers in developed countries. Poor sanitation and a lack of access to health care might account for the high death rate from infections and parasites in developing countries. In developed countries, a longer life expectancy as well as a fatty diet, smoking, and a lack of exercise might be factors in the high incidence of circulatory diseases and cancers.

For more test practice online . . .

TEST PRACTICE
CLASSZONE.COM

**Directions:** Use the following passage and your knowledge of world geography to answer the questions below.

**Subregions of Canada**

Canada and the United States share a similar history and culture. Canada's location in the northern latitudes, however, has affected its population distribution and its economic growth in ways that make the country different from the United States.

1   The chart below lists the four subregions of Canada. Complete the chart by briefly describing the population and economic activities of each subregion. (Note that some of the answers have been written for you.)

| Subregion | Population | Economic activities |
|---|---|---|
| **Atlantic Provinces** | small population due to rugged terrain and severe weather; most people living in coastal cities | logging, fishing, mining |
| **Core Provinces— Quebec and Ontario** | | agriculture, mining, manufacturing |
| **Prairie Provinces** | populated by diverse immigrant groups | |
| **Pacific Province and the Territories** | | logging, mining, and hydroelectric production in British Columbia; mining, fishing, and logging in territories |

2   In a short essay, compare and contrast population distribution in Canada with population distribution in the United States. Note any similarities between subregions of Canada and subregions of the United States, and describe the outstanding differences.

# Document-Based Questions

A document-based question (DBQ) requires you to analyze and interpret a variety of documents. These documents often are accompanied by short-answer questions. You use these answers and information from the documents to write an essay on a specified subject.

**1** Read the "Context" section to get a sense of the issue addressed in the question.

**2** Read the "Task" section and note the action words. This will help you understand exactly what the essay question requires.

**3** Study and analyze each document. Consider what connection the documents have to the essay question. Take notes on your ideas.

**4** Read and answer the document-specific questions. Think about how these questions connect to the essay topic.

## Introduction

**1** **Context:** In recent years, population densities in the urban areas of the United States have been falling. This is due, in large part, to urban sprawl—widespread low-density urban development, such as strip malls, large office buildings, and housing subdivisions, in areas well beyond city boundaries.

**2** **Task:** ⟨Define⟩ the term *urban sprawl* and ⟨explain⟩ why this recent development has become an issue of concern, particularly in the Sunbelt states.

## Part 1: Short Answer

Study each document carefully and answer the questions that follow.

**3** **Document 1: Urban Sprawl in the Southwest United States**

Copyright © Gary Layda/Metropolitan Planning Department of Nashville–Davidson County

**4** **How does this photograph illustrate urban sprawl?**

*The photograph shows low-density urban development well beyond city boundaries—a huge single-family housing subdivision butting up against the mountains.*

## Document 2: Developed Land in the United States

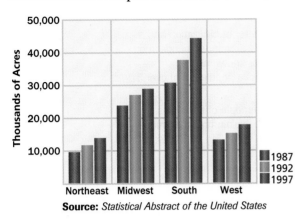

**Source:** *Statistical Abstract of the United States*

### What trends does the bar graph show?

*The area of developed land is increasing in all regions of the United States, but particularly in the South.*

## Document 3: The Impact of Sprawl in the United States

| | |
|---|---|
| **Sprawl increases traffic.** | Sprawl lengthens trips and forces people to drive more. |
| **Sprawl increases pollution.** | As sprawl increases, people rely more and more on cars and driving. Cars are a major source of air pollution. |
| **Sprawl increases the risk of flooding.** | Developments sometimes are built on floodplains and in wetland areas. |
| **Sprawl consumes parks, farms, and open space.** | Over one million acres of parks, farms, and open space are developed each year to accommodate sprawl. |
| **Sprawl drains the tax coffers.** | Sprawl requires millions of tax dollars for new infrastructure. These tax dollars could be spent on improving existing communities. |
| **Sprawl overcrowds schools** | Sprawl puts more children in suburban schools, causing overcrowding. |

**Source:** The Sierra Club

### What is the environmental impact of the sprawl-related increase in traffic?

*The increase in traffic causes an increase in air pollution.*

## Part 2: Essay

**5** Using information from the documents, your answers to the questions in Part 1, and your knowledge of world geography, write an essay that defines the term *urban sprawl* and explains why this recent development has become an issue of concern, particularly in the Sunbelt states.

**5** Carefully read the essay question. Then write an outline for your essay.

**6** Write your essay. Be sure that it has an introductory paragraph that introduces your argument, main body paragraphs that explain it, and a concluding paragraph that restates your position. In your essay, include quotations or details from specific documents to support your ideas. Add other supporting facts or details that you know from your study of world geography.

**6**
**Essay Rubric** The best essays will point out that urban sprawl involves widespread low-density urban development (such as strip malls, large office buildings, and housing subdivisions) in areas well beyond city boundaries (Document 1). They will go on to mention that this largely unplanned and uncontrolled development is cause for concern for several reasons. These include increased traffic and related air pollution, increased risk of flooding, increased costs to government, and school overcrowding (Document 3). They will conclude by pointing out that the rapid increase in the amount of developed land in the South indicates that urban sprawl is of particular concern in the Sunbelt states (Document 2).

## Introduction

**Context:** For more than 2,500 years, the city of Istanbul has been a center of civilization and a place of passage, where languages, crafts, goods, and necessities have exchanged hands and enriched the cultures of the world. It began as Byzantium and was later known as Constantinople. Istanbul today is the commercial center of Turkey. It has a population of over 8 million people.

**Task:** Discuss how the Istanbul of today is like and unlike the Constantinople of the 1300s. Discuss its role as a crossroads that connects vastly different cultures. Explain how the unique location of Istanbul is important to its development as a world port.

## Part 1: Short Answer

Study each document carefully and answer the questions that follow.

**Document 1: Constantinople, Center of Trade and Travel in the 1300s**

[Constantinople] is enormous in size, and in two parts separated by a great river. . . . The part of the city on the eastern bank of the river is called Istanbul. . . . Its bazaars and streets are spacious and paved with flagstones; each bazaar has gates which are closed upon it at night, and the majority of the artisans and sellers in them are women. The city lies at the foot of a hill which projects about nine miles into the sea. . . . Round this hill runs the city-wall, which is very strong and cannot be taken by assault from the sea front. Within its circuit there [are] about thirteen inhabited villages. The principal church is in the midst of this part of the city. The second part, on the western bank of the river . . . is reserved to the Frankish Christians who dwell there. They are of different kinds, including Genoese, Venetians, Romans and people of France. . . . They are all men of commerce and their harbour is one of the largest in the world; I saw there about a hundred galleys and other large ships.

—Excerpt from *The Adventures of Ibn Battuta: A Muslim Traveler of the 14th Century*, translated and edited by Ross W. Dunn (Berkeley: University of California Press, 1989), page 3. Reprinted by permission of the University of California Press.

What are three of the characteristics of Constantinople described by Ibn Battúta that might explain its long history as a major commercial, cultural, religious, and political center to the world?

Document 2: Istanbul, Turkey, June 16, 2000, Satellite Image

**The urban areas appear blue-green; vegetation appears red; water, blue. Istanbul is divided by the Bosporus Strait, which is a deep, twisting waterway, about 19 miles long, and about 800 yards wide at places. The city is a major port for Europe and Asia.**

NASA/GSFC/MITI/ERSDAC/JAROS, and
U.S./Japan ASTER Science Team

**What geographic factors explain the growth of Istanbul into a large city?**

Document 3: Number of Ships Traveling the Bosporus, 1995–2000

| Years | Tankers | Total Passages | Monthly Average | Daily Average |
|-------|---------|----------------|-----------------|---------------|
| 1995 | unknown | 46,954 | 3,912 | 128 |
| 1996 | 4,248 | 49,952 | 4,162 | 137 |
| 1997 | 4,303 | 50,942 | 4,245 | 142 |
| 1998 | 5,142 | 49,304 | 4,109 | 137 |
| 1999 | 4,452 | 47,906 | 3,992 | 133 |
| 2000 | 4,937 | 48,079 | 4,007 | 134 |

**Source:** "Number of Ships Traveling the Bosporus," from the Turkish Maritime Pilots' Association Web site. Reprinted by permission of the Turkish Maritime Pilots Association.

**How does the chart show that Istanbul is a major port?**

## Part 2: Essay

Using information from the documents, your answers to the questions in Part 1, and your knowledge of world geography, write an essay that discusses how the Istanbul of today is like and unlike the Constantinople of the 1300s. Discuss its role as a crossroads that connects vastly different cultures. Explain how the unique location of Istanbul is important to its development as a world port.

# RAND McNALLY
# World Atlas

# Contents

## Complete Legend for Physical and Political Maps

### Symbols

Lake

Salt Lake

Seasonal Lake

River

\ Waterfall

— Canal

△ Mountain Peak

▲ Highest Mountain Peak

### Cities

■ **Los Angeles** — City over 1,000,000 population

▣ **Calgary** — City of 250,000 to 1,000,000 population

• Haifa — City under 250,000 population

⊛ *Paris* — National Capital

★ **Vancouver** — Secondary Capital (State, Province, or Territory)

### Type Styles Used to Name Features

**CHINA** — Country

O N T A R I O — State, Province, or Territory

**PUERTO RICO (U.S.)** — Possession

A T L A N T I C O C E A N — Ocean or Sea

*A l p s* — Physical Feature

*Borneo* — Island

### Boundaries

International Boundary

Secondary Boundary

### Land Elevation and Water Depths

**Land Elevation**

| Meters | | Feet |
|---|---|---|
| 3,000 and over -- | | -- 9,840 and over |
| 2,000 - 3,000 -- | | -- 6,560 - 9,840 |
| 500 - 2,000 -- | | -- 1,640 - 6,560 |
| 200 - 500 -- | | -- 656 - 1,640 |
| 0 - 200 -- | | -- 0 - 656 |

**Water Depth**

| | | |
|---|---|---|
| Less than 200 -- | | -- Less than 656 |
| 200 - 2,000 -- | | -- 656 - 6,560 |
| Over 2,000 -- | | -- Over 6,560 |

ATLAS

ARCTIC OCEAN

Greenland

Baffin
Island

Baffin
Bay

Jan

Iceland

Faroe Is.

Yukon

Mackenzie

Canadian Shield

Hudson
Bay

Newfoundland

Mt. McKinley △
20,320 Ft.
6,194m

NORTH

Rocky Mountains

Great Plains

Aleutian Islands

Vancouver

AMERICA

St. Lawrence

Azores

Los Angeles

Colorado

Appalachian Mts.

Mississippi

Washington D.C.

Cape Hatteras

ATLANTIC

Canary
Islands

Midway Is.

Baja
California

Gulf of Mexico

Tropic of Cancer

Hawaiian
Islands

Yucatan
Peninsula

Cuba

Hispaniola

Puerto Rico

Jamaica

Caribbean
Sea

Cape
Verde
Islands

Cape Verde

PACIFIC

Orinoco

Trinidad

OCEAN

Palmyra

Galapagos Islands

Amazon

Amazon

SOUTH

Equator

Basin

AMERICA

Kiribati

Marquesas Is.

Mato Grosso
Plateau

St. Helena

Samoa
Islands

Andes

Rio de Janeiro

Tonga
Is.

Cook
Islands

Tahiti

Tropic of Capricorn

Easter Island

Paraná

Archipiélago
Juan Fernández

△Mt. Aconcagua
22,831 Ft.
6,959m

Buenos Aires

N

Chatham Is.

Patagonia

Falkland Is.

South
Georgia

0        1000        2000 Miles

0    1000    2000    3000 Kilometers

Copyright by Rand McNally & Co.
Robinson Projection

Tierra del Fuego

South
Sandwich Is.

Cape Horn

South
Orkney Is.

Antarctic Circle

South
Shetland Is.

Antarctic
Peninsula

Weddell
Sea

Ross
Sea

Marie
Byrd
Land

△ Vinson Massif
16,066 Ft.
4,897m

ATLAS

ARCTIC OCEAN

Baffin
Bay

GREENLAND
(Den.)

Arctic Circle

RUSSIA          ALASKA
                Yukon (U.S.)
Anchorage•

ICELAND

FAROE IS.
(Den.)

IRELAND

Aleutian Islands

C A N A D A

Hudson
Bay

Newfoundland

Vancouver

Missouri

Montréal
Ottawa⊛

PORTUGAL

Azores
(Port.)

Chicago•

UNITED STATES

New York
Washington D.C.

Colorado

Casablanca•

Los Angeles•

ATLANTIC

Canary
Islands
(Sp.)

Houston•

MIDWAY IS.
(U.S.)

Tropic of Cancer

Gulf of Mexico

BAHAMAS

MEXICO

MAURITANIA

Hawaiian
Islands
(U.S)

Mexico City⊛

CUBA
HAITI    DOM. REP.
         PUERTO RICO (U.S.)
JAMAICA  Caribbean
         Sea

CAPE
VERDE

SENEGAL

P A C I F I C

BELIZE
GUAT. HOND.
EL. SAL. NIC.

GAMBIA
GUINEA-BISSAU

SIERRA LEONE

COSTA
RICA
PANAMA

Caracas⊛
VENEZUELA

TRINIDAD AND TOBAGO

GUYANA
SURINAME
FRENCH GUIANA

LIBERIA

COLOMBIA

Galapagos Islands
(Ecuador)

ECUADOR

Amazon

B R A Z I L

O C E A N

Equator

KIRIBATI

PERU

Lima⊛

SAMOA

O C E A N

AMERICAN
SAMOA

COOK
ISLANDS (N.Z.)

TONGA

FRENCH POLYNESIA

Tropic of Capricorn

BOLIVIA

PARAGUAY

Rio de Janeiro

ST. HELENA
(U.K.)

Easter Island
(Chile)

ARGENTINA

N

URUGUAY

Santiago⊛

Buenos⊛
Aires

0        1000        2000 Miles
0   1000   2000   3000 Kilometers
Copyright by Rand McNally & Co.
Robinson Projection

FALKLAND IS.
(U.K.)

South
Georgia
(U.K.)

South
Orkney Is.
(U.K.)

Antarctic Circle

South
Shetland Is.
(U.K.)

Weddell
Sea

ATLAS

**ARCTIC OCEAN**

Franz Josef Land (r.)

Novaya Zemlya

FINLAND

SWEDEN EST. LAT.
LITH.
Volga
Moscow

GERMANY POLAND BELARUS
CZ
AUS HUNG UKRAINE
SLVK MOLD.
CRO ROM.
BOS BUL.
ALB MA.
ITC GREECE
Rome
TURKEY

Black Sea

GEO.
ARM. AZER.

ALB. MA.

Mediterranean Sea

Crete CYPRUS LEB.
SYRIA
ISRAEL
JORDAN
IRAQ

TUNISIA

Cairo

LIBYA EGYPT

NIGER

CHAD SUDAN

MA

CENTRAL
AFRICAN
REPUBLIC

CAMEROON

ERIA

Jos

GABON

OF
GO

DEM. REP.
OF CONGO

Congo

RWANDA
BURUNDI

UGANDA

KENYA

TANZANIA

ANGOLA

ZAMBIA

NAMIBIA ZIMBABWE

BOTSWANA

MOZAMBIQUE

SWAZILAND

SOUTH
AFRICA LESOTHO

ape Town

**RUSSIA**

Yenisey

Ob

Novosibirsk

KAZAKHSTAN

UZBEKISTAN

TURKMENISTAN
KYRG.
TAJIK.

IRAN AFGHANISTAN

KUWAIT

SAUDI
ARABIA QATAR
U.A.E.

OMAN

YEMEN

Red Sea

ERITREA

DJIBOUTI

ETHIOPIA

SOMALIA

Addis
Ababa

SEYCHELLES

COMOROS

MADAGASCAR

REUNION
(Fr.)

Lena

MONGOLIA

CHINA

Beijing

PAKISTAN

NEPAL
Ganges
BHU.
BNGL.

INDIA

Mumbai
(Bombay)

Arabian
Sea

Bay of
Bengal

MALDIVES

Kolkata
(Calcutta)

MYANMAR

LAOS

THAILAND

Bangkok

SRI LANKA

CAMBODIA

VIETNAM

Chang Jiang
(Yangtze)

Guangzhou

Shanghai

TAIWAN

South China
Sea

Sea of Japan

NORTH
KOREA

SOUTH
KOREA

JAPAN
Tokyo

PACIFIC

Tropic of Cancer

NORTHERN
MARIANA ISLANDS
(U.S.)

GUAM (U.S.)

PHILIPPINES

PALAU

OCEAN

WAKE ISLAND
(U.S.)

MARSHALL
ISLANDS

FED. STATES OF
MICRONESIA

BRUNEI

MALAYSIA

SINGAPORE

Borneo

Sumatra

Jakarta

Java

INDONESIA

New Guinea

PAPUA
NEW GUINEA

EAST TIMOR

SOLOMON
ISLANDS

Equator

INDIAN

Darwin

Coral Sea

VANUATU

NEW CALEDONIA
(Fr.)

FIJI

Tropic of Capricorn

OCEAN

AUSTRALIA

Perth

Darling

Sydney

Melbourne

NEW ZEALAND
Wellington

Tasmania

Kerguelen
Islands
(Fr.)

Antarctic Circle

ANTARCTICA

Bering
Sea

Sea of Okhotsk

15° 30° 45° 60° 75° 90° 105° 120° 135° 150° 165° 180°

75°

60°

45°

30°

15°

0°

15°

30°

45°

60°

75°

RAND McNALLY

A5

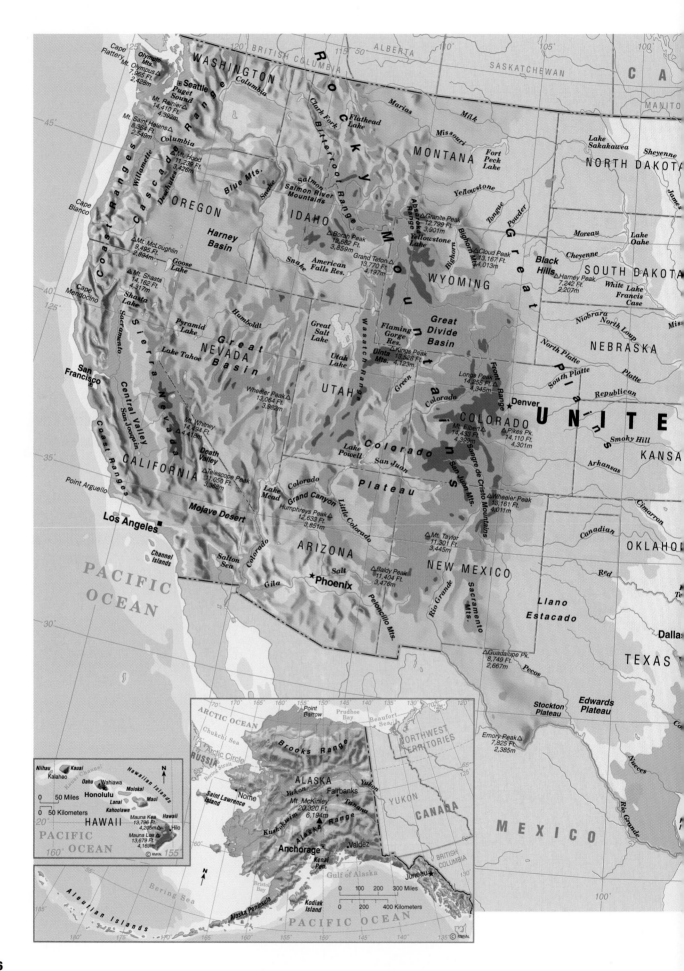

D A
ONTARIO
Lake
Nipigon
QUÉBEC
Lake of
the
Woods
NEW
BRUNSWICK
St. Lawrence
Isle Royale
Keweenaw
Peninsula
Whitefish
Point
Lake Superior
Great
Lakes
Mt. Katahdin
5,268 Ft.
1,606m
MAINE
Moosehead
Lake
NESOTA
MINNESOTA
Upper Peninsula
MICHIGAN
Montréal
VERMONT
Lake
Champlain
White
Mts.
Mt. Washington
6,288 Ft.
1,917m
Gulf of
Maine
neapolis
Minneapolis
Georgian
Bay
Bruce
Peninsula
Lake Huron
Saginaw Bay
Adirondack
Mountains
NEW
HAMPSHIRE
Chippewa
WISCONSIN
Lake
Winnebago
Muskegon
Lower Peninsula
Grand
Toronto
Lake Ontario
Niagara
Falls
NEW YORK
Green Mts.
Connecticut
MASS.
Boston
Cape Cod
Wisconsin
Lake Michigan
Catskill
Mts.
Hudson
CONNECTICUT R.I.
Nantucket
Island
IOWA
Iowa
Detroit
Lake Erie
Maumee
Allegheny
Plateau
PENNSYLVANIA
Susquehanna
Long Island
New York
Des Moines
Chicago
INDIANA
OHIO
Scioto
Allegheny Mountains
Philadelphia
NEW JERSEY
S T A T E S
Illinois
White
ILLINOIS
Ohio
WEST
VIRGINIA
Washington D.C.
James
VIRGINIA
DELAWARE
MARYLAND
Delaware Bay
ota
Mississippi
Lake of
the Ozarks
Missouri
St. Louis
Appalachian Mountains
Chesapeake Bay
Albemarle
Sound
MISSOURI
Green
Lake
Cumberland
KENTUCKY
Cumberland
Roanoke
Blue Ridge Mountains
Cape Hatteras
Ozark Plateau
White
Kentucky
Lake
Mt. Mitchell
6,684 Ft.
2,037m
Piedmont
NORTH
CAROLINA
Pamlico Sound
daho
Boston
Mts.
Kentucky Lake
Cumberland Plateau
TENNESSEE
Cape Lookout
70°
chita Mts.
Ouachita
Arkansas
ARKANSAS
Tennessee
Appalachian
Cape Fear
Coastal Plain
Cape Fear
ATLANTIC
ame
arn
es.
Yazoo
Mississippi
SOUTH
CAROLINA
Pee Dee
OCEAN
Toledo
Bend
Res.
Red
MISSISSIPPI
Tombigbee
ALABAMA
Clarks
Hill
Lake
Santee
Savannah
GEORGIA
Atlanta
Pearl
Sea Islands
N
LOUISIANA
Alabama
Flint
Chattahoochee
Altamaha
0   100   200   300 Miles
0   100   200   300   400 Kilometers
Copyright by Rand McNally & Co.
Alber's Conic Equal Area Projection
ousen
Houston
New
Orleans
Cape
San Blas
Apalachee
Bay
Suwannee
Atchafalaya
Bay
Mississippi
Delta
Cape Canaveral
GULF OF MEXICO
Tampa Bay
FLORIDA
Lake
Okeechobee
The
Everglades
Miami
Cape Sable
Florida Keys

67°    66°
19°
ATLANTIC
OCEAN
N
Arecibo
San
Juan
Mayaguez
Caguas
Ponce
18°
PUERTO RICO
(U.S.)
0   25   50 Miles
0   25   50 Kilometers
Caribbean
Sea

85°   80°   50°   75°   70°   45°   40°   35°   30°   25°
90°   85°   80°   75°

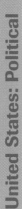

RAND McNALLY

**D A**

ONTARIO

QUÉBEC

NEW BRUNSWICK

Lake Nipigon

Lake of the Woods

International Falls

Duluth

MINNESOTA

•Cloud

•nneapolis St. Paul★

Mankato

•Rochester

IOWA

Des Moines ★

Waterloo

Dubuque

Cedar Rapids

•Davenport

Moline•

Rockford•

Isle Royale

Lake Superior

Marquette

MICHIGAN

Sault Ste. Marie

Georgian Bay

Lake Huron

Lake Michigan

WISCONSIN

Green Bay

Appleton

OshKosh

Sheboygan

Milwaukee

Madison★

Racine•

Eau Claire

Traverse City

Saginaw

Grand Rapids•

•Flint

Lansing•

Detroit

Ann Arbor

Kalamazoo

Lake Erie

MAINE

Moosehead Lake

•Bangor

•Augusta

St. Lawrence

Montréal

Ottawa

Lake Champlain

Burlington•

VERMONT

Montpelier★

Concord★

NEW HAMPSHIRE

Manchester•

Portland•

Gulf of Maine

Toronto★

Lake Ontario

Rochester•

Buffalo•

NEW YORK

Syracuse

Binghamton

Albany★

Watertown•

Worcester

MASSACHUSETTS

•Boston

Providence

CONNECTICUT R.I.

Hartford★

Bridgeport•

Nantucket Island

Long Island

Peoria•

Springfield★

ILLINOIS

Aurora•

Chicago■

Gary•

South Bend•

Fort Wayne•

Lima•

INDIANA

Bloomington•

Muncie•

Indianapolis■

Dayton•

Terre Haute•

Bloomington•

OHIO

Columbus★

Springfield•

Cincinnati■

Toledo■

Cleveland•

Akron•

Youngstown

Erie•

Oil City•

PENNSYLVANIA

Scranton•

Pittsburgh■

Harrisburg★

Allentown•

Susquehanna

New York★

Newark

Trenton★

Philadelphia■

NEW JERSEY

Wilmington•

DELAWARE

Dover★

MARYLAND

Baltimore■

Annapolis★

Delaware Bay

Mississippi

Illinois

St. Joseph•

•as City

•ka

Kansas City

Jefferson City•

Columbia•

MISSOURI

Springfield•

Cape Girardeau•

St. Louis★

Decatur•

Evansville•

Owensboro•

Wabash

Ohio

Louisville■

Frankfort★

Lexington•

KENTUCKY

Missouri

Huntington•

Charleston•

WEST VIRGINIA

Washington D.C.★

VIRGINIA

Richmond★

Roanoke•

Newport News•

Norfolk•

Virginia Beach

Albemarle Sound

Cumberland

Kentucky Lake

Clarksville•

Nashville★

Knoxville•

TENNESSEE

Chattanooga•

Memphis■

Huntsville•

Johnson City•

Winston-Salem•

Greensboro•

Durham•

Raleigh★

Asheville•

NORTH CAROLINA

Charlotte■

Roanoke

Pamlico

Greenville•

Wilmington•

ATLANTIC OCEAN

•as

•St. Joseph

Fayetteville•

Jonesboro•

Fort Smith•

Little Rock•

ARKANSAS

Pine Bluff•

Arkansas

xarkana

yler•

am urn es.

Ouachita

Shreveport•

Monroe•

LOUISIANA

Toledo Bend Res.

Jackson•

MISSISSIPPI

Tombigbee

Mississippi

Tuscaloosa•

Birmingham■

Montgomery★

ALABAMA

Athens•

Atlanta★

Macon•

Columbus•

GEORGIA

Albany•

Augusta•

Chattahoochee

Altamaha

Savannah

Charleston•

Greenville•

SOUTH CAROLINA

Columbia★

Savannah•

N

•aumont

Houston●

Galveston•

Hattiesburg•

Lake Charles•

Lafayette•

Baton Rouge★

Gulfport•

Mobile•

Pensacola•

New Orleans■

Dothan•

Tallahassee★

Jacksonville■

GULF OF MEXICO

Gainesville•

Daytona Beach•

Orlando•

Tampa■

Lakeland•

St. Petersburg•

FLORIDA

Lake Okeechobee

Fort Myers•

West Palm Beach

Fort Lauderdale•

Miami■

Key West•

0    100    200    300 Miles

0    100    200    300    400 Kilometers

Copyright by Rand McNally & Co.
Alber's Conic Equal Area Projection

ATLANTIC OCEAN

19°

67°    66°

N

Arecibo•

San Juan★

Mayagüez•    Caguas•

Ponce•

PUERTO RICO (U.S.)

18°

0    25    50 Miles

0    25    50 Kilometers

Caribbean Sea

© RMcN.

95°    90°    85°    80°    75°

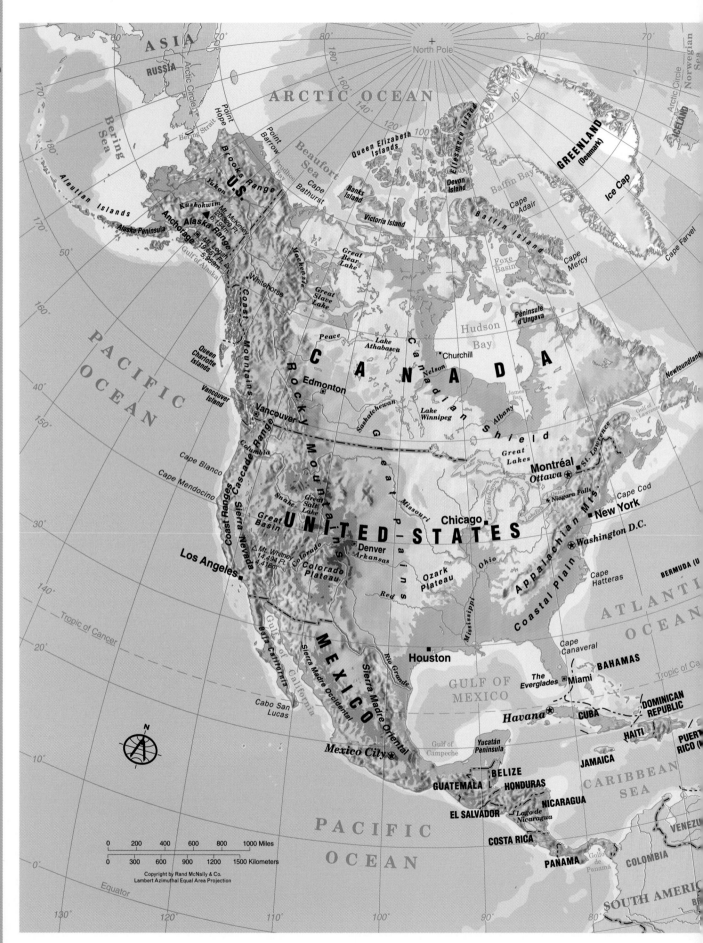

ASIA

RUSSIA

Arctic Circle

Bering Strait

Point Hope

ARCTIC OCEAN

North Pole

Beaufort Sea

Point Barrow

Prudhoe Bay

Cape Bathurst

Queen Elizabeth Islands

Banks Island

Ellesmere Island

Devon Island

GREENLAND (Denmark)

Ice Cap

ICELAND

Bering Sea

Brooks Range

U.S.

Yukon

Kuskokwim

Mt. McKinley 20,320 Ft. 6,194m

Alaska Range

Anchorage

Mt. Logan 19,551 Ft. 5,959m

Gulf of Alaska

Victoria Island

Mackenzie

Great Bear Lake

Baffin Island

Cape Adair

Baffin Bay

Cape Mercy

Cape Farvel

Aleutian Islands

Alaska Peninsula

Whitehorse

Coast Mountains

Great Slave Lake

Peace

Lake Athabasca

Hudson Bay

Foxe Basin

Péninsule d'Ungava

PACIFIC OCEAN

Queen Charlotte Islands

Vancouver Island

Rocky Mountains

C A N A D A

Edmonton

Saskatchewan

Churchill

Nelson

Lake Winnipeg

James Bay

Albany

Canadian Shield

Newfoundland

Cape Blanco

Cape Mendocino

Vancouver

Columbia

Cascade Range

Snake

Great Salt Lake

Great Basin

UNITED STATES

Great Plains

Missouri

Lake Superior

Great Lakes

Lake Michigan

Lake Huron

Lake Erie

Montréal

Ottawa

Lake Ontario

Niagara Falls

St. Lawrence

Gulf of St. Lawrence

Cape Cod

Coast Ranges

Sierra Nevada

Mt. Whitney 14,494 Ft. 4,418m

Colorado

Colorado Plateau

Denver

Arkansas

Red

Ozark Plateau

Mississippi

Ohio

Appalachian Mts.

Chicago

New York

Washington D.C.

Coastal Plain

Cape Hatteras

ATLANTIC OCEAN

BERMUDA (U)

Los Angeles

Gulf of California

Baja California

MEXICO

Sierra Madre Occidental

Sierra Madre Oriental

Rio Grande

Houston

GULF OF MEXICO

Cape Canaveral

The Everglades

Miami

BAHAMAS

Tropic of Cancer

Cabo San Lucas

Gulf of Campeche

Yucatán Peninsula

Mexico City

Havana

CUBA

DOMINICAN REPUBLIC

HAITI

PUERTO RICO (U

JAMAICA

CARIBBEAN SEA

BELIZE

GUATEMALA

HONDURAS

EL SALVADOR

NICARAGUA

Lago de Nicaragua

COSTA RICA

PANAMA

Golfo de Panamá

COLOMBIA

VENEZUELA

PACIFIC OCEAN

SOUTH AMERICA

N

| | | | | |
|---|---|---|---|---|
| 0 | 200 | 400 | 600 | 800 | 1000 Miles |
| 0 | 300 | 600 | 900 | 1200 | 1500 Kilometers |

Copyright by Rand McNally & Co.
Lambert Azimuthal Equal Area Projection

Equator

ASIA

RUSSIA

Arctic Circle

Bering
Strait

ARCTIC OCEAN

North Pole

Beaufort
Sea

Queen Elizabeth
Islands

Ellesmere Island

GREENLAND
(Denmark)

ICELAND
Reykjavík

Arctic Circle

Prudhoe
Bay

Aleutian Islands

Banks
Island

Devon
Island

Baffin Bay

Godthåb

Anchorage
Fairbanks
Yukon
Valdez
Juneau
Whitehorse

U.S.

Victoria Island

Baffin Island

PACIFIC

Gulf of Alaska

Mackenzie

Great
Bear
Lake

Great
Slave
Lake
Yellowknife

Hudson
Bay

OCEAN

Peace

CANADA

Newfoundland

Edmonton

Nelson

Lake
Winnipeg

St. John's

Victoria
Vancouver
Seattle

Calgary
Saskatoon
Saskatchewan
Regina

Gulf of
St. Lawrence

Saint John
Halifax

Spokane

Winnipeg

Thunder Bay

Québec

Columbia

Missouri

Lake Superior

Montréal
Ottawa
St. Lawrence

Portland

Billings

Minneapolis

Milwaukee
Chicago
Detroit

Toronto

Boston

New York

Sacramento
San Francisco

Great
Salt
Lake

UNITED STATES

Omaha

Lake Michigan

Cleveland

Philadelphia
Washington D.C.

Las Vegas

Denver
Colorado
Arkansas

Kansas City
St. Louis

Indianapolis
Ohio

Cincinnati

Norfolk

Los Angeles
San Diego
Tijuana

Albuquerque

Oklahoma
City
Red

Nashville

Charlotte

BERMUDA (U.K.)

ATLANTIC

Phoenix

Memphis

Atlanta

Ciudad
Juárez

Dallas

Mississippi

Jacksonville

OCEAN

Hermosillo

MEXICO

Gulf of

Houston

San Antonio

New Orleans

Tampa

Miami

BAHAMAS
Nassau

Tropic of Cancer

30°

Chihuahua

Rio Grande

Culiacan

Torreón
Monterrey

Tropic of Cancer

GULF OF
MEXICO

California

San Luis Potosí

Mérida

Cancún

Havana

CUBA

DOMINICAN
REPUBLIC

PUERTO
RICO
(U.S.)

Guadalajara
León

Mexico City
Puebla
Veracruz

JAMAICA
Kingston

HAITI
Port-au-
Prince

Santo
Domingo

CARIBBEAN

Acapulco

BELIZE
Belmopan

Caracas

GUATEMALA

HONDURAS

SEA

PACIFIC

Guatemala City

Tegucigalpa
Lago de NICARAGUA
Nicaragua

Panama
City

VENEZUELA

San Salvador
EL SALVADOR
Managua

OCEAN

COSTA RICA
San José

PANAMA

Golfo
de
Panamá

COLOMBIA
Bogotá

SOUTH AMERICA
BRAZIL

N

0     200    400    600    800   1000 Miles

0     300    600    900   1200   1500 Kilometers

Copyright by Rand McNally & Co.
Lambert Azimuthal Equal Area Projection

Equator

RAND M?NALLY

ICELAND

Horn

Fontur

Surtsey

Arctic Circle

NORWEGIAN SEA

Lofoten Islands

Kebnekaise
6,926 Ft.
2,111m

Luleälven

Scandinavian
Peninsula

Umeälven

Gulf of B

FAROE ISLANDS
(Den.)

NORWAY

SWEDEN

Galdhøpiggen
8,100 Ft.
2,469m

Glomma

Klarälven

Dalälven

Stockholm

ATLANTIC

OCEAN

Hebrides

Orkney
Islands

Grampian
Mts.

UNITED

KINGDOM

Cheviot
Hills

NORTH
SEA

Skagerrak

DENMARK

Vänern

Vättern

Öland

BALTIC S

Ireland

Irish
Sea

IRELAND

Great
Britain

St. George's Channel

Thames

London

Bornholm
(Den.)

NETHERLANDS

Elbe

Northern Eur

Berlin

Oder

R

English Channel

Strait of Dover

GERMANY

POLAND

BELGIUM

Rhine

LUX.

Paris

Paris
Basin

Loire

Seine

CZECH
REPUBLIC

Bohemian
Forest

SLOVAK

FRANCE

Saone

Jura

Black
Forest

Danube

AUSTRIA

HUNGARY

Bay of Biscay

Dordogne

Massif
Central

Rhône

Mt. Blanc
15,771 Ft.
4,808m

SWITZERLAND

LIECH.

Alps

Drava

Great Hun
Plai

Cantabrian Mts.

Pyrenees

ANDORRA

Po

SLOVENIA

CROATIA

Duero

Iberian Mts.

Ebro

Apennines

SAN
MARINO

Dinaric Alps

BOSNIA AND
HERZEGOVINA

Bal

Douro

Iberian

MONACO

ADRIATIC SEA

YUGOS

Lisbon

PORTUGAL

Peninsula

SPAIN

Tagus

Sierra Morena

Corsica
(Fr.)

Rome

ITALY

ALBANIA

Balearic Islands

Minorca

Sardinia
(It.)

Pind

Strait of Gibraltar

Ibiza

Majorca

△Vesuvius
4,190 Ft.
1,277m

GIBRALTAR
(U.K.)

Algiers

TYRRHENIAN
SEA

MEDITERRAN

Mt. Etna
10,902 Ft.
3,323m △
Sicily

IONIAN
SEA

AFRICA

MOROCCO

ALGERIA

TUNISIA

MALTA

0    100    200    300    400 Miles
0    200    400    600 Kilometers

Copyright by Rand McNally & Co.
Lambert Conformal Conic Projection

N

Murmansk

Kola
Peninsula
Ponoy

WHITE SEA

Timan Ridge

Pechora

Ob'

Mezen

Northern Dvina

Irtysh

Onega

Sukhona

Northern Uvals
(Uplands)

Kama

Ural Mountains

d

NLAND

Lake
Onega

Helsinki

of Finland

Lake
Ladoga

Rybinsk
Res.

RUSSIA

ASIA

TONIA

Lake
Peipus

Valdai
Hills

⊛ Moscow

Oka

LATVIA

Plain

HUANIA

Neman

a-ID

Central
Russian
Upland

Don

Khoper

Ural

KAZAKHSTAN

Caspian Depression

Syr Darya

Aral Sea

UZBEKISTAN

BELARUS

Pripyat

Dnieper

Lowland

Volga

Amu Darya

Kiev ⊛

Dniester

Donets Basin

Dnieper

UKRAINE

MOLDOVA

Sea of Azov

Crimean
Peninsula

C A S P I A N

TURKMENISTAN

MANIA

sylvanian Alps

Danube

Caucasus

Mt. Elbrus
18,510 Ft.
5,642m

Baku ⊛

S E A

eninsula

B L A C K   S E A

GEORGIA

BULGARIA

ARMENIA

AZERBAIJAN

Tehran ⊛

Istanbul

AZER.

t. Olympus
570 Ft.
917m

TURKEY

IRAN

REECE

IRAQ

Euphrates

EGEAN SEA

N

SYRIA

Rhodes

NORTH
CYPRUS

LEBANON

Tigris

Crete

SEA

CYPRUS

ICELAND
Reykjavik

Arctic Circle

NORWEGIAN SEA

FAROE ISLANDS (Den.)

Trondheim

Umeå

NORWAY  SWEDEN

Bergen

Oslo

Stockholm

Aberdeen

SCOTLAND

Glasgow

Edinburgh

UNITED

NORTH SEA

DENMARK

Skagerrak

Vänern  Vättern

Göteborg

BALTIC

Copenhagen

LITHUA

Kaliningrad  RUS

Gdańsk

POLAND

NORTHERN IRELAND

Belfast

Irish Sea

KINGDOM

Dublin

IRELAND

Cork

Liverpool

Manchester

WALES

St. George's Channel

Birmingham

ENGLAND

Cardiff

Thames

Plymouth

London

NETHERLANDS

Amsterdam

The Hague

Hamburg

Elbe

Berlin

Szczecin

GERMANY

Oder

Dresden

Wroclaw

Warsaw

Wisła

English Channel

Strait of Dover

Le Havre

Brussels

BELGIUM

Cologne

Bonn

Frankfurt

Rhine

Prague

CZECH REPUBLIC

Krak

Luxembourg

LUX.

Paris

Nantes

Loire

Seine

Strasbourg

Stuttgart

Danube

Munich

SLOVAKIA

Bratislava

Vienna

AUSTRIA

Budapest

HUNGARY

Belgra

FRANCE

Zürich

Bern

LIECH.

SWITZERLAND

Geneva

Lyon

Rhône

SLOVENIA

Ljubljana

Zagreb

A Coruña

Bay of Biscay

Gijón

Bilbao

Porto

Toulouse

Bordeaux

Turin

Milan

Venice

Po

CROATIA

Genoa

Nice

Marseille

MONACO

Florence

SAN MARINO

BOSNIA AND HERZEGOVINA

Sarajevo

YUGOSLA

Valladolid

PORTUGAL

Lisbon

Tagus

Madrid

SPAIN

ANDORRA

Zaragoza

Ebro

Barcelona

Corsica (Fr.)

Rome

VATICAN CITY

ITALY

ADRIATIC SEA

Skopje

ALBANIA

MA DO

Valencia

Córdoba

Palma

Sardinia (It.)

Naples

Bari

Tiranë

Seville

Málaga

GIBRALTAR (U.K.)

Cagliari

TYRRHENIAN SEA

Strait of Gibraltar

Rabat

Algiers

MEDITERRA

Palermo

Sicily

Catania

IONIAN SEA

MOROCCO

AFRICA

ALGERIA

TUNISIA

Tunis

Valletta

MALTA

NE

ATLANTIC OCEAN

0  100  200  300  400 Miles
0    200    400    600 Kilometers

Copyright by Rand McNally & Co.
Lambert Conformal Conic Projection

Murmansk

WHITE SEA

Arkhangel'sk

*Northern Dvína*

Syktyvkar

R U S S I A

Perm'

Petrozavodsk
*Lake
Onega*

Kirov

Izhevsk

Ufa

A S I A

St. Petersburg

elsinki

*Finland*

Cherepovets
*Rybinsk
Res.*

Nizhniy
Novgorod

Kazan'

Yaroslavl'

A S I A

llinn

NIA

*Lake
Peipus*

Tver'

*Oka*

Samara

ga

LATVIA

Moscow ✪

Ryazan'

Penza

KAZAKHSTAN

*Syr Darýá*

Vitsyebsk

Tula

Don

Lipetsk

Saratov

*Ural*

*Aral Sea*

ius

✪ *Minsk*

Bryansk

Voronezh

UZBEKISTAN

BELARUS

Homyel'

Volgograd

Astrakhan'

*Amu Darya*

Chernobyl

✪ Kiev

Kharkiv

Luhans'k

*Volga*

C A S P I A N

'viv

UKRAINE

*Dnieper*

Dnipro-
petrovs'k

Donets'k

Rostov

TURKMENISTAN

niester

Vinnytsya

Kryvyy Rih

Zaporizhzhya

Mariupol'

S E A

MOLDOVA

Iaşi

✪ *Chişinău*

Krasnodar

Stavropol'

uj-Napoca

Odesa

*Sea of Azov*

Ashgabat

MANIA

Galaţi

Simferopol'

Grozny

Bakur

Sevastopol'

GEORGIA

✪ *Tbilisi*

Bucharest

B L A C K   S E A

AZERBAIJAN

be

BULGARIA

Varna

ARMENIA

Sofia

AZER.

Plovdiv

*Yerevan*

✪ Tehran

IRAN

Istanbul

essaloníki

*Ankara*

TURKEY

IRAQ

EECE

*Baghdad*

thens

SYRIA

*Euphrates*

AEGEAN

NORTH
CYPRUS

*Nicosia*

*Tigris*

N

SEA

CYPRUS

*Beirut* LEBANON

Crete

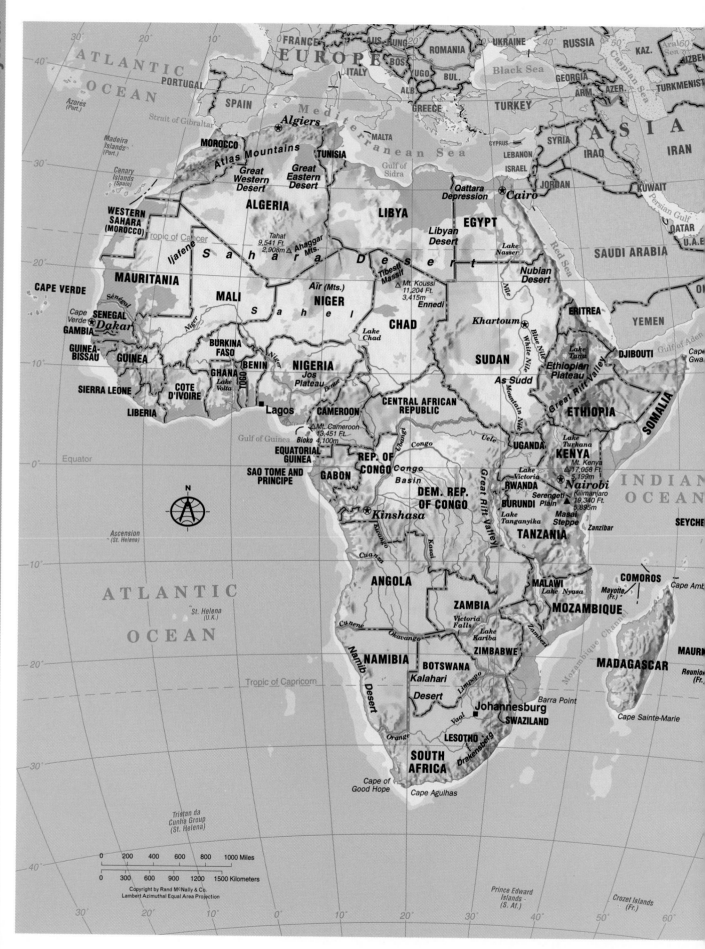

ATLANTIC
OCEAN

PORTUGAL

Azores
(Port.)

FRANCE

EUROPE

AUS. HUNG.
ROMANIA
BOS.
YUGO.
BUL.

RUSSIA
UKRAINE

KAZ.

Aral
Sea

SPAIN

ITALY

Black Sea

GEORGIA

Caspian Sea

TURKMENIST

ALB.

Strait of Gibraltar

Mediterranean Sea

GREECE

TURKEY

ARM. AZER.

Madeira
Islands
(Port.)

MOROCCO

Algiers

MALTA

CYPRUS

SYRIA

IRAQ

IRAN

Canary
Islands
(Spain)

Atlas Mountains

TUNISIA

LEBANON

ISRAEL

JORDAN

KUWAIT

A S I A

WESTERN
SAHARA
(MOROCCO)

Great
Western
Desert

Great
Eastern
Desert

ALGERIA

LIBYA

Qattara
Depression

Cairo

EGYPT

QATAR

U.A.E.

Tropic of Cancer

Ijafene

S   a   h   a   r   a

Tahat
9,541 Ft.
2,908m   Ahaggar
Mts.

Libyan
Desert

Lake
Nasser

Red Sea

SAUDI ARABIA

O

MAURITANIA

MALI

Aïr (Mts.)

NIGER

D   e   s   e   r   t

Tibesti
Massif
Mt. Koussi
11,204 Ft.
3,415m
Ennedi

Nubian
Desert

YEMEN

Gulf of Aden

CAPE VERDE

S   a   h   e   l

Nile

ERITREA

Cape
Verde

SENEGAL

Sénégal

Dakar

CHAD

Lake
Chad

Khartoum

SUDAN

Blue Nile

White Nile

Lake
Tana

DJIBOUTI

Cape
Gwa

GAMBIA

BURKINA
FASO

Niger

Niger

NIGERIA

BENIN

Ethiopian
Plateau

GUINEA-
BISSAU

GUINEA

As Sudd

Great Rift Valley

GHANA

Lake
Volta

Jos
Plateau

Benue

CENTRAL AFRICAN
REPUBLIC

Mountain Nile

ETHIOPIA

SOMALIA

SIERRA LEONE

COTE
D'IVOIRE

TOGO

LIBERIA

Lagos

CAMEROON

Mt. Cameroon
13,451 Ft.
Bioko  4,100m

Ubangi

Congo

Uele

UGANDA

Lake
Turkana

KENYA

Mt. Kenya
17,058 Ft.
5,199m

Gulf of Guinea

EQUATORIAL
GUINEA

REP. OF
CONGO

Congo
Basin

Lake
Victoria

Kilimanjaro
19,340 Ft.
5,895m

INDIAN

Equator

SAO TOME AND
PRINCIPE

GABON

DEM. REP.
OF CONGO

Great Rift Valley

RWANDA

Nairobi

Serengeti
Plain

OCEAN

Kinshasa

BURUNDI

Masai
Steppe

N

Kwango

Lake
Tanganyika

TANZANIA

Zanzibar

SEYCHE

Ascension
(St. Helena)

Kasai

Cuanza

MALAWI

COMOROS

Cape Amb

Lake Nyasa

ATLANTIC

St. Helena
(U.K.)

Cuando

ANGOLA

ZAMBIA

Mayotte
(Fr.)

MOZAMBIQUE

MAUR

Cunene

Victoria
Falls

Lake
Kariba

Mozambique Channel

OCEAN

Okavango

ZIMBABWE

Zambezi

MADAGASCAR

Reunion
(Fr.)

Tropic of Capricorn

NAMIBIA

BOTSWANA

Namib
Desert

Kalahari
Desert

Limpopo

Barra Point

Johannesburg

Cape Sainte-Marie

Orange

Vaal

SWAZILAND

LESOTHO

Drakensberg

SOUTH
AFRICA

Cape of
Good Hope

Cape Agulhas

Tristan da
Cunha Group
(St. Helena)

0   200   400   600   800   1000 Miles

0   300   600   900   1200   1500 Kilometers

Copyright by Rand McNally & Co.
Lambert Azimuthal Equal Area Projection

Prince Edward
Islands
(S. Af.)

Crozet Islands
(Fr.)

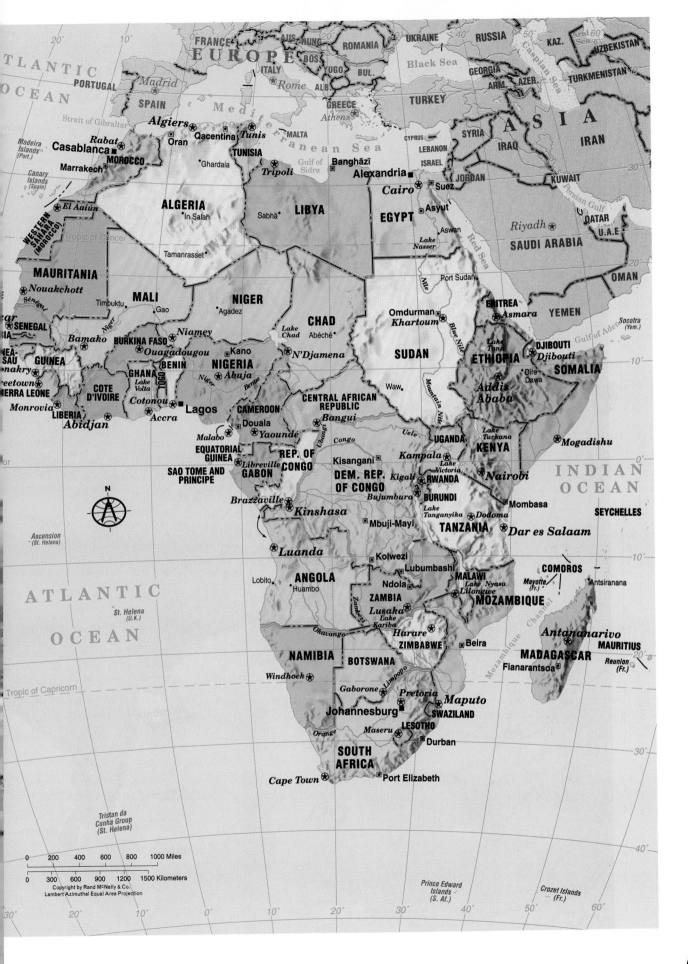

RAND McNALLY

RAND MCNALLY

New Siberian Islands

East Siberian Sea

Laptev Sea

Yana

Lena

gara

nynoyarsk

Lake Baikal

Irkutsk

Yenisei

Chita

Ulaanbaatar

MONGOLIA

CHINA

Lhasa

Chengdu

Kunming

Lanzhou

Xi'an

Taiyuan

Tianjin

Beijing

Shenyang

Changchun

Qiqihar

Harbin

Yakutsk

Amur

Khabarovsk

Vladivostok

Sapporo

Hokkaido

Sea of Japan

Honshu

Tokyo

Nagoya

Osaka

JAPAN

Shikoku

Kyushu

NORTH KOREA

Seoul

SOUTH KOREA

Pusan

Yellow Sea

Jinan

Nanjing

Wuhan

Shanghai

Hangzhou

East China Sea

Chongqing

Fuzhou

Taipei

TAIWAN

Kaohsiung

Guangzhou

Hong Kong

Nanning

Guiyang

Chang (Yangtze)

Huang

Huang

Macadan

Palana

Kamchatka Peninsula

Petropavlovsk-Kamchatskiy

Sea of Okhotsk

Sakhalin

Kuril Islands

ALEUTIAN ISLANDS (U.S.)

Bering Sea

Anadyr

PACIFIC OCEAN

Tropic of Cancer

NORTHERN MARIANA ISLANDS (U.S.)

GUAM (U.S.)

FEDERATED STATES OF MICRONESIA

Philippine Sea

Luzon Strait

Luzon

PHILIPPINES

Manila

Samar

Cebu

Mindanao

Davao

PALAU

Equator

Hainan Island

Gulf of Tonkin

Hanoi

LAOS

Vientiane

Da Nang

VIETNAM

Ho Chi Minh City

Phnom Penh

CAMBODIA

THAILAND

Bangkok

Gulf of Thailand

Mekong

South China Sea

Sulu Sea

Celebes Sea

Manado

New Guinea

PAPUA NEW GUINEA

MYANMAR

Yangon

Chittagong

naka

Brahmaputra

Andaman Sea

Nicobar Islands (India)

Medan

Sumatra

Palembang

MALAYSIA

Kuala Lumpur

Singapore

Bandar Seri Begawan

BRUNEI

MALAYSIA

Borneo

Banjarmasin

Celebes

Ceram

Banda Sea

INDONESIA

Java Sea

Jakarta

Bandung

Surabaya

Java

EAST TIMOR (UN Admin.)

Timor

Timor Sea

Arafura Sea

Gulf of Carpentaria

Coral Sea

AUSTRALIA

A23

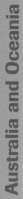

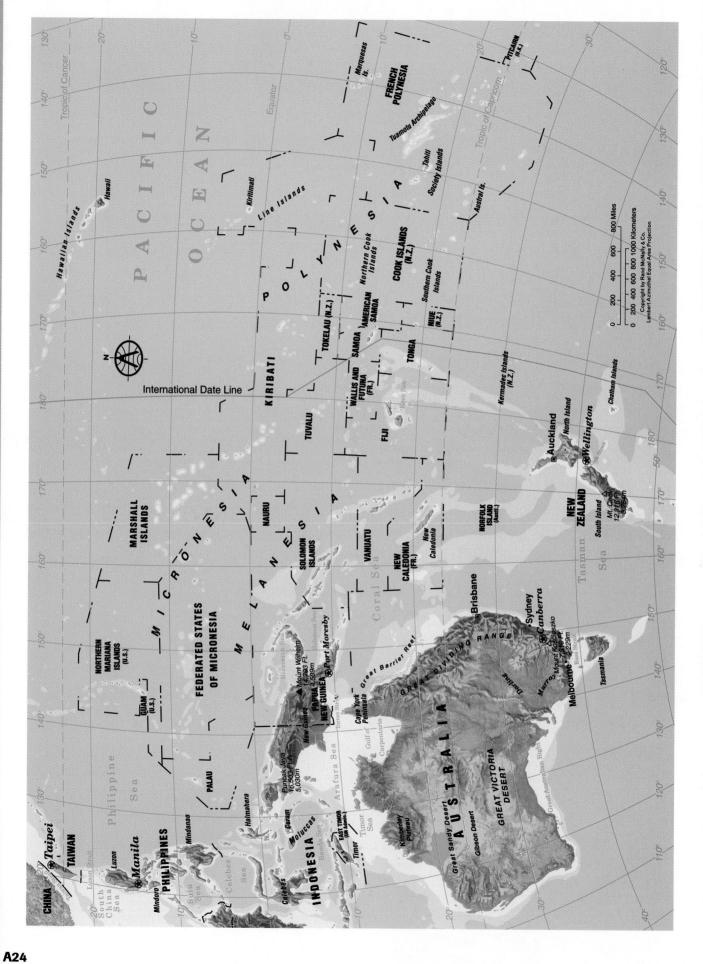

Tropic of Cancer

PACIFIC OCEAN

Equator

Tropic of Capricorn

Hawaiian Islands

Hawaii

Marquesas Is.

FRENCH POLYNESIA

Tuamotu Archipelago

Tahiti

Society Islands

Austral Is.

Kiritimati

Line Islands

POLYNESIA

Northern Cook Islands

COOK ISLANDS (N.Z.)

Southern Cook Islands

PITCAIRN (U.K.)

N

International Date Line

TOKELAU (N.Z.)

AMERICAN SAMOA

SAMOA

NIUE (N.Z.)

KIRIBATI

WALLIS AND FUTUNA (FR.)

TONGA

Koro Sea

MARSHALL ISLANDS

MICRONESIA

NAURU

TUVALU

FIJI

Kermadec Islands (N.Z.)

Chatham Islands

Auckland

North Island

Wellington

NEW ZEALAND

South Island

Mt. Cook 12,316 Ft. 3,754m

NORTHERN MARIANA ISLANDS (U.S.)

GUAM (U.S.)

FEDERATED STATES OF MICRONESIA

MELANESIA

SOLOMON ISLANDS

VANUATU

NEW CALEDONIA (FR.)

New Caledonia

NORFOLK ISLAND (Austl.)

Tasman Sea

PHILIPPINES

Manila

Mindanao

PALAU

Halmahera

Ceram

Moluccas

Celebes Sea

Celebes

New Guinea

Puncak Jaya 16,503 Ft. 5,030m

Mount Wilhelm 14,793 Ft. 4,509m

PAPUA NEW GUINEA

Port Moresby

Blanche Bay

Solomon Sea

Bismarck Sea

Coral Sea

Great Barrier Reef

GREAT DIVIDING RANGE

Brisbane

Sydney

Canberra

Mount Kosciuszko 7,310 Ft. 2,229m

Melbourne

Tasmania

Bass Strait

Murray

Darling

CHINA

Taipei

TAIWAN

Luzon Strait

Mindoro

Luzon

South China Sea

Philippine Sea

Sulu Sea

INDONESIA

Timor

EAST TIMOR (UN Admin.)

Banda Sea

Timor Sea

Arafura Sea

Gulf of Carpentaria

Cape York Peninsula

Torres Strait

AUSTRALIA

Great Sandy Desert

Gibson Desert

GREAT VICTORIA DESERT

Kimberley Plateau

Great Australian Bight

0   200   400   600   800 1000 Kilometers
0   200   400   600   800 Miles

Copyright by Rand McNally & Co.
Lambert Azimuthal Equal Area Projection

# North Pole

ALASKA (U.S.)
Brooks Range
Barrow
Point Barrow
Chukchi Sea
Wrangell I.
East Siberian Sea
Srednekolymsk
Indigirka
New Siberian I.
New Siberian Islands
Kotelny I.
Verhoyansk
Yana
Verkhoyansk
Lena
RUSSIA
Mts. Aldan
CANADA
Inuvik
man Wells
Beaufort Sea
Tiksi
Olenëk
great Bear lake
Amundsen Gulf
Banks I.
QUEEN ELIZABETH ISLANDS
ARCTIC OCEAN
Laptev Sea
Anabar
80°
Kotuj
Khatanga
160°
170°
70°
180°
170°
160°
Aldan
130°
VICTORIA I.
Melville
Prince Patrick Island
uktutiak
Prince of Wales I.
Ellef Ringnes I.
North Magnetic Pole
Axel Heiberg I.
Somerset
Devon I.
North Pole
Taymyr Peninsula
Lake Taymyr
Khatanga
100°
90°
Severnaya Zemlya
ELLESMERE I.
Gulf of Boothia
110°
Dikson
80°
BAFFIN I.
Bylot I.
Etah
Thule
Alert
Peary Land
Franz Josef Land
Kara Sea
70°
Baffin Bay
Davis Strait
GREENLAND (Den.)
Disko
Godhavn
80°
Novaya Zemlya
Vorkuta
60°
odthab
Gunnbjorn Field 12,139 Ft. 3,700m
SPITSBERGEN
SVALBARD (Nor.)
Greenland Sea
Barents Sea
Pechora
Angmagssalik
Jan Mayen (Nor.)
North Cape
Hammerfest
Murmansk
Kola Peninsula
Arhangel'sk
NORWAY FINLAND
50°
40°
20°
10°
10°
20°

0  200  400  600 Miles
0  200  400  600  800  1000 Kilometers
Copyright by Rand McNally & Co.
Azimuthal Equidistant Projection

# South Pole

Strait of Magellan
Cape Horn
Drake Passage
FALKLAND ISLANDS (U.K.)
50°
40°
40°
30°
PACIFIC OCEAN
Antarctic Circle
South Shetland Islands (U.K.)
Graham Land
Adelaide I.
Alexander I.
Antarctic Peninsula
Larsen Ice Shelf
South Orkney Islands (U.K.)
South Georgia (U.K.)
Scotia Sea
ATLANTIC OCEAN
South Sandwich Islands (U.K.)
30°
Thurston I.
Bellingshausen Sea
Amundsen Sea
Ellsworth Land
20°
Mt. Sidley 13,717 Ft. 4,181m
Ellsworth Mts.
Vinson Massif 16,066 Ft. 4,897m
Ronne Ice Shelf
Weddell Sea
Marie Byrd Land
Berkner I.
Filchner Ice Shelf
Cape Norvegia
10°
Rockefeller Plateau
Pensacola Mts.
Coats Land
Mölig Hofmann Mts.
Queen Maud Land
0°
Roosevelt I.
Ross Sea
Mt. Kirkpatrick 14,856 Ft. 4,528m
South Pole
10°
Cape Adare
Mt. Erebus 12,451 Ft. 3,795m
Ross Ice Shelf
Transantarctic Mountains
Ser Rondane Mts.
Victoria Land
ANTARCTICA
20°
Macquarie Island (Austl.)
George V Coast
80°
Wilkes Land
American Highland
Lambert Glacier
Enderby Land
Napier Mts.
Cape Ann
Antarctic Circle
30°
South Magnetic Pole
Amery Ice Shelf
70°
Cape Darnley
Prince Edward Is. (S. Afr.)
Cape Poinsett
INDIAN OCEAN
Crozet Archipelago (Fr.)
50°
40°

0  200  400  600  800  1000 Miles
0  300  600  900  1200  1500 Kilometres
Copyright by Rand McNally & Co.
Polar Stereographic Projection

RAND McNALLY

A25

# Unit

# The Basics of Geography

The earth is a unique planet capable of supporting a wide variety of life forms. Human beings adapt and alter the environments on earth.

**PHYSICAL GEOGRAPHY** Internal and external forces constantly change the earth's surface. Here the volcano Arenal, located in Costa Rica, spews molten rock that will cool and alter the land.

BASICS

**HUMAN GEOGRAPHY** Pictured here is Adnan Nevic, the child officially identified by the United Nations as the six billionth person on earth. He was born on October 12, 1999, in Sarajevo, Bosnia.

*The Basics of Geography* **3**

# PHYSICAL GEOGRAPHY
# Looking at the Earth

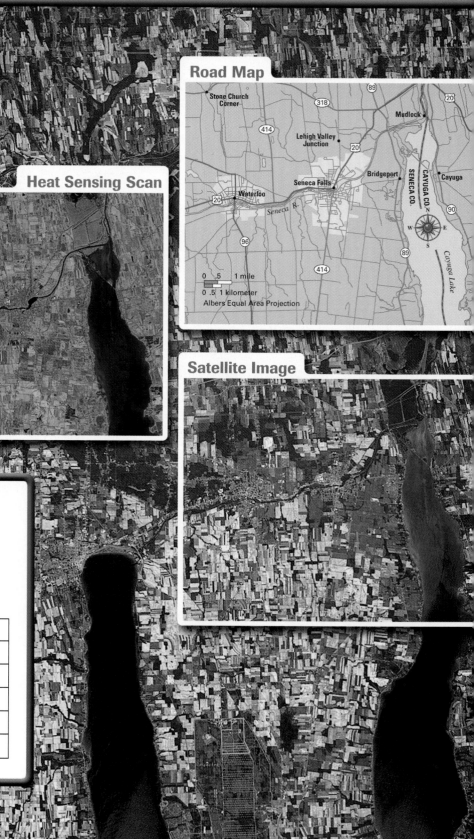

**Road Map**

**Heat Sensing Scan**

**Satellite Image**

Seneca Falls, New York, is represented in a road map, a heat sensing (thermal) scan, and a satellite image.

## Geo**Focus**

### How do geographers view the world?

**Taking Notes** Copy the graphic organizer below into your notebook. Use it to record information about the work of geographers and the themes of geography.

| 5 Themes: |
| --- |
| |
| |

| Tools: |
| --- |
| |
| |

# The Five Themes of Geography

## Main Ides

**Main Ideas**
- Geographers view the world in terms of the use of space.
- Geographers study the world by looking at location, place, region, movement, and human-environment interaction.

**Places & Terms**

geography

absolute location

relative location

hemisphere

equator

prime meridian

latitude

longitude

**A HUMAN PERSPECTIVE** Between 1838 and 1842, Captain Charles Wilkes led an American expedition to the South Pacific and Antarctica. At one stop at a South Sea island, a friendly islander drew a map on the wooden deck planks of the ship. To Wilkes's amazement, the map accurately showed the location of the Tuamotu Archipelago—a chain of about 80 coral islands that stretches more than 1,000 miles across the South Pacific. The islander relied on personal experience sailing in the area and a mental map to accurately show the positions of the islands.

## The Geographer's Perspective

Maps like the one that the islander drew are important tools in geography. The word *geography* comes from the Greek word *geographia,* which means "to describe the earth." Geographers study the world in a different way than do other social scientists. Historians look at events over time. Geographers, on the other hand, view the world by looking at the use of space on the earth and the interactions that take place there. They look for patterns and connections between people and the land that they live on. **Geography,** then, is the study of the distribution and interaction of physical and human features on the earth.

**METHODS OF GEOGRAPHY** Geographers use a variety of tools to study the use of space on earth. The most common one is a map. Maps are visual representations of a portion of the earth. Maps do not have to be written down to be useful. Since people began roaming the earth, they have created mental maps—maps that they carry in their minds. You use a mental map every day as you go to and from school.

The maps that you are probably most familiar with appear in printed form, such as in road atlases and books. In recent years, more maps have appeared in electronic media such as CD-ROMs and on the Internet.

Geographers also use photographs to gain visual evidence about a place. They organize information into charts, graphs, or tables to learn about geographic patterns and to understand changes over time. They may also construct scale models to make study of the real world easier. Sometimes they use graphic models to illustrate an idea.

Other basic tools used by geographers are the five themes of geography, which also describe patterns and connections in the use of space. These themes organize information about geography into five distinct categories, shown at right. These themes are important to geographic study. They help the geographer to describe the use of space.

**The Five Themes**

**Location**
Where is it?

**Place**
What is it like?

**Region**
How are places similar or different?

**Movement**
How do people, goods, and ideas move from one location to another?

**Human-Environment Interaction**
How do people relate to the physical world?

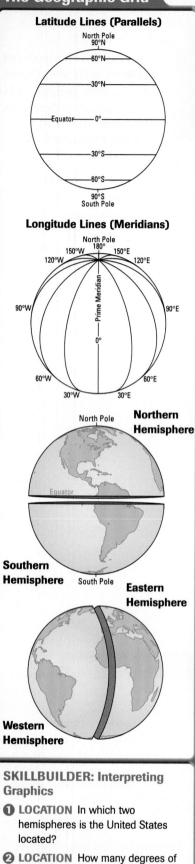

## The Geographic Grid

**Latitude Lines (Parallels)**

North Pole
90°N
60°N
30°N
Equator 0°
30°S
60°S
90°S
South Pole

**Longitude Lines (Meridians)**

North Pole
180°
150°W 150°E
120°W 120°E
Prime Meridian
90°W 90°E
0°
60°W 60°E
30°W 30°E

**Northern Hemisphere**

North Pole

Equator

**Southern Hemisphere** South Pole

**Eastern Hemisphere**

**Western Hemisphere**

**SKILLBUILDER: Interpreting Graphics**

❶ **LOCATION** In which two hemispheres is the United States located?

❷ **LOCATION** How many degrees of latitude are there?

# Theme: Location

The geographic question "Where is it?" refers to location. Geographers describe location in two ways. **Absolute location** is the exact place on earth where a geographic feature, such as a city, is found. **Relative location** describes a place in comparison to other places around it.

**ABSOLUTE LOCATION** To describe absolute location, geographers use a grid system of imaginary lines for precisely locating places on the earth's surface. (See the diagram at left.) Earth is divided into two equal halves. Each half of the globe is called a **hemisphere.** Because the earth is round, a hemisphere can be north and south, or east and west. The **equator** is the imaginary line that divides the north and south halves. The **prime meridian** is the imaginary line dividing the earth east and west. Sometimes this line is called the Greenwich meridian (GREHN•ich muh•RIHD•ee•uhn) line because the line runs through Greenwich, England. Ⓐ

**LATITUDE LINES** To locate places north or south, geographers use a set of imaginary lines that run parallel to the equator. These lines are called **latitude** lines. The equator is designated as the zero-degree line for latitude. Lines north of the equator are called north latitude lines, and lines south of the equator are called south latitude lines.

**LONGITUDE LINES** To complete the grid system, geographers use a set of imaginary lines that go around the earth over the poles. These lines, called **longitude** lines, mark positions in the east and west hemispheres. The prime meridian is the zero-degree line for longitude.

Each site on the earth can have only one absolute location. To find an absolute location using the grid system, you need to find the point where the latitude and longitude lines cross. For example, the absolute location of Melbourne, Australia, is 37° South latitude, 145° East longitude. To see how latitude and longitude lines cross and to learn more about absolute location, see page 17 in the Geography Skills Handbook.

**RELATIVE LOCATION** Relative location describes how a place is related to its surrounding environment. For example, you may tell a person that the library is three blocks west of the park. This helps the person find the library—if he or she knows where the park is located. Using relative location may help you become familiar with the specific characteristics of a place. Learning that Cairo, Egypt, is located near the mouth of the Nile River in Africa, for example, tells you something about Cairo, the Nile River, and even Africa itself.

**Geographic Thinking**

**Making Comparisons**
Ⓐ How is the equator different from the prime meridian?

Overlooking the entrance to Guanabara Bay, Sugarloaf Mountain is a prominent landform in the skyline of Rio.

Leisure boats rest in the harbor of Botafogo Bay. There is a large commercial shipyard industry in Rio.

Headquarters of corporations and expensive housing compete for space in the scenic part of the city.

**PLACE** Rio de Janeiro, once the capital of Brazil, lies on the western shore of Guanabara Bay. **How would location on a bay affect the economy of a city?**

## Theme: Place

The question "What is it like?" refers to place. Place includes the physical features and cultural characteristics of a location. All locations on earth have physical features that set them apart, such as climate, landforms, and vegetation. Other features are the product of humans interacting with the environment, such as by building dams, highways, or houses. Still others are the result of humans interacting with animals or with each other. In the photograph above, you can see place features of Rio de Janeiro. Since a location's culture and its use of space may change over time, the description of a place may also change.

## Theme: Region

The question "How are places similar or different?" refers to region. A region is an area of the earth's surface with similar characteristics. Regions usually have more than one characteristic that unifies them. These may include physical, political, economic, or cultural characteristics. For example, the Sunbelt in the southern United States is a physical region. Geographers categorize regions in three ways: formal, functional, and perceptual regions. 🔲

🌐 **Geographic Thinking**

**Using the Atlas**
🅱 Refer to the U.S. map on pages A8–A9. What states might be included in the Sunbelt?

**FORMAL REGIONS** A formal region is defined by a limited number of related characteristics. For example, the Sahel region of Africa is a desert area characterized by specific climate, vegetation, and land use patterns. In this textbook, the regions you'll explore generally are defined by continental area and by similar cultural styles. The following are considered formal regions:

- The United States and Canada
- Latin America
- Europe
- Russia and the Republics
- Africa
- Southwest Asia
- South Asia
- East Asia
- Southeast Asia, Oceania, and Antarctica

*The Five Themes of Geography* **7**

**FUNCTIONAL REGIONS** A functional region is organized around a set of interactions and connections between places. Usually a functional region is characterized by a hub, or central place, and links to that central place. For example, a city and its suburbs may form a functional region. Highways, commuter railroads, subways, and bus lines move people from the suburbs to the city for jobs and other activities. Because the city and its suburbs are connected by a great deal of movement back and forth, they form a functional region. ▶

**PERCEPTUAL REGIONS** A perceptual region is a region in which people perceive, or see, the characteristics of the region in the same way. However, the set of characteristics may not be precisely the same for all people. For example, although many people are familiar with the region called the American Midwest, they sometimes differ on how that region is defined. Some people believe the Midwest begins in Ohio. Others believe the region begins in the middle of Illinois.

**Geographic Thinking**

**Seeing Patterns**
◀ How might areas within a city form a functional region?

## Theme: Human–Environment Interaction

The question "How do people relate to the physical world?" refers to the relationship between humans and their environment. People learn to use what the environment offers them and to change that environment to meet their needs. They also learn to live with aspects of the environment that they cannot control, such as climate.

People living in similar environments do not respond to them in the same way. For example, some people view a hot, sunny climate near a body of water as ideal for recreational activities. Others may see this as an opportunity for raising citrus, olives, or grapes. Human beings work to alter their environments to make them better places or to provide needed goods. People may drain swamps or dig irrigation ditches to grow crops in a particular environment. Sometimes the alterations create new problems, such as pollution. As you study geography, you will learn about many ways humans interact with their environment.

**HUMAN–ENVIRONMENT INTERACTION**
Neighbors and friends use sandbags to hold back floodwaters during the Great Mississippi Flood of 1993.
**In what ways do floods alter the landscape?**

# Theme: Movement

The question "How do people, goods, and ideas move from one location to another?" refers to movement. Geographers are interested in the ways people, goods, and ideas move from place to place. Think about the clothing you wear, the music you listen to, or the places you go for entertainment. All of these things involve movement from one place to another. Geographers analyze movement by looking at three types of distance: linear distance, time distance, and psychological distance.

**LINEAR DISTANCE AND TIME DISTANCE** Linear distance simply means how far across the earth a person, an idea, or a product travels. Physical geography can affect linear distance by forcing a shift in a route to avoid impassable land or water.

Time distance is the amount of time it takes for a person, an idea, or a product to travel. Modern inventions have shortened time distances. For example, in the 1800s, pioneers traveled up to six months to reach California. Today you can get there by airplane from almost any U.S. location in under six hours. With the use of the Internet, ideas can travel around the world in seconds.

**PSYCHOLOGICAL DISTANCE** Psychological distance refers to the way people view distance. When you were younger, some locations seemed very far away. As you grew older, the distance to these locations probably seemed to shrink. Studies show that, as we become familiar with a place, we think it is closer than it actually is. Less familiar places seem to be further away. Psychological distance may influence decisions about many different human activities.

Across the world, people make important choices based on linear distance, time distance, and psychological distance. These choices make up patterns that geographers can study. In the next section, you'll read about the tools they use to study these patterns.

**Geographic Thinking**

**Seeing Patterns**
D How do interstate highways affect linear distance and time distance?

---

## SECTION 1 Assessment

### ❶ Places & Terms

Explain the meaning of each of the following terms.

- geography
- hemisphere
- equator
- prime meridian
- latitude
- longitude

### ❷ Taking Notes

**REGION** Review the notes you took for this section.

| 5 Themes: |
|---|
|  |
|  |

- What is a region?
- What are three types of regions?

### ❸ Main Ideas

a. What are the five themes of geography?

b. How is place different from location?

c. Why do geographers study human-environment interaction?

### ❹ Geographic Thinking

**Making Generalizations**
How is the study of geography different from the study of history? **Think about:**

- use of space on earth
- relationships between people and the environment

**S** **See Skillbuilder Handbook, page R6.**

---

**GeoActivity**

**EXPLORING LOCAL GEOGRAPHY** Using the five themes of geography, develop a **brochure** describing your community. Use pictures or sketches, maps, and other data to complete your descriptions.

# The Geographer's Tools

**A HUMAN PERSPECTIVE** At noon on a sunny midsummer day, sometime around 255 B.C., Eratosthenes drove a stake into the ground at the mouth of the Nile River in Alexandria, Egypt. He then noted the angle of the shadow cast by the stake. Meanwhile at Syene (modern-day Aswan, Egypt), another person drove a stake into the ground—but it cast no shadow. Using the angle of the first shadow and the distance between Syene and Alexandria, Eratosthenes calculated the circumference of the earth. By today's measurements, he was off by about 15 percent, but he was remarkably accurate considering the simple tools he used. Eratosthenes was one of the earliest geographers to use tools and critical thinking to measure and describe the earth.

## Maps and Globes

A geographer's tools include maps, globes, and data that can be displayed in a variety of ways. The oldest known map is a Babylonian clay tablet created about 2,500 years ago. The tablet is about four inches high and shows the Babylonian world surrounded by water. Over the centuries, mapmaking evolved into a very complex task. However, a map's function has remained the same—to show locations of places, landforms, and bodies of water, and where they are in relation to other parts of the earth.

**TWO OR THREE DIMENSIONS** A **globe** is a three-dimensional representation of the earth. It provides a way to view the earth as it travels through space. But since the earth is a sphere, we can see only one half of it at any time. For certain tasks, globes are not very practical because they are not easily portable.

People often prefer to use **maps,** which are two-dimensional graphic representations of selected parts of the earth's surface. Maps are easily portable and can be drawn to any scale needed. The disadvantage of a map is that distortion occurs as the earth's surface is flattened to create the map. A **cartographer,** or mapmaker, reduces some types of distortion by using different types of map projections. A **map projection** is a way of drawing the earth's surface that reduces distortion caused by presenting a round earth on flat paper. To learn more about map projections, see the Geography Skills Handbook, pages 18–19.

This globe, created circa 1492, is turned to show Africa and Europe.

**TYPES OF MAPS** The three types of maps are general reference maps, thematic maps, and navigational maps. A general reference map is sometimes called a **topographic map,** which is a representation of natural and man-made features on the earth. Thematic maps emphasize specific kinds of information, such as climate or population density. Sailors and pilots use the third type of map—navigation maps. You can learn more about using different maps in the Geography Skills Handbook, pages 20–23.

**BACKGROUND**
Navigational maps, often referred to as charts, help their users to plot a course through air or water.

## The Science of Mapmaking

A cartographer decides what type of map to create by considering how the map will be used. Keeping that purpose in mind, he or she then determines how much detail to show and what size the map should be.

**SURVEYING** The first step in making a map is to complete a field survey. Surveyors observe, measure, and record what they see in a specific area. Today, most mapping is done by remote sensing, the gathering of geographic information from a distance by an instrument that is not physically in contact with the mapping site. These data are gathered primarily by aerial photography or by satellites.

The data gathered includes information such as elevation, differences in land cover, and variations in temperature. This information is recorded and converted to a gray image. Cartographers then use these data and computer software to construct maps. See the illustration below to learn more about satellite surveying.

### How Satellites Gather Map Data

1. As the satellite orbits the earth, a scanner constantly records data from the earth's surface.

2. Instruments measure invisible electromagnetic waves emitted by each object on earth. Because these waves are unique for every object, computers can analyze and identify them.

3. The data collected is converted first to code and then to pixels—electronic dots. Computer software then converts the pixels into usable images.

The first step in mapmaking is collecting data. Remote sensors gather information for constructing maps.

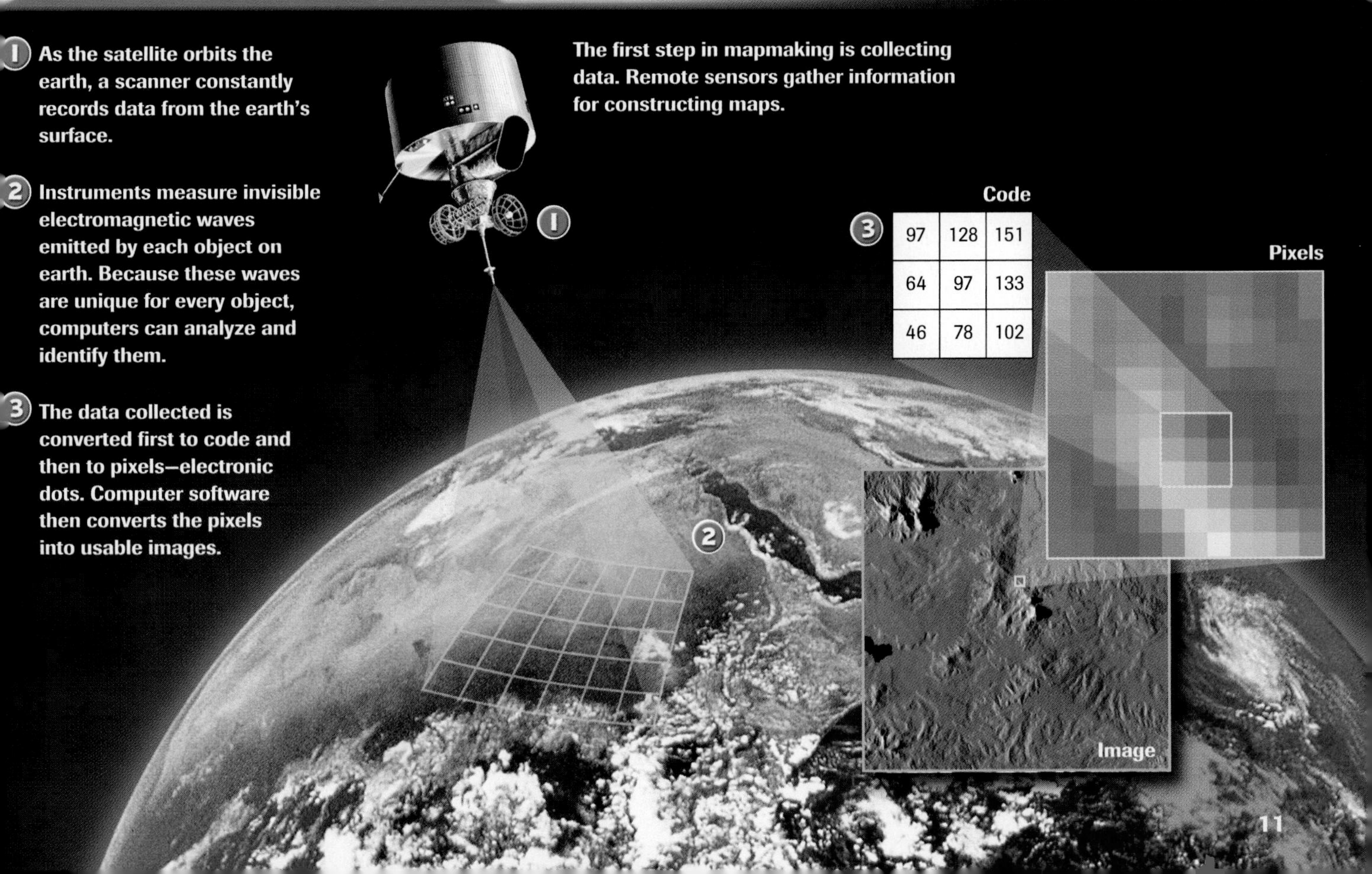

**Code**

| 97 | 128 | 151 |
| 64 | 97 | 133 |
| 46 | 78 | 102 |

**Pixels**

**Image**

**SATELLITES** Today, geographers rely heavily on satellites to provide geographic data. Two of the best-known satellites are Landsat and GOES. **Landsat** is actually a series of satellites that orbit more than 100 miles above the earth. Each time a satellite makes an orbit, it picks up data in an area 115 miles wide. Landsat can scan the entire earth in 16 days.

Geostationary Operational Environment Satellite (GOES) is a weather satellite. This satellite flies in orbit at the same speed as the earth's rotation. By doing so, it always views the same area. It gathers images of atmospheric conditions that are useful in forecasting the weather.

## Geographic Information Systems

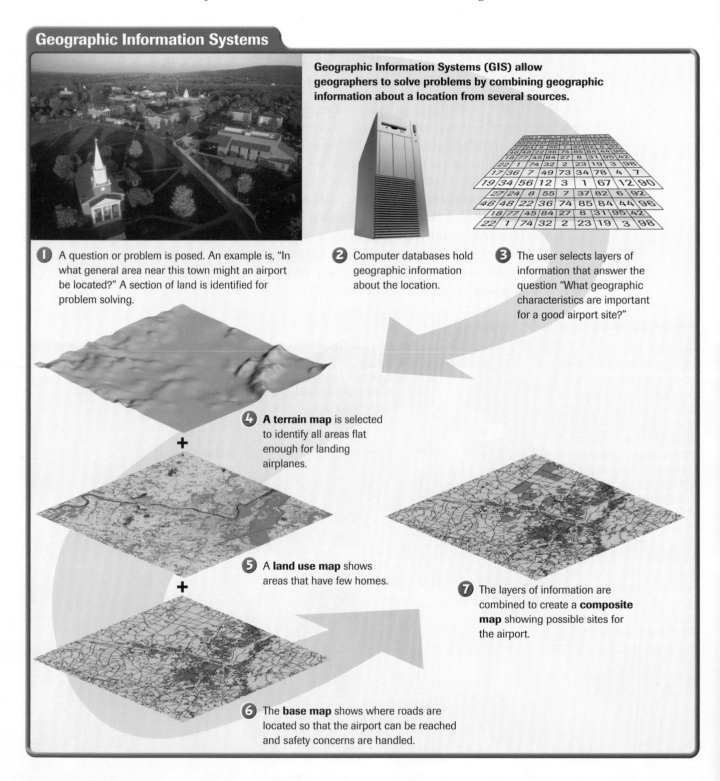

Geographic Information Systems (GIS) allow geographers to solve problems by combining geographic information about a location from several sources.

**1** A question or problem is posed. An example is, "In what general area near this town might an airport be located?" A section of land is identified for problem solving.

**2** Computer databases hold geographic information about the location.

**3** The user selects layers of information that answer the question "What geographic characteristics are important for a good airport site?"

**4** **A terrain map** is selected to identify all areas flat enough for landing airplanes.

**5** A **land use map** shows areas that have few homes.

**6** The **base map** shows where roads are located so that the airport can be reached and safety concerns are handled.

**7** The layers of information are combined to create a **composite map** showing possible sites for the airport.

**GEOGRAPHIC INFORMATION SYSTEMS** The newest tool in the geographer's toolbox is **Geographic Information Systems (GIS).** GIS stores information about the world in a digital database. GIS has the ability to combine information from a variety of sources and display it in ways that allow the user to visualize the use of space in different ways.

When using the system, geographers must look at a problem and decide what types of geographic information would help them solve the problem. The information could include maps, aerial photographs, satellite images, or other data. Next, they select the appropriate layers of information. Then, GIS creates a composite map combining the information. Study the diagram on page 12 to learn more about the way GIS works.

**GLOBAL POSITIONING SYSTEM (GPS)** A familiar tool of geographers is GPS or Global Positioning System. It was originally developed to help military forces know exactly where they were on the earth's surface. The system uses a series of 24 satellites called Navstars, which beam information to the earth. The exact position—latitude, longitude, altitude, and time—is displayed on a hand–held receiver. Hikers, explorers, sailors, and drivers use GPS devices to determine location. They are also used to track animals. ◁◺

Geographers use a variety of other tools including photographs, cross sections, models, cartograms, and population pyramids. These tools help geographers to visualize and display information for analysis. They are looking for patterns and connections in the data they find. You will learn how to use these tools in the Geography Skills Handbook, which follows, and in the Map and Graph Skills pages in this book.

**MOVEMENT** Scientists use a GPS device to track this brown bear in Minnesota.
**What other uses could be found for a GPS device?**

---

◉ **Geographic Thinking** ◂

**Making Comparisons**
Ⓐ▶ How might the military use both GOES and GPS?

---

★SECTION 2▶ **Assessment**

**❶ Places & Terms**

Explain the meaning of each of the following terms.

- globe
- map
- cartographer
- map projection
- topographic map
- GIS

**❷ Taking Notes**

**REGION** Review the notes you took for this section.

| Tools: |
| --- |
|  |
|  |

- How would a globe show a region differently than a map?
- How does GIS aid in understanding a region?

**❸ Main Ideas**

a. What are the three basic types of maps?

b. What are some geographers' tools in addition to maps and globes?

c. How does a cartographer decide which type of map is needed?

**❹ Geographic Thinking**

**Making Generalizations**
How does modern technology help geographers? **Think about:**

- digital information
- satellite images

Ⓢ **See Skillbuilder Handbook, page R6.**

---

**GeoActivity**

**MAKING COMPARISONS** Choose a place on the earth and in an atlas, and find three maps that show the place in three different ways. Create a **chart** that lists the similarities and differences in the way the place is shown on the three maps.

---

This handbook covers the basic map skills and information that geographers rely on as they investigate the world—and the skills you will need as you study geography.

## Finding Location

Mapmaking depends on surveying the earth's surface. Until recently, that activity could only happen on land or sea. Today, aerial photography and satellite imaging are the most popular ways to gather data.

A personal **GPS** device provides the absolute location to the user.

Nigerian surveyors use a **theodolite,** a type of surveying instrument. It precisely measures angles and distances on the earth.

**Magnetic compasses** introduced by the Chinese around the 1100s helped to accurately determine direction.

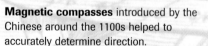

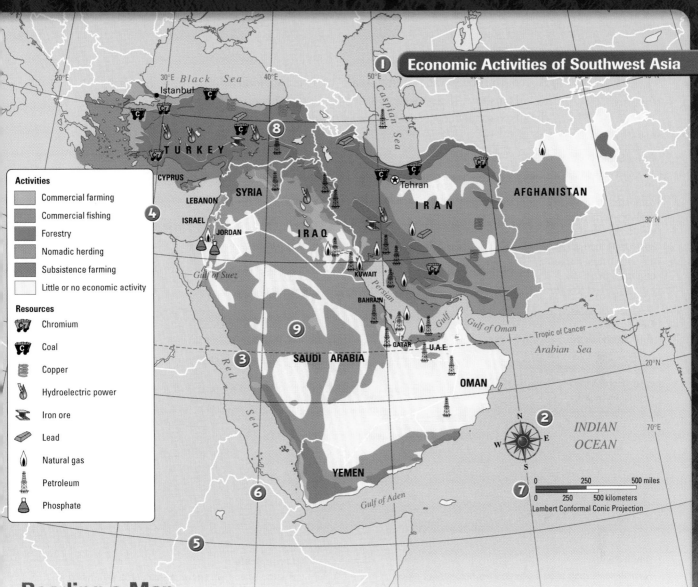

**Activities**

- Commercial farming
- Commercial fishing
- Forestry
- Nomadic herding
- Subsistence farming
- Little or no economic activity

**Resources**

- Chromium
- Coal
- Copper
- Hydroelectric power
- Iron ore
- Lead
- Natural gas
- Petroleum
- Phosphate

INDIAN OCEAN

0        250        500 miles
0    250    500 kilometers
Lambert Conformal Conic Projection

# Reading a Map

All maps have these elements, which are necessary to read and understand them.

**① TITLE** The title explains the subject of the map and gives you an idea of what information the map conveys.

**② COMPASS ROSE** The compass rose shows you the north (N), south (S), east (E), and west (W) directions on the map. Sometimes only north is indicated.

**③ LABELS** Labels are words or phrases that explain features on the map.

**④ LEGEND** A legend or key lists and explains the symbols and use of color on the map.

**⑤ LINES OF LATITUDE** These are imaginary lines that measure distance north or south of the equator.

**⑥ LINES OF LONGITUDE** These are imaginary lines that measure distance east or west of the prime meridian.

**⑦ SCALE** A scale shows the ratio between a unit of length on the map and a unit of distance on the earth.

**⑧ SYMBOLS** Symbols represent such items as capital cities, economic activities, or natural resources. Check the map legend for more details.

**⑨ COLORS** Colors represent a variety of information on a map. The map legend indicates what the colors mean.

# Scale

A geographer decides what scale to use by determining how much detail to show. If many details are needed, a large scale is used. If fewer details are needed, a small scale is used.

**Ratio Scale**
This shows the ratio of distance on the map compared to real earth measurement. Here, 1 inch on the map equals 30,000,000 inches (500 miles) in actual distance on the earth.

**Bar Scale**
This bar shows the ratio of distance on the map to distance on the earth. Here, 1 inch equals 500 miles.

**EASTERN UNITED STATES**
Scale: 1:30,000,000
1"= 500 miles

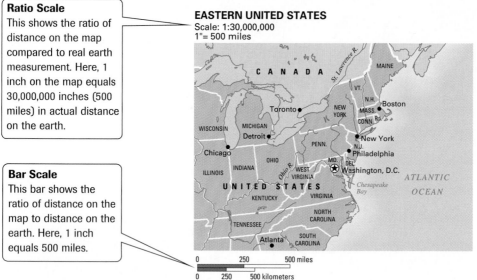

0    250    500 miles
0    250    500 kilometers
Azimuthal Equidistant Projection

**Small Scale**
A small scale map shows a large area but without much detail. A small scale is used to see relative location in a region or between regions.

**WASHINGTON, D.C., METRO AREA**
Scale: 1:3,000,000
1"= 50 miles

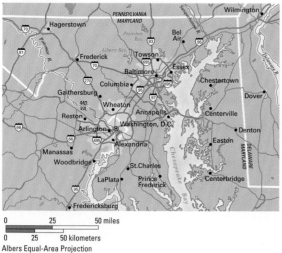

0    25    50 miles
0    25    50 kilometers
Albers Equal-Area Projection

**Large Scale**
A large scale map shows a small area with much more detail. A large scale is used to see relative location within a region.

**WASHINGTON, D.C.**
Scale: 1:62,500
1"= 1 mile

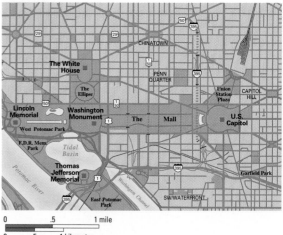

0    .5    1 mile
0    .5    1 kilometer
Albers Equal-Area Projection

# Using the Geographic Grid

As you learned in Chapter 1, geographers use a grid system to identify absolute location. The grid system uses two kinds of imaginary lines:

- latitude lines, also called parallels because they run parallel to the equator
- longitude lines, also called meridians because, like the prime meridian, they run from pole to pole

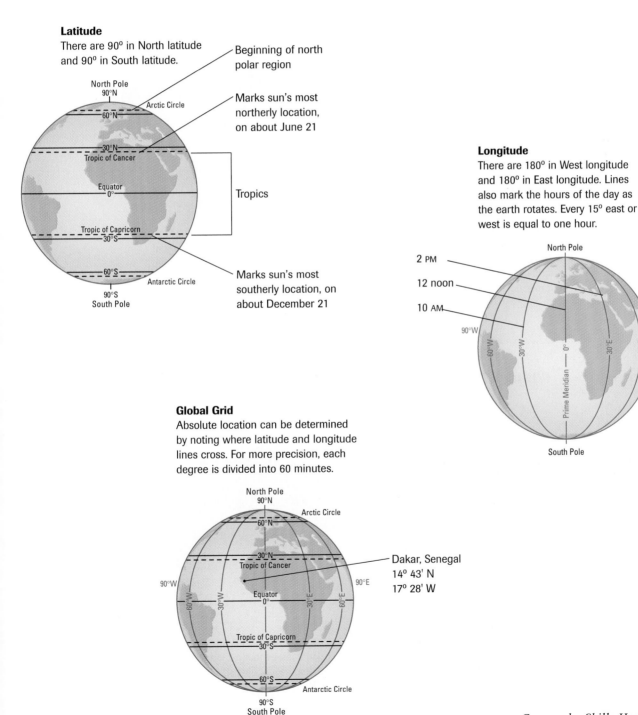

**Latitude**
There are 90° in North latitude and 90° in South latitude.

Beginning of north polar region

Marks sun's most northerly location, on about June 21

Tropics

Marks sun's most southerly location, on about December 21

**Longitude**
There are 180° in West longitude and 180° in East longitude. Lines also mark the hours of the day as the earth rotates. Every 15° east or west is equal to one hour.

2 PM
12 noon
10 AM

**Global Grid**
Absolute location can be determined by noting where latitude and longitude lines cross. For more precision, each degree is divided into 60 minutes.

Dakar, Senegal
14° 43' N
17° 28' W

# Projections

A projection is a way of showing the curved surface of the earth on a flat map. Because the earth is a sphere, a flat map will distort some aspect of the earth's surface. Distance, shape, direction, or area may be distorted by a projection. Be sure to check the projection of a map so you are aware of how the areas are distorted.

## PLANAR PROJECTIONS

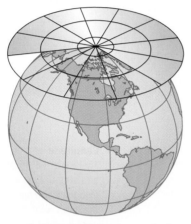

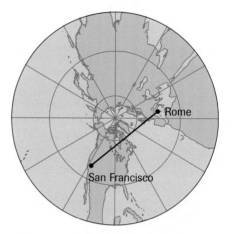

A planar projection is a projection on a flat surface. This projection is also called an azimuthal projection. It distorts size and shape. To the right is a type of planar projection.

The **azimuthal** projection shows the earth so that a line from the central point to any other point on the map gives the shortest distance between the two points. Size and shape are distorted.

## CONICAL PROJECTIONS

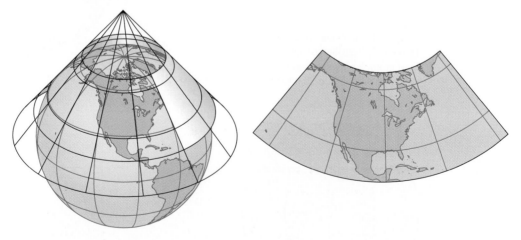

A conical projection is a projection onto a cone. This projection shows shape fairly accurately, but it distorts landmasses at the edges of the map.

Conical projections are often used to show landmasses that extend over large areas going east and west.

## CYLINDRICAL PROJECTIONS

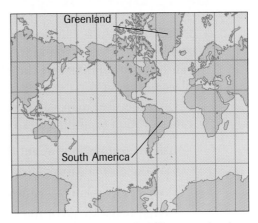

A cylindrical projection is a projection onto a cylinder. This projection shows the entire earth on one map. Included here are three types of cylindrical projections.

In the cylindrical projection called **Mercator,** the shapes of the continents are distorted at the poles and somewhat compressed near the equator. For example, the island of Greenland is actually one-eighth the size of South America.

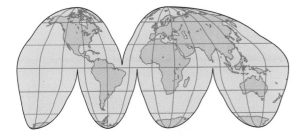

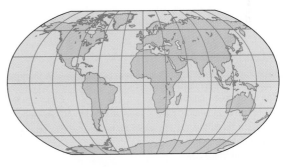

The cylindrical projection called **homolosine** is sometimes called an "interrupted map," because the oceans are divided. This projection shows the accurate shapes and sizes of the landmasses, but distances on the map are not correct.

A **Robinson** projection is a type of cylindrical projection, commonly used in textbooks. It shows the entire earth with nearly the true sizes and shapes of the continents and oceans. However, the shapes of the landforms near the poles appear flat.

## Map Practice

Use pages 14–19 to help you answer these questions. Look at the map on page 15 to answer questions 1–3.

**1.** How are colors used on this map?

**2.** Is the map a large-scale or a small-scale map? How do you know?

**3.** What is the approximate longitude of Tehran?

**4.** What are the names of three lines of latitude besides the equator?

**5.** Which projections show shape of landmasses most accurately?

**MAKING COMPARISONS** Look at the maps in the atlas in this book. Create a **database** that shows the projection and scale of each map. Write a summary of your findings.

# Using Different Types of Maps

**PHYSICAL MAPS** Physical maps help you see the types of landforms and bodies of water found in a specific area. By studying the map, you can begin to understand the relative location and characteristics of a place or region.

On a physical map, color, shading, or contour lines are used to indicate elevation or altitude, also called relief.

Ask these questions about the physical features shown on a map:

• Where on the earth's surface is this area located?

• What is its relative location?

• What is the shape of the region?

• In which direction do the rivers flow? How might the direction of flow affect travel and transportation in the region?

• Are there mountains or deserts? How do they affect the people living in the area?

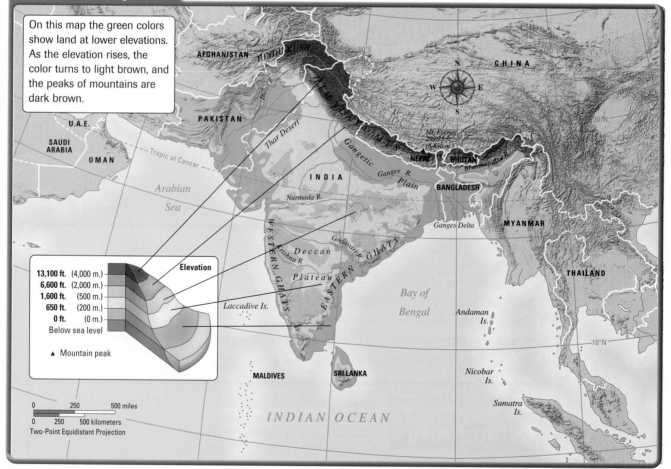

**South Asia: Physical**

On this map the green colors show land at lower elevations. As the elevation rises, the color turns to light brown, and the peaks of mountains are dark brown.

AFGHANISTAN
HINDU KUSH
CHINA
PAKISTAN
Indus R.
Thar Desert
U.A.E.
SAUDI ARABIA
OMAN
Tropic of Cancer
Ganges R.
Mt. Everest 29,035 ft. (8,850 m.)
NEPAL
BHUTAN
Brahmaputra R.
INDIA
Ganges R. Plain
BANGLADESH
Arabian Sea
Narmada R.
Ganges Delta
MYANMAR
WESTERN GHATS
Deccan
Godavari R.
Krishna R.
Plateau
EASTERN GHATS
Bay of Bengal
THAILAND
Laccadive Is.
Andaman Is.
MALDIVES
SRI LANKA
Nicobar Is.
Sumatra Is.
INDIAN OCEAN

**Elevation**
13,100 ft. (4,000 m.)
6,600 ft. (2,000 m.)
1,600 ft. (500 m.)
650 ft. (200 m.)
0 ft. (0 m.)
Below sea level

▲ Mountain peak

0    250    500 miles
0    250    500 kilometers
Two-Point Equidistant Projection

**POLITICAL MAPS** Political maps show features on the earth's surface that humans created. Included on a political map may be cities, states, provinces, territories, or countries.

Ask these questions about the political features shown on a map:

- Where on the earth's surface is this area located?
- What is its relative location? How might the location affect the economy or foreign policy of a place?
- What is the shape and size of the country? How might shape or size affect the people living in the country?
- Who are the neighbors in the region, country, state, or city?
- How populated does the area seem to be? How might that affect activities there?

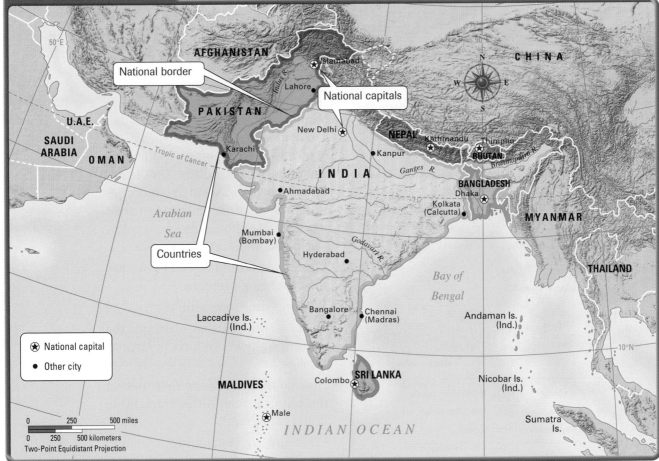

South Asia: Political

# Thematic Maps

Geographers also rely on thematic maps, which focus on specific types of information. For example, in this textbook you will see thematic maps that show climate, vegetation, natural resources, population density, and economic activities. Some thematic maps illustrate historical trends, and others may focus on the movement of people or ideas. These maps may be presented in a variety of ways.

## Cultural Legacy of the Roman Empire

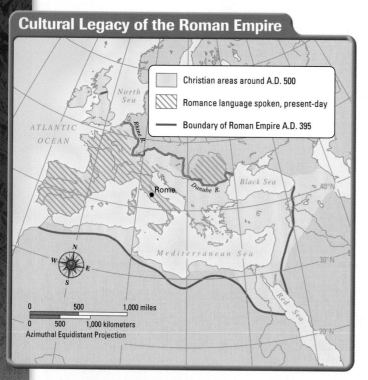

Christian areas around A.D. 500

Romance language spoken, present-day

Boundary of Roman Empire A.D. 395

0    500    1,000 miles
0    500    1,000 kilometers
Azimuthal Equidistant Projection

**QUALITATIVE MAPS** Qualitative maps use colors, symbols, dots, or lines to help you see patterns related to a specific idea. The map shown to the left shows the influence of the Roman Empire on Europe, North Africa, and Southwest Asia. Use the suggestions below to help you interpret a map.

• Check the title to identify the theme and data being presented.

• Study the legend to understand the theme and the information presented.

• Look at physical or political features of the area. How might the theme of the map affect them?

• What are the relationships among the data?

**CARTOGRAMS** In a cartogram, geographers present information about a country based on a set of data other than land area. The size of each country is drawn in proportion to that data rather than to its land size. On the cartogram shown to the left, the countries are represented on the basis of their oil reserves. Use the suggestions below to help you interpret a cartogram.

• Check the title and legend to identify the data being presented.

• What do sizes represent?

• Look at the relative sizes of the countries shown. Which is largest? smallest?

• How do the sizes of the countries on the physical map differ from those in the cartogram?

• What are the relationships among the data?

## Estimated World Oil Reserves

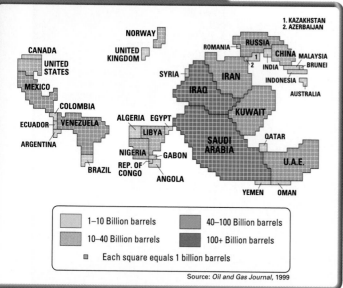

1–10 Billion barrels
10–40 Billion barrels
40–100 Billion barrels
100+ Billion barrels
■  Each square equals 1 billion barrels

Source: *Oil and Gas Journal*, 1999

**FLOW-LINE MAPS** Flow-line maps illustrate movement of people, goods, ideas, animals, or even glaciers. The information is usually shown in a series of arrows. Location, direction, and scope of movement can be seen. The width of the arrow may show how extensive the flow is. Often the information is given over a period of time. The map shown to the right portrays the movement of the Bantu peoples in Africa. Use the suggestions below to help you interpret a flow-line map.

- Check the title and legend to identify the data being presented.
- Over what period of time did the movement occur?
- In what direction did the movement occur?
- How extensive was the movement?

Remember that the purpose of a map is to show a location and provide additional information. Be sure to look at the type of map, scale, and projection. Knowing how maps present the information will help you interpret the map and the ideas it presents.

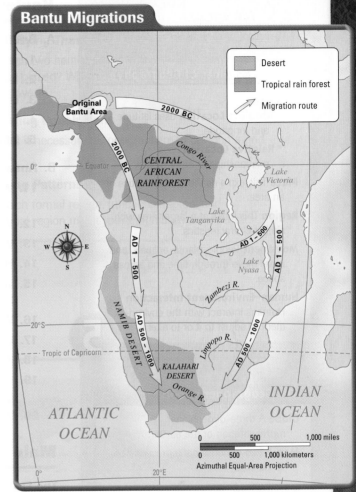

**Bantu Migrations**

Legend:
- Desert
- Tropical rain forest
- Migration route

Azimuthal Equal-Area Projection

**Map Practice**

Use pages 20–23 to help you answer these questions. Use the maps on pages 20–21 to answer questions 1–3.

**1.** In what direction does the Ganges River flow?

**2.** China is the northern neighbor of which countries?

**3.** Which city is closer to the Thar Desert–Lahore, Pakistan or New Delhi, India?

**4.** Why are so few nations shown on the cartogram?

**5.** Which of the thematic maps would best show the location of climate zones?

**GeoActivity**

**EXPLORING LOCAL GEOGRAPHY** Obtain a physical–political map of your state. Use the data on it to create two separate **maps.** One should show physical features only, and one should show political features only.

# PHYSICAL GEOGRAPHY
# A Living Planet

Third planet from the Sun: Earth appears as a blue and white ball in the darkness of space.

## GeoFocus

### What forces shape the earth?

**Taking Notes** Copy the graphic organizer below into your notebook. Use it to record information from the chapter about the structure of the earth.

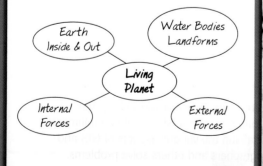

Earth Inside & Out

Water Bodies Landforms

Living Planet

Internal Forces

External Forces

# The Earth Inside and Out

## Main Ideas

• The earth is the only habitable planet in the sun's solar system.

• The drifting of the continents shaped the world we live in today.

## Places & Terms

| | |
|---|---|
| **continent** | **atmosphere** |
| **solar system** | **lithosphere** |
| **core** | **hydrosphere** |
| **mantle** | **biosphere** |
| **magma** | **continental drift** |
| **crust** | |

BASICS

**A HUMAN PERSPECTIVE** A quick look at a world map will convince you that the **continents,** landmasses above water on earth, fit together like a huge jigsaw puzzle. South America and Africa are good examples. With imagination, you can see how other continents might fit together as well. The first person to suggest that the seven continents were once all one supercontinent was Englishman Francis Bacon in 1620. Bacon's idea received support in the early 1900s, when scientists found rocks in Africa that matched rocks in South America. Other evidence also supported the idea of a supercontinent millions of years ago.

## The Solar System

The "home address" of the earth is the third planet in the solar system of the sun, which is a medium-sized star on the edge of the Milky Way galaxy. Its distance from the sun is 93 million miles. The **solar system** consists of the sun and nine known planets, as well as other celestial bodies that orbit the sun. The solar system also contains comets, spheres covered with ice and dust that leave trails of vapor as they race through space. Asteroids—large chunks of rocky material—are found in space as well. As you can see in the diagram, our solar system has an asteroid belt between the orbits of Jupiter and Mars.

**LOCATION** This not-to-scale illustration shows the nine planets and other objects in our solar system.
**What is the earth's relative location in the solar system?**

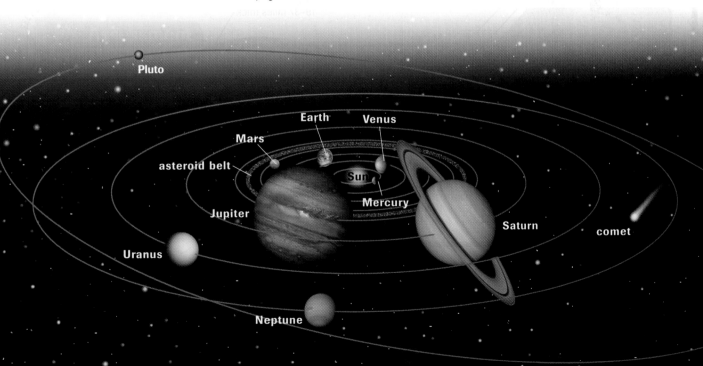

Pluto · Earth · Venus · Mars · asteroid belt · Sun · Mercury · Jupiter · Saturn · comet · Uranus · Neptune

# Disasters!

## Asteroid Hit!

For years, scientists speculated that the extinction of dinosaurs was due to one very large "environmental event." Today we know that event was most likely the impact of an asteroid about six miles wide. Sixty-five million years ago it slammed into the earth traveling a thousand times faster than a rifle bullet. Fallout from the asteriod impact changed the environment so drastically that 50 to 70 percent of all living species on earth were wiped out.

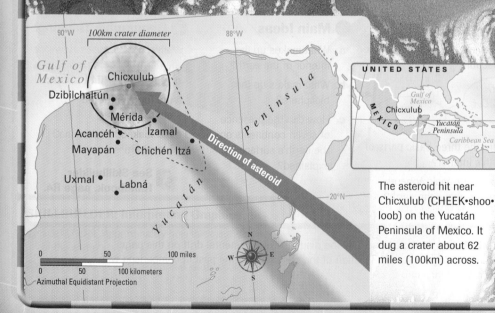

90°W  |  88°W

100km crater diameter

*Gulf of Mexico*

Chicxulub

Dzibilchaltún

Mérida

Acancéh

Mayapán

Izamal

Chichén Itzá

*P e n i n s u l a*

Direction of asteroid

Uxmal

Labná

*Y u c a t á n*

20°N

0   50   100 miles
0   50   100 kilometers
Azimuthal Equidistant Projection

**UNITED STATES**

*Gulf of Mexico*

MEXICO

Chicxulub

*Yucatán Peninsula*

*Caribbean Sea*

The asteroid hit near Chicxulub (CHEEK•shoo•loob) on the Yucatán Peninsula of Mexico. It dug a crater about 62 miles (100km) across.

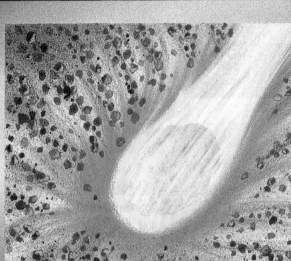

The asteroid plows into the earth at 150,000 mph, vaporizing limestone and seawater. It creates an immense fireball that causes fires thousands of miles away.

The Earth's skies are darkened for several months by 25 trillion tons of rock, dust, and smoke from the impact. Acid rain created by vaporized minerals poisons lakes and rivers. Food chains collapse, and plants and animals die.

A thick layer of carbon dioxide is trapped in the atmosphere, creating a "greenhouse effect" for perhaps a thousand years or more. Ferns, burrowing mammals, and some freshwater animals survive. Some even thrive in the new climate.

## GeoActivities

### CREATING A FRONT PAGE

With a small group, use the Internet to research the Chicxulub event. Then create the front page of a **newspaper** describing the event.

- Create a map showing the impact area.
- Add an article describing the destruction caused by the asteroid.
- Write an interview with a scientist who predicts event results.

**RESEARCH LINKS**
CLASSZONE.COM

## GeoData

### ASTEROIDS

- Asteroids are small planetary bodies that orbit the sun.
- There are an estimated 50,000 asteroids in our solar system.
- Asteroids range in size from 20 feet to 580 miles in diameter.
- Fragments of asteroids that reach the earth are called meteorites.

### TUNGUSKA EVENT

On June 30, 1908, at about 7:30 A.M., an explosion occurred over the Tunguska region of Siberia. This event might have been an asteroid hit.

- The force of the explosion was estimated at between 10 and 20 megatons of TNT.
- The fireball and explosion were seen and felt 500 miles away.
- Five hundred thousand acres of forest were flattened and burned.
- More than 600 grazing reindeer were roasted instantly.
- No crater could be found.

**CAPE**
a point of land extending
into an ocean or lake

**VOLCANO**
an opening in the earth, usually raised, through
which gases and lava escape from the earth's interior

**SEA LEVEL**
level of the ocean's surface, used as a
reference point when measuring the
height or depth of the earth's surface

**STRAIT**
a narrow channel connecting
two larger bodies of water

**BAY**
part of an ocean or lake
partially enclosed by land

**HARBOR**
a sheltered area of water deep
enough for docking ships

**(RIVER) MOUTH**
the place where a river flows
into a lake or an ocean

**MARSH**
soft, wet, low-lying, grassy
land that serves as a transition
between water and land

**ISLAND**
a body of land surrounded
by water

**DELTA**
a triangular area of land formed from
deposits at the mouth of a river

**FLOOD PLAIN**
flat land near the edges of
rivers formed by mud and
silt deposited by floods

**SWAMP**
a lowland region that
is saturated by water

**OASIS**
a spot of fertile land in a
desert, fed by water from
wells or underground springs

**BUTTE**
a raised, flat area of land
with steep cliffs, smaller
than a mesa

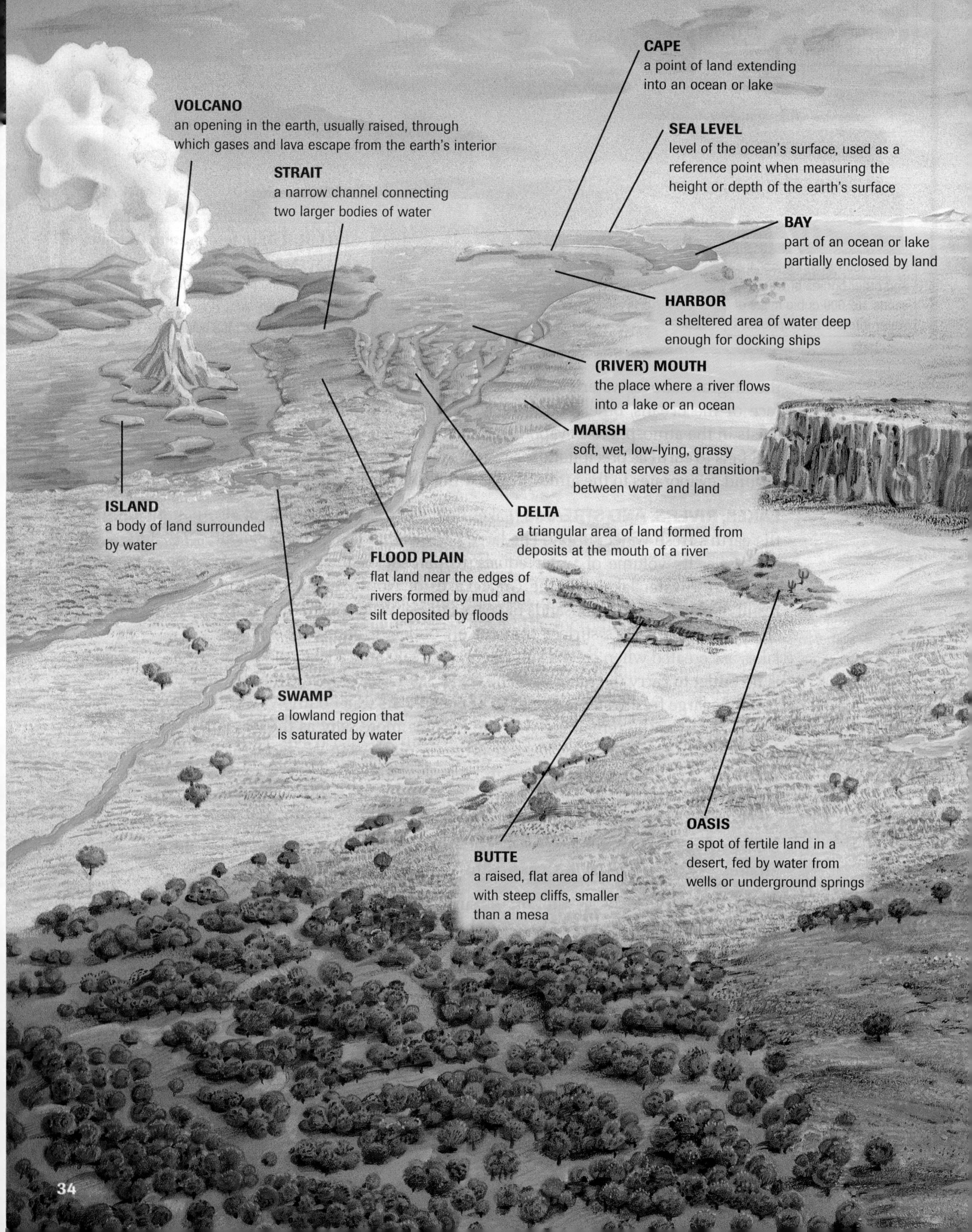

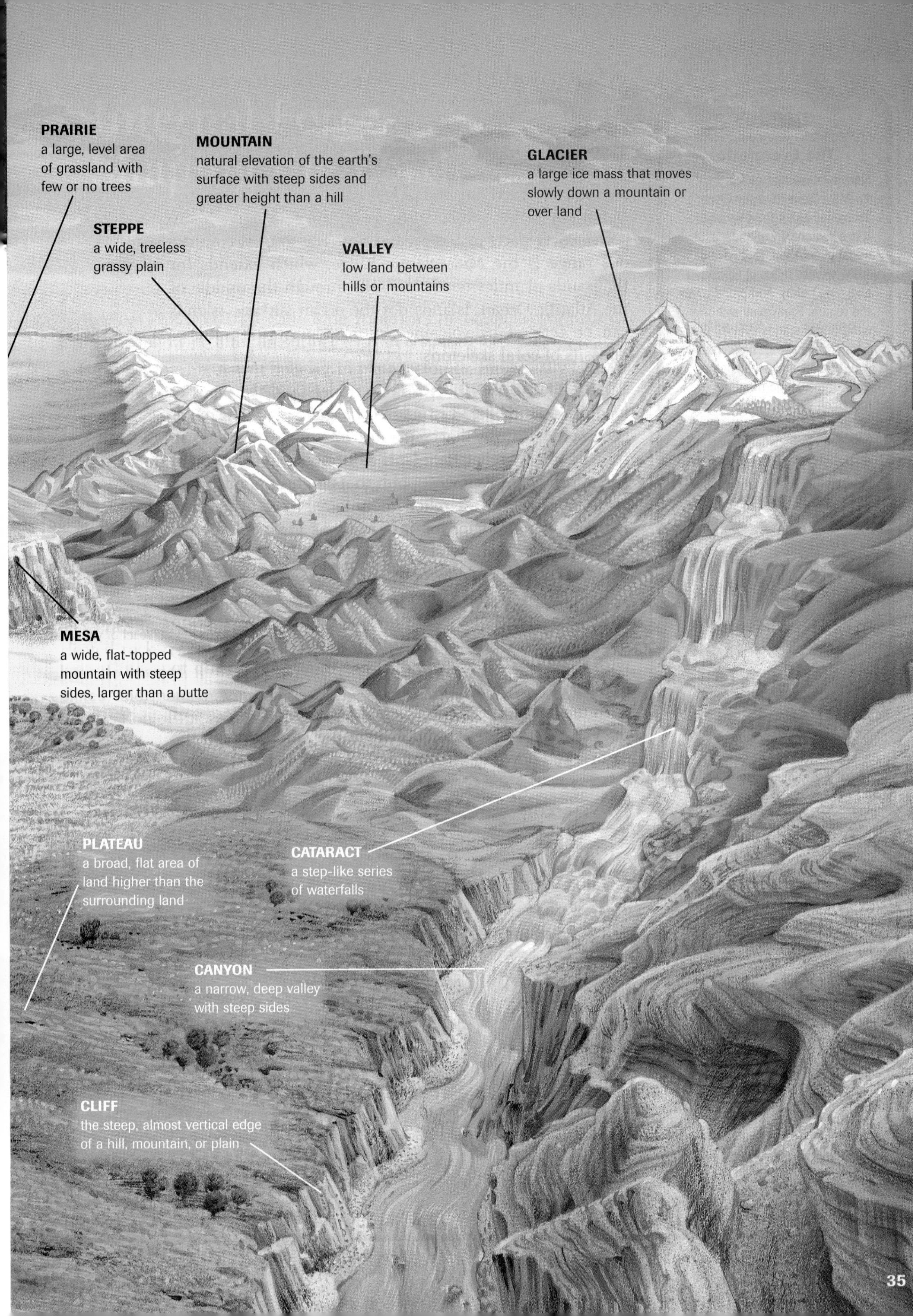

**PRAIRIE**
a large, level area
of grassland with
few or no trees

**STEPPE**
a wide, treeless
grassy plain

**MOUNTAIN**
natural elevation of the earth's
surface with steep sides and
greater height than a hill

**VALLEY**
low land between
hills or mountains

**GLACIER**
a large ice mass that moves
slowly down a mountain or
over land

**MESA**
a wide, flat-topped
mountain with steep
sides, larger than a butte

**PLATEAU**
a broad, flat area of
land higher than the
surrounding land

**CATARACT**
a step-like series
of waterfalls

**CANYON**
a narrow, deep valley
with steep sides

**CLIFF**
the steep, almost vertical edge
of a hill, mountain, or plain

**LOCATION** Victims of the 1995 earthquake in Kobe, Japan, wait out aftershocks. More than 5,000 people died in this quake. **Why does the location of Japan make it vulnerable to earthquakes?**

**EARTHQUAKE DAMAGE** Earthquakes result in squeezing, stretching, and shearing motions of the earth's crust that damage land and structures.

The changes are most noticeable in places where people live. Landslides, displacement of land, fires (from broken gas lines), and collapsed buildings are major outcomes of the ground motion. Aftershocks, or smaller-magnitude quakes, may occur after an initial shock and can sometimes continue for days afterward.

An earthquake is the sudden release of energy in the form of motion. C.F. Richter developed a scale to measure the amount of energy released. The **Richter Scale** uses information collected by seismographs to determine the relative strength of an earthquake. The scale has no absolute upper limit. Most people would not notice a quake that measured 2 on the scale. A 4.5 quake will probably be reported in the news. A major quake has a measurement of 7 or more. The largest quake ever measured was 8.9 in the Kermadec Islands of the South Pacific in 1986.

**TSUNAMI** Sometimes an earthquake causes a **tsunami** (tsu·NAH·mee), a giant wave in the ocean. A tsunami can travel from the epicenter of a quake at speeds of up to 450 miles per hour, producing waves of 50 to 100 feet or higher. The world record for a tsunami was set in 1971 off the Ryukyu Islands near Japan, where the wall of water reached 238 feet—more than 20 stories high. Tsunamis may travel across wide stretches of the ocean and do damage on distant shores. For example, in 1960 a quake near Chile created a tsunami that caused damage in Japan, almost half a world away. A tsunami from a quake near Alaska killed 159 people in Hilo, Hawaii, in 1946.

## Volcanoes

Volcanoes are among the most spectacular of natural events. Magma, gases, and water from the lower part of the crust or the mantle collect in underground chambers. Eventually the materials pour out of a crack in the earth's surface called a **volcano.** Most volcanoes are found along the tectonic plate boundaries.

**VOLCANIC ACTION** When the magma flows out onto the land slowly, it may spread across an area and cool. Magma that has reached the earth's surface is called **lava.** The most dramatic volcanic action is an eruption, in which hot lava, gases, ash, dust, and rocks explode out of vents in the earth's crust. Often a hill or a mountain is created by lava. The landform may also be called a volcano.

Volcanoes do not erupt on a predictable schedule; they may be active over many years and then stop. Sometimes they remain inactive for

**Geographic Thinking**

**Using the Atlas**
Using the map on pages A2–3, calculate the distance these two tsunamis traveled.

long periods of time—as long as hundreds of years—before becoming active again.

**RING OF FIRE** The **Ring of Fire,** a zone around the rim of the Pacific Ocean, is the location of the vast majority of active volcanoes. You can see the zone on the map on page 37. Eight major tectonic plates meet in this zone. Volcanic action and earthquakes occur frequently there. Other volcanoes are located far from the margins of tectonic plates. They appear over "hot spots" where magma from deep in the mantle rises and melts through the lithosphere, as in volcanoes in the Hawaiian Islands.

Hot springs and geysers are indicators of high temperatures in the earth's crust. Hot springs occur when ground water circulates near a magma chamber. The water heats up and rises to the surface. The hot springs and pools of Yellowstone Park are examples of this type of activity. A geyser is a hot spring that occasionally erupts with steam jets and boiling water. Old Faithful, a geyser in Yellowstone, erupts regularly, but most geysers are irregular in their eruptions. Countries with hot springs and geysers include the United States, Iceland, and Japan. **C**

Not all volcanic action is bad. Volcanic ash produces fertile soil. In some parts of the world, the hot springs, steam, and heat generated by the magma are tapped for energy. In Iceland, for example, volcanic heat and steam are used for heating and hot water in the city of Reykjavik.

Internal forces have a major role in shaping the earth. In the next section, you will learn how external forces also change the landscape.

**Geographic Thinking**

**Seeing Patterns**
▶ Why do the United States, Iceland, and Japan have geysers?

## Geography TODAY

### An Island Is Born

On May 14, 2000, a team of scientists observed the birth of a new island in the South Pacific. On that day Kavachi, a volcano in the Solomon Islands, erupted for the first time since 1991. The volcano is located about 18 miles from the boundary of the Indo-Australian plate and the Pacific plate.

For at least 20 hours, the volcano erupted every 5 to 7 minutes, shooting ash and glowing lava blocks 230 feet into the air (shown below). The peak of the volcano is under water, about 2,100 feet above the sea floor. A sandy, ashen beach is forming about 6 feet below the surface of the ocean.

---

**SECTION 3** **Assessment**

**① Places & Terms**

Explain the meaning of each of the following terms.

- tectonic plate
- fault
- earthquake
- seismograph
- epicenter
- volcano

**② Taking Notes**

**MOVEMENT** Review the notes you took for this section.

- What are four types of plate movement?
- How are folds and faults created?

**③ Main Ideas**

a. How does the movement of tectonic plates shape the earth's surface?

b. When does a volcano occur?

c. How do earthquakes cause damage?

**④ Geographic Thinking**

**Making Generalizations**
Why do volcanoes and earthquakes occur along the Ring of Fire? **Think about:**

- tectonic plate movement
- movement of magma

**RESEARCH LINKS**
CLASSZONE.COM

**GeoActivity**

**SEEING PATTERNS** Use the Internet to find information on the top 10 most deadly volcanoes in history. Create a **database** showing the information by continent. Summarize your findings about the location of deadly quakes in two sentences.

# External Forces Shaping the Earth

## Main Ideas
- Wind, heat, cold, glaciers, rivers, and floods alter the surface of the earth.
- The results of weathering and erosion change the way humans interact with the environment.

## Places & Terms

| | |
|---|---|
| weathering | delta |
| sediment | loess |
| mechanical weathering | glacier |
| chemical weathering | glaciation |
| erosion | moraine |
| | humus |

**A HUMAN PERSPECTIVE** In Egypt, a seasonal dry wind is called khamsin ("fifty") for the number of days the season occurs. During khamsin, wind-driven sandstorms kill and injure people, close businesses and airports, and strip topsoil and seed from the ground. Sandstorms are not limited to the desert areas of Africa and Southwest Asia. For instance, a five-hour storm recently blasted Jingchang, China, causing millions of dollars of damage and killing about 300 people. Sandstorms are among the external forces that change the shape of the earth and affect the lives of the people in their paths.

## Weathering

In the last section, you learned about forces within the earth that changed the land. External forces, such as weathering and erosion, also alter landscapes and in some instances create the soil that is needed for plant life. **Weathering** refers to physical and chemical processes that change the characteristics of rock on or near the earth's surface. Weathering occurs slowly over many years and even centuries. Weathering processes create smaller and smaller pieces of rock called **sediment.** Sediment is mostly identifiable as either mud, sand, or silt, which is very fine particles of rock.

**MECHANICAL WEATHERING** Processes that break rock into smaller pieces are referred to as **mechanical weathering.** Mechanical weathering does not change the composition of the rock—only its size. For example, when ice crystals build up in the crack of a rock, they can actually create enough pressure to fracture the rock into smaller pieces. All sorts of agents can break apart rocks. Frost and even plant roots dig into crevices in the rock, splitting it. Human activities, like road construction or drilling and blasting in mining, are also mechanical weathering forces. Eventually, the smaller broken material will be combined with organic material to become soil.

**MOVEMENT** A natural arch frames a view of the Grand Canyon in Arizona. The canyon's depth was created by water erosion, and the width by rain and wind erosion. **What has happened to the sediment created by weathering in the canyon?**

**CHEMICAL WEATHERING** <u>**Chemical weathering**</u> occurs when rock is changed into a new substance as a result of interaction between elements in the air or water and the minerals in the rock. Decomposition, or breakup, can happen in several ways. Some minerals react to oxygen in the air and begin to crumble. That is what happens when iron rusts, for example.

Other minerals break down when combined with water or carbon dioxide, which form weak acids within the rock. When sulfur and nitrogen oxides mix with water, acid rain is formed. The increase of acid rain in the 20th century is believed to be speeding up some decomposition. The location and the climate in which the rocks are located have a great deal to do with how rocks decompose. Climates that are warm and moist will produce more chemical weathering than do cool dry areas. Rocks in cold dry and hot dry areas generally experience more mechanical weathering than chemical weathering. ◄A

**⊕ Geographic Thinking◄**

**Making Comparisons**

**A▷** Why would chemical weathering be rare in a desert area?

# Erosion

<u>**Erosion**</u> occurs when weathered material is moved by the action of wind, water, ice, or gravity. For erosion to occur, a transporting agent, such as water, must be present. Glaciers, waves, stream flow, or blowing winds cause erosion by grinding rock into smaller pieces. Material moved from one location to another results in the lowering of some locations and increased elevation in others. For example, water might carry topsoil from a hill into a river and gradually cause the river to become more narrow. Erosion in its many forms reshapes landforms and coastal regions, as well as riverbeds and riverbanks.

**WATER EROSION** One form of water erosion occurs as water flows in a stream or river. The motion picks up loose material and moves it downstream. The greater the force of water, the greater the ability of the water to transport tiny rock particles, or sediment. Another form of erosion is abrasion, the grinding away of rock by transported particles. The heavier the load of sediment, the greater the abrasion on the banks and riverbed. A third eroding action of water occurs when the water dissolves chemical elements in the rock. The composition of the rock changes as a result.

Most streams erode both vertically and horizontally—that is, the valley cut by a stream gets deeper and wider, forming a V-shaped valley. As the water slows, it drops the sediment it is carrying. When a river enters the ocean, the sediment is deposited in a fan-like landform called a <u>**delta.**</u>

Wave action along coastlines also changes the land. Waves can reduce or increase beaches. Sediment deposited by wave action may build up sandbars or islands. Wave action is so powerful that in some locations, it erodes about three feet of beach per year. For some unfortunate people, a beach house with an ocean view

**BACKGROUND**
The term *delta* is used because the shape of the landform resembles the Greek letter delta (Δ).

## Geography TODAY

### Moving the Cape Hatteras Lighthouse

Coastal erosion led to one of the great moving projects of the 20th century. The Cape Hatteras Lighthouse (shown below), the tallest brick lighthouse in the nation, was dangerously close to disappearing into the sea. Built in 1870 on Hatteras Island off the coast of North Carolina, the lighthouse stood 1,500 feet from the sea. By 1987, it was only 160 feet away. The only way to save the historic lighthouse was to move it.

In the summer of 1999, the structure was slowly moved—10 to 355 feet per day—to a new location 1,600 feet from the sea. But erosion will also take beach from the new location, and by 2018, as much as 404 feet may be gone.

## VISUAL SUMMARY
### A LIVING PLANET

### The Earth Inside and Out

- The earth's interior is made up of a series of layers that float on one another.
- The exterior of the earth is the crust.
- The presence of air and water make life on earth possible.

### Bodies of Water and Landforms

- Almost three-fourths of the earth is covered with water.
- The hydrologic cycle circulates water.
- Landforms on the land and under the ocean are similar.

### Internal Forces Shaping the Earth

- Huge plates on the earth's crust move because of the circulation of magma.
- Earthquakes and volcanoes are the results of plate movement.

### External Forces Shaping the Earth

- Weathering and erosion cause changes in the earth's surface and build soil.
- Actions of wind, water, ice, and gravity shape the earth's surface.

## Reviewing Places & Terms

**A. Briefly explain the importance of each of the following.**

1. continent
2. magma
3. hydrologic cycle
4. landform
5. relief
6. tectonic plate
7. earthquake
8. volcano
9. weathering
10. erosion

**B. Answer the questions about vocabulary in complete sentences.**

11. How are continents and tectonic plates related?
12. Where is magma found?
13. Lava is a form of which term listed above?
14. What is an example of a landform?
15. What does relief tell you about a landform?
16. What is the purpose of the hydrologic cycle?
17. What causes earthquakes?
18. How are magma and volcanoes related?
19. What are the two types of weathering?
20. What must be present for erosion to occur?

## Main Ideas

### The Earth Inside and Out (pp. 27–31)

1. What layers are found in the earth's interior?
2. What is the continental drift theory?

### Bodies of Water and Landforms (pp. 32–36)

3. How does water reach a drainage basin?
4. What is topography?

### Internal Forces Shaping the Earth (pp. 37–41)

5. What are three types of plate boundaries?
6. How are the Richter scale and a seismograph used?
7. What is the Ring of Fire?

### External Forces Shaping the Earth (pp. 42–45)

8. What is the difference between weathering and erosion?
9. What are three transporting agents of erosion?
10. Why are there many different types of soil?

# Critical Thinking

## 1. Using Your Notes

Use your completed chart to answer these questions.

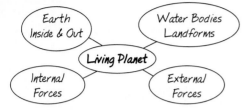

a. Why is water a critical element on the earth?

b. How do internal and external forces shape the earth?

## 2. Geographic Themes

a. **MOVEMENT** How does the movement of wind, water, or ice reshape the earth's surface?

b. **HUMAN–ENVIRONMENT INTERACTION** How do volcanoes and earthquakes affect human life?

## 3. Identifying Themes

What might be the hazards of living near the Ring of Fire? Which of the five themes apply to this situation?

## 4. Determining Cause and Effect

What is the relationship between tectonic plates, earthquakes, and volcanoes?

## 5. Making Comparisons

How is a valley created by water different from a valley created by a glacier?

Additional Test Practice, pp. S1–S37

**TEST PRACTICE**
CLASSZONE.COM

---

# Geographic Skills: Interpreting Charts

## Ten Most Deadly Earthquakes in the 20th Century

Use the information in the chart to answer the following questions.

1. **LOCATION** Which location suffered two deadly earthquakes in the 20th century?

2. **MOVEMENT** How is the magnitude of a quake related to loss of life?

3. **PLACE** What reasons might there be for so great a loss of life in Tangshan, China?

## GeoActivity

Using a base map of the world and an atlas, plot the locations of the ten most deadly earthquakes. Write a sentence describing the pattern you see in the locations.

| Date | Location | Deaths | Magnitude* |
|------|----------|--------|------------|
| 1976, July 27 | Tangshan, China | 255,000 | 8.0 |
| 1920, Dec. 16 | Gansu, China | 200,000 | 8.6 |
| 1927, May 22 | Nan-Shan, China | 200,000 | 8.3 |
| 1923, Sept. 1 | Yokohama, Japan | 143,000 | 8.3 |
| 1908, Dec. 28 | Messina, Italy | 83,000 | 7.5 |
| 1932, Dec. 25 | Gansu, China | 70,000 | 7.6 |
| 1970, May 31 | Northern Peru | 66,000 | 7.8 |
| 1935, May 30 | Quetta, India | 50,000 | 7.5 |
| 1990, June 20 | Western Iran | 40,000 | 7.7 |
| 1988, Dec. 7 | Armenia | 25,000 | 7.0 |

*Magnitude of earthquakes measured on the Richter scale developed in 1935.
SOURCES: Global Volcanism Network, Smithsonian Institution, U.S. Geological Survey, *World Almanac*

---

## INTERNET ACTIVITY

Use the links at **classzone.com** to do research about volcanic action. Focus on a variety of volcanic activities, including eruptions, geysers, hot springs, and island formation.

**Creating a Multimedia Presentation** Put together a presentation about the variety of volcanic activity. Include diagrams of several different types of activity and give examples of locations where the activity takes place.

Chapter 3

SECTION 1
Seasons and Weather

SECTION 2
Climate

SECTION 3
World Climate Regions

SECTION 4
Soils and Vegetation

PHYSICAL GEOGRAPHY

# Climate and Vegetation

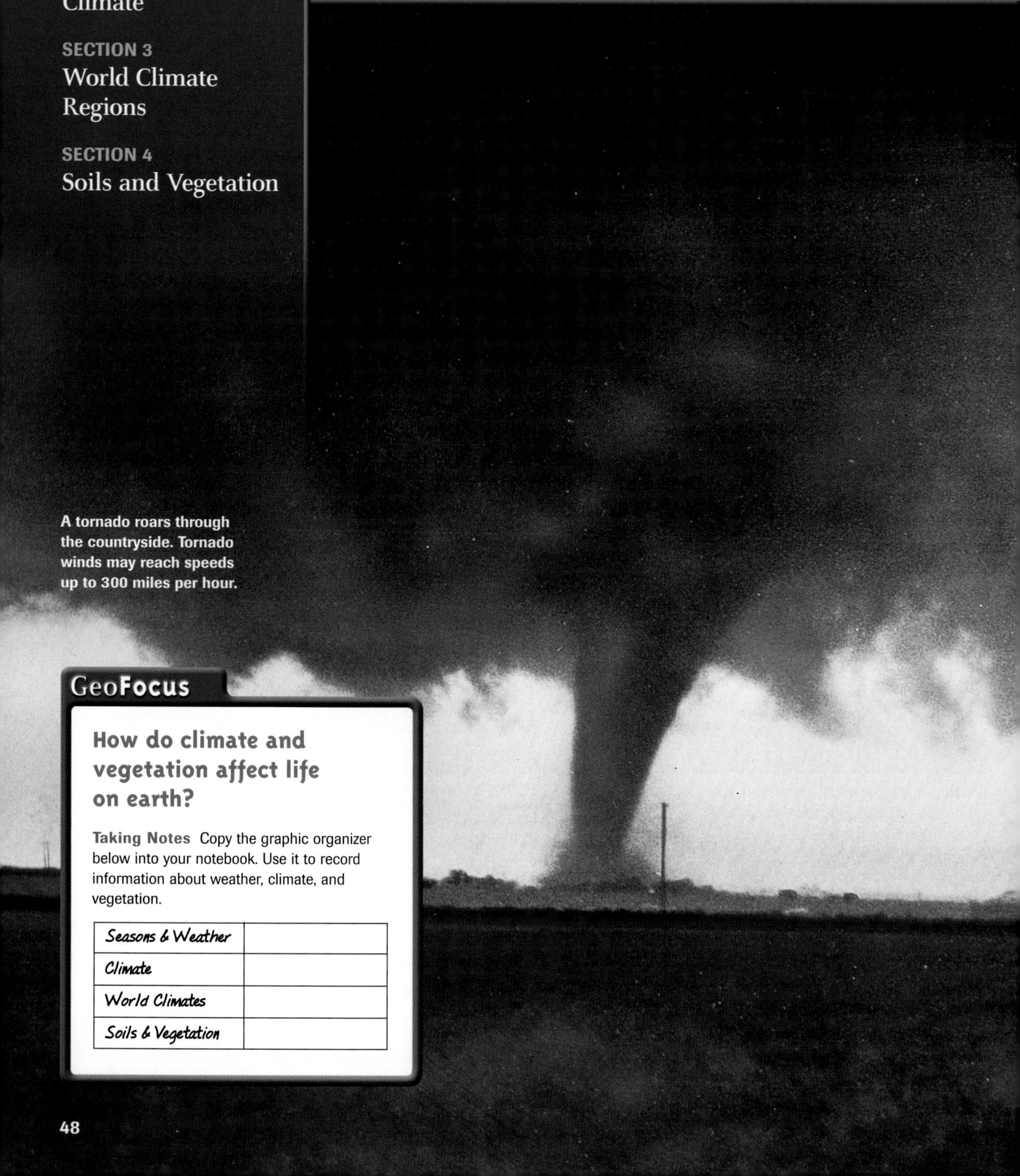

A tornado roars through the countryside. Tornado winds may reach speeds up to 300 miles per hour.

## GeoFocus

### How do climate and vegetation affect life on earth?

**Taking Notes** Copy the graphic organizer below into your notebook. Use it to record information about weather, climate, and vegetation.

| | |
|---|---|
| *Seasons & Weather* | |
| *Climate* | |
| *World Climates* | |
| *Soils & Vegetation* | |

# Seasons and Weather

## Main Ideas

- Seasons and weather occur because of the changing position of the earth in relation to the sun.
- Weather extremes are related to location on earth.

## Places & Terms

| | |
|---|---|
| solstice | hurricane |
| equinox | typhoon |
| weather | tornado |
| climate | blizzard |
| precipitation | drought |
| rain shadow | |

BASICS

**A HUMAN PERSPECTIVE** The smell of thousands of decaying corpses hung in the air in what was once the thriving seaport of Galveston, Texas. The day before, winds estimated at 130 miles per hour roared through the city. A storm surge of seawater more than 15 feet high pushed a wall of debris across the island of Galveston. Through this turmoil, Isaac Cline's family huddled in their home. A trolley trestle rammed the house until at last it collapsed, and the waves poured in. Cline survived, but some of his family did not. With a toll of 8,000 human lives, the "Great Galveston Hurricane" would be the deadliest hurricane to hit the United States. The storm date was August 8, 1900.

## Seasons

Hurricanes occur frequently in the southern and eastern United States during summer and fall. During these seasons, storm systems with strong winds form over warm ocean water.

**EARTH'S TILT** Seasons have an enormous impact on us, affecting the conditions in the atmosphere and on the earth that create our weather. As the earth revolves around the sun, it is tilted at a 23.5° angle in relation to the sun. Because of the earth's revolution and its tilt, different parts of the earth receive the direct rays of the sun for more hours of the day at certain times in the year. This causes the changing seasons on the earth. Notice in the diagram to the right that the northern half of the earth tilts toward the sun in summer and away from the sun in winter.

Two lines of latitude—the tropic of Cancer and the tropic of Capricorn—mark the points farthest north and south that the sun's rays shine directly overhead at noon. The day on which this occurs is called a **solstice.** In the Northern Hemisphere, the summer solstice, or the beginning of summer, is the longest day of the year. Winter solstice, the beginning of winter, is the shortest.

Another signal of seasonal change are the equinoxes. Twice a year on the **equinox,** the days and nights all over the world are equal in length. The equinoxes mark the beginning of spring and autumn.

### Seasons: Northern Hemisphere

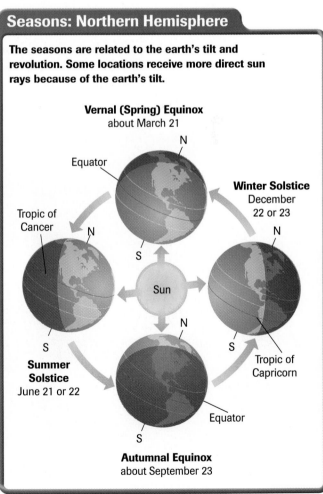

The seasons are related to the earth's tilt and revolution. Some locations receive more direct sun rays because of the earth's tilt.

**Vernal (Spring) Equinox**
about March 21

**Winter Solstice**
December 22 or 23

**Summer Solstice**
June 21 or 22

**Autumnal Equinox**
about September 23

Equator
Tropic of Cancer
Sun
Tropic of Capricorn
Equator

# Weather

Weather and climate are often confused. **Weather** is the condition of the atmosphere at a particular location and time. **Climate** is the term for weather conditions at a particular location over a long period of time. Northern Russia, for example, has a cold climate. ▶

**WHAT CAUSES THE WEATHER?** Daily weather is the complex result of several conditions. For example, the amount of solar energy received by a location varies according to the earth's position in relation to the sun. Large masses of air absorb and distribute this solar energy, which in turn affects the weather. Other factors include:

- **water vapor** This determines whether there will be **precipitation—** falling water droplets in the form of rain, sleet, snow, or hail.
- **cloud cover** Clouds may hold water vapor.
- **landforms and bodies of water** Water heats slowly but also loses heat slowly. Land heats rapidly but loses heat quickly as well.
- **elevation** As elevation above sea level increases, the air becomes thinner and loses its ability to hold moisture.
- **air movement** Winds move the air and the solar energy and moisture that it holds. As a result, weather can change very rapidly.

**PRECIPITATION** Precipitation depends on the amount of water vapor in the air and the movement of that air. As warm air rises, it cools and loses its ability to hold water vapor. The water vapor condenses, and the water droplets form into clouds. When the amount of water in a cloud is too heavy for the air to hold, rain or snow falls from the cloud. Geographers classify precipitation as convectional, orographic, or frontal, as illustrated in the diagram below.

🌐 **Geographic Thinking** ◀

**Making Comparisons**
◀ Why might geographers be more interested in the climate of a place than its weather?

## Types of Precipitation

**Convectional** Typical of hot climates, convection occurs after morning sunshine heats warm moist air. Clouds form in the afternoon and rain falls.

**Orographic** Associated with mountain areas, orographic storms drop more rain on the windward side of a mountain and create a rain shadow on the leeward side.

**Frontal** Mid-latitude frontal storms feature cold dense air masses that push lighter warm air masses upward, causing precipitation to form.

Convectional precipitation occurs in hot, moist climates where the sun quickly heats the air. The heated air rises, and by afternoon clouds form and rain falls. Orographic precipitation falls on the windward side of hills or mountains that block moist air and force it upward. The air cools and rain or snow falls. The land on the leeward side is called a **rain shadow** because it gets little rain from the descending dry air. Frontal movement causes most precipitation in the middle latitudes. A front is the boundary between two air masses of different temperatures or density. Rain or snow occurs when lighter, warm air is pushed upward by the colder, denser air. The rising air cools, water vapor condenses, and precipitation falls.

## Weather Extremes

As air masses warm and cool and move across the earth's surface, they create weather. Sometimes the clashes between air masses cause storms, which can be severe. They disrupt the usual patterns of life and often cause major property damage and loss of human life. Hurricanes, tornadoes, blizzards, droughts, and floods are examples of extreme weather.

**HURRICANES** Storms that form over warm, tropical ocean waters are called **hurricanes**—also known as **typhoons** in Asia. These storms are called different names around the globe: tropical cyclones, willy-willies (Australia), *baguios* (Philippines), and *chubascos* (Mexico). Hurricanes are one way heat from the tropics is moved out of the region. Air flowing over an ocean with a water temperature of 80°F or higher picks up huge amounts of moisture and heat energy. As these water-laden winds flow into a low-pressure core, they tighten to form an "eye." The eye is usually 10 to 20 miles across and has clear, calm skies. But the winds moving around the eye may be as strong as 200 miles per hour.

The clouds and winds stretch over a vast area, sometimes as wide as 500 miles. Upper air currents blowing from the east steer the hurricanes in a westerly direction. As the hurricane hits land, it pounds the area with howling winds and very heavy rains. It may also cause a storm surge along coastal regions. This wall of seawater, pushed ashore by the winds, may rise to 16 feet or more. The low-lying coastal regions of Bangladesh in South Asia are especially vulnerable to storm surges from tropical cyclones. ◀ⓑ

**TORNADOES** Unlike hurricanes, which take days to develop, tornadoes form quickly and sometimes without warning. A **tornado,** or twister, is a powerful funnel-shaped column of spiraling air.

**Geographic Thinking**◀

**Using the Atlas**
ⓑ▶ Use the map on page A20. On which river delta is Bangladesh located?

**MOVEMENT** A pair of typhoons move across the Pacific Ocean. Notice the "eye" in each storm. **What is the weather inside the "eye" like?**

*Pacific Ocean*

# Climate

**Main Ideas**
- Climate reflects the seasonal patterns of weather for a location over a long period of time.
- Global climatic changes may be natural or human-made.

**Places & Terms**
**convection**
**El Niño**
**greenhouse effect**

**A HUMAN PERSPECTIVE** Nineteenth-century fishermen along the Peruvian coast called the event El Niño—the Spanish name for the infant Jesus—because the event occurred near Christmastime. Every two to seven years, the waters off the Peruvian coast became warmer than usual, resulting in poor fishing. Eventually, 20th-century scientists studying worldwide climate changes confirmed the truth of this folk knowledge. They discovered that El Niño brought about changes in global weather patterns that disrupted not only fishing, but also other economic activities. Droughts and floods in Asia, Africa, and North America seemed to be related to El Niño. Scientists recognized that weather and climate conditions are not isolated but are connected parts of the global climate system.

## Factors Affecting Climate

Four major factors influence the climate of a region: wind and ocean currents, latitude, elevation, and topography.

**WIND CURRENTS** Wind and ocean currents help distribute the sun's heat from one part of the world to another through **convection,** the transfer of heat in the atmosphere by upward motion of the air. As sunlight heats the atmosphere, the air expands, creating a zone of low air pressure. Cooler dense air in a nearby high-pressure zone rushes into the low-pressure area, causing wind.

Global wind patterns are caused by the same kind of circulation on a larger scale. The hot air flows toward the poles, and the cold air moves toward the equator. The winds would blow in straight lines, but since the earth rotates they are turned at an angle. In the Northern Hemisphere, they turn to the right. In the Southern Hemisphere, they turn to the left. This bending of the winds is called the Coriolis effect.

The map to the right shows that the wind patterns are mirror images of each other in the Northern and Southern Hemispheres. Winds are identified by the direction from which they blow; a north wind blows from the north to the south.

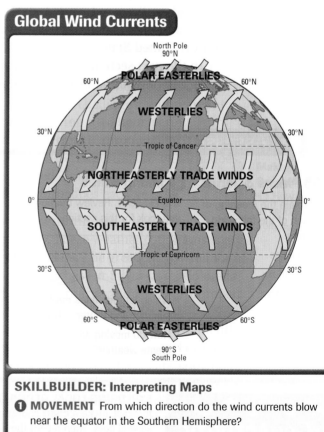

**Global Wind Currents**

**SKILLBUILDER: Interpreting Maps**
❶ **MOVEMENT** From which direction do the wind currents blow near the equator in the Southern Hemisphere?
❷ **LOCATION** Between which latitudes do the westerlies blow?

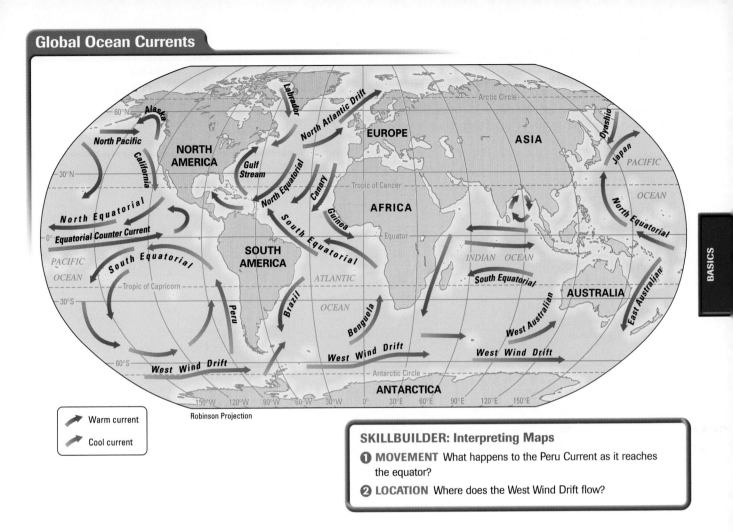

Robinson Projection

Warm current

Cool current

**SKILLBUILDER: Interpreting Maps**

❶ **MOVEMENT** What happens to the Peru Current as it reaches the equator?

❷ **LOCATION** Where does the West Wind Drift flow?

**OCEAN CURRENTS** Ocean currents are like rivers flowing in the ocean. Moving in large circular systems, warm waters flow away from the equator toward the poles, and cold water flows back toward the equator. Winds blowing over the ocean currents affect the climate of the lands that the winds cross. For example, the warmth of the Gulf Stream and the North Atlantic Drift help keep the temperature of Europe moderate. Even though much of Europe is as far north as Canada, it enjoys a much milder climate than Canada.

Ocean currents affect not only the temperature of an area, but also the amount of precipitation received. Cold ocean currents flowing along a coastal region chill the air and sometimes prevent warm air and the moisture it holds from falling to earth. The Atacama Desert in South America and the Namib Desert in Africa, for example, were formed partly because of cold ocean currents nearby. ◀

**Geographic Thinking** ◀

**Making Comparisons**

Ⓐ How are wind and ocean currents similar in their effect on climate?

**ZONES OF LATITUDE** Geographers divide the earth into three general zones of latitude: low or tropical, middle or temperate, and high or polar. Tropical zones are found on either side of the equator. They extend to the tropic of Cancer in the Northern Hemisphere and the tropic of Capricorn in the Southern Hemisphere. Lands in tropical zones are hot all year long. In some areas, a shift in wind patterns causes variations in the seasons. For example, Tanzania experiences both a rainy season and a dry season as Indian Ocean winds blow in or away from the land.

Latitude and elevation influence climate. Notice that as you move along the latitude line, the climates at the lower altitude change. However, the greater the altitude, the fewer the climate zones no matter what latitude a location may be.

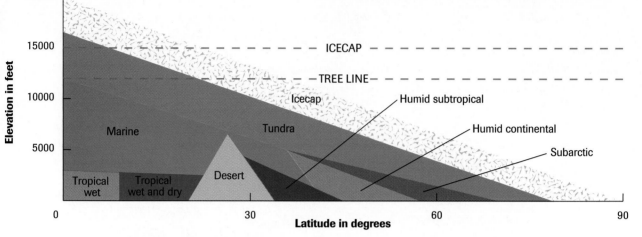

Adapted from *Physical Geography* by Ralph Scott.

The high-latitude polar zones, which encircle the North Pole and South Pole, are cold all year. Summer temperatures in the polar regions may reach a high of only 50°F.

The earth's two temperate zones lie at the middle latitudes, between the tropics and the polar regions. Within the temperate zones, climates can vary greatly, ranging from relatively hot to relatively cold. These variations occur because solar heating is greater in the summer than in the winter. So summers are much warmer.

**ELEVATION** Another factor in determining the climate of a region is elevation, or distance above sea level. You would think that the closer you get to the sun, the hotter it would become. But as altitude increases, the air temperature drops about 3.5°F for every 1,000 feet. Therefore, the climate gets colder as you climb a mountain or other elevated location. Climates above 12,000 feet become like those in Arctic areas—with snow and ice. For example, Mt. Kilimanjaro in east Africa is capped by snow all year long. The diagram above will help you see how latitude and elevation are related.

**TOPOGRAPHY** Landforms also affect the climate. This is especially true of mountain areas. Remember that moisture-laden winds cool as they move up the side of a mountain, eventually releasing rain or snow. By the time the winds reach the other side of the mountain, they are dry and become warmer as they flow down the mountain.

## Changes in Climate

Climates change over time. Scientists studying ice-core samples from thousands of years ago have noted a variety of changes in temperature and precipitation. Some of the changes in climate appear to be natural while others are the result of human activities.

**EL NIÑO** The warming of the waters off the west coast of South America—known as **El Niño**—is a natural change in the climate. About every two to seven years, prevailing easterly winds that blow over the central Pacific Ocean slow or reverse direction, changing the ocean temperature and affecting the weather worldwide. Normally, these easterlies bring seasonal rains and push warm ocean water toward Asia and Australia. In El Niño years, however, the winds push warm water and heavy rains toward the Americas. This can cause floods and mudslides there, while Australia and Asia experience drought conditions.

When the reverse occurs—that is, when the winds blow the warmer water to the lands on the western Pacific rim—the event is called La Niña. La Niña causes increases in precipitation in places such as India and increased dryness along the Pacific coasts of the Americas.

## El Niño and La Niña

**El Niño and La Niña act to transfer the heat on the earth's surface and in the atmosphere to other parts of the globe.**

**SKILLBUILDER: Interpreting Graphics**

❶ **MOVEMENT** In which direction do winds and water move in El Niño?

❷ **LOCATION** Where does flooding occur during La Niña?

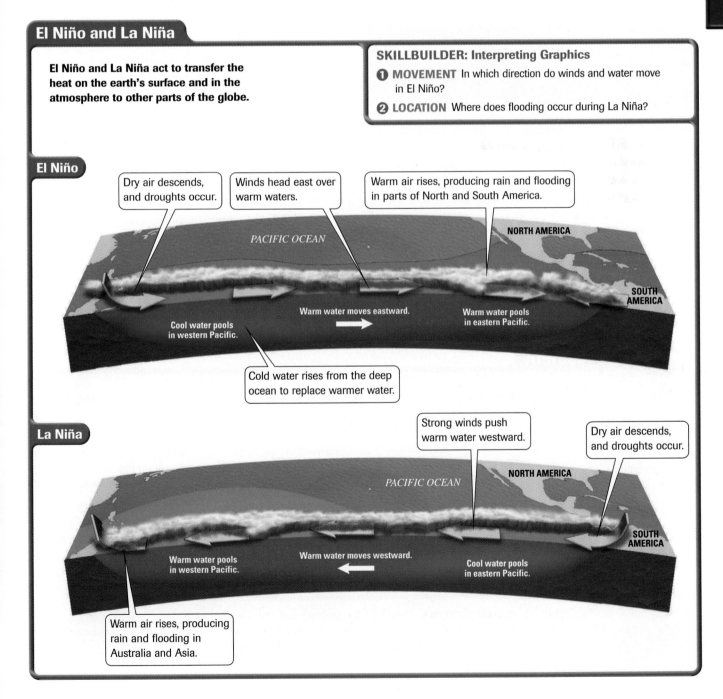

**El Niño**

Dry air descends, and droughts occur.

Winds head east over warm waters.

Warm air rises, producing rain and flooding in parts of North and South America.

*PACIFIC OCEAN*

NORTH AMERICA

SOUTH AMERICA

Cool water pools in western Pacific.

Warm water moves eastward.

Warm water pools in eastern Pacific.

Cold water rises from the deep ocean to replace warmer water.

**La Niña**

Strong winds push warm water westward.

Dry air descends, and droughts occur.

*PACIFIC OCEAN*

NORTH AMERICA

SOUTH AMERICA

Warm water pools in western Pacific.

Warm water moves westward.

Cool water pools in eastern Pacific.

Warm air rises, producing rain and flooding in Australia and Asia.

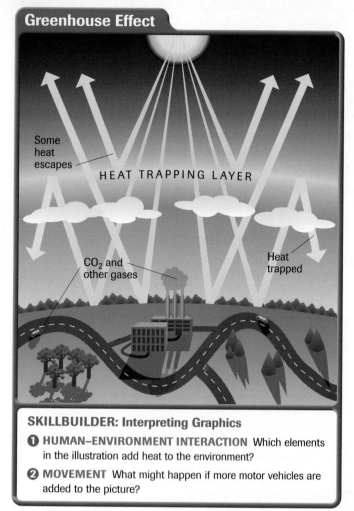

**Greenhouse Effect**

Some heat escapes

HEAT TRAPPING LAYER

$CO_2$ and other gases

Heat trapped

**SKILLBUILDER: Interpreting Graphics**

❶ **HUMAN–ENVIRONMENT INTERACTION** Which elements in the illustration add heat to the environment?

❷ **MOVEMENT** What might happen if more motor vehicles are added to the picture?

**GLOBAL WARMING** Although controversy exists over the causes of global warming, scientists agree that air temperatures are increasing. Since the late 1800s, the temperature of the earth has increased by one degree. However, estimates for the next century suggest that the increase will be almost 3.5 degrees.

Some scientists believe that this warming is part of the earth's natural warming and cooling cycles. For example, 18,000 to 20,000 years ago, the earth was in the last of several ice ages, when vast glaciers advanced over huge portions of the land mass.

Other scientists argue that global temperature increases are caused by the **greenhouse effect.** The layer of gases released by the burning of coal and petroleum traps some solar energy, causing higher temperatures in the same way that a greenhouse traps solar energy.

As more and more nations become industrialized, the amount of greenhouse gases will also increase. Scientists predict that, if global warming continues, ice caps will melt, flooding some coastal areas, covering islands, and changing the global climate. In the next section, you will learn about world climate regions.

**BACKGROUND**
The air temperature in the period between about 1500 and 1850 was so much cooler than today that it is known as a "Little Ice Age."

---

**SECTION 2 Assessment**

❶ **Places & Terms**

Explain the meaning of each of the following terms.

• convection
• El Niño
• greenhouse effect

❷ **Taking Notes**

**MOVEMENT** Review the notes you took for this section.

Climate

• What are four factors that affect climate?
• What are examples of forces that produce climate changes?

❸ **Main Ideas**

a. What role do wind and ocean currents play in climate?

b. How do latitude and altitude affect climate?

c. How do El Niño and La Niña affect climate?

❹ **Geographic Thinking**

**Drawing Conclusions**
Which of the factors affecting climate has the greatest impact on the climate in your region? **Think about:**

• the four factors affecting climate
• the climate where you live

**RESEARCH LINKS**
CLASSZONE.COM

**GeoActivity**

**SEEING PATTERNS** Review the information and diagram about El Niño and La Niña on page 57. Use the Internet to find more information on these events. Create a **multimedia presentation** explaining one of the events and how it affects the world-wide weather conditions.

# World Climate Regions

## Main Ideas

- Temperature and precipitation define climate regions.
- Broad climate definitions help to identify variations in weather at a location over the course of a year.

## Places & Terms

**tundra**

**permafrost**

BASICS

**A HUMAN PERSPECTIVE** Songs have been written celebrating April in Paris. Springtime there is mild, with temperatures in the 50°F range. But no songs have been written about April in Winnipeg, Canada. Temperatures in April there are only slightly above freezing. If you look at the two locations on a map, you will find the cities are almost the same distance north of the equator. To understand why two cities at the same latitude are so different, you need to understand climate regions. When studying climate, one of the key words is location.

## Defining a Climate Region

Climate regions act like a code that tells geographers much about an area without giving many local details. To define a climate region, geographers must make generalizations about what the typical weather conditions are like over many years in a location.

The two most significant factors in defining different climates are temperature and precipitation. A place's location on a continent, its topography, and its elevation may also have an impact on the climate.

Geographers use a variety of methods to describe climate patterns. The most common method uses latitude to help define the climate. There are five general climate regions: tropical (low-latitude), dry, mid-latitude, high latitude, and highland. Dry and highland climates occur at several different latitudes. Within the five regions, there are variations that geographers divide into smaller zones. You can see the varied climate regions on the map on pages 60–61.

Although the map shows a distinct line between each of the climate regions, in reality there are transition zones between the regions. As you read about climate regions, refer to the climate map. You should see the latitude-related patterns that emerge in world climate regions.

**PLACE** This highland climate zone in Patagonia, South America, has several different climate regions, including tundra and subartic.

**DESERT** Some people think a desert is nothing but sand dunes. However, deserts are categorized according to the amount of rainfall, rather than by landforms, and can be hot or cool/cold. Deserts receive less than ten inches of rain per year. Hot deserts, like the Sahara and the Arabian Desert, regularly have low humidity and high temperatures during the day. At night, temperatures drop because the dry air cannot hold heat well.

Cool/cold deserts are found in the mid-latitudes mostly in the Northern Hemisphere, often in the rain shadow of nearby mountain ranges. Summer temperatures are warm to hot, and winter temperatures range from quite cool to below freezing.

**MEDITERRANEAN** This climate subregion is named for the land around the Mediterranean Sea where it is located. It also exists elsewhere, such as the west coast of the United States and parts of Australia. Its summers are dry and hot, and its winters cool and rainy. This climate region supports a dense population and rich agricultural activity.

**MARINE WEST COAST** This climate subregion, which is located close to the ocean, is frequently cloudy, foggy, and damp. The winds over the warm ocean moderate the temperatures and keep them relatively constant. Parts of the west coast of the United States and Canada and most of Western Europe experience this climate. Precipitation in marine west coast climate regions is evenly distributed throughout the year. Industrial regions with marine west coast climate may have smog (a mixture of smoke and fog).

PLACE These Italian vineyards thrive in the hot dry summers and cool rainy winters of the Mediterranean climate. The climate also supports the cultivation of citrus fruit, olives, and vegetables.

**Geographic Thinking**

**Making Comparisons**
Ⓐ How are Mediterranean and marine west coast climates different?

**HUMID SUBTROPICAL** Long periods of summer heat and humidity characterize the humid subtropics. These areas are found on the east coast of continents and are often subject to hurricanes in late summer and autumn. The southeastern part of the United States and large areas of China are examples. Winters are mild to cool, depending on latitude. The climate is very suitable for raising crops, especially rice.

**HUMID CONTINENTAL** A great variety in temperature and precipitation characterizes this climate, which is found in the mid-latitude interiors of Northern Hemisphere continents. For example, Winnipeg, Manitoba, in Canada is located deep in the North American continent. It has a humid continental climate. Air masses chilled by Arctic ice and snow flow south over these areas and frequently collide with tropical air masses, causing changing weather conditions. These areas experience four seasons. However, the length of each season is determined by the region's latitude.

**SUBARCTIC** Evergreen forests called taiga cover the lands in the subarctic subregion, especially in Canada and Russia. Huge temperature variations occur in this subregion between summer and winter. Although the summers are short and cool, the winters are always very cold.

Temperatures at freezing or below freezing last five to eight months of the year.

**TUNDRA** The flat, treeless lands forming a ring around the Arctic Ocean are called **tundra.** The climate subregion is also called tundra. It is almost exclusively located in the Northern Hemisphere. Very little precipitation falls here, usually less than 15 inches per year. The land has **permafrost**—that is, the subsoil is constantly frozen. In the summer, which lasts for only a few weeks, the temperature may reach slightly above 40°F. **B**

**ICE CAP** Snow, ice, and permanently freezing temperatures characterize the region, which is so cold that it rarely snows. These subregions are sometimes called polar deserts since they receive less than ten inches of precipitation a year. The coldest temperature ever recorded, 128.6°F below zero, was on the ice cap at Vostok, Antarctica.

**HIGHLANDS** The highlands climate varies with latitude, elevation, other topography, and continental location. In rugged mountain areas such as the Andes of South America, climates can vary based on such factors as whether a slope faces north or south and whether it is exposed to winds carrying moisture.

Understanding climate helps you understand about the general weather conditions in an area. In the next section, you will learn about the variety of soils and vegetation on the earth.

**REGION** Life is hard during the long, cold, and dark winter in the subarctic. The only places where the temperatures are colder are the icecaps of Greenland and the Antarctic.

---

## SECTION 3 Assessment

**① Places & Terms**

Identify and explain where in the region these would be found.

- tundra
- permafrost

**② Taking Notes**

**REGION** Review the notes you took for this section.

*World Climates*

- What are the five basic climate regions?
- What are the factors that determine climate?

**③ Main Ideas**

a. How do tropical climates differ from each other?

b. How do desert regions differ from each other?

c. How are Humid subtropical and Mediterranean climates different from each other?

**④ Geographic Thinking**

**Making Generalizations**
How are the climates of the Northern Hemisphere different from the climates of the Southern Hemisphere?
**Think about:**

- sizes and locations of the continents

**S** See Skillbuilder Handbook, page R6.

---

**GeoActivity**

**MAKING COMPARISONS** Study the descriptions of climates in this chapter. Then either draw pictures or find pictures that illustrate the climates. Using a hanger and string, create a **mobile** displaying world climate regions.

# Interpreting Climographs

How many seasons are in a year where you live? In some parts of the world the climate is the same all year long. Other places have only two seasons—wet and dry. Still others experience changes in temperature and precipitation almost every month. A climograph allows you to quickly determine what the climate is like in a place. If you have two climographs you may compare two different places.

**THE LANGUAGE OF GRAPHS** A **climograph** shows the average daily temperature and precipitation for each month of the year for a specific location. This information shows what the climate is like over a year. Use the green line on the graph to find the average temperature and the blue bars to find average rainfall.

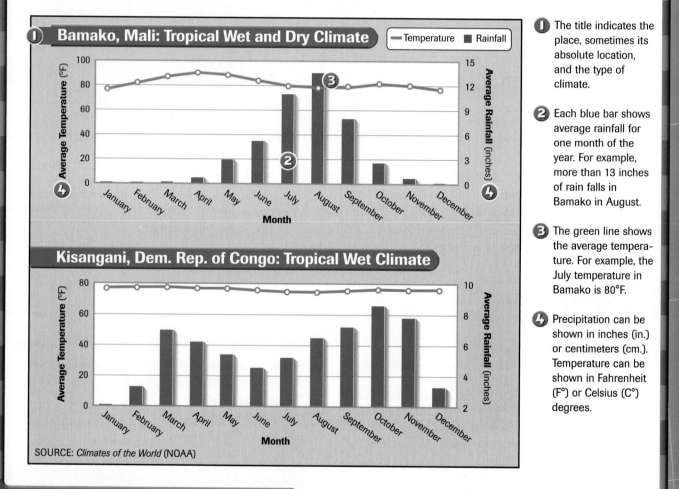

**① Bamako, Mali: Tropical Wet and Dry Climate** — Temperature ■ Rainfall

**Kisangani, Dem. Rep. of Congo: Tropical Wet Climate**

SOURCE: *Climates of the World* (NOAA)

**①** The title indicates the place, sometimes its absolute location, and the type of climate.

**②** Each blue bar shows average rainfall for one month of the year. For example, more than 13 inches of rain falls in Bamako in August.

**③** The green line shows the average temperature. For example, the July temperature in Bamako is 80°F.

**④** Precipitation can be shown in inches (in.) or centimeters (cm.). Temperature can be shown in Fahrenheit (F°) or Celsius (C°) degrees.

## Map and Graph Skills Assessment

**1. Analyzing Data**
What information is shown on each side of the vertical axis?

**2. Analyzing Data**
What are the rainy months in Bamako? How much rain falls in the rainiest month?

**3. Drawing Conclusions**
How is the tropical wet and dry climate of Bamako different from the tropical wet climate of Kisangani?

# Soils and Vegetation

## Main Ideas
- Soil and climate help to determine the vegetation of a region.
- Human land use alters the vegetation in both positive and negative ways.

## Places & Terms

| | |
|---|---|
| ecosystem | coniferous |
| biome | savanna |
| deciduous | steppe |
| rain forest | |

BASICS

**A HUMAN PERSPECTIVE** In the 1870s, a settler described prairie land in Tazewell County, Illinois, as having western meadow lilies "as high as a boy's head," rippling waves of wildflowers, and grass so dense that a man on horseback 30 yards away could not be seen. At that time, the land produced crops of grains, such as corn, wheat, and oats. In most places in the world where people have settled, the land continues to be used for agricultural purposes, such as farming, herding, and timber production. Soil and vegetation have a direct impact on which of those activities the people living in a region can perform.

## Soil Regions

Soil is a thin layer of weathered rock, humus, air, and water. It shapes human existence in many ways. The world's food supply depends greatly on the top six inches of soil (sometimes called topsoil). Such factors as depth, texture, and humus content of the soil determine the type of vegetation that can be supported in a region. That, in turn, helps to influence which human activities may take place there. As you study the chart below, notice the relationship of climate to the characteristics of the soil. Soil characteristics and climate are major influences in vegetation regions.

## Vegetation Regions

Vegetation regions are natural environments that provide the stage for human activities such as farming, raising livestock, and producing timber. Soil, temperature, and moisture influence the type of vegetation that thrives naturally in a region. Vegetation patterns are identified on the basis of the ecosystems they support. An **ecosystem** is an interdependent community of plants and animals. The ecosystem of a region is referred to as a **biome.** Biomes are further divided into forest, grassland, desert, and tundra.

### Soil Differences

| Soil Characteristic | Wet Climate | Dry Climate | Warm Climate | Cold Climate |
|---|---|---|---|---|
| Depth | deep | shallow | deep | shallow |
| Texture | intermediate to fine | coarse | fine | coarse |
| Weathering | chemical | physical | rapid | slow |
| Humus Content | variable | low | low | abundant |
| Acidity | acidic | not acidic | less acidity | higher acidity |

SOURCE: *Physical Geography*, Ralph Scott

**SKILLBUILDER: Interpreting Charts**

❶ **PLACE** What characteristics would soil in a cold, dry climate most likely have?

❷ **REGION** How does the soil in warm and wet climates differ from the soil in cold and dry climates in terms of depth and texture?

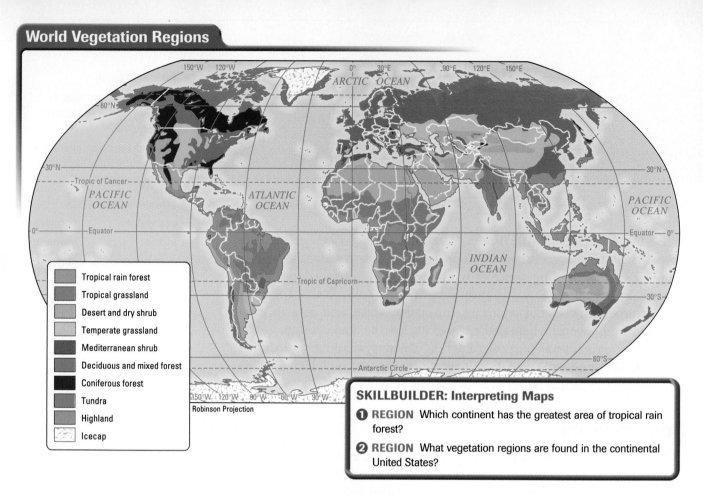

Tropical rain forest
Tropical grassland
Desert and dry shrub
Temperate grassland
Mediterranean shrub
Deciduous and mixed forest
Coniferous forest
Tundra
Highland
Icecap

Robinson Projection

**SKILLBUILDER: Interpreting Maps**

❶ **REGION** Which continent has the greatest area of tropical rain forest?

❷ **REGION** What vegetation regions are found in the continental United States?

**FORESTLANDS** Forest regions are categorized by the types of trees they support—broadleaf or needleleaf. Broadleaf trees, such as maple, oak, birch, and cottonwood, are also called **deciduous** trees. The **rain forest** is located in the tropical zone and is covered with a heavy concentration of broadleaf trees. In the tropical rain forest region, some broadleaf trees stay green all year. In the deciduous region, trees shed their leaves at least once during the year. This region is located almost exclusively in the Northern Hemisphere. Sometimes deciduous trees are mixed with needleleaf trees, such as pine, fir, and cedar, to form a mixed forest region. Needleleaf trees are also called **coniferous** trees because they are cone bearing. They are found in huge stands in northern regions of North America, Asia, and Europe.

**GRASSLANDS** Grasslands, mostly flat regions dotted with a few trees, are called by different terms. In the tropical grassland region, the flat, grassy, mostly treeless plains are called **savanna.** In the Northern Hemisphere, the terms **steppe** or prairie are used to identify temperate grasslands. Vast areas of Eurasia are covered with steppe. In the Southern Hemisphere, the temperate grasslands may be referred to as pampas. Ⓐ

**DESERT AND TUNDRA** The plants that live in these extreme climates are specially adapted to tolerate the dry or cold conditions. In the tundra, plants that hug the ground, such as mosses and lichen, are best adapted to survive the cold dry climate. In the desert, plants that can conserve water and withstand heat, such as cacti, sagebrush, or other shrubs, dot the landscape.

**Geographic Thinking**

**Seeing Patterns**
Ⓐ Study the map above. What patterns do you see in the relationship of forestlands to grasslands?

Before

After

# Human Impact on the Environment

As you can imagine, the impact of human activities on soil and vegetation is immense. Throughout this book, you will read about the ways that human beings either have adapted to the land or have altered it to meet their needs. Human activities that affect the environment include building dams or irrigation systems, planting food crops, or slashing and burning the vegetation.

The two photographs above show you an example of a human-environment interaction. The photograph to the left shows Glen Canyon on the Colorado River before a dam was built to create a huge lake. The lake—Lake Powell—was created to provide irrigation water, hydroelectric power, and recreational facilities. The photograph on the right shows a part of Lake Powell today. It is 186 miles long, has 1,900 miles of shoreline, and in places is 500 feet deep. As you can see, this human activity has caused changes in the environment.

The next chapter will help you understand the human side of geography and its relationship to the physical world.

**HUMAN–ENVIRONMENT INTERACTION** Photographs of Glen Canyon show the same site before and after it was filled with the waters of Lake Powell. **How has the landscape changed as the result of the creation of the lake?**

## SECTION 4 Assessment

**❶ Places & Terms**

Explain the meaning of each of the following terms.

- ecosystem
- biome
- rain forest
- savanna
- steppe

**❷ Taking Notes**

**REGION** Review the notes you took for this section.

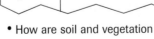

Soils & Vegetation

- How are soil and vegetation linked?
- What are the four types of biomes?

**❸ Main Ideas**

a. What soil factors influence type of vegetation in a region?

b. What is the difference between coniferous and deciduous trees?

c. What is unique about vegetation in the desert and tundra regions?

**❹ Geographic Thinking**

**Making Inferences** What impact have humans had on soil and vegetation? **Think about:**

- altering the land to meet needs
- careless use of the land

**RESEARCH LINKS**
CLASSZONE.COM

GeoActivity

**EXPLORING LOCAL GEOGRAPHY** Use the Internet to find out about the current vegetation of your state and what it was like before becoming populated. Draw two **maps** to show the contrast between the two time periods. Write a sentence summarizing what you learned.

## VISUAL SUMMARY
### CLIMATE AND VEGETATION

### Seasons and Weather

- Seasons occur because of the earth's revolution and tilt.
- Weather is the condition of the atmosphere on a daily basis.
- Weather extremes disrupt normal patterns of living.

### Climate

- Climate is the atmospheric condition over a long period of time.
- Climate is affected by wind and ocean currents, latitude, elevation, and topography.
- Global climate changes include El Niño and the greenhouse effect.

### World Climate Regions

- There are five basic climate regions: tropical, dry, mid-latitude, high latitude, and highland.
- The two most significant factors in climate are temperature and precipitation.

### Soils and Vegetation

- Soil characteristics include texture, depth, and humus content.
- Soil and climate are major influences on vegetation regions.
- Vegetation patterns are based on ecosystems.

## Reviewing Places & Terms

**A. Briefly explain the importance of each of the following.**

1. weather
2. climate
3. precipitaton
4. convection
5. El Niño
6. greenhouse effect
7. ecosystem
8. biome
9. rain forest
10. savanna

**B. Answer the questions about vocabulary in complete sentences.**

11. In what type of situation would it be more important to know about weather instead of climate?
12. How are climate and weather related?
13. Which of the above terms deal with types of vegetation?
14. What role does convection play in precipitation?
15. Which of the above terms deals with increases in average global temperature?
16. Which of the above terms has to do with dramatic changes in Pacific Ocean water temperature?
17. What is the relative location of rain forests?
18. What does savanna have in common with steppe and prairie?
19. Which of the above terms could be affected by the greenhouse effect?
20. What is the relationship between an ecosystem and a biome?

## Main Ideas

### Seasons and Weather (pp. 49-53)

1. What causes the changing seasons on earth?
2. What are the major factors that cause weather?
3. What are the different types of precipitation?

### Climate (pp. 54-58)

4. What are four factors that influence climate?
5. How do ocean currents affect climate?
6. What might be some causes of global warming?

### World Climate Regions (pp. 59-64)

7. What general information about climate is included in a description of a climate region?
8. What are the five basic climate regions?

### Soils and Vegetation (pp. 65-67)

9. How does climate affect soil?
10. How are forestlands defined?

# Critical Thinking

## 1. Using Your Notes

Use your completed chart to answer these questions.

| Seasons & Weather | |
| --- | --- |
| Climate | |
| World Climates | |
| Soils & Vegetation | |

a. How are seasons, weather, and climate connected to each other?

b. How would knowing about the climate of a region help you determine the vegetation of the region?

## 2. Geographic Themes

a. **REGION** Why are there few subarctic climate zones in the Southern Hemisphere?

b. **LOCATION** How does location affect climate?

## 3. Identifying Themes

How might the climate of an area be affected by global warming? Which of the five themes apply to this situation?

## 4. Drawing Conclusions

What is incorrect about defining a desert by landforms such as sand dunes?

## 5. Making Inferences

Why is a hurricane such a deadly storm?

Additional Test Practice, pp. S1–S37

**TEST PRACTICE**
CLASSZONE.COM

# Geographic Skills: Interpreting Graphs

## Temperature Variations

Use the graph to answer the following questions.

1. **MOVEMENT** Which decade (10-year span) had the highest temperatures?

2. **MOVEMENT** In approximately which year did temperatures begin to consistently rise above the average?

3. **HUMAN–ENVIRONMENT INTERACTION** What impact might the greenhouse effect have on the temperature changes?

## GeoActivity

Using straws, devise a three-dimensional model to show the information on the graph. Be sure to provide time frames and temperature information on your model.

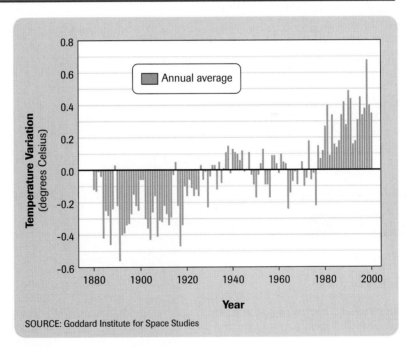

SOURCE: Goddard Institute for Space Studies

## INTERNET ACTIVITY

Use the links at **classzone.com** to do research about global warming. Choose one of the nine regions in this textbook. Focus on determining the effects of global warming on the region, especially on coastal areas.

**Creating a Multimedia Presentation** Combine charts, maps, or other visual images in an electronic presentation showing how the earth will be affected by global warming.

# HUMAN GEOGRAPHY
# People and Places

**Petroglyphs like this one from the Fremont culture (found in Dinosaur National Monument) offer evidence of human life in the desert of the Colorado Plateau.**

## GeoFocus

### What is human geography about?

**Taking Notes** Copy the graphic organizer below into your notebook. Use it to record information about human geography.

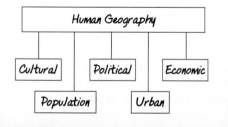

# The Elements of Culture

**Main Ideas**
- Human beings are members of social groups with shared and unique sets of behaviors and attitudes.
- Language and religion are two very important aspects of culture.

**Places & Terms**

culture

society

ethnic group

innovation

diffusion

cultural hearth

acculturation

dialect

religion

**BASICS**

**A HUMAN PERSPECTIVE** In an article titled "The 100% American," anthropologist Ralph Linton described how a typical American, in eating breakfast, had borrowed from other cultures.

> He has coffee, an Abyssinian plant, with cream and sugar. Both the domestication of cows and the idea of milking them originated in the Near East, while sugar was first made in India. . . . As a side dish he may have the egg of a species of bird domesticated in Indo-China, or thin strips of the flesh of an animal domesticated in Eastern Asia.

Borrowing from other cultures is common around the world, even if we are not aware of it.

## Defining Culture

What makes us similar to some people in the world but different from most others? The answer is culture. **Culture** is the total of knowledge, attitudes, and behaviors shared by and passed on by the members of a specific group. Culture acts as a blueprint for how a group of people should behave if they want to fit in with the group. It ties us to one group and separates us from other groups—and helps us to solve the problems that all humans face. Culture involves the following factors:

- food and shelter
- religion
- relationships to family and others
- language
- education
- security/protection
- political and social organization
- creative expression

A group that shares a geographic region, a sense of identity, and a culture is called a **society.** Sometimes you will hear the term **ethnic group** used to refer to a specific group that shares a language, customs, and a common heritage. An ethnic group has an identity as a separate group of people within the region where they live. For example, the San peoples—known as the Bushmen of the Kalahari Desert in Africa—live in a specific territory, speak their own language, and have a social organization distinct from other groups living in the region.

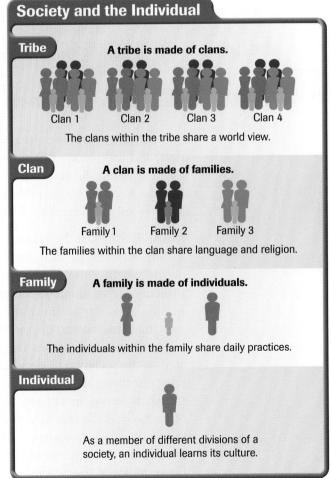

**Society and the Individual**

**Tribe**
**A tribe is made of clans.**

Clan 1    Clan 2    Clan 3    Clan 4

The clans within the tribe share a world view.

**Clan**
**A clan is made of families.**

Family 1    Family 2    Family 3

The families within the clan share language and religion.

**Family**
**A family is made of individuals.**

The individuals within the family share daily practices.

**Individual**

As a member of different divisions of a society, an individual learns its culture.

# Culture Change and Exchange

Cultures and societies are always in the process of changing. Change comes very slowly to some societies and rapidly to others. It can come about through innovation or the spread of ideas or behaviors from one culture to another.

**INNOVATION** Taking existing technology and resources and creating something new to meet a need is called **innovation.** For example, to solve the need for storage of goods, some societies invented baskets woven from reeds because reeds were abundant. Other cultures developed clay pots to solve the same problem.

Innovation and invention may happen on purpose or by accident. History is filled with examples of "accidents" that changed the life of a society. For example, the first cooked meat may have happened by accident, but it led to the practice of cooking most food rather than eating it raw.

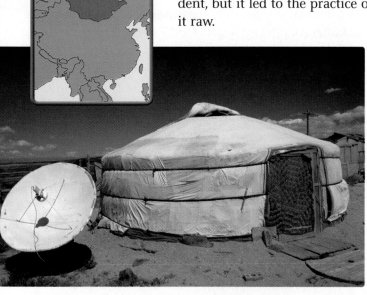

**MOVEMENT** A satellite dish brings the outside world to a Mongolian family living in this traditional house called a yurt. **How does this picture show acculturation?**

**DIFFUSION** Good ideas or inventions are hard to keep secret—they spread when people from different societies, or their ideas and inventions, come into contact with one another. This spread of ideas, inventions, or patterns of behavior is called **diffusion.** In an age of electronic technology, diffusion can happen very quickly. Television and the Internet speed ideas and facilitate the sale of goods around the globe. Almost no group of people can avoid some kind of contact with other societies. **A**

A **cultural hearth** is a site of innovation from which basic ideas, materials, and technology diffuse to many cultures. River civilizations such as those along the Indus River in South Asia, Huang He in East Asia, the Nile River in Africa, and the Tigris and Euphrates in Southwest Asia are the best known cultural hearths.

**ACCULTURATION** Exposure to an innovation does not guarantee that a society will accept that innovation. Individuals in the society must decide whether the innovation is useful and consistent with its basic principles. **Acculturation** occurs when a society changes because it accepts or adopts an innovation. An example of acculturation might be wearing jeans instead of traditional garments.

Sometimes individuals or a group adopt innovations that radically change the society. The resulting changes may have a positive or a negative effect on the society, depending on how the change came about. If change is forced on a group, it may have negative consequences. On the other hand, if the individuals or a group accept the change, it may lead to a better life for everyone. For example, the lives of thousands of people in Somalia were saved when they were persuaded to be vaccinated for smallpox in the 1970s.

**Geographic Thinking**

**Seeing Patterns**
**A** In which locations would diffusion happen less frequently?

# Language

Language is one of the most important aspects of culture because it allows the people within a culture to communicate with each other. Language reflects all aspects of culture, including the physical area occupied by the society. For example, a society that lives in the subarctic or tundra region may have many different words to describe various forms of snow. However, those words would be useless for a culture in a place with no snow.

**LANGUAGE AND IDENTITY** Language helps establish a cultural identity. It builds a group identity and a sense of unity among those who speak the language. If a language is spoken throughout a political region, a spirit of unity and sometimes nationalism (a strong feeling of pride in one's nation) grows. Language can also divide people. If more than one language is spoken in an area, but one language seems to be favored, then conflict sometimes results. In Canada, for example, where both English and French are spoken, French Canadians pressured the government to recognize both French and English as official languages.

**LANGUAGE FAMILIES** Geographers estimate that between 3,000 and 6,500 languages are spoken across the world today. The languages are categorized by placing them with other similar languages in language families. (See page 74.) Today's languages evolved from earlier languages. One of the earlier languages, called Nostratic, developed in the area known today as Turkey. Nostratic is believed to be the basis of the Indo-European languages that you see on the chart on page 74. Languages as different as English, Russian, Hindi, and Greek all developed from the Indo-European family.

Versions of a language are called dialects. A **dialect** reflects changes in speech patterns related to class, region, or other cultural changes. For example, in the United States, dialects might include a Southern drawl, a Boston accent, or even street slang.

**LANGUAGE DIFFUSION** Like other aspects of culture, language can be diffused in many ways. It may follow trade routes or even be invented. For example, Swahili developed as a trade language between Arabic traders and Bantu-speaking tribes on Africa's east coast. Sometimes a blended language develops to aid communication among groups speaking several languages. In Louisiana, the presence of French, African, and North American peoples resulted in a blended language called Louisiana Creole.

A second way diffusion occurs is through migration. As people settle in new locations, the language they carry with them sometimes takes hold in the region. For example, colonists from Europe brought the English, Spanish, French, and Dutch languages to North and South America, Afric, Australia, and parts of Asia.

**BACKGROUND**
The language spoken by the largest number of native speakers is Mandarin Chinese, with an estimated 885 million speakers.

## 5 THEMES

**MOVEMENT**

### Spanglish

As more and more Spanish-speaking people moved to the United States, a blended language developed—Spanglish. The new language takes some English words and "Spanish-izes" them. In turn, some Spanish words are "English-ized."

Spanglish frequently shows up when a speaker doesn't know the correct terms in one language. Take the phrase, "click the mouse." In Spanglish, click may become "clickea" or mouse might be "el mouse" or "el raton." The final result might be "clickea el raton," or "click el mouse."

This switching back and forth between languages is called code switching and is common with many foreign language speakers.

**MEDICAL SPANGLISH**

TRUDY ESPINOZA-ABRAMS

How to Examine a Spanish-Speaking Patient Without Knowing a Single Word of Spanish

MedMaster

Levels of economic development are measured in goods and services available in a country. In this graphic, the possessions of three families reflect economic development levels.

**DEVELOPING NATION**
**Mali** (family of 11)
5 ceramic pots
2 water kettles
2 sieves for sifting grain
1 bicycle
1 radio

**NATION IN TRANSITION**
**Cuba** (family of 9)
4 bicycles
3 televisions
2 stereos
3 radios
1 VCR

# Economic Support Systems

Producing and distributing goods and services requires a series of support systems. The most important of these services is infrastructure.

**INFRASTRUCTURE** A nation's **infrastructure** consists of the basic support systems needed to keep an economy going, including power, communications, transportation, water, sanitation, and education systems. The more sophisticated the infrastructure, the more developed the country.

One of the most important systems in the infrastructure is transportation. Geographers look at the patterns of roads and highways, ports, and airports to get an idea of how transportation affects economic growth. For example, the country of Honduras has only one major north-south highway. The highway leads to port cities where a major export, bananas, is shipped out of the country. Areas not accessible to the major highway remain undeveloped. ▶

Communications systems give geographers an idea of how a country is linked internally as well as with the outside world. Countries with a strong economy are linked internally and externally by high-speed Internet and satellite communications.

The level of available technology and access to it is also an indicator of the development of a country. A country may have valuable natural resources but be unable to profit from them because its people lack the skills to make use of them. Technology may be available, but a country may lack educated workers to run and maintain sophisticated equipment.

# Measuring Economic Development

Geographers use a variety of standards to make comparisons among economies. One is **per capita income,** the average amount of money earned by each person in a political unit. Another way of comparing economies examines levels of development based on economic activities such as industry and commerce. Still others use a standard of living that reflects a society's purchasing power, health, and level of education.

**GNP AND GDP** A commonly-used statistic to measure the economy of a country is the **gross national product (GNP).** The **GNP** is the total value of all goods and services produced by a country over a year or some other specified period of time.

Because economies have become so interconnected, the GNP may reflect the value of goods or services produced in one country by a com-

**Geographic Thinking**

**Using the Atlas**
◀ Use the map on page A13. What are the port cities of Honduras?

3 bicycles    1 microwave oven
3 radios      1 motor vehicle
1 telephone   1 computer
1 television    1 VCR

SOURCE: *Material World: A Global Family Portrait* by Peter Menzel

pany based in another country. For example, the value of sport shoes produced in Thailand by an American company is counted as U.S. production, even though the shoes were not produced in the United States. To adjust for situations like this, a second statistic is used—**GDP, or gross domestic product**—which is the total value of all goods and services produced *within* a country in a given period of time.

**DEVELOPMENT LEVELS** Countries of the world have different levels of economic development. Developing nations are nations that have a low GDP and limited development on all levels of economic activities. These countries lack an industrial base and struggle to provide their residents with items to meet their basic needs.

**BACKGROUND**
Developing countries that have greatly improved their GDP are called countries in transition.

Developed nations, on the other hand, are countries with a high per capita income and varied economy, especially with quaternary activities such as computer software development. Western European nations, Japan, Canada, and the United States have highly developed economies.

In this chapter, you've learned that human geography is a complex mix of human activities and the earth's resources. As you study the regions of the world, remember that a geographer views those regions by looking at the space and the interactions that take place there.

---

## SECTION 5 Assessment

### ① Places & Terms

Explain the meaning of each of the following terms.

- economy
- natural resources
- infrastructure
- per capita income
- GDP

### ② Taking Notes

**PLACE** Review the notes you took for this section.

> Human Geography
> └ Economic

- What are the four basic economic systems?
- What are the three types of resources?

### ③ Main Ideas

**a.** What are the basic activities in each of the four economic activity levels?

**b.** What role do natural resources play in the economy of a country?

**c.** What systems are a part of a country's infrastructure?

### ④ Geographic Thinking

**Drawing Conclusions** Fossil fuels are non-renewable resources. What does this suggest about worldwide supplies of this energy?
**Think about:**

- industrial need for power
- alternative sources of power

---

**GeoActivity**

**MAKING COMPARISONS** Study the types of economic systems on page 91. Create a series of **illustrations** showing the differences among the systems. Be sure your illustrations show the role of the consumer and the government in determining what goods or services are produced in each type of economy.

# VISUAL SUMMARY
## PEOPLE AND PLACES

### The Elements of Culture

- All human groups have a culture.
- Language and religion are a part of culture.

### Population Geography

- The world's population is expanding rapidly.
- Most of the world's population lives in the Northern Hemisphere.

### Political Geography

- Size, shape, and location influence political geography.
- States of the world have a variety of political systems.

### Urban Geography

- Urban areas have expanded rapidly and now are home to about one half of the world's population.
- Functions of cities are similar.
- Land use patterns are unique to a place.

### Economic Geography

- Resources, available technology, and economic systems shape the economy of a state.
- Economic activities are based on how goods or services are produced and traded.

## Reviewing Places & Terms

**A. Briefly explain the importance of each of the following.**

1. culture
2. diffusion
3. rate of natural increase
4. population density
5. state
6. nation
7. urbanization
8. economy
9. infrastructure
10. GDP

**B. Answer the questions about vocabulary in complete sentences.**

11. What is the growth in the number of cities called?
12. Which term above refers to the blueprint for the behaviors of a group?
13. How is the birthrate different from the rate of natural increase?
14. How is population density determined?
15. How is a nation different from a state?
16. Which term refers to the spread of ideas, innovations and inventions, and patterns of behavior?
17. How are the economy and the infrastructure related to each other?
18. What does the GDP number tell you about a country's economy?
19. Which terms above are associated with population geography?
20. What are some examples of infrastructure?

## Main Ideas

### The Elements of Culture (pp. 71–77)

1. What is the purpose of culture?
2. Why is language so important to a culture?

### Population Geography (pp. 78–82)

3. What geographic factors influence population distribution?
4. How is population density different from population distribution?

### Political Geography (pp. 83–86)

5. What are the geographic characteristics of a state?
6. What is the difference between a country with a democracy and one with a dictatorship?

### Urban Geography (pp. 87–90)

7. What are some characteristics of city locations?
8. What are the basic land use patterns in cities?

### Economic Geography (pp. 91–95)

9. Why does a country need an infrastructure?
10. How are natural resources related to a country's economy?

# Critical Thinking

## 1. Using Your Notes

Use your completed chart to answer these questions.

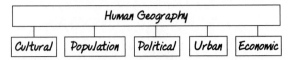

| Human Geography | | | | |
| --- | --- | --- | --- | --- |
| Cultural | Population | Political | Urban | Economic |

a. Which type of human geography focuses on how goods and services are produced and distributed by a country?

b. What do population geographers study?

## 2. Geographic Themes

a. **MOVEMENT** How might migration affect both population distribution and density?

b. **PLACE** What are some characteristics of an urban area?

## 3. Identifying Themes

How do landform and climate affect the distribution of population? Which of the five themes apply to this situation?

## 4. Making Inferences

Why might two groups of people living in the same area develop different cultures?

## 5. Identifying and Solving Problems

What reasons might countries have to form a regional political unit?

Additional Test Practice, pp. S1–S37

**TEST PRACTICE**
CLASSZONE.COM

## Geographic Skills: Interpreting Maps

### Dominant World Cities*

Use the map to answer the following questions.

1. **REGION** Which continent has the most dominant world cities shown?

2. **REGION** Which continents do not have dominant world cities?

3. **MOVEMENT** Into which continent does the most activity appear to flow? Give a reason for your answer.

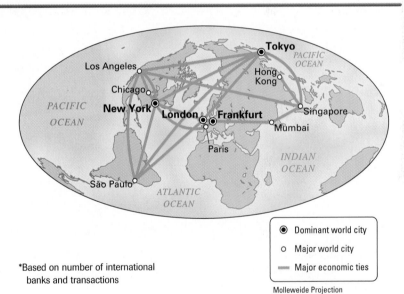

*Based on number of international banks and transactions

- ◉ Dominant world city
- ○ Major world city
- — Major economic ties

Molleweide Projection

## GeoActivity

Using a blank map of the world, mark in the cities shown on this map. Then go to page 80. Add the cities with more than 12 million shown on that map. On the back of your map, write two observations about the cities on your map.

## INTERNET ACTIVITY

Use the links at **classzone.com** to do research about population growth. Focus on the projected growth by 2050. Identify ten places where predicted growth will be the greatest and ten with little predicted growth.

**Creating a Database** Create a **database** showing your findings about worldwide growth. Create separate databases for the fastest growth and for the slowest growth. Be sure to label your databases.

# Unit 2

# The United States and Canada

**The United States and Canada are two of the world's largest countries with vast lands and abundant resources. They occupy four-fifths of the continent of North America.**

MOVEMENT Thousands of cars enter and leave Chicago, Illinois, daily. They use the vast expressway system that links the city to its surrounding suburbs and to interstate highways.

PLACE Cowhands and tourists from around the world gather in the western Canadian city of Calgary, Alberta, each July for the Calgary Stampede—the world's largest rodeo.

## GeoData

**LOCATION** The United States and Canada extend from the Atlantic Ocean to the Pacific Ocean and from the Arctic Ocean to the Gulf of Mexico (only the United States).

**REGION** The two countries are often referred to as Anglo America, because both were once British colonies and also share a common language—English.

**MOVEMENT** Both countries were settled by immigrants from all over the world, beginning with their first settlers who migrated from Asia after the last Ice Age.

**For more information on the United States and Canada . . .**

**RESEARCH LINKS**
CLASSZONE.COM

**LOCATION** The majestic falls of the Niagara River are shared by both the United States and Canada. The American Falls, to the left, are in New York state; Horseshoe Falls, to the right, are in Ontario, Canada.

*The United States and Canada* **99**

# Today's Issues in the United States and Canada

Today, the United States and Canada face the issues previewed here. As you read Chapters 5, 6, and 7, you will learn helpful background information. You will study the issues themselves in Chapter 8.

In a small group, answer the questions below. Then have a class discussion of your answers.

## Exploring the Issues

1. **TERRORISM** Consider news stories that you have heard about terrorist groups in other countries. Make a list of the countries and the type of terrorist activity in each.

2. **URBAN SPRAWL** Why is the ever-expanding spread, or sprawl, of cities and suburbs a problem? What can be done to improve the quality of life in these areas?

3. **DIVERSE SOCIETIES** Search the Internet for information about diversity in the United States or Canada. What strategies or actions are being taken to help these many cultures unify?

For more on these issues in the United States and Canada . . .

CURRENT EVENTS
CLASSZONE.COM

TERRORISM

**How can a country protect itself from terrorism?**

A surprise attack, such as the one on the World Trade Center in New York City, is just one way terrorists attempt to intimidate governments and civilian populations to further their objectives.

URBAN SPRAWL

## How can urban sprawl be controlled?

Urban communities, such as Las Vegas shown here, are trying to solve problems caused by urban areas spreading farther and farther out.

# CASESTUDY

DIVERSE SOCIETIES

## How can many cultures form a unified nation?

The diverse population of the United States is reflected in this group of California students. How to bring many cultures together as one nation is a continuing challenge for the United States, and for Canada, as well.

# Patterns of Physical Geography

Use the Unit Atlas to add to your knowledge of the United States and Canada. As you look at the maps and charts, notice geographic patterns and specific details about the region.

After studying the illustrations, graphs, and physical map on these two pages, jot down answers to the following questions in your notebook.

## Making Comparisons

**1.** Compare the world's longest river, the Nile, to the Mississippi. How much difference is there in the lengths of the two rivers?

**2.** Compare the landmass and population of the United States to those of Canada. What statement can be made about the two countries?

**3.** Compare the mountain peaks of the United States to those of Canada. What statement can be made about the height of these mountains?

For updated statistics on the United States and Canada . . .

**DATA UPDATE**
CLASSZONE.COM

## Comparing Data

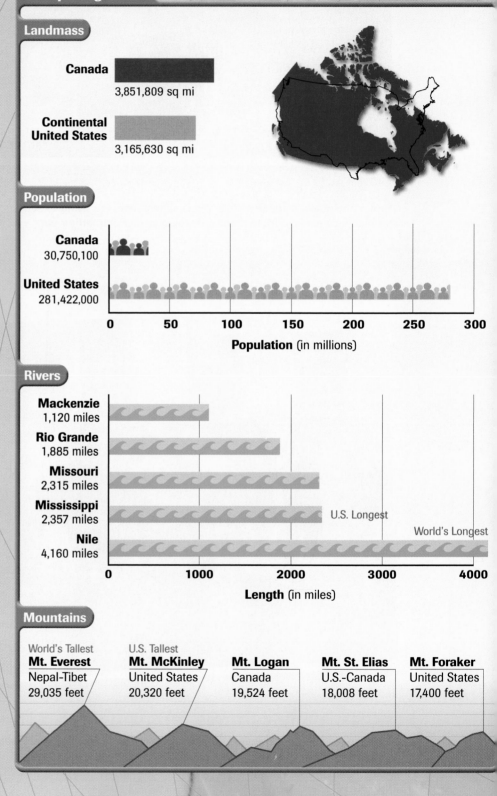

### Landmass

**Canada**
3,851,809 sq mi

**Continental United States**
3,165,630 sq mi

### Population

**Canada**
30,750,100

**United States**
281,422,000

0    50    100    150    200    250    300
**Population** (in millions)

### Rivers

**Mackenzie**
1,120 miles

**Rio Grande**
1,885 miles

**Missouri**
2,315 miles

**Mississippi**
2,357 miles — U.S. Longest

**Nile**
4,160 miles — World's Longest

0    1000    2000    3000    4000
**Length** (in miles)

### Mountains

World's Tallest
**Mt. Everest**
Nepal-Tibet
29,035 feet

U.S. Tallest
**Mt. McKinley**
United States
20,320 feet

**Mt. Logan**
Canada
19,524 feet

**Mt. St. Elias**
U.S.-Canada
18,008 feet

**Mt. Foraker**
United States
17,400 feet

US & CANADA

**Elevation**

| | |
|---|---|
| 13,100 ft. | (4,000 m.) |
| 6,600 ft. | (2,000 m.) |
| 1,600 ft. | (500 m.) |
| 650 ft. | (200 m.) |
| 0 ft. | (0 m.) |
| Below sea level | |

▲ Mountain peak

▢ Glacier

0   250   500 miles
0   250   500 kilometers
Azimuthal Equal–Area Projection

HAWAII
0   75   150 miles
0   75   150 kilometers

# Patterns of Human Geography

After the coming of European settlers in the 17th century, the political map of North America changed quickly and significantly. Study the historical and political maps of the United States and Canada on these two pages. In your notebook, answer these questions.

## Making Comparisons

1. What differences do you notice when you compare the map of 1600 with the map of the United States and Canada today?

2. Which names of native peoples are found as geographic names on the map on page 105?

3. Which country was more sparsely settled by native peoples in 1600?

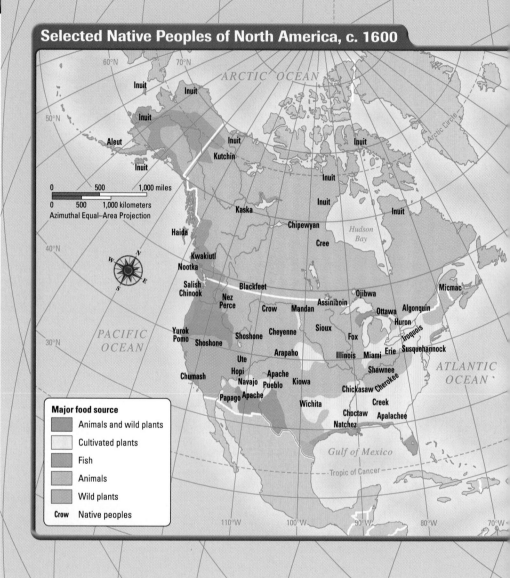

**Selected Native Peoples of North America, c. 1600**

500 miles
1,000 miles
0 500 1,000 kilometers
Azimuthal Equal–Area Projection

**Major food source**

| | |
|---|---|
| | Animals and wild plants |
| | Cultivated plants |
| | Fish |
| | Animals |
| | Wild plants |
| **Crow** | Native peoples |

ARCTIC OCEAN

Inuit, Aleut, Kutchin, Kaska, Haida, Chipewyan, Cree, Kwakiutl, Nootka, Salish, Chinook, Blackfeet, Nez Perce, Crow, Mandan, Assiniboin, Ojibwa, Ottawa, Algonquin, Huron, Iroquois, Micmac, Yurok, Pomo, Shoshone, Cheyenne, Sioux, Fox, Arapaho, Illinois, Miami, Erie, Susquehannock, Ute, Hopi, Apache, Navajo, Pueblo, Kiowa, Shawnee, Chumash, Papago, Apache, Wichita, Chickasaw, Cherokee, Creek, Choctaw, Apalachee, Natchez

PACIFIC OCEAN

ATLANTIC OCEAN

Hudson Bay

Gulf of Mexico

Tropic of Cancer

RUSSIA

*ARCTIC OCEAN*

*Chukchi Sea*

*Bering Sea*

Bering Strait

*Beaufort Sea*

GREENLAND (Den.)

ICELAND

*Greenland Sea*

Denmark Strait

Arctic Circle

ALASKA (U.S.)

Anchorage

Yukon R.

*Gulf of Alaska*

YUKON TERRITORY

NORTHWEST TERRITORIES

Mackenzie R.

Great Bear Lake

Great Slave Lake

Lake Athabasca

NUNAVUT

*Baffin Bay*

*Davis Strait*

*Labrador Sea*

US & CANADA

BRITISH COLUMBIA

ALBERTA

SASKATCHEWAN

MANITOBA

*Hudson Bay*

*James Bay*

ONTARIO

QUEBEC

NEWFOUNDLAND

Lake Winnipeg

C A N A D A

Vancouver

Seattle
WASHINGTON

Calgary

Edmonton

Winnipeg

Columbia R.

L. Superior

PRINCE EDWARD ISLAND

NEW BRUNSWICK

NOVA SCOTIA

MAINE

Gulf of St. Lawrence

St. Lawrence R.

Montreal
VT.
N.H.
MASS.
R.I.
CONN.

OREGON

MONTANA

N. DAKOTA

MINN.

WIS.

Ottawa
Toronto

L. Michigan
L. Huron
L. Ontario
L. Erie

IDAHO

S. DAKOTA

Mississippi R.

Minneapolis

MICH.

Detroit

N.Y.
New York
Boston

Philadelphia
N.J.
DEL.
MD.

WYOMING

Salt Lake City

NEBRASKA

IOWA

Missouri R.

Chicago

IND. OHIO

PENN.

*PACIFIC*

San Francisco

NEVADA

UTAH

U N I T E D   S T A T E S

COLORADO

Kansas City

St. Louis

ILL.

Ohio R.

W.VA.

Washington, D.C.

VIRGINIA

*OCEAN*

CALIFORNIA

Colorado R.

KANSAS

MO.

KENTUCKY

N.C.

Bermuda (U.K.)

Los Angeles

ARIZONA

NEW MEXICO

OKLAHOMA

ARK.

TENNESSEE

S.C.

San Diego

Phoenix

Mississippi R.

Atlanta

*ATLANTIC*

Dallas

MISS.

ALA.

GEORGIA

Rio Grande

TEXAS

LA.

*OCEAN*

Gulf of California

Houston

New Orleans

FLORIDA

BAHAMAS

*Tropic of Cancer*

Miami

MEXICO

*Gulf of Mexico*

CUBA

DOMINICAN REPUBLIC

HAITI

*Caribbean Sea*

BELIZE

HONDURAS

GUATEMALA
EL SALVADOR

NICARAGUA

PANAMA

COSTA RICA

COLOMBIA

☒ National capital

• Other city

| 0 | 250 | 500 miles |
| 0 | 250 | 500 kilometers |

Azimuthal Equal–Area Projection

*Hawaiian Islands*

PACIFIC OCEAN

Nihau

Kauai

Oahu

Honolulu

Molokai
Lanai
Kahoolawe

Maui

HAWAII

Hawaii

| 0 | 75 | 150 miles |
| 0 | 75 | 150 kilometers |

N
W   E
S

# Regional Patterns

These pages contain three thematic maps and an infographic. The infographic illustrates economic connections between the United States and Canada. The maps show economic activities, population density, and areas affected by natural hazards.

Study these two pages and then answer the questions below in your notebook.

## Making Comparisons

**1.** Where are the areas of greatest population density found in each country? Do settlement patterns have any relationship to the threat of natural hazards?

**2.** Where are manufacturing and trade concentrated in the United States and Canada? Why might this be so?

## Canada-U.S. Connections

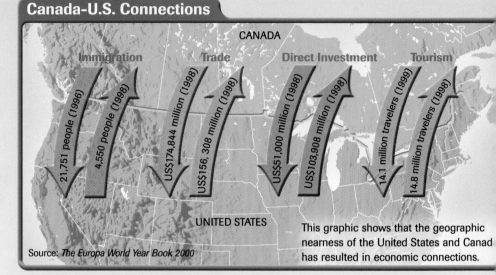

Source: *The Europa World Year Book 2000*

This graphic shows that the geographic nearness of the United States and Canad has resulted in economic connections.

## Economic Activities of the U.S. and Canada

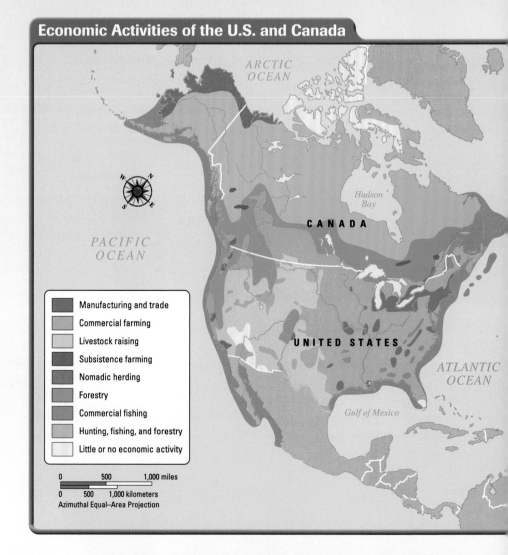

- Manufacturing and trade
- Commercial farming
- Livestock raising
- Subsistence farming
- Nomadic herding
- Forestry
- Commercial fishing
- Hunting, fishing, and forestry
- Little or no economic activity

0  500  1,000 miles
0  500  1,000 kilometers
Azimuthal Equal–Area Projection

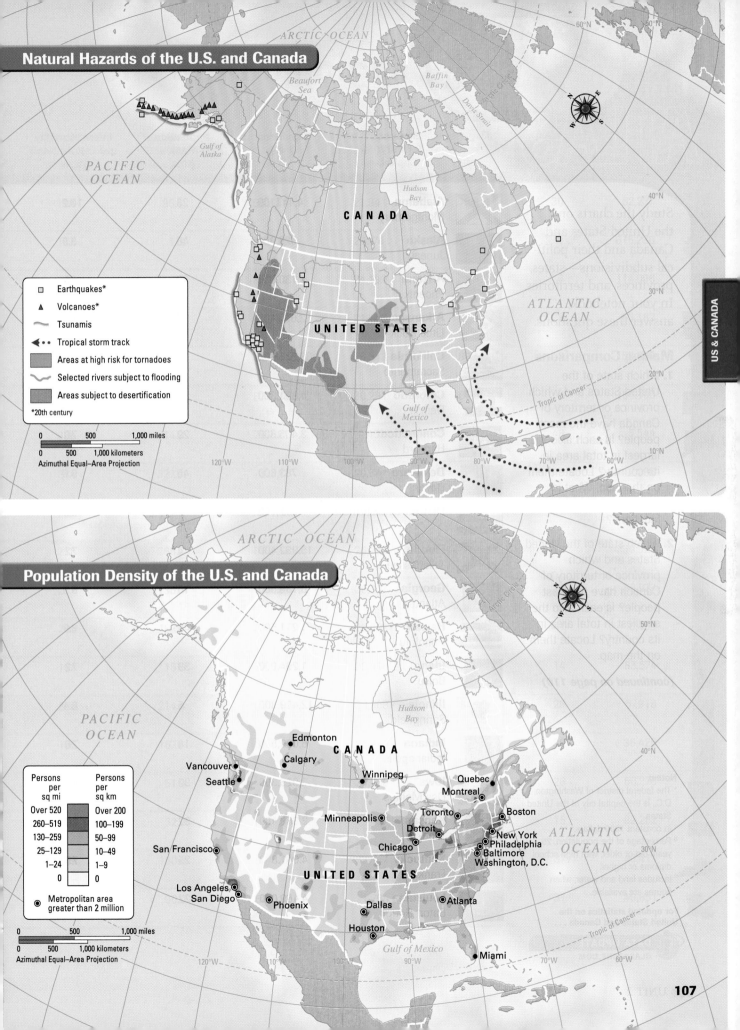

# Natural Hazards of the U.S. and Canada

**Legend:**
- □ Earthquakes*
- ▲ Volcanoes*
- ～ Tsunamis
- ◄•• Tropical storm track
- Areas at high risk for tornadoes
- Selected rivers subject to flooding
- Areas subject to desertification

*20th century

0        500      1,000 miles
0    500    1,000 kilometers
Azimuthal Equal–Area Projection

ARCTIC OCEAN
PACIFIC OCEAN
Beaufort Sea
Gulf of Alaska
Baffin Bay
Hudson Bay
CANADA
UNITED STATES
Gulf of Mexico
ATLANTIC OCEAN
Tropic of Cancer
60°N, 50°N, 40°N, 30°N, 20°N, 10°N
120°W, 110°W, 100°W, 90°W, 80°W, 70°W, 60°W

US & CANADA

# Population Density of the U.S. and Canada

**Persons per sq mi / Persons per sq km:**
- Over 520 / Over 200
- 260–519 / 100–199
- 130–259 / 50–99
- 25–129 / 10–49
- 1–24 / 1–9
- 0 / 0

◉ Metropolitan area greater than 2 million

0        500      1,000 miles
0    500    1,000 kilometers
Azimuthal Equal–Area Projection

ARCTIC OCEAN
PACIFIC OCEAN
Arctic Circle
Hudson Bay
CANADA
UNITED STATES
ATLANTIC OCEAN
Gulf of Mexico
Tropic of Cancer

Edmonton
Calgary
Vancouver
Seattle
Winnipeg
Quebec
Montreal
Minneapolis
Toronto
Boston
Detroit
Chicago
New York
Philadelphia
San Francisco
Baltimore
Washington, D.C.
Los Angeles
San Diego
Phoenix
Dallas
Atlanta
Houston
Miami

50°N, 40°N, 30°N
120°W, 110°W, 100°W, 90°W, 80°W, 70°W, 60°W

**107**

## Making Comparisons
### (continued)

**3.** Which six states of the United States and which three provinces or territories of Canada have the highest per capita income? Locate them on the map. What factors might account for this?

**4.** Which are the six most highly urbanized states of the United States? In which three provinces or territories of Canada do at least 80 percent of the people live in urban areas? Are these states and provinces or territories the same as those that have the highest per capita incomes?

*(continued on page 112)*

| Flag | State or Territory/ Capital | Population (2000) | Population Rank (2000) | Infant Mortality (per 1,000 live births) (1998) |
|---|---|---|---|---|
| | **Maine** Augusta | 1,274,900 | 40 | 6.3 |
| | **Maryland** Annapolis | 5,296,500 | 19 | 8.6 |
| | **Massachusetts** Boston | 6,349,100 | 13 | 5.1 |
| | **Michigan** Lansing | 9,938,400 | 8 | 8.2 |
| | **Minnesota** St. Paul | 4,919,479 | 21 | 5.9 |
| | **Mississippi** Jackson | 2,844,700 | 31 | 10.1 |
| | **Missouri** Jefferson City | 5,595,200 | 17 | 7.7 |
| | **Montana** Helena | 902,200 | 44 | 7.4 |
| | **Nebraska** Lincoln | 1,711,300 | 38 | 7.3 |
| | **Nevada** Carson City | 1,998,300 | 35 | 7.0 |
| | **New Hampshire** Concord | 1,235,800 | 41 | 4.4 |
| | **New Jersey** Trenton | 8,414,400 | 9 | 6.4 |
| | **New Mexico** Santa Fe | 1,819,00 | 36 | 7.2 |
| | **New York** Albany | 18,976,500 | 3 | 6.3 |
| | **North Carolina** Raleigh | 8,049,300 | 11 | 9.3 |
| | **North Dakota** Bismarck | 642,200 | 47 | 8.6 |
| | **Ohio** Columbus | 11,353,100 | 7 | 8.0 |
| | **Oklahoma** Oklahoma City | 3,450,700 | 27 | 8.5 |
| | **Oregon** Salem | 3,421,400 | 28 | 5.4 |

**Notes:**
[a] In constant 1996 dollars.
[b] Percentage of the population, 25 years old or older, with high school diploma or higher.
[c] Includes land and water, when figures are available.

| Doctors (per 100,000 pop.) (1998–1999) | Population Density (per square mile) | Urban/Rural Population (%) (1990) | Per Capita Income[a] ($US) (1999) | High School Graduates[b] (%) (1998) | Area Rank (2000) | Total Area[c] (square miles) | |
|---|---|---|---|---|---|---|---|
| 223 | 37.8 | 45 / 55 | 23,867 | 86.7 | 39 | 33,741 | |
| 374 | 430.7 | 81 / 19 | 30,757 | 84.7 | 42 | 12,297 | |
| 412 | 687.1 | 84 / 16 | 34,168 | 85.6 | 45 | 9,241 | |
| 224 | 102.8 | 71 / 29 | 26,625 | 85.4 | 11 | 96,705 | |
| 249 | 56.6 | 70 / 30 | 29,281 | 89.4 | 12 | 86,943 | |
| 163 | 58.9 | 47 / 53 | 19,608 | 77.3 | 32 | 48,286 | |
| 230 | 80.3 | 69 / 31 | 25,040 | 82.9 | 21 | 69,709 | |
| 190 | 6.1 | 53 / 47 | 21,337 | 89.1 | 4 | 147,046 | |
| 218 | 22.1 | 66 / 34 | 26,235 | 87.7 | 16 | 77,358 | |
| 173 | 18.1 | 88 / 12 | 29,022 | 89.1 | 7 | 110,567 | |
| 237 | 133.1 | 51 / 49 | 29,552 | 84.0 | 44 | 9,283 | |
| 295 | 1,024.3 | 89 / 11 | 34,525 | 86.5 | 46 | 8,215 | |
| 212 | 15.0 | 73 / 37 | 21,097 | 79.6 | 5 | 121,598 | |
| 387 | 351.5 | 84 / 16 | 32,459 | 81.5 | 27 | 53,989 | |
| 232 | 153.0 | 50 / 50 | 25,072 | 81.4 | 29 | 52,672 | |
| 222 | 9.1 | 53 / 47 | 22,488 | 84.3 | 18 | 70,704 | |
| 235 | 253.3 | 74 / 26 | 25,895 | 86.2 | 34 | 44,828 | |
| 169 | 49.4 | 68 / 32 | 21,802 | 84.6 | 20 | 69,903 | |
| 225 | 35.2 | 71 / 29 | 25,947 | 85.5 | 10 | 97,132 | |

# Regional Data File

| Flag | Province or Territory/ Capital | Population (2000) | Population Rank (2000) | Infant Mortality (per 1,000 live births) (1997) |
|---|---|---|---|---|
| | **Alberta** Edmonton | 2,997,200 | 4 | 4.8 |
| | **British Columbia** Victoria | 4,063,800 | 3 | 4.7 |
| | **Manitoba** Winnipeg | 1,147,900 | 5 | 7.5 |
| | **New Brunswick** Fredericton | 756,600 | 8 | 5.7 |
| | **Newfoundland** St. John's | 538,800 | 9 | 5.2 |
| | **Northwest Territories** Yellowknife | 42,100 | 11 | 10.9 |
| | **Nova Scotia** Halifax | 941,000 | 7 | 4.4 |
| | **Nunavut** Iqaluit | 27,700 | 13 | N/A |
| | **Ontario** Toronto | 11,669,300 | 1 | 5.5 |
| | **Prince Edward Island** Charlottetown | 138,900 | 10 | 4.4 |
| | **Quebec** Quebec City | 7,372,400 | 2 | 5.6 |
| | **Saskatchewan** Regina | 1,023,600 | 6 | 8.9 |
| | **Yukon Territory** Whitehorse | 30,700 | 12 | 8.4 |
| | **Canada** Ottawa, Ontario | 30,750,100 | — | 5.5 |
| | **United States** Washington, D.C. | 281,422,000 | — | 7.0 |

## Making Comparisons

### (continued)

**7.** Which state and which province or territory is the most densely populated? Which state and which territory is the least densely populated? Are the most densely populated the smallest in area and the least populated the largest in area?

**Sources:**
Bureau of Economic Analysis, U.S. Dept. of Commerce
Canadian Institute for Health Information, online
Census 2000, U.S. Census Bureau, online
*Digest of Educational Statistics 2000,* online
*Europa World Year Book 2000*
*Merriam-Webster's Geographical Dictionary,* 1997
Northwest Territories Bureau of Statistics, online
Pan-American Health Organization, online
*Statistical Abstract of the United States, 1999 and 2000*
Statistics Canada, online
*World Factbook 2000,* CIA online
N/A = not available

**Notes:**
ᵃ In constant 1996 dollars.
ᵇ Percentage of the population, 25 years old or older, with high school diploma or higher.
ᶜ Includes land and water, when figures are available.

| Doctors (per 100,000 pop.) (1998) | Population Density (per square mile) | Urban/Rural Population (%) (1996) | Per Capita Income[a] ($US) (1996) | High School Graduates[b] (%) (1998) | Area Rank (2000) | Total Area[c] (square miles) | |
|---|---|---|---|---|---|---|---|
| 162 | 11.7 | 80 / 20 | 30,038 | 86 | 6 | 255,285 | |
| 193 | 11.1 | 82 / 18 | 31,592 | 87 | 5 | 366,255 | |
| 177 | 4.6 | 72 / 28 | 26,829 | 79 | 8 | 250,934 | |
| 153 | 26.7 | 49 / 51 | 26,607 | 78 | 11 | 28,345 | |
| 171 | 12.4 | 57 / 43 | 27,692 | 71 | 10 | 43,359 | |
| 92 | 0.08 | 42 / 58 | 33,738 (1994) | 64 (1996) | 3 | 503,951 | |
| 196 | 44.0 | 55 / 45 | 25,712 | 78 | 12 | 21,425 | |
| N/A | 0.03 | N/A | 27,421 (1994) | N/A | 1 | 818,959 | |
| 178 | 28.3 | 83 / 17 | 32,537 | 84 | 4 | 412,582 | |
| 128 | 49.4 | 44 / 56 | 25,534 | 74 | 13 | 2,814 | |
| 211 | 12.4 | 78 / 22 | 28,826 | 78 | 2 | 594,860 | |
| 149 | 4.1 | 63 / 34 | 26,463 | 82 | 7 | 251,700 | |
| 149 | 0.2 | 60 / 40 | 36,130 | 67 (1996) | 9 | 186,661 | |
| | | | | | | | |
| 185 | 8.0 | 78 / 22 | 23,000 (1999) | 82 | — | 3,851,809 | |
| 251 | 74.3 | 76 / 24 | 33,900 (1999) | 83 | — | 3,787,319 | |

# PHYSICAL GEOGRAPHY OF THE UNITED STATES and CANADA
# A Land of Contrasts

The 3,593-foot El Capitan is one of many cliffs that soar above the valley floor in California's Yosemite National Park.

## GeoFocus

**What is alike and what is different about the lands of the United States and Canada?**

**Taking Notes** Copy the graphic organizer below into your notebook. Use it to record information from the chapter about the physical geography of the United States and Canada.

| Landforms | |
|---|---|
| Resources | |
| Climate and Vegetation | |
| Human-Environment Interaction | |

# Landforms and Resources

**Main Ideas**
- The United States and Canada have vast lands and abundant resources.
- These two countries share many of the same landforms.

**Places & Terms**
**Appalachian Mountains**
**Great Plains**
**Canadian Shield**
**Rocky Mountains**
**Great Lakes**
**Mackenzie River**

**US & CANADA**

**CONNECT TO THE ISSUES**
**URBAN SPRAWL** Urban development in the United States is generally determined by the location of landforms and the abundance of natural resources.

**A HUMAN PERSPECTIVE** The beauty and abundance of the land was a source of wonder to early explorers of North America. One who traveled the Atlantic coast referred to the "amazing extent of uncultivated land, covered with forests, and intermixed with vast lakes and marshes." A 17th–century French expedition described "a beautiful river, large, broad, and deep" (the Mississippi). Still others found "an unbounded prairie" (the Great Plains), "shining mountains" (the Rocky Mountains), and "an infinite number of fish" (along the Pacific coast). To the continent's first settlers, the land was "strong and it was beautiful all around," according to an old Native American song.

## Landscape Influenced Development

The United States and Canada occupy the central and northern four-fifths of the continent of North America. Culturally, the region is known as Anglo America because both countries were colonies of Great Britain at one time and because most of the people speak English. (The southern one-fifth of the continent—Mexico—is part of Latin America.) The two countries are bound together not only by physical geography and cultural heritage, but also by strong economic and political ties.

**VAST LANDS** The United States and Canada extend across North America from the Atlantic Ocean on the east to the Pacific on the west, and from the Arctic Ocean on the north to the Gulf of Mexico on the south (only the United States). In total area, each ranks among the largest countries of the world. Canada ranks second, behind Russia, and the United States is third. Together, they fill one-eighth of the land surface of the earth.

**ABUNDANT RESOURCES** In addition to their huge landmass, the United States and Canada are rich in natural resources. They have fertile soils, ample supplies of water, vast forests, and large deposits of a variety of minerals. This geographic richness has for centuries attracted immigrants from around the world and has enabled both countries to develop into global economic powers.

**LOCATION** Pittsburgh, Pennsylvania, is located where the Allegheny and Monongahela rivers meet to form the Ohio River.

**117**

# Landform Regions of the U.S. and Canada

**1** East Quoddy Head in New Brunswick

**2** Great Regina Plain in Saskatchewan

**3** Cypress Gardens in Florida

ARCTIC OCEAN

170°E
180°
160°W
50°N
40°N
PACIFIC
OCEAN
30°N

ARCTIC COASTAL PLAIN

INTERMOUNTAIN BASINS AND PLATEAUS

ROCKY MOUNTAINS

PACIFIC MOUNTAINS AND VALLEYS

INTERMOUNTAIN BASINS AND PLATEAUS

Mackenzie R.

Columbia R.

Colorado R.

Rio Grande

CANADIAN SHIELD

INTERIOR PLAINS

GREAT PLAINS

Hudson Bay

ARCTIC COASTAL PLAIN

Mississippi R.

L. Superior
L. Michigan
L. Huron
L. Erie
L. Ontario
St. Lawrence R.

Missouri R.

Ohio R.

INTERIOR HIGHLANDS

Mississippi R.

GULF-ATLANTIC COASTAL PLAIN

APPALACHIAN HIGHLANDS

PIEDMONT

ATLANTIC OCEAN

Gulf of Mexico

Tropic of Cancer

60°N
40°W
50°N
50°W
50°N
40°N
30°N

0°
130°W
120°W
110°W
100°W
90°W

0    250    500 miles
0    250    500 kilometers
Azimuthal Equal-Area Projection

# Many and Varied Landforms

All major types of landforms are found in the United States and Canada. If you look at the map on the opposite page, you will see that both countries share many of these landforms. The most prominent are eastern and western mountain chains and enormous interior plains.

**THE EASTERN LOWLANDS**  A flat, coastal plain runs along the Atlantic Ocean and the Gulf of Mexico. One section, called the Atlantic Coastal Plain, begins as narrow lowland in the northeastern United States and widens as it extends southward into Florida. This area features many excellent harbors. A broader section of the plain—the Gulf Coastal Plain—stretches along the Gulf of Mexico from Florida into Texas. The Mississippi River empties into the Gulf from this region.

Between these plains and the nearby Appalachian (A•puh•LAY•chun) Highlands is a low plateau called the Piedmont (PEED•MAHNT). This area of rolling hills contains many fast-flowing rivers and streams.

**BACKGROUND**
The word *piedmont* comes from *pied,* meaning "foot," and *mont,* for "mountain." A piedmont is found at the foot of a mountain chain.

**THE APPALACHIAN HIGHLANDS**  West of the coastal plain are the Appalachian highlands. The gently sloping **Appalachian Mountains** are in this region. They are one of the two major mountain chains in the United States and Canada. Both chains run north to south. The Appalachian Mountains extend some 1,600 miles from Newfoundland in Canada to Alabama. There are several mountain ranges in the Appalachian system. Among them are the Green and the Catskill mountains in the north and the Blue Ridge and the Great Smoky mountains in the south.

Because the Appalachians are very old—more than 400 million years old—they have been eroded by the elements. Many peaks are only between 1,200 and 2,400 feet high. The Appalachian Trail, a scenic hiking path 2,160 miles long, spans almost the entire length of the chain.

**THE INTERIOR LOWLANDS**  A huge expanse of mainly level land covers the interior of North America. It was flattened by huge glaciers thousands of years ago. The terrain includes lowlands, rolling hills, thousands of lakes and rivers, and some of the world's most fertile soils.

The interior lowlands are divided into three subregions: the Interior Plains, the Great Plains, and the Canadian Shield. The Interior Plains spread out from the Appalachians to about 300 miles west of the Mississippi River. They gradually rise from a few hundred feet above sea level to about 2,000 feet. To the west are the **Great Plains,** a largely treeless area that continues the ascent to about 4,000 feet. The **Canadian Shield** lies farther north. This rocky, mainly flat area covers nearly 2 million square miles around Hudson Bay. It averages 1,500 feet above sea level but reaches over 5,000 feet in Labrador. ◁

**THE WESTERN MOUNTAINS, PLATEAUS, AND BASINS**  West of the plains are the massive, rugged **Rocky Mountains,** the other major mountain system of the

**Geographic Thinking**

**Making Comparisons**
▲ Which of the interior lowlands has the highest elevation?

**5 THEMES**

**PLACE**

**Death Valley**

Death Valley is hot—very, very hot. Temperatures can top 130°F. Few forms of life can survive its intense heat for long periods. Land features called Dead Man Pass, Funeral Mountains, and Starvation Canyon are reminders of the danger.

Death Valley (shown below) is located at the western edge of the Great Basin in California. It is the hottest point in North America. And at 282 feet below sea level, it also is the lowest point in the Western Hemisphere.

REGION This West Virginia coal mine is in one of the world's most important coal-producing regions—the Appalachian highlands. **What other region in North America is an important coal producer?**

The United States and Canada also have huge forests. About one-half of Canada is covered by woodlands, as is one-third of the United States. Canada's forests cover more land than those of the United States, but the United States has more kinds of trees because of its more varied climate. Both countries are major producers of lumber and forest products.

**MINERALS AND FOSSIL FUELS** As you saw on the map on page 120, the United States and Canada have large quantities and varieties of minerals and fossil fuels. These resources gave both countries the means to industrialize rapidly.

Valuable deposits of iron ore, nickel, copper, gold, and uranium are found in the Canadian Shield. Scattered among the western mountains are gold, silver, copper, and uranium. Both countries also have substantial deposits of coal, natural gas, and oil, and well-developed networks for distributing these energy-producing fossil fuels. Important coal-producing areas are the Appalachian highlands and the northern Great Plains. Significant deposits of oil and natural gas are found in the Great Plains, Alaska, and along the Gulf of Mexico. **D**

The United States is the world's biggest consumer of energy resources. Its need for these fuels is so great that it is a major importer. In fact, most of Canada's energy exports go to its neighbor to the south.

In the next section, you will read how some landforms of the United States and Canada have affected climate and vegetation patterns.

**Geographic Thinking**

**Seeing Patterns**
**D** Why are oil and natural gas important to highly-industrialized nations?

---

**Assessment**

### ① Places & Terms

Identify and explain where in the region these would be found.

- Appalachian Mountains
- Great Plains
- Canadian Shield
- Rocky Mountains
- Great Lakes

### ② Taking Notes

LOCATION Review the notes you took for this section.

| Landforms | |
|-----------|--|
| Resources | |

- What is the relative location of the Great Lakes?
- What is the relative location of most of Canada's islands?

### ③ Main Ideas

a. What landforms are shared by the United States and Canada?

b. Why are the Great Lakes important to both the United States and Canada?

c. Why do most of Canada's energy exports go to the United States?

### ④ Geographic Thinking

**Making Generalizations** What makes the United States and Canada leading industrial nations? **Think about:**

- available resources
- oceans and waterways

**S** **See Skillbuilder Handbook, page R6.**

---

**EXPLORING LOCAL GEOGRAPHY** Using the maps on pages 103 and 118, identify the landforms located in your state. Then draw a **sketch map** of your state showing the major landforms and water bodies.

# Climate and Vegetation

**Main Ideas**

- Almost every type of climate is found in the 50 United States because they extend over such a large area north to south.
- Canada's cold climate is related to its location in the far northern latitudes.

**Places & Terms**

**permafrost**

**prevailing westerlies**

**Everglades**

**CONNECT TO THE ISSUES**

URBAN SPRAWL The rapid spread of urban sprawl has led to the loss of much vegetation in both the United States and Canada.

**A HUMAN PERSPECTIVE** A little gold and bitter cold—that is what thousands of prospectors found in Alaska and the Yukon Territory during the Klondike gold rushes of the 1890s. Most of these fortune hunters were unprepared for the harsh climate and inhospitable land of the far north. Winters were long and cold, the ground frozen. Ice fogs, blizzards, and avalanches were regular occurrences. You could lose fingers and toes—even your life—in the cold. But hardy souls stuck it out. Legend has it that one miner, Bishop Stringer, kept himself alive by boiling his sealskin and walrus-sole boots and then drinking the broth.

## Shared Climates and Vegetation

The United States and Canada have more in common than just frigid winter temperatures where Alaska meets northwestern Canada. Other shared climate and vegetation zones are found along their joint border at the southern end of Canada and the northern end of the United States.

If you look at the map on page 125, you will see that the United States has more climate zones than Canada. This variety, ranging from tundra to tropical, occurs because the country extends over such a large area north to south. Most of the United States is located in the mid-latitudes, where the climates are moderate. Canada is colder because so much of it lies far north in the higher latitudes.

**COLDER CLIMATES** The Arctic coast of Alaska and Canada have tundra climate and vegetation. Winters are long and bitterly cold, while summers are brief and chilly. Even in July, temperatures are only around 40°F. The land is a huge, treeless plain. Much of the rest of Canada and Alaska have a subarctic climate, with very cold winters and short, mild summers. A vast forest of needle-leafed evergreens covers the area. In some places, there is **permafrost**, or permanently frozen ground.

The Rocky Mountains and the Pacific ranges have highland climate and vegetation. Temperature and vegetation vary with elevation and latitude. Generally, the temperature is colder and the vegetation is more sparse in the higher, more northerly mountains. The mountains also influence the temperature and precipitation of surrounding lower areas. For example, the

MOVEMENT The snowmobile has replaced the dogsled as transportation in many parts of the Northwest Territories. Here, a mother picks up her children from school.

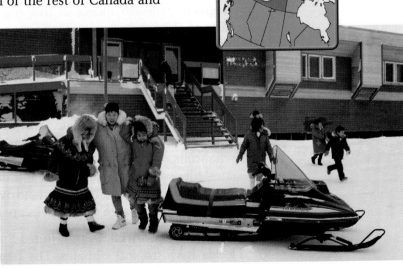

**REGION** Deadly ice storms like this one in Watertown, New York, create chaos each winter, especially in heavily populated areas. **What are some of the hazards of this form of extreme weather?**

a few degrees in the 70s°F. Mount Waialeale (wy·AH·lay·AH·lay) on Kauai island receives about 460 inches of rain annually, and is one of the wettest spots on earth. Southern Florida has a tropical wet and dry climate. It is nearly always warm, but has wet and dry seasons. Vegetation is mainly tall grasses and scattered trees, like those in the **Everglades,** a huge swampland that covers some 4,000 square miles. ▶

**Geographic Thinking**

**Making Comparisons**
Ⓒ How do climate and vegetation differ between Mediterranean and tropical climates?

## Effects of Extreme Weather

Weather in the United States and Canada can be harsh and sometimes deadly. You can see the areas affected by extreme weather and climate conditions by looking at the natural hazards map on page 107.

In both cold and mild climates, severe storms can trigger widespread devastation. Warm air from the Gulf of Mexico and cold Canadian air masses sometimes clash over the plains region to produce violent thunderstorms, tornadoes, and blizzards. As you read in Unit 1, tornadoes strike so often in an area of the Great Plains that it is called "Tornado Alley." In summer and fall, hurricanes that sweep along the Atlantic and Gulf coasts can cause great damage. Winter snowstorms may bring normal life to a temporary halt in many cities, such as the one shown in the photo on this page.

Disasters can also result from too much precipitation in a short time or too little over a long period. Heavy rainfall can cause flooding. Lands along major rivers, such as the Mississippi, are especially at risk. Too little rain or too much heat may bring on droughts and dust storms or spark destructive forest fires.

In this section, you read about the varied climates and vegetation of the United States and Canada. In the next section, you will learn how physical geography has shaped life in these countries.

## SECTION 2 Assessment

### ❶ Places & Terms

Identify and explain where in the region these would be found.

- permafrost
- prevailing westerlies
- Everglades

### ❷ Taking Notes

**REGION** Review the notes you took for this section.

*Climate and Vegetation*

- What climate regions do the United States and Canada share?
- What climate regions are found in the United States but not in Canada?

### ❸ Main Ideas

**a.** How do the prevailing westerlies change the climate of parts of the United States and Canada?

**b.** In which region would you find the dry climates?

**c.** In which climate type would you find the Everglades?

### ❹ Geographic Thinking

**Seeing Patterns** Why doesn't all of Alaska have cold, snowy winters? **Think about:**

- location
- prevailing westerlies

**RESEARCH LINKS**
CLASSZONE.COM

**GeoActivity**

**MAKING COMPARISONS** Make a list of five Canadian cities and five U.S. cities. Then use the Internet to find out the average monthly temperature and monthly rainfall for each city. Create a **database** with the information. Then summarize your findings.

# Human–Environment Interaction

> **Main Ideas**
> - Humans have dramatically changed the face of North America.
> - European settlements in the United States and Canada expanded from east to west.

### Places & Terms

**nomad**

**Beringia**

**St. Lawrence Seaway**

**lock**

**CONNECT TO THE ISSUES**

**URBAN SPRAWL** The spreading of cities and suburbs over wider areas—urban sprawl—is causing problems.

**US & CANADA**

**A HUMAN PERSPECTIVE** The sun-baked American Southwest was a harsh environment for its early inhabitants, the ancestors of today's Pueblo peoples. But these early settlers made good use of available resources. From the land, they took clay and stone building materials. They built multi-room, apartment-like dwellings in cliffs. This gave protection against daytime heat, nighttime cold, and human and animal enemies. From plants and animals, the early settlers got food and clothing. They survived because they adapted to their environment.

## Settlement and Agriculture Alter the Land

Before humans came, North American landforms were changed only by natural forces, such as weathering and erosion. That changed when the first settlers—the ancestors of the native peoples of North America—arrived thousands of years ago.

**SETTLEMENT** The first inhabitants of the area of North America now known as the United States and Canada were **nomads,** people who move from place to place. Most archaeologists believe that they probably migrated from Asia over **Beringia,** a land bridge that once connected Siberia and Alaska. These migrants moved about the land. They hunted game, fished, and gathered edible wild plants. Since water was necessary for survival, these first Americans made temporary settlements along coastlines and near rivers and streams. They adjusted to extremes of temperature and climate. They also adapted to the region's many natural environments, including mountains, forests, plains, and deserts.

**AGRICULTURE** Many early settlements became permanent after agriculture replaced hunting and gathering as the primary method of food production about 3,000 years ago. When people began to cultivate crops, they changed the landscape to meet their needs. In wooded areas, early farmers cut down trees for lumber to build houses and to burn as fuel. To plant crops, they plowed the rich soil of river valleys and flood plains using hoes of wood, stone, and bone. They dug ditches for irrigation. Vegetables they first cultivated—corn, beans, and squash—are now staples around the world.

Agriculture remains an important economic activity in the United States and Canada. In fact, both countries are leading exporters of agricultural products.

**REGION** Irrigation has opened land in dry areas to farming. Tracts such as these in New Mexico are watered by a method called center-pivot, which taps underground water.
**What are some other ways water can be brought to dry land?**

127

Chapter

6

SECTION 1
History and
Government of
the United States

SECTION 2
Economy and Culture
of the United States

SECTION 3
Subregions of
the United States

# HUMAN GEOGRAPHY OF THE UNITED STATES
## Shaping an Abundant Land

**Four Subregions of the United States**

ALASKA

CANADA

PACIFIC
OCEAN

WASHINGTON
OREGON
IDAHO
CALIFORNIA
NEVADA
MONTANA
WYOMING
UTAH
ARIZONA
NEW
MEXICO
N. DAKOTA
S. DAKOTA
NEBRASKA
COLORADO
KANSAS
OKLAHOMA
TEXAS
MINN.
WIS.
IOWA
MO.
ARK.
LA.
MISS.
MICHIGAN
ILL. IND.
KENTUCKY
TENNESSEE
ALA.
GEORGIA
OHIO
W.VA.
VIRGINIA
N. CAROLINA
S. CAROLINA
FLORIDA
MAINE
VT. N.H.
N.Y. MASS.
R.I.
PENN. CONN.
N.J.
DEL.
MD.
D.C.

L. Superior
L. Michigan
Huron
Erie
Ontario

ATLANTIC
OCEAN

Gulf of Mexico

Tropic of Cancer

PACIFIC OCEAN

HAWAII

| 0 | 75 | 150 miles |
| 0 | 75 | 150 kilometers |

160°W    158°W    156°W    154°W

| 0 | 250 | 500 miles |
| 0 | 250 | 500 kilometers |

Azimuthal Equal-Area Projection

PACIFIC
OCEAN

- Northeast
- South
- Midwest
- West

## GeoFocus

### What factors shaped the development of the United States?

**Taking Notes** In your notebook, copy a cluster diagram like the one shown. As you read, take notes about the history, economy, culture, and modern life of the United States and its subregions.

# History and Government of the United States

## Main Ideas

- The United States is a "nation of immigrants," settled by people from all over the world.
- The United States is the most diverse and highly industrialized and urbanized nation in the world.

## Places & Terms

**migration**

**Columbian Exchange**

**Louisiana Purchase**

**frontier**

**suburb**

**representative democracy**

## CONNECT TO THE ISSUES

**TERRORISM** Beginning in the late 20th century, the United States has been subjected to terrorist attacks by individuals and groups opposed to its policies.

**A HUMAN PERSPECTIVE** Women were North America's first farmers. In all early cultures except the hunter-gatherer culture of the Southwest, women cultivated the land. They discovered which wild plants could be used as food for the family. They planted the seeds, tended the garden, harvested the crops, and prepared food for meals. Corn, beans, and squash were the first of these foods. Women also learned which leaves, bark, roots, stems, and berries could be used for medicines. Their efforts helped to ensure the survival of human settlement in North America—and the part of the land that became the United States.

## Creating a Nation

The United States occupies nearly two-fifths of North America. It is the world's third largest country in both land area and population. It is rich in natural resources and is also fortunate to have a moderate climate, fertile soil, and plentiful water supplies. For thousands of years, this bounty has attracted waves of immigrants who came to find a better life. This continuing immigration is a recurring theme in the country's history; so is the constant **migration,** or movement, of peoples within the United States.

**MANY PEOPLES SETTLE THE LAND** As you read in Chapter 5, the first inhabitants of North America were believed to be nomads who came from Asia at least 13,000 or more years ago. These people settled the continent, spreading south along the Pacific coast and east to the Atlantic. Over the centuries, they developed separate cultures, as the map on page 104 shows. These native peoples occupied the land undisturbed until the 15th century, when Europeans began to explore what they called the "New World." The Spanish arrived first. They searched the present-day Southeast and Southwest for gold and other treasure. In 1565, they founded St. Augustine, Florida, the oldest permanent European settlement in the United States.

The French and English came later. France was interested in fisheries and the fur trade. In the early 1600s, the French settled along the northern Atlantic Coast and the St. Lawrence River in what is now Canada. The English arrived at about the same time. During the 1600s and 1700s,

**HUMAN-ENVIRONMENT INTERACTION** Early Native American settlers in the Southwest often built their dwellings into canyon walls. The dwellings shown are in Mesa Verde National Park in Colorado.
**Why did the earliest settlers choose such locations for their dwellings?**

US & CANADA

## The Columbian Exchange

**THE AMERICAS TO EUROPE, AFRICA, AND ASIA**

Pumpkins · Potatoes · Tomatoes · Vanilla

Pineapple · Corn · Beans · Squash

Cacao · Peppers · Tobacco · Peanuts

Turkeys · Sweet Potatoes

**EUROPE, AFRICA, AND ASIA TO THE AMERICAS**

Citrus Fruits · Grapes · Bananas · Sugar Cane · Honey Bees · Coffee Beans · Peaches, Pears · Onions · Olives · Turnips

**Grains**
•Wheat
•Rice
•Barley
•Oats

**Livestock**
• Cattle
• Sheep
• Pigs
• Horses

**Diseases**
• Smallpox
• Influenza
• Typhus
• Measles
• Malaria
• Diphtheria
• Whooping Cough

**MOVEMENT** This infographic shows how plants, animals, and diseases were transferred between the Eastern and Western hemispheres as trade followed the voyages of Christopher Columbus to the Americas.

they settled to the south—on rivers and bays along the Atlantic coast from present-day Maine to Georgia. The English made their first permanent settlement in Jamestown, Virginia, in 1607.

European colonies often displaced Native Americans. In 1617, the Europeans brought Africans to America to work as slave laborers on cotton and tobacco plantations in the South. The coming of the Europeans also began what historians call the **Columbian Exchange.** The infographic above shows how the arrival of Europeans in the Western Hemisphere affected the lives of both Europeans and the native peoples.

**ESTABLISHING AND MAINTAINING THE UNION** The French and the English eventually fought in North America over trade and territory. In 1763, Great Britain gained control of all of North America east of the Mississippi River. But its control was short-lived. Britain's 13 American colonies soon began to resent the policies forced on them by a government thousands of miles away across the Atlantic. Their protests led to the American Revolution (1775–1783) and the founding of the United States of America. The new nation grew rapidly, and settlers pushed westward to the Mississippi. In 1803, the United States nearly doubled in size when the government purchased the vast plains region between the Mississippi and the Rocky Mountains from France. This territory became known as the **Louisiana Purchase.**

In the early 1800s, immigrants from Western Europe arrived in great numbers. They settled in cities in the Northeast, where industrialization was beginning. One such city was Lowell, Massachusetts, which had become a booming textile center by the 1840s. The newcomers also moved to rich farmlands in what is now the Midwest.

Meanwhile, sectionalism was growing. People were placing loyalty to their region, or section, above loyalty to the nation. The result was rising political and economic tensions between an agricultural South dependent on slave labor and the more industrialized North. These tensions led to the Civil War (1861–1865). It took four years of bloody fighting and many more years of political conflict to reunite the country.

**BACKGROUND** About 600,000 Africans were brought to the United States to work as slave laborers from 1617 until the importation of slaves was banned in 1808.

## An Industrial and Urban Society

In the second half of the 19th century, millions of Americans were on the move. They settled on newly opened lands west of the Mississippi and in the rapidly industrializing cities of the North and Midwest.

**WESTWARD MOVEMENT** From departure points such as Independence, Missouri, hundreds of thousands of pioneers left in covered wagons bound for the West. They blazed trails that crossed prairie, plains, desert, and mountains, moving toward the Pacific. A wagon train on the Oregon Trail might have taken up to six months to reach its destination 2,000 miles away.

To make way for white settlers, the U.S. government removed Native Americans from their lands by treaty, or by force. In Chapter 5, you read that the first transcontinental railroad across the United States was completed in 1869. Railroads brought people to the West, and western cattle and products to markets in the East. By 1890, about 17 million people lived between the Mississippi and the Pacific. The free, open land that had been available and suitable for settlement—the **frontier**—was now fully settled.

**INDUSTRIALIZATION AND URBANIZATION** As the West was being settled, immigrants—mainly from Western and Eastern Europe—poured into the United States. About 14 million came from 1860 to 1900.

Some joined the movement to the West. Others settled in urban areas undergoing industrialization. Cities such as New York, Boston, Pittsburgh, Cleveland, Detroit, and Chicago expanded rapidly. Both recent immigrants and large numbers of Americans from rural areas came to cities such as these to work in textile, steel, oil, food processing, and other industries. The United States was being transformed from a rural, agricultural nation to an urban, industrialized one.

## World Power and Domestic Change

As the 20th century began, the United States was the dominant economic and political power in the Western Hemisphere. By the century's end, it would be the world's sole superpower.

**LOOKING BEYOND ITS BORDERS** The United States had tried to avoid involvement in foreign affairs during its decades of growth. Because of its ample natural and human resources, it had been almost self-sufficient from its founding. Its farms grew the food necessary for survival, and the nation's factories produced the manufactured goods it needed. It was also protected

**Geographic Thinking**

**Using the Atlas**

**A** Refer to the map on page 103. What landforms must be crossed by pioneers going from Independence, Missouri, to the Pacific coast?

**Development of the West**

**1803** The United States purchases French territory west of the Mississippi.

**1804–1806 Lewis and Clark** expedition explores the area of the Louisiana Purchase.

**1840s Wagon trains** begin moving pioneers to the West.

**1869** A symbolic **"golden spike"** is used to mark the completion of a transcontinental railroad across the United States.

**1890** Land available for settlement on the western frontier has nearly disappeared.

**1898** The United States continues its westward expansion, annexing Hawaii.

## Growth of Technology

**1913**
Use of an **assembly line** in Ford auto plants streamlines manufacturing.

**1920**
Regular radio programming by station KDKA in Pittsburgh begins the era of mass communication.

**1947**
The first mass television audience watches baseball's World Series.

**1959**
The development of the **integrated circuit** would make the widespread use of computers possible.

**1961**
U.S. manned exploration of space starts as Alan B. Shepard, Jr., is launched into suborbit of the Earth.

**1969**
The U.S. Department of Defense develops a computer network that later leads to the Internet.

**2000**
Mapping **human genetic material (DNA)** is a breakthrough in biotechnology.

**DNA**

---

from foreign conflicts by two vast oceans—the Atlantic and the Pacific. But a global economic depression and two world wars brought significant changes. When World War II ended in 1945, the United States was the only major nation that had escaped physical damage and had a healthy economy.

**SOCIAL CHANGE AND TECHNOLOGICAL GROWTH** The last half of the 20th century was a time of rapid social change. Americans were on the move. Large numbers of people began migrating from cities to surrounding **suburbs,** the communities outside of a city. Some Americans left the colder climates of the Northeast and Midwest for the warmer South and West. Also, immigrants continued to arrive by the hundreds of thousands. But now they came mainly from the countries of Latin America and Asia. **B**

These years saw much social unrest, especially during the 1960s and 1970s. The civil rights movement fought to gain equal rights for African Americans. The feminist movement sought equality for women. Also, many students and others protested U.S. involvement in a war between Communist and non-Communist forces in Vietnam (1955–75).

During this period, the U.S. economy boomed, despite some periods of economic downturn, or recession. The economy, too, was being transformed. Changes in technology altered the way goods were produced. The use of computers revolutionized the workplace. Providing services and information technology surpassed industrial production in importance. The United States also became the world's greatest economic power. Today, it plays a major role in a global economy that is increasingly competitive.

**LIVING IN A GLOBAL SOCIETY** Meanwhile, American political influence spread throughout the world after the Second World War. The United States became the leader of the world's non-Communist nations. Their goal was to stop the spread of communism, spearheaded by the Soviet Union (now Russia). A competition for world influence called the Cold War (roughly 1945–1991) followed. When communism in Europe collapsed in 1991, the United States emerged as the world's sole superpower. As such, it has used its diplomatic and military power to try to keep the peace and to further American interests in the international community.

**Geographic Thinking**

**Seeing Patterns**
**B** What kinds of movement were taking place in the United States in the last half of the 20th century?

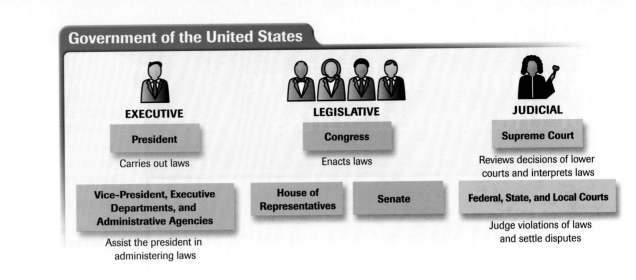

**Government of the United States**

| EXECUTIVE | LEGISLATIVE | JUDICIAL |
|---|---|---|
| **President** | **Congress** | **Supreme Court** |
| Carries out laws | Enacts laws | Reviews decisions of lower courts and interprets laws |
| **Vice-President, Executive Departments, and Administrative Agencies** | **House of Representatives** · **Senate** | **Federal, State, and Local Courts** |
| Assist the president in administering laws | | Judge violations of laws and settle disputes |

## Governing the People

One of the strengths of the United States is the political system created by the U.S. Constitution, drawn up in 1787. The United States is a **representative democracy,** where the people rule through elected representatives. It is also a federal republic, where powers are divided among the federal, or national, government and various state governments.

As you can see on the chart above, there are three separate and equal branches of the federal government. The executive branch, headed by the president, carries out the laws. The president also approves or vetoes proposed laws. The legislative branch makes the laws, and the judicial branch interprets the laws by reviewing decisions of lower courts. The 50 states also have executive, legislative, and judicial branches. They exercise powers not specifically granted to the federal government by the Constitution.

In this section, you read about the history and government of the United States. In the next, you will learn about its economy and culture.

**Geography Thinking**

**Making Comparisor**

**B** What do major cities of Midwest have common with those of the Northeast?

## SECTION Assessment

**1 Places & Terms**

Explain the meaning of each of the following terms.
• migration
• Columbian Exchange
• Louisiana Purchase
• frontier
• suburb
• representative democracy

**2 Taking Notes**

**MOVEMENT** Review the notes you took for this section.

History and Government ⟶ The United States

• Where did people migrate from to populate North America?
• Where did people move after the frontier was fully settled?

**3 Main Ideas**

a. Why did the United States attract so many immigrants?

b. How was the United States able to become a world power?

c. How are the powers of government in the United States divided?

**4 Geographic Thinking**

**Making Inferences** How did the physical geography of the United States contribute to its economic growth? **Think about:**

• land and mineral resources
• its relative global location

**S** **See Skillbuilder Handbook, page R4.**

**GeoActivity**

**EXPLORING LOCAL GEOGRAPHY** Make a list of physical features that would have attracted settlement to your area. Then do research or call your local historical society to find out when your community was founded and what groups settled there. Combine your findings in a **report** about your community.

# The South

**The South** is a subregion that covers about one-fourth of the land area of the United States and contains more than one-third of its population. Among its 16 states are 11 that made up the Confederacy during the Civil War. One of these states—Texas—is sometimes included in an area of the West called the Southwest. The South's warm climate, fertile soils, and many natural resources have shaped its development.

**THE OLD SOUTH**  Like the Northeast, the South was also the site of early European settlement. In fact, Virginia was England's first American colony. The South has a mix of cultures that reflects the diversity of its early settlers. In addition to people of British heritage, there are the descendants of Africans brought as slave laborers and Hispanics whose families first migrated from Mexico to Texas. Cajuns of French-Canadian origin and Creoles of French, Spanish, and African descent are found in Louisiana, while Florida is home to many Hispanics who came from Cuba.

Once a rural agricultural area, the South is rapidly changing and its cities growing. Along with the Southwest, it is often referred to as the "sunbelt" because of its climate.

**THE NEW SOUTH**  Agriculture was the South's first economic activity, and cotton, tobacco, fruits, peanuts, and rice are still grown there. Also, livestock production is important in states such as Texas and Arkansas. The South's humid subtropical climate at first hindered industrialization. But the widespread use of air conditioning beginning in the 1950s and the region's vast stores of energy resources—oil, coal, natural gas, and water—gave a boost to industry.

In recent times, the South has attracted many manufacturing and service industries fleeing the harsh weather of the "rust belt." Major industries include petroleum, steel, chemicals, food processing, textiles, and electronics. The South's climate draws millions of tourists and retirees, too. Atlanta, Georgia—a financial, trade, and transportation center—is the hub of the New South. Miami, Tampa-St. Petersburg, New Orleans, Houston, Dallas-Fort Worth, and San Antonio are other rapidly growing **metropolitan areas**—large cities and nearby suburbs and towns.

# The West

Look on the map on page 134, and you will see that **the West** is a far-flung subregion consisting of 13 states. It stretches from the Great Plains to the Pacific Ocean and includes Alaska to the north and Hawaii in the Pacific. The West covers about one-half of the land area of the United States but has only about one-fifth of the population. It is a region of dramatic and varied landscapes.

People settle in the West today as they did during its frontier days: wherever landforms and climate are favorable. Some areas, such as its many deserts, are sparsely settled. California, on the other hand, is the

**BACKGROUND**
Washington, Oregon, and Idaho are often called the Northwest. California, Arizona, New Mexico, Nevada, Colorado, Utah, and Texas are called the Southwest.

country's most populous state because of excellent farmland, good harbors, and a mild climate. The West is the most rapidly growing region in the United States. Los Angeles, the country's second largest city, is the West's cultural and commercial center.

**BACKGROUND**
According to the 2000 census, the population of the West grew by 20 percent from 1990.

**DEVELOPING THE WEST** The West's growth in the 20th century was helped by air conditioning and by irrigation. The map on this page, for example, shows how water from the Colorado River in Arizona has been diverted to serve many areas. Water supply aided development of inland cities such as Las Vegas, Tucson, and Phoenix.

The economic activities of the West are as varied as its climate and landscape. Among them are farming, ranching, food processing, logging, fishing, mining, oil refining, tourism, filmmaking, and the production of computers. Many cities with good harbors, including Seattle, Los Angeles, and Long Beach, make foreign trade—especially with Asia—important.

You read about the subregions of the United States in this section. In the next chapter, you will learn about the human geography of Canada.

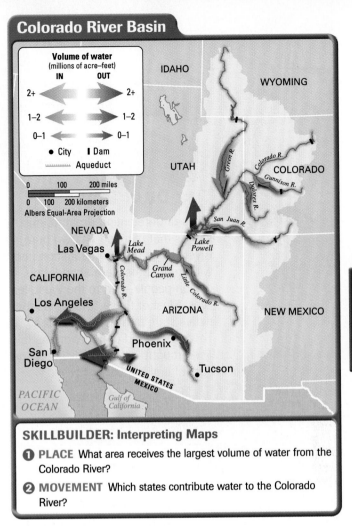

## Colorado River Basin

**Volume of water**
(millions of acre–feet)
IN          OUT

| 2+ | 2+ |
| 1–2 | 1–2 |
| 0–1 | 0–1 |

● City          ▮ Dam
‗‗‗‗‗ Aqueduct

0   100   200 miles
0   100   200 kilometers
Albers Equal-Area Projection

**SKILLBUILDER: Interpreting Maps**

❶ **PLACE** What area receives the largest volume of water from the Colorado River?

❷ **MOVEMENT** Which states contribute water to the Colorado River?

## Assessment

### ❶ Places & Terms

Explain the meaning of each of the following terms.
• New England
• megalopolis
• the Midwest
• the South
• metropolitan area
• the West

### ❷ Taking Notes

**REGION** Review the notes you took for this section.

• What are the four subregions of the United States?
• Which subregion is the largest in land area?

### ❸ Main Ideas

**a.** Why is the Northeast one of the most heavily industrialized and urbanized areas?

**b.** How is the economy of the Midwest changing?

**c.** What helped the economy of the West to grow?

### ❹ Geographic Thinking

**Seeing Patterns** How has air conditioning changed the economic activities of the subregions of the United States? **Think about:**

• the South and the West
• the "rust belt" and the "sunbelt"

**RESEARCH LINKS**
CLASSZONE.COM

**GeoActivity**

**MAKING COMPARISONS** Use the Internet to find more information on the economies of the four subregions. Create a **database** comparing the top five industries in each of the four subregions.

US & CANADA

# Disasters!

## The Dust Bowl

Years of unrelenting drought, misuse of the land, and the miles-high dust storms that resulted (shown here) devastated the Great Plains in the 1930s. Rivers dried up, and heat scorched the earth. As livestock died and crops withered, farms were abandoned. Thousands of families—more than two million people—fled to the West, leaving behind their farms and their former lives. Most of these "Okies," as they were called (referring to Oklahoma, the native state of many), made their way over hundreds of miles to California. There they tried to find work as migrant farm laborers and restart their lives. The drought lasted nearly a decade, and it took years for this productive agricultural region to recover.

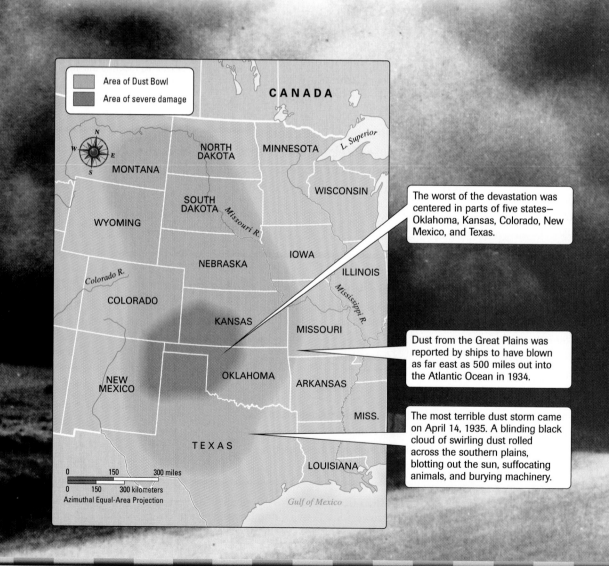

Area of Dust Bowl
Area of severe damage

CANADA

L. Superior

NORTH DAKOTA
MINNESOTA
MONTANA
WISCONSIN
SOUTH DAKOTA
Missouri R.
WYOMING
IOWA
NEBRASKA
ILLINOIS
Colorado R.
Mississippi R.
COLORADO
KANSAS
MISSOURI
NEW MEXICO
OKLAHOMA
ARKANSAS
MISS.
TEXAS
LOUISIANA
Gulf of Mexico

0   150   300 miles
0   150   300 kilometers
Azimuthal Equal-Area Projection

The worst of the devastation was centered in parts of five states—Oklahoma, Kansas, Colorado, New Mexico, and Texas.

Dust from the Great Plains was reported by ships to have blown as far east as 500 miles out into the Atlantic Ocean in 1934.

The most terrible dust storm came on April 14, 1935. A blinding black cloud of swirling dust rolled across the southern plains, blotting out the sun, suffocating animals, and burying machinery.

Thousands of farms like this one in Cimarron County, Oklahoma, were turned into dust-covered wastelands by the drought and dust storms of the 1930s.

Migrants from the Dust Bowl were forced to live any way they could while trying to find jobs picking vegetables or fruit. This mother and her seven children lived in a tent in a California migrant camp, eating vegetables found on the ground and birds they killed.

## GeoActivity

**REMEMBERING THE VICTIMS**
Use the Internet to find personal accounts of Dust Bowl families. Then create a **Documentary Proposal** about one of them.

- Begin with a brief overview of how the drought affected the family.
- Add a sketch map showing where they lived and copies of any photos available, with captions for each.
- Present your proposal to a panel of student producers.

**RESEARCH LINKS**
CLASSZONE.COM

## GeoData

### CAUSES
- Years of poor agricultural practices, such as overplowing and overgrazing, stripped away about 96 million acres of grasslands in the southern plains.
- Seven years of drought, or dry weather, turned the soil to dust.

### EFFECTS
- Hundreds of millions of tons of soil were blown away.
- Crops withered and livestock died.
- More than 2 million plains people abandoned their farms.

### PREVENTIVE MEASURES
Experts in crop production and soil management proposed the use of scientific farming methods, including

- contour plowing, or plowing across a hill rather than up and down, to stop wind and water erosion
- terracing, or planting crops in stair-stepped rows, to prevent soil erosion
- planting trees to hold the soil in place and to slow the force of the wind

# Comparing Cultures

## Transportation

As you have read, one of the five themes of geography is movement—how people move themselves and their goods across the Earth's surface. The earliest humans moved by foot from place to place. Later, they used animals, both to ride and as pack animals. Needing to cross streams, ancient people built primitive boats from available materials, such as wood and reeds. Over the centuries, advances in technology from wheeled vehicles to the steam engine to the construction of lighter-than-air craft has enabled people in different regions to meet the challenges posed by their environments.

Canada

Vietnam

Algeria

Peru

**In North African countries like Algeria,** camels are often called "ships of the desert" because they can carry freight and people across long distances. The Arabian, or one-humped, camel shown here in the Sahara Desert can cover 40 miles a day for four days carrying 400 pounds.

**Flat, smooth roadways crisscrossing Vietnam** make it easy for these workers to transport hundreds of fish traps from workshops to customers on the coast by bicycle.

**Geograp...
Thinking**

**Using the At...**
Ⓐ Look at th...
map on page...
Which bodies...
water do the
Atlantic Provi...
border?

**In the northernmost reaches of Canada,** roads are scarce. So, vast distances between places are more easily covered by small planes that can touch down on land or water, like this one flying into Cochrane, Ontario.

**This crescent-shaped boat on Lake Titicaca in Peru** is made from a reedlike plant. Native peoples of the region have made these boats for centuries.

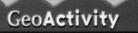

## GeoActivity

### RESEARCHING TRANSPORTATION

Working with a partner, use the Internet to research transportation around the world. Then prepare a report that shows the design of a **Web page** highlighting some aspect of world transportation.

• Create text to present the information you have found.

• Select suitable images.

• Locate appropriate links for visitors to your Web site.

**RESEARCH LINKS**
CLASSZONE.COM

## GeoData

### LAND TRANSPORTATION

• In the United States, there is one car for every two persons; in Somalia, one for every 500.

• One of the world's longest single rail systems, Russia's Trans-Siberian Railway, covers a distance of 5,867 miles from Moscow to the port of Nakhodka.

• Snowmobiles have replaced dogsleds as transport in remote, cold climates of North America.

• China has more bicycles—about 540,000,000—than any other country.

• Animals, including dogs, horses, donkeys, mules, camels, and elephants, still provide transport for many people around the world.

### AIR TRANSPORTATION

• Airliners carried 137 million passengers on more than 1 million flights from the United States to other countries from June 1999 to June 2000.

### WATER TRANSPORTATION

• Some modern cruise ships and ocean liners are more than 900 feet long and can carry upwards of 2,000 passengers on a voyage.

the map on page 160 shows, they supply a wide variety of products. Toronto, located on the shores of Lake Ontario, is not only the country's most populous city but also its banking and financial hub. Montreal, located on the St. Lawrence River, is Canada's second largest city. It is the center of economic and political activity in Quebec province.

## The Prairie Provinces

To the west of the hustle and bustle of Ontario and Quebec lie the **Prairie Provinces**—Manitoba, Saskatchewan, and Alberta.

**CANADA'S BREADBASKET** Canada's Prairie Provinces are part of the Great Plains of North America. These three provinces are the center of the nation's agricultural yield. They account for 50 percent of Canada's agricultural production. The land of the Prairie Provinces, however, consists of more than just fertile soil. About 60 percent of Canada's mineral output comes from this region of the country. Alberta itself has the nation's largest known deposits of coal and oil and produces 90 percent of Canada's natural gas.

**A CULTURAL MIX** The people of the Prairie Provinces are a diverse group. Manitoba has large numbers of Scots-Irish, Germans, Scandinavians, Ukrainians, and Poles. The town of St. Boniface boasts the largest French-Canadian population outside Quebec. The population of Saskatchewan also includes immigrants from South and East Asia and is home to the métis. Alberta is perhaps the most diverse of all. In addition to European immigrants, this province also has significant Indian, Japanese, Lebanese, and Vietnamese populations. ▶B

**Geographic Thinking◀**

**Seeing Patterns**
◀B Why might Alberta have attracted such a diverse population?

## The Pacific Province and the Territories

The province of British Columbia along with the three territories—Yukon Territory, Northwest Territories, and Nunavut—make up Canada's western and northern lands.

REGION The vast fertile plains of the Prairie Provinces, shown here in Regina, Saskatchewan, provide wheat for Canadians and the world.

PIONEER

**BRITISH COLUMBIA** Canada's westernmost province is **British Columbia.** Nearly all of it lies within the Rocky Mountain range. As a result, three-fourths of the province is 3,000 feet or more above sea level. More than half of the land is densely forested, and nearly one-third is frozen tundra, snowfields, and glaciers. Most of the population is found in the southwest. This is the location of British Columbia's two largest cities, Victoria and Vancouver. The economy is built on logging, mining, and hydroelectric-power production. Vancouver is Canada's largest port and has a prosperous shipping trade. ◀C

**Geographic Thinking** ◀

**Using the Atlas**

▶ Using a world map, locate Vancouver. Where might many of the goods shipped from its port be headed?

**THE TERRITORIES** Canada's three territories make up 41 percent of the country's land mass. Yet, they are too sparsely populated to be provinces. The Yukon Territory, with a population around 30,000, lies north of British Columbia and is largely an unspoiled wilderness. Directly east is the Northwest Territories, an area that extends into the Arctic. It has a population of about 41,000 people.

**Nunavut** was carved out of the eastern half of the Northwest Territories in 1999. It is home to many of Canada's Inuit. (See "Geography Today" on this page.) Even though the land is rugged and climatic conditions are severe, economic activities take place in the territories. Mining, fishing, and some logging are the principal industries, and these widely scattered activities explain why the settlements are so dispersed.

In this chapter and the last, you read about the human geography of the United States and Canada. In the next chapter, you will learn about some of the issues that are facing those countries today.

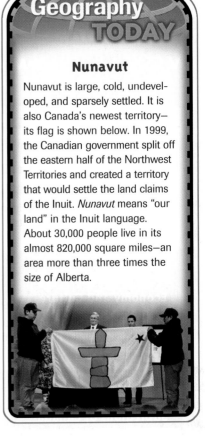

## Geography TODAY

### Nunavut

Nunavut is large, cold, undeveloped, and sparsely settled. It is also Canada's newest territory—its flag is shown below. In 1999, the Canadian government split off the eastern half of the Northwest Territories and created a territory that would settle the land claims of the Inuit. *Nunavut* means "our land" in the Inuit language. About 30,000 people live in its almost 820,000 square miles—an area more than three times the size of Alberta.

---

SECTION **3** ▶ **Assessment**

**① Places & Terms**

Identify and explain where in the region these would be found.

• Atlantic Provinces
• Quebec
• Ontario
• Prairie Provinces
• British Columbia

**② Taking Notes**

**REGION** Review the notes you took for this section.

Canada

Subregions

• What is the major economic activity of the Atlantic Provinces?
• Which provinces make up the Prairie Provinces?

**③ Main Ideas**

a. Why is the population of the Atlantic Provinces so small?

b. Why are Ontario and Quebec called the heartland of Canada?

c. What economic activities take place in British Columbia?

**④ Geographic Thinking**

**Making Inferences** Which subregions have the greatest potential for economic growth? **Think about:**

• already developed subregions
• each subregion's natural resources

S **See Skillbuilder Handbook, page R4.**

---

**GeoActivity**

**MAKING COMPARISONS** Review the differences among the subregions of Canada. Create a **brochure** that illustrates the economic activities, population characteristics, and major cities of the subregions.

# Unit 3

# Latin America

Latin America includes parts of North America, Central America and the Caribbean, and South America. The region covers many latitudes from north to south of the equator.

HUMAN–ENVIRONMENT INTERACTION Chacobo Indians make the dugout canoes they use to explore in the Amazon River basin in northern Bolivia.

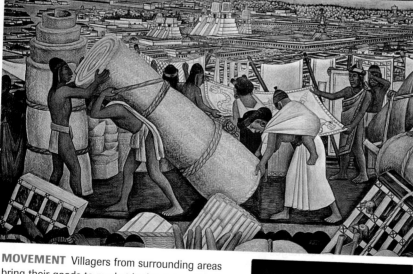

MOVEMENT Villagers from surrounding areas bring their goods to market in the Aztec city of Tenochtitlán, depicted in this mural by Diego Rivera.

## GeoData

**LOCATION** Latin America extends from Mexico southward across the equator to nearly reach Antarctica in the Southern Hemisphere.

**REGION** It is called "Latin America" because the two main languages spoken there—Spanish and Portuguese—developed from Latin.

**REGION** This region is bordered by two oceans (Atlantic and Pacific), the Gulf of Mexico, and the Caribbean Sea.

**For more information on Latin America . . .**

**RESEARCH LINKS**
CLASSZONE.COM

**PLACE** Sugarloaf Mountain is a famous landmark that looks out over Guanabara Bay in Rio de Janeiro, Brazil. The statue of Christ atop the mountain reflects the importance of the Catholic faith to millions of Latin Americans.

PHYSICAL GEOGRAPHY OF LATIN AMERICA

# From the Andes to the Amazon

Angel Falls in eastern Venezuela is the world's tallest waterfall. Named after James Angel, an American pilot who spotted it from his airplane in 1935, it is 3,212 feet tall.

## GeoFocus

### What effect has physical geography had on the settling of Latin America?

**Taking Notes** Copy the graphic organizer below into your notebook. Use it to record information from the chapter about the physical geography of Latin America.

| | |
|---|---|
| Landforms | |
| Resources | |
| Climate and Vegetation | |
| Human-Environment Interaction | |

# Landforms and Resources

## Main Ideas

- Latin America's landforms include highlands, lowlands, mountains, and plains.
- The Andes Mountains and the Amazon River are the region's most remarkable physical features.

### Places & Terms

**Andes Mountains**

**llanos**

**cerrado**

**pampas**

**Orinoco River**

**Amazon River**

**Paraná River**

### CONNECT TO THE ISSUES

RESOURCES People in Latin America have often struggled over the best way to develop and use natural resources.

**A HUMAN PERSPECTIVE** Simón Bolívar was a general who led the South American wars of independence against Spain. In August 1819, Bolívar led approximately 2,500 soldiers on a daring march from Venezuela over the mountains into present-day Colombia. Coming from this direction, over the massive barrier of the Andes Mountains, Bolívar and his troops were able to advance unseen. Bolívar's soldiers surprised the Spanish army and won a great victory. Military leaders such as Bolívar were able to use the geography of the region to help the South American republics win their independence from Spain.

## Mountains and Highlands

Latin America has an enormous span from north to south, as you can see from the map on page 191. It reaches from the border between the United States and Mexico down to Tierra del Fuego at the southern-most tip of South America, a distance of about 7,000 miles. It covers part of North America, all of Central and South America, and the Caribbean Islands. Its highlands, lowlands, rain forests, and plains are bounded by the Atlantic and Pacific oceans, the Gulf of Mexico, and the Caribbean Sea. The mountains of Latin America form one of the great ranges of the world.

**THE ANDES MOUNTAINS** The **Andes Mountains** of the South American continent are part of a chain of mountain ranges that run through the western portion of North, Central, and South America. This range is called the Rockies in the United States, the Sierra Madre in Mexico, and the Andes in South America. There are many active volcanoes throughout the region.

All along the west and south coasts of South America, the Andes Mountains are a barrier to movement into the interior. As a result, more settlement in South America has occurred along the eastern and northern coasts.

Even so, the mountain ranges of Latin America were the home of some of the most important civilizations in the hemisphere, including the Inca in Peru.

MOVEMENT Two sure-footed guanacos climb the foothills of the Andes in Patagonia, a region that includes parts of Argentina and Chile.

# Disasters!

## Volcano on Montserrat

Montserrat is an island in the Caribbean. One of the outstanding features of the island is its large volcano located in the Soufriere Hills. The volcano had been dormant for approximately five centuries when it began to erupt in 1995. The eruptions continued through 1996 and became particularly severe in 1997. The large map of the island (below) shows the area affected by the eruptions. The dates on the map show the expanding "zones of exclusion." A zone of exclusion is an area too dangerous for people to enter. Two-thirds of the island is now uninhabitable.

ATLANTIC OCEAN

Montserrat

Caribbean Sea

SOUTH AMERICA

Soufriere Hills

June '97

October '96

February '9

Sept '97

July '97

Plymouth

Plymouth, the capital and largest city on the island of Montserrat, lies downwind of Soufrière Hills volcano. As a result, it has been covered with a gray shroud of ash.

Fiery eruptions illuminated the nighttime sky as lava and ashes poured out of the volcano's cone.

## GeoActivity

**MAKING A PRESENTATION**

Working with a partner, use the Internet to research a volcanic eruption on the chart below. Then create a **presentation** about the eruption.

- Create a diagram showing the extent of the eruption, the damage caused by it, and the number of lives lost.
- Add a map of the region affected by the eruption.
- Write a report explaining how the eruption affected people.

**RESEARCH LINKS**
CLASSZONE.COM

## GeoData

**OTHER FAMOUS VOLCANOES**

 **A.D. 79**
Mount Vesuvius erupted, and thousands of people died when they were buried under ash and mud or breathed the poisonous fumes.

 **1707**
Mount Fuji erupted. It is the highest and most sacred mountain in Japan.

**1943**
Paricutin was a volcano that formed in the middle of a cornfield in Mexico. It last erupted in 1943.

 **1980**
Mt. St. Helens in Washington State erupted with tremendous force. The eruption lasted nine hours and killed 60 people.

 **2000**
Popocatépetl in Mexico erupted in its biggest explosion in a thousand years.

# Unit 4

# Europe

Europe is the world's second smallest continent. Located in the Northern Hemisphere, Europe has great diversity of landforms and cultures.

**LOCATION** The dazzling White Cliffs of Dover in England face the English Channel. The cliffs are made of soft chalk and are slowly eroding.

**REGION** Many people view the Ural Mountains as the eastern border of Europe, but for historic and cultural reasons, Russia and other former republics of the Soviet Union are in Unit 5.

**PLACE** Europe's coastline is longer than that of Africa, the world's second largest continent.

**HUMAN-ENVIRONMENT INTERACTION** Historically, Europeans used the oceans and seas to make voyages for exploration and trade. Their culture spread around the world.

**For more information on Europe . . .**

**RESEARCH LINKS**
CLASSZONE.COM

EUROPE

**PLACE** The Eiffel Tower stands 984 feet above the Paris skyline. It was completed in 1889 for an International Exposition celebrating the French Revolution.

**MOVEMENT** Europeans are wildly enthusiastic about soccer. Teams and fans travel to matches held all over the world. In this game, held during the 1998 World Cup matches, Germany played Italy.

# Today's Issues in Europe

Today, Europe faces the issues previewed here. As you read Chapters 12 and 13, you will learn helpful background information. You will study the issues themselves in Chapter 14.

In a small group, answer the questions below. Then participate in a class discussion of your answers.

## Exploring the Issues

**1. CONFLICT** Search a print or online newspaper for articles about ethnic or religious conflicts in Europe today. What do these conflicts have in common? How are they different?

**2. POLLUTION** Make a list of possible pollution problems faced by Europe and those faced by the United States. How are these problems similar? Different?

**3. UNIFICATION** To help you understand the issues involved in unifying Europe, compare Europe to the United States. Imagine what might occur if each U.S. state were its own country. List five problems that might result.

For more on these issues in Europe . . .

CURRENT EVENTS
CLASSZONE.COM

CONFLICT

## How can people resolve their differences?

In central Bosnia, a child stands near the ruins of a Muslim mosque. Bosnian Croats destroyed the mosque during an "ethnic cleansing" campaign to drive out Muslims during the 1992–1995 Bosnian war.

## How can Europeans clean up their environment?

On February 13, 2000, cyanide-polluted water from a Romanian mine reached Hungary. The cyanide killed thousands of fish, some of which are shown here washed up on the banks of the Tisza River.

## CASESTUDY

### Will there be a United States of Europe?

Over the centuries, wars and conflicts have ravaged Europe, but since 1950, Europe's nations have begun working together. As the new century begins, economics may be the key to uniting Europe.

UNIFICATION

THIS MUST BE THE STEERING COMMITTEE

EURO

# Patterns of Physical Geography

Use the Unit Atlas to add to your knowledge of Europe. As you look at the maps and charts, notice geographic patterns and specific details about the region. For example, the chart gives details about the rivers and mountains of Europe.

After studying the graphs and physical map on these two pages, jot down answers to the questions below in your notebook.

## Making Comparisons

**1.** Compare Europe's size and population to that of the United States. Based on that data, how might the population densities of the two compare?

**2.** Compare Europe's longest river, the Danube, to the Mississippi. How much difference is there in the lengths?

**3.** Which countries have many mountains? How might those mountains affect human life there?

**For updated statistics on Europe . . .**

**DATA UPDATE**
CLASSZONE.COM

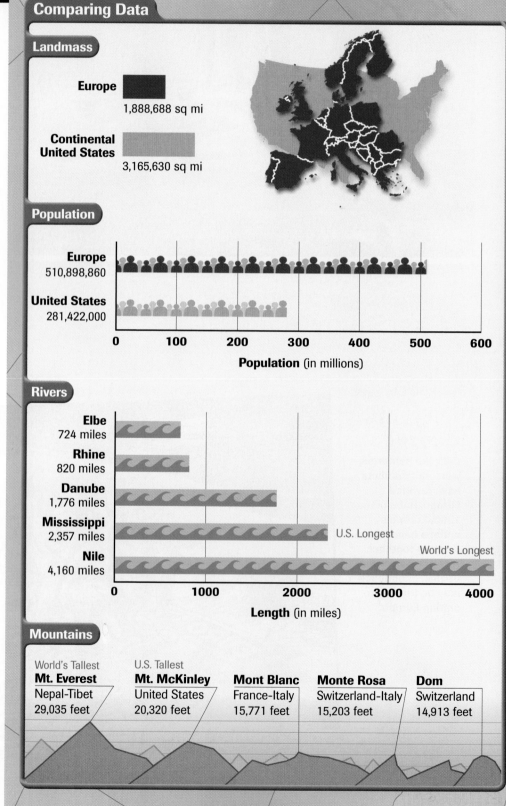

## Comparing Data

### Landmass

**Europe**
1,888,688 sq mi

**Continental United States**
3,165,630 sq mi

### Population

**Europe**
510,898,860

**United States**
281,422,000

Population (in millions)
0   100   200   300   400   500   600

### Rivers

**Elbe**
724 miles

**Rhine**
820 miles

**Danube**
1,776 miles

**Mississippi**
2,357 miles  — U.S. Longest

**Nile**
4,160 miles  — World's Longest

Length (in miles)
0   1000   2000   3000   4000

### Mountains

| World's Tallest | U.S. Tallest | | | |
| **Mt. Everest** | **Mt. McKinley** | **Mont Blanc** | **Monte Rosa** | **Dom** |
| Nepal-Tibet | United States | France-Italy | Switzerland-Italy | Switzerland |
| 29,035 feet | 20,320 feet | 15,771 feet | 15,203 feet | 14,913 feet |

ICELAND

Norwegian Sea

Arctic Circle

Faroe Is.

Shetland Is.

Orkney Is.

Hebrides

HIGHLANDS

North Sea

Gulf of Bothnia

FINLAND

NORWAY

SWEDEN

Baltic Sea

ESTONIA

RUSSIA

LATVIA

LITHUANIA

RUSSIA

BELARUS

Gotland

Öland I.

Jutland

DENMARK

IRELAND

BRITISH ISLES

UNITED KINGDOM

Land's End

English Channel

Channel Is.

ATLANTIC OCEAN

NETHERLANDS

IJSSELMEER

BELGIUM

LUXEMBOURG

Rhine R.

Elbe R.

GERMANY

NORTHERN EUROPEAN PLAIN

Vistula R.

Oder R.

POLAND

UKRAINE

Loire R.

Seine R.

BLACK FOREST

CZECH REPUBLIC

Danube R.

SLOVAKIA

CARPATHIAN MTS.

MOLDOVA

FRANCE

LIECHTENSTEIN

SWITZERLAND

AUSTRIA

HUNGARY

ROMANIA

Cape Finisterre

Bay of Biscay

MASSIF CENTRAL

A L P S

Mt. Blanc 15,771 ft. (4,807 m.)

Rhône R.

Po R.

SLOVENIA

CROATIA

PORTUGAL

Ebro R.

PYRENEES

ANDORRA

MONACO

SAN MARINO

BOSNIA & HERZEGOVINA

YUGOSLAVIA

Danube R.

BALKAN MTS.

Black Sea

Tagus R.

MESETA

Corsica

Elba

APENNINES

Adriatic Sea

BULGARIA

MACEDONIA

Majorca

Minorca

VATICAN CITY

ITALY

SPAIN

Cape St. Vincent

Balearic Is.

Sardinia

Tyrrhenian Sea

ALBANIA

GREECE

TURKEY

Strait of Gibraltar

M e d i t e r r a n e a n

Mt. Etna 10,902 ft. (3,323 m.)

Sea

Aegean Sea

PELOPONNESUS

Cyclades

Sicily

Rhodes

ALGERIA

TUNISIA

MALTA

Crete

N W E S

### Elevation

13,100 ft. (4,000 m.)
6,600 ft. (2,000 m.)
1,600 ft. (500 m.)
650 ft. (200 m.)
0 ft. (0 m.)
Below sea level

▲ Mountain peak

Glacier

0 250 500 miles

0 250 500 kilometers

Azimuthal Equidistant Projection

LIBYA

EGYPT

EUROPE

263

After World War I (1914–1918), the political map of Europe changed radically. Empires disappeared, and new countries were born. Study the political maps of Europe in 1914 and Europe today to see what changes took place in the 20th century. Then answer these questions in your notebook.

### Making Comparisons

**1.** Which nations appear on the map of Europe today but don't appear on the 1914 map?

**2.** Which nations existed in 1914 but no longer exist today?

**3.** Which nations are larger now than they were in 1914?

**4.** Which nations are smaller than they were in 1914?

**Europe, 1914**

This map shows the nations of Europe in 1914, before the outbreak of World War I.

Reykjavík
20°W
**ICELAND**
10°W
0°
10°E
Arctic Circle

*Norwegian Sea*

Faroe
Islands
(Den.)

Trondheim

Shetland Is.
(Br.)

**NORWAY**

Bergen

Oslo
**SWEDEN**

**FINLAND**

Tampere

Helsinki

60°N

Gulf of
Bothnia

Göteborg

Stockholm

**ESTONIA**

**RUSSIA**

Glasgow
*North
Sea*

**LATVIA**

Belfast
Edinburgh

Dublin
**IRELAND**
**UNITED
KINGDOM**

Cork

**DENMARK**

Copenhagen

*Baltic
Sea*

**LITHUANIA**

**RUSSIA**

**BELARUS**

**NETHERLANDS**
Hamburg

Amsterdam
Berlin

**POLAND**

Poznań

Warsaw

Portsmouth

London

Brussels
**BELGIUM**
**GERMANY**

**LUXEMBOURG**

Frankfurt

Prague

Luxembourg

**CZECH REPUBLIC**

**SLOVAKIA**

Bratislava

**UKRAINE**

50°N

*English Channel*

**ATLANTIC
OCEAN**

Nantes
Paris

**FRANCE**

**LIECHTENSTEIN**

Vienna
Graz

**AUSTRIA**

**MOLDOVA**

Bern
**SWITZERLAND**

Budapest

**HUNGARY**

**ROMANIA**

*Bay
of
Biscay*

Bordeaux

Milan

**SLOVENIA**
Ljubljana

Venice

Zagreb

**CROATIA**

Bucharest

**PORTUGAL**

Marseille

**ITALY**

**SAN
MARINO**

**BOSNIA &
HERZEGOVINA**

Belgrade

*Black
Sea*

**MONACO**

Sarajevo

**YUGOSLAVIA**

**BULGARIA**

*Adriatic*

**SPAIN**
**ANDORRA**

Madrid

Corsica
(Fr.)

**VATICAN
CITY**

Barcelona

Rome

Sofia

Skopje

**MACEDONIA**

40°N

Lisbon

Seville

Naples

Tiranë

**ALBANIA**

Balearic Islands
(Sp.)

Sardinia
(It.)

*Tyrrhenian
Sea*

*Sea*

**GREECE**

*Aegean
Sea*

**TURKEY**

**MEDITERRANEAN**

**MOROCCO**

Sicily
(It.)

**MALTA**

Valletta

Athens

N
W        E
S

Crete
(Gr.)

**ALGERIA**

★ National capital

● Other city

0          250          500 miles

0       250      500 kilometers

Azimuthal Equidisant Projection

**TUNISIA**

10°E

20°E

**LIBYA**

**EGYPT**

*Mediterranean Sea*

EUROPE

# PHYSICAL GEOGRAPHY OF EUROPE
## The Peninsula of Peninsulas

Sognafjord, north of the
city of Bergen, Norway,
has only about five and a
half hours of light per
day in mid-December.

## GeoFocus

### What effect does physical geography have on the lives of Europeans?

**Taking Notes** Copy the graphic organizer
below into your notebook. Use it to record
information from the chapter about the
physical geography of Europe.

| Landforms | |
|---|---|
| Resources | |
| Climate and Vegetation | |
| Human–Environment Interaction | |

# Landforms and Resources

**Main Ideas**

• Europe is composed of many peninsulas and islands.

• Europe's landforms also include large plains and mountain ranges.

**Places & Terms**

fjord                *Massif Central*

uplands            peat

*Meseta*

**CONNECT TO THE ISSUES**

**UNIFICATION** Resources helped Western Europe develop industry before other regions. The European Union began in Western Europe.

**A HUMAN PERSPECTIVE** Elephants in Europe? In 218 B.C., Hannibal, a general from Carthage in North Africa, attacked the Roman Empire, which was at war with Carthage. He moved 38 war elephants and an estimated 60,000 troops across the Mediterranean Sea to Spain. To reach Italy, his armies had to cross the Pyrenees Mountains, the Rhone River, and the Alps. Hannibal used rafts to float the elephants across the Rhone. In the Alps, steep paths and slick ice caused men and animals to fall to their deaths. Despite this, Hannibal arrived in Italy with 26,000 men and a few elephants, and he defeated Rome in many battles. His crossing of the Alps was a triumph over geographic barriers.

## Peninsulas and Islands

On a map you will see that Europe is a large peninsula stretching to the west of Asia. Europe itself has many smaller peninsulas, so it is sometimes called a "peninsula of peninsulas." Because of these peninsulas, most locations in Europe are no more than 300 miles from an ocean or sea. As you can imagine, the European way of life involves using these bodies of water for both business and pleasure.

**NORTHERN PENINSULAS** In northern Europe is the Scandinavian Peninsula. Occupied by the nations of Norway and Sweden, it is bounded by the Norwegian Sea, the North Sea, and the Baltic Sea. More than almost any other place in Europe, this peninsula shows the results of the movement of glaciers during the Ice Age. The glaciers scoured away the rich topsoil and left only thin, rocky soil that is hard to farm.

In Norway, glaciers also carved out **fjords** (fyawrdz), which are steep U-shaped valleys that connect to the sea and that filled with seawater after the glaciers melted. Fjords provide excellent harbors for fishing boats. The fjords are often separated by narrow peninsulas.

The Jutland Peninsula is directly across the North Sea from Scandinavia. Jutland forms the largest part of Denmark and a small part of Germany. This peninsula is an extension of a broad

**Major European Peninsulas**

0       250       500 miles
0     250     500 kilometers
Azimuthal Equidistant Projection

*Norwegian Sea*

SCANDINAVIAN PENINSULA

ATLANTIC OCEAN

North Sea

JUTLAND PENINSULA

Baltic Sea

Bay of Biscay

ALPS

PYRENEES

IBERIAN PENINSULA

ITALIAN PENINSULA

Adriatic Sea

BALKAN PENINSULA

Black Sea

Mediterranean Sea

**SKILLBUILDER: Interpreting Maps**

❶ **LOCATION** Where are Europe's major peninsulas located in relation to each other?

❷ **REGION** Why might each peninsula be considered a region?

# Disasters!

## Bubonic Plague

By the 1300s, Italian merchants were growing rich from the trade in luxury goods from Asia. Then in October 1347, trading ships sailed into the port of Messina, Sicily, carrying a terrifying cargo—the disease we now call bubonic plague. Over the next four years, the plague spread along trade routes throughout Europe. An estimated 25 million Europeans died, about one-fourth to one-third of the population. In terms of its death toll, the plague (also called the Black Death) was the worst disaster Europe ever suffered.

### Spread of the Bubonic Plague

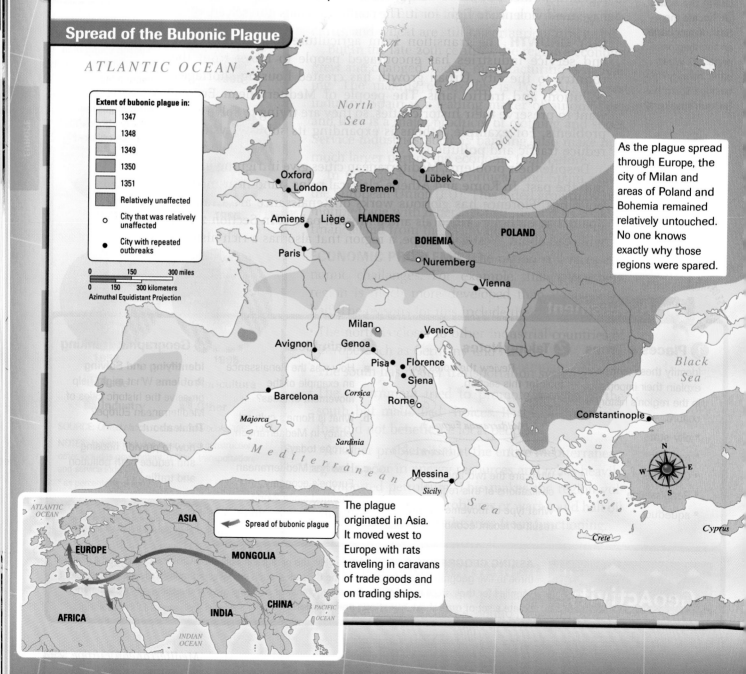

ATLANTIC OCEAN

**Extent of bubonic plague in:**
- 1347
- 1348
- 1349
- 1350
- 1351
- Relatively unaffected
- ○ City that was relatively unaffected
- ● City with repeated outbreaks

0    150    300 miles
0    150    300 kilometers
Azimuthal Equidistant Projection

North Sea

Baltic Sea

Oxford
London
Bremen
Lübek
Amiens
Liège
FLANDERS
POLAND
BOHEMIA
Paris
Nuremberg
Vienna
Milan
Venice
Avignon
Genoa
Pisa
Florence
Siena
Barcelona
Corsica
Rome
Majorca
Sardinia
Mediterranean Sea
Messina
Sicily
Constantinople
Black Sea
Crete
Cyprus

As the plague spread through Europe, the city of Milan and areas of Poland and Bohemia remained relatively untouched. No one knows exactly why those regions were spared.

ATLANTIC OCEAN
ASIA
→ Spread of bubonic plague
EUROPE
MONGOLIA
AFRICA
INDIA
CHINA
PACIFIC OCEAN
INDIAN OCEAN

The plague originated in Asia. It moved west to Europe with rats traveling in caravans of trade goods and on trading ships.

## Transmission of the Plague

① The bacterium that causes bubonic plague, *Yersinia pestis,* lives in the guts of fleas. The fleas bite rats and feed on their blood, infecting them with the disease.

② Sometimes, an infected rat comes into contact with humans. Because the rat is dying, the fleas jump onto the humans to feed off them.

③ People catch bubonic plague from flea bites. In some, the plague enters their lungs, becoming pneumonic plague. These victims cough, sneeze, and spit up infected blood and saliva—spreading the disease more quickly.

## GeoActivity

**UNDERSTANDING EPIDEMICS**

Working with a partner, use the Internet to research an epidemic on the time line below and create a **presentation** about it.

- Create a diagram showing the symptoms of the disease and the methods of treating it.
- Add a map of the region affected by this epidemic.
- Last, write a report explaining how the epidemic affected society.

**RESEARCH LINKS**
CLASSZONE.COM

## GeoData

**PREVENTIVE MEASURES**

In the 1300s, most doctors recommended these methods of purifying the air to prevent plague:

- Burn richly scented incense.
- Fill the house with flowers.
- Sprinkle the floors with vinegar.
- Have doctors wear a bird mask with perfume in the beak.

**OTHER DISASTROUS EPIDEMICS**

**1507–1518**
Smallpox killed one-third to one-half of the people of Cuba, Haiti, and Puerto Rico.

**1918–1919**
About 30 million people died from an influenza outbreak that spread around the world.

**2000**
A UN report said that AIDS had killed 19 million people worldwide. Seven African countries had 20 percent of their population infected.

# Western Europe

**Main Ideas**

- France and the Germanic countries developed very different cultures.
- These cultural differences led to conflicts that shaped the history of Western Europe.

**Places & Terms**

| | |
|---|---|
| **Benelux** | **nationalism** |
| **Reformation** | **Holocaust** |
| **feudalism** | **Berlin Wall** |

**CONNECT TO THE ISSUES**

**UNIFICATION** France and Germany have resolved their past conflicts and now cooperate in the European Union.

**A HUMAN PERSPECTIVE** Today, the French call Émile Durkheim the father of French sociology (the study of society). But he wasn't always honored. During World War I, some French patriots considered him a disloyal foreigner. Why? Perhaps it was because he had a German last name and came from Lorraine, a region that had switched between French and German rule many times. France and Germany have long had a deep rivalry, based in part on cultural differences.

## A History of Cultural Divisions

France and Germany are the dominant countries in Western Europe. They are the two largest countries, and their access to resources, ports, and trade routes helped them to build productive economies.

French culture is strong in France and Monaco; German culture is strong in Germany, Austria, and Liechtenstein. Switzerland and the **Benelux** countries of Belgium, the Netherlands, and Luxembourg have their own cultures—but also have been influenced by Germany and France. Western Europe's cultural divisions have historic roots.

**ROME TO CHARLEMAGNE** One cultural division, language, dates from ancient times. By 50 B.C., the Roman Empire had conquered the Celtic tribes in what is now France. French is one of the Romance languages that evolved from Latin (Rome's language). But Rome never fully conquered the Germanic tribes that migrated into the lands east of France. Germanic languages are still spoken there. (See the chart on page 297.)

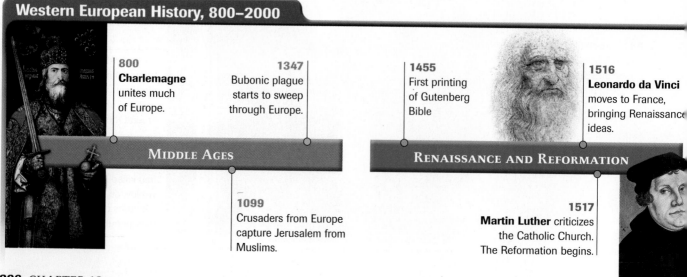

## Western European History, 800–2000

**800** **Charlemagne** unites much of Europe.

**1347** Bubonic plague starts to sweep through Europe.

**1455** First printing of Gutenberg Bible

**1516** **Leonardo da Vinci** moves to France, bringing Renaissance ideas.

**MIDDLE AGES**

**RENAISSANCE AND REFORMATION**

**1099** Crusaders from Europe capture Jerusalem from Muslims.

**1517** **Martin Luther** criticizes the Catholic Church. The Reformation begins.

In the late 700s, a Germanic king, Charlemagne, conquered most of the region. However, his empire began to fall apart soon after his death. Western Europe remained a region of small, competing kingdoms.

**THE REFORMATION** A religious movement created new differences. During the Renaissance (see Section 1), scholars questioned authority. Some people even began to question the Catholic Church. In 1517, Martin Luther published 95 statements that criticized church practices that he believed were wrong. That began the **Reformation**, a period when many Christians broke away from the Catholic Church and started Protestant churches. Mutual hostility led Catholics and Protestants to fight religious wars that tore Europe apart.

Today, France is mostly Catholic. The Netherlands, Switzerland, and Germany contain both Protestants and Catholics. In Germany, Protestants live mainly in the north and Catholics in the south of the country.

**CONNECT TO THE ISSUES**

CONFLICT

A Why might conflict result if neighboring countries adopt different religions?

## The Rise of Nation-States

The period between the fall of Rome and the Renaissance is called the Middle Ages. During this time, Europeans gradually developed the nation-state, an independent nation of people with a common culture.

**NATIONALISM** During the centuries after Rome fell, **feudalism** gradually developed in Europe. This was a political system in which powerful lords owned most of the land. They gave some land to nobles in exchange for military service by those nobles. Over time, strong kings gained power over feudal lords, and nationalism evolved. **Nationalism** is the belief that people should be loyal to their nation, the people with whom they share land, culture, and history.

Nationalism often causes groups to want their own countries, so it contributed to the rise of modern nation-states. France was one of the

**5 THEMES**

**REGION**

**Diversity of Languages**

| Nation | Languages Spoken |
| --- | --- |
| Austria | German |
| Belgium | Flemish, French, German |
| Germany | German |
| France | French |
| Liechtenstein | German, Alemannic dialect |
| Luxembourg | Luxembourgian, German, French |
| Monaco | French, English, Italian, Monegasque dialect |
| Netherlands | Dutch |
| Switzerland | German, French, Italian, Romansch |

SOURCE: *The National Geographic Desk Reference, World Book*

EUROPE

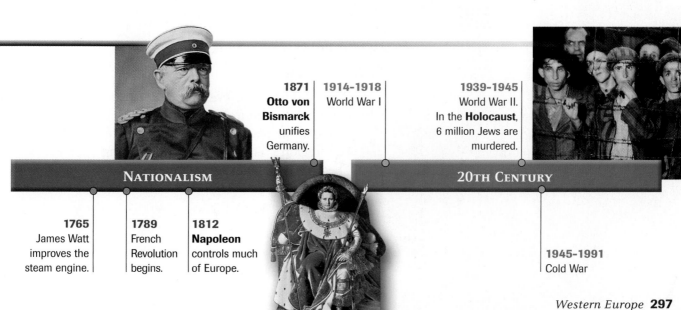

**NATIONALISM**

**1765**
James Watt improves the steam engine.

**1789**
French Revolution begins.

**1812**
**Napoleon** controls much of Europe.

**1871**
**Otto von Bismarck** unifies Germany.

**1914–1918**
World War I

**20TH CENTURY**

**1939–1945**
World War II. In the **Holocaust**, 6 million Jews are murdered.

**1945–1991**
Cold War

*Western Europe* **297**

first nation-states. By the late 1600s, French kings held absolute power, which they often used to benefit themselves, not their people. In 1789, the people began a rebellion—the French Revolution. They deposed the king and formed a republic. But in a few years, an army officer named Napoleon Bonaparte seized power. In 1804, he made himself emperor. Napoleon tried to conquer all of Europe but was defeated.

The nation-states of Europe became strong rivals. From the 1600s to 1945, wars repeatedly broke out between France and Austria or between France and the German states (later Germany). Germany did not unify as a nation until 1871. It was one of many European countries affected by a new wave of nationalism in the 1800s.

Western Europe also experienced industrial growth in the 1800s. Industrialism caused European nations to set up colonies in other lands in order to gain raw materials and markets. Many European nations saw each other as rivals in the race to gain colonies. You will learn more about the effects of colonialism as you read this book. **B**

**Seeing Patterns**
**B** Why might industrialism cause a country to want colonies?

**MODERN CONFLICTS** The nationalistic rivalry and competition for colonies among European nations helped cause World War I. The Allied Powers (including France) fought the Central Powers (Germany, Austria-Hungary, and their allies). The Allied Powers won and imposed harsh terms on Germany. German resentment over those terms helped cause World War II, in which Germany, led by Adolf Hitler and the Nazis, tried to conquer Europe. The Nazis also carried out the **Holocaust**, a program of mass murder of European Jews and other minorities. In 1945, the Allies defeated Germany.

**BACKGROUND**
The Nazis were a political party that created a government that controlled all aspects of German life. They held many racist beliefs.

After the war, Germany was split into two nations. West Germany was allied with non-Communist Europe and the United States. East Germany was allied with the Communist Soviet Union. The capital city of Berlin, located in East Germany, was also divided, cut in two by the **Berlin Wall**. In 1989, anti-Communist reforms swept Europe, and in response to protests, East Germany opened the Berlin Wall.

In 1990, the two Germanys reunited under a democratic government. In recent years, France and Germany have tried to end the rivalry that so often led to war. These two nations were leaders in the movement toward establishing the European Union. (See the Case Study on pages 326–329.)

## Economics: Diversity and Luxury

Since the Middle Ages, Western Europe has been rich in agriculture, and in the 1800s, it was one of the first regions to industrialize. The region's economy remains strong because it includes agriculture and manufacturing, plus high-tech and service industries.

**REGION** Picturesque old castles, such as the Castle Reichenstein in Germany, were built for defense purposes. Now they are tourist attractions.
**Why do you think this castle was built on a hillside?**

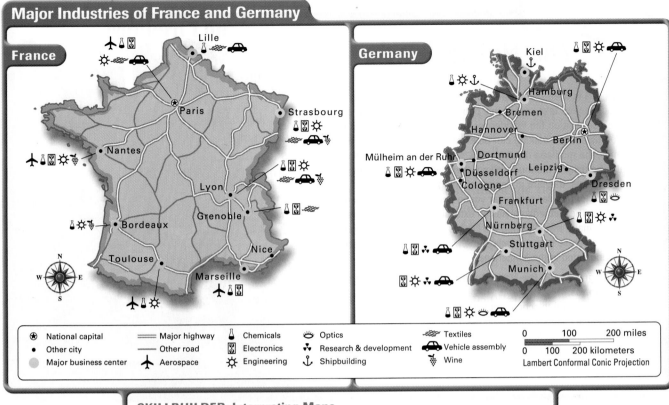

## Major Industries of France and Germany

**France**

Lille
Paris
Strasbourg
Nantes
Lyon
Grenoble
Bordeaux
Nice
Toulouse
Marseille

**Germany**

Kiel
Hamburg
Bremen
Hannover
Berlin
Mülheim an der Ruhr
Dortmund
Düsseldorf
Leipzig
Cologne
Dresden
Frankfurt
Nürnberg
Stuttgart
Munich

|  |  | |  |  |
|---|---|---|---|---|
| ⊛ | National capital | | 🧪 | Chemicals |
| ● | Other city | | 🗄 | Electronics |
| ⬤ | Major business center | | ☼ | Engineering |
| ═══ | Major highway | | 👁 | Optics |
| ─── | Other road | | ⚛ | Research & development |
| ✈ | Aerospace | | ⚓ | Shipbuilding |

Textiles
Vehicle assembly
Wine

0   100   200 miles
0   100   200 kilometers
Lambert Conformal Conic Projection

---

**SKILLBUILDER: Interpreting Maps**

❶ **LOCATION** What is the relative location of business centers? Give possible reasons.

❷ **MOVEMENT** Use the Unit Atlas to find the border between France and Germany. Which French and German cities might make good international trading partners?

---

**AGRICULTURE TO HIGH-TECH** Dairy farming and livestock provide most of the agricultural income in Belgium, France, the Netherlands, and Switzerland. These countries produce and export dairy products. In addition, France is the largest producer of agricultural products in Western Europe. Its major crops include wheat, grapes, and vegetables.

Western Europe was a leader in developing industry because it was rich in coal and iron ore. Today, the region has three of Europe's top manufacturing nations: France, Germany, and the Netherlands. The maps above show the major industries of France and Germany.

High-tech and service industries are also very important. Electronics is a major product of the Netherlands. Germany also produces electronics, as well as scientific instruments. France has one of the world's fastest passenger trains, the TGV (*train à grande vitesse*, or high-speed train), and a space program. France also relies heavily on nuclear energy. Nuclear plants produce nearly 75 percent of its electricity. ◀

Switzerland specializes in the service industry of banking. One reason for this is that Switzerland refuses to fight in wars, so people believe that money is safer there.

**TOURISM AND LUXURY** Because of its varied scenery, mild climate, and historic sites, Western Europe is popular with tourists. Tourism is a major part of the French, Swiss, and Austrian economies.

Western Europe exports luxury goods to the world. For example, some German cars and Swiss watches are considered status symbols.

**Geographic Thinking**

**Making Comparisons**

▶ Which high-tech industry do Germany and the Netherlands have in common?

# Comparing Cultures

## Geographic Sports Challenges

Over time, humans have found ways to enjoy even the most forbidding climates and terrains. Some popular sports evolved from activities that people used to overcome geographic challenges, such as mountains or snowy climates. Other sports were created to take advantage of special geographic features, such as recurring winds or waves. On these two pages, you will learn about geographically inspired sports from around the world.

**Surfing, shown here off the coast of Australia,** dates back to prehistoric times. It may have originated when Polynesian sailors of the Pacific Islands needed to reach land from large canoes floating offshore.

**Skiing originated as a means of travel in northern Europe,** and ski jumping probably evolved in hilly Norway. In 1924, ski jumping became an Olympic sport. Competitors are judged not only on how far they jump but also on the technique they use.

**Acapulco, Mexico, is famous for its cliff diving.** This dangerous sport often involves diving from heights nearly three times higher than those used in Olympic platform diving. Cliff divers have been killed by hitting their heads on rocks.

**The Iditarod Sled Dog Race is held in Alaska.** Susan Butcher, shown here, was the first person to have won it three years in a row. The Inuit people first used sled dogs to travel across snow-covered terrain; racing evolved later.

## GeoData

**Skiing**
• Skis that are more than 4,000 years old have been found in Scandinavian bogs.
• Skiing was once a military skill. Norwegian troops skied in the Battle of Oslo in 1200.

**Surfing**
• The explorer James Cook first reported seeing surfing in 1778.
• European missionaries banned surfing in 1821. It was revived in 1920 by a Hawaiian, Duke Kahanamoku.

**Cliff Diving**
• Women did not compete at Acapulco until 1996.
• Divers enter the water at speeds of up to 65 mph.

**Sled Dog Racing**
• The Iditarod honors a 1925 emergency mission to deliver medicine to Nome, Alaska.
• During the 1985 race, a moose charged across Susan Butcher's path. The collision that resulted killed 2 dogs and wounded 13 other dogs.

# Unit 5

# Russia and the Republics

Between 1922 and 1991, Russia and most of the Republics were part of the Union of Soviet Socialist Republics (USSR), also known as the Soviet Union.

**LOCATION** Shoppers stroll around Russia's famous State Department Store. The mall, which opened in 1893, is located in Moscow, the capital of Russia.

**REGION** Russia and the Republics cross over 11 time zones and cover nearly one-sixth of the earth's land surface.

**LOCATION** Most of the region is hundreds of miles from the open sea.

**HUMAN-ENVIRONMENT INTERACTION** Freezing temperatures can continue so long that people use frozen rivers as roadways.

**For more information on Russia and the Republics . . .**

**RESEARCH LINKS**
CLASSZONE.COM

RUSSIA & REP.

**PLACE** The Caucasus Mountains stretch between the Black and Caspian seas. A great variety of peoples have settled in the region surrounding the mountains.

**MOVEMENT** Invaders from Arabia brought Islam to the southern areas of the region by the 8th century. Beautiful mosques adorn many of the region's cities.

# Today's Issues in Russia and the Republics

Today, Russia and the Republics face the issues previewed here. As you read Chapters 15 and 16, you will learn helpful background information. You will study the issues themselves in Chapter 17.

In a small group, answer the questions below. Then participate in a class discussion of your answers.

## Exploring the Issues

**1. CONFLICT** Search a newspaper for articles about conflicts in Russia and the Republics today. What do these conflicts have in common? How are they different?

**2. ECONOMIC CHANGE** Think about the different economic systems you learned about in Chapter 4. How might changing from a command economy to a market economy be difficult?

**3. NUCLEAR LEGACY** What impact could Soviet nuclear programs have on the region's economy?

For more on these issues in Russia and the Republics . . .

i **CURRENT EVENTS**
CLASSZONE.COM

**CONFLICT**

## How do new nations establish law and order?

After the collapse of the Soviet Union in 1991, groups in different parts of the region took up arms to fight for independence. This photo shows a woman and child from a region of Russia called Chechnya. Russia invaded Chechnya twice in the 1990s to end an independence movement in the region.

## How does a nation change its economic system?

For more than 70 years, the Soviet government made all the important economic decisions in the region. This cartoon illustrates a major economic challenge faced by the region's new leaders, as demonstrated here by former Russian president Boris Yeltsin. The leaders are trying to move their nations from a command economy to a market economy.

## CASESTUDY

### How have Soviet decisions affected new leaders?

In 1965, Soviet officials exploded a nuclear bomb to create this lake in Kazakhstan. The blast exposed nearby residents to harmful radiation. The region's new leaders inherited many problems caused by Soviet nuclear programs.

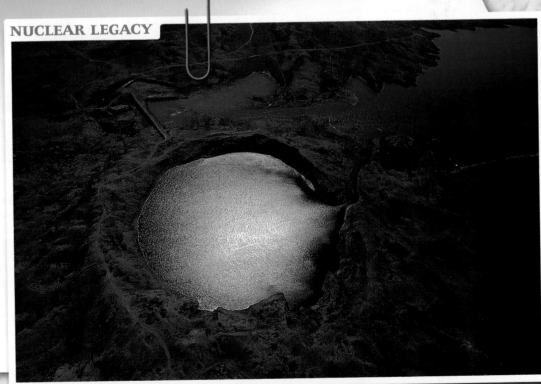

NUCLEAR LEGACY

PHYSICAL GEOGRAPHY OF
RUSSIA AND THE REPUBLICS

# A Land of Extremes

Russia's Lake Baikal is the
world's deepest lake and
holds over 20 percent of the
earth's fresh water. Russians
treasure Lake Baikal as
much as Americans treasure
the Grand Canyon.

## GeoFocus

**How do the extremes of
physical geography in Russia
and the Republics affect the
lives of the region's people?**

**Taking Notes** Copy the graphic organizer
below into your notebook. Use it to record
information from the chapter about the physical
geography of Russia and the Republics.

| Landforms | |
| --- | --- |
| Resources | |
| Climate and Vegetation | |
| Human-Environment Interaction | |

# Landforms and Resources

## Main Ideas

- Flat plains stretch across the western and central areas of the region. In the south and east, the terrain is more mountainous.
- Many resources in Russia and the Republics are in hard-to-reach regions with brutal climates.

## Places & Terms

chernozem

Ural Mountains

Eurasia

Transcaucasia

Central Asia

Siberia

## CONNECT TO THE ISSUES

ECONOMIC CHANGE
Leaders must strike a balance between environmental protection and economic growth.

**A HUMAN PERSPECTIVE** Russia and the Republics occupy a tremendous expanse of territory—approximately three times the land area of the United States. The region sprawls across the continents of both Europe and Asia and crosses 11 time zones. When laborers in the western city of Kaliningrad are leaving their jobs after a day's work, herders on the region's Pacific coast are just beginning to awaken their animals for the next day's grazing.

## Northern Landforms

The geography of Russia and the Republics is the geography of nearly one-sixth of the earth's land surface—over eight and a half million square miles. In spite of this huge size, the region's landforms follow a simple overall pattern. You can divide the northern two-thirds of the region into four different areas. Moving from west to east, they are the Northern European Plain, the West Siberian Plain, the Central Siberian Plateau, and the Russian Far East. (See the physical map on pages 336–337 of the Unit Atlas.)

**THE NORTHERN EUROPEAN PLAIN** The Northern European Plain is an extensive lowland area. It stretches for over 1,000 miles from the western border of Russia and the Republics to the Ural Mountains.

One of the world's most fertile soils—**chernozem,** or black earth—is abundant on this plain. It sometimes occurs in layers three feet deep or more. Because of the high quality of its soil, many of the region's agricultural areas are located on this plain.

Nearly 75 percent of the region's 290 million people live on this plain. Three of the region's largest cities are located there: Moscow, Russia's capital; St. Petersburg; and Kiev, the capital of Ukraine.

**PLACE** Ukraine, which lies on the Northern European Plain, has been called the region's breadbasket because of the enormous grain crops produced on its farms.

# HUMAN GEOGRAPHY OF RUSSIA AND THE REPUBLICS
# A Diverse Heritage

## Three Subregions of Russia and the Republics

Russia and the Western Republics
Transcaucasia
Central Asia

500    1,000 miles
500    1,000 kilometers
Two-Point Equidistant Projection

## GeoFocus

### How did Russia's expansion affect the region's geography?

**Taking Notes** In your notebook, copy a cluster diagram like the one shown. As you read, take notes about the history, economics, culture, and modern life of each subregion of Russia and the Republics.

# Russia and the Western Republics

## 1

**Main Ideas**

• From modest beginnings, Russia expanded to become the largest country in the world.

• The rise and fall of the Soviet Union affected the world's political geography.

**Places & Terms**

**Baltic Republics**

**czar**

**Russian Revolution**

**USSR**

**Cold War**

**command economy**

**collective farm**

**CONNECT TO THE ISSUES**

ECONOMIC CHANGE The region is struggling to move from a command economy to a market economy.

**A HUMAN PERSPECTIVE** Early in the 1500s, the Russian leader Ivan the Great put an end to two centuries of foreign rule in his homeland. Russia then entered a period of explosive growth. From its center in Moscow, Russia expanded at a rate of about 55 square miles a day for the next four centuries. During the expansion, Russians made so much progress toward the east that they swallowed up a future U.S. state, Alaska. Russia had taken control of the territory by the late 18th century but did not sell it to the United States until 1867.

## A History of Expansion

Russia's growth had lasting effects on nearby lands and peoples. You can see these effects even today in the republics to its west: Belarus, Moldova, Ukraine and the **Baltic Republics** of Estonia, Latvia and Lithuania. But Russian expansion not only affected its neighbors. It also had an impact on the entire world's political geography.

**BIRTH OF AN EMPIRE** The Russian state began in the region between the Baltic and Black seas. In the ninth century, Vikings from Scandinavia came to the region to take advantage of the river trade between the two seas. They established a settlement near what is now Kiev, a city near the Dnieper River. In time, the Vikings adopted the customs of the local Slavic population. Soon the settlement began to expand.

Expansion was halted in the 13th century with the arrival of invaders from Mongolia, called Tatars. The ferocity of those Mongol warriors is legendary. It is said that "like molten lava, they destroyed everything in their path." The Tatars sacked Kiev between 1237 and 1240.

The Mongols controlled the region until the 1500s, when Ivan the Great, the powerful prince of Moscow, put an end to their rule. Russia continued once again to expand to the east. By the end of the 17th century, it had built an empire that extended to the Pacific Ocean. As the leaders of Russia added more territory to their empire, they also added more people. Many of these people belonged to different ethnic groups, spoke different languages, and practiced different religions.

**MOVEMENT** This Mongol armor from the 14th or 15th century includes a case for bow and arrows. Mongol warriors were skilled archers, even on horseback.

RUSSIA & REP.

# Comparing Cultures

## Homes and Shelters

The geography of the region in which people live influences the nature of their homes and shelters. People who live in forested areas, for example, might build log cabins. People living in grasslands, on the other hand, may use thatch—plant stalks and leaves—to build their homes. On these two pages, you will learn how homes in different parts of the world reflect local geographic possibilities and limitations.

Greenland

Kyrgyzstan

Spain

Indonesia

**Arctic peoples in Canada and Greenland** take advantage of their environment by using blocks of snow to build dome-shaped winter shelters called igloos. They sometimes add windows made with sheets of ice or seal intestines.

**The portable yurts of Kyrgyz herders** are suited to their nomadic lifestyle.

The Korowai of Irian Jaya, Indonesia, live in tree houses that protect them from rival tribes, as well as the insects, scorpions, and snakes of the rain forest.

People in the Spanish town of Guadix have turned underground caves into homes to protect against the region's extreme temperatures.

## GeoActivity

**CREATING AN EXHIBIT**
Working with a partner, use the Internet to do research on homes in a region other than those shown on these two pages. Create an **exhibit** that shows the relationship between the region and its homes.

- Construct a model of the homes you are researching.
- Add a world map to the exhibit that shows where the homes are located.

**RESEARCH LINKS**
CLASSZONE.COM

## GeoData

**Igloos**
- The blocks of snow in an igloo are about 2 feet high, 4 feet long, and 8 inches thick.
- An experienced builder can finish an igloo in one to two hours.

**Caves**
- About 50 percent of Guadix's inhabitants live underground.
- Some of Guadix's caves are quite luxurious, with marble floors, modern kitchens, fax machines, and Internet connections.

**Tree Houses**
- The Korowai people build tree houses as high as 150 feet above ground.
- Korowai tree houses have separate areas for men and women, each with its own entrance.

**Yurts**
- A nomadic family can set up their yurt in approximately a half-hour.
- Felt—the material used to cover yurts—is a fabric of compressed animal fibers, such as wool or fur.

Africa is the world's second largest continent. Its unique location—almost centered over the equator—affects its vegetation, climate, and population patterns.

**LOCATION**
A man prays in front of the pyramids at Giza in Egypt.

**MOVEMENT**
People travel to a market outside of Mali's Great Mosque in Djenné. The mosque is one of the world's largest mud-brick buildings.

**REGION** Around 650 million of Africa's 800 million people live south of the Sahara. They are divided into more than 800 ethnic groups, each with its own language, religion, and culture.

**HUMAN-ENVIRONMENT INTERACTION** Roughly two-thirds of all Africans live in rural areas or small villages and earn a living as farmers.

**PLACE** The ancient Romans called the continent Africa, possibly from the Latin *aprica,* meaning "sunny," or the Greek *aphrike,* meaning "without cold."

**For more information on Africa . . .**

RESEARCH LINKS
CLASSZONE.COM

**PLACE** Africa's tallest mountain, Mount Kilimanjaro, towers above northeastern Tanzania as a giraffe roams the grassy plain below.

# Disasters!

## Famine in Somalia

Famine—an extreme and long-term shortage of food—causes widespread hunger and sometimes death to millions of people. Natural causes, such as weather, plant diseases, and massive insect infestations, can cause famine. Drought is the most common natural cause. In addition, human beings can cause famine. Wars and political violence often destroy crops and prevent the adequate distribution of food. The worst famines usually involve a combination of both human and natural causes. The Horn of Africa, which includes Ethiopia and Somalia, has been the site of recent famines in the 1980s and 1990s.

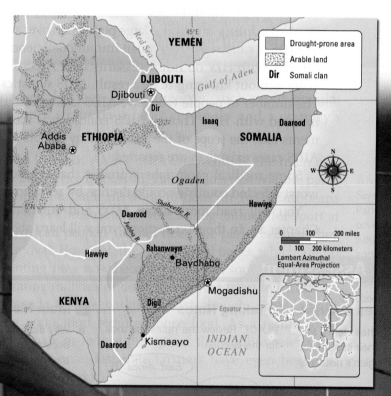

## Natural Causes

A lack of rain in successive seasons resulted in drought. Drought prevented the growth of enough food to feed the country's population.

## Human Causes

Somali gunmen often looted relief shipments and then extracted payment for protecting relief workers. Other political causes, such as disagreements between warring factions, also prevented the delivery of food supplies.

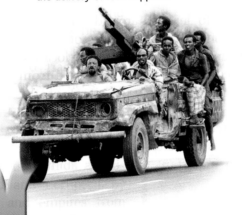

**Results**

Thirsty Somalis plead for water delivered by the International Red Cross in Baidoa, Somalia, in 1992. Aid agencies estimated that famine killed between 25 and 50 people a day in this town in 1992.

## GeoActivity

**UNDERSTANDING FAMINE**
Working with a partner, use the Internet to research different international aid organizations. Then write a **news report** about those organizations.

• Create a visual aid comparing the various groups.

• Include information about how the groups are funded.

**RESEARCH LINKS**
CLASSZONE.COM

## GeoData

**FAMINE IN SOMALIA**
In the early 1990s, more than 300,000 Somalis died of famine, and another 30,000 died in a related civil war.

• Principal causes included drought, desertification, and civil war.

• Underlying causes, such as increased growth of cash crops and reliance on livestock, stemmed from a history of foreign intervention dating back to Italian and British colonization in the 19th century.

**OTHER FAMINES**

**1876–1878 India**
Drought caused famine that killed about five million people.

**1932–1934 Soviet Union**
Between six and eight million peasants died because of actions by the government.

**1958–1960 China**
Around 20 million people died during government reforms.

**Southwest Asia, sometimes called
a cradle of civilization, is the home
of oil rich lands, vast deserts, and
difficult political problems.**

**HUMAN-ENVIRONMENT INTERACTION**
Flares of burning natural gas are common
sights at oil wells in the Al-Ghawar oil field
in Saudi Arabia.

**PLACE** Two holy places in Jerusalem, Israel, can be
seen in this photograph: a shrine known as the Dome of
the Rock, which is sacred to Muslims, and the Western
Wall, a spot sacred to Jews.

## GeoData

**REGION** More than half of the world's oil reserves are found in this region.

**HUMAN-ENVIRONMENT INTERACTION** Some experts believe that the freshwater supplies of the Arabian peninsula will be exhausted in the next 25 to 30 years.

**LOCATION** Southwest Asia connects three continents: Europe, Asia, and Africa.

**For more information on Southwest Asia . . .**

**RESEARCH LINKS**
CLASSZONE.COM

**SW ASIA**

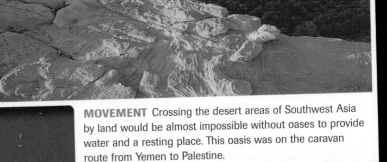

**MOVEMENT** Crossing the desert areas of Southwest Asia by land would be almost impossible without oases to provide water and a resting place. This oasis was on the caravan route from Yemen to Palestine.

# Today's Issues in Southwest Asia

Today, Southwest Asia faces the issues previewed here. As you read Chapters 21 and 22, you will learn helpful background information. You will study the issues themselves in Chapter 23.

In a small group, answer the questions below. Then participate in a class discussion of your answers.

## Exploring the Issues

1. **POPULATION RELOCATION** Think about why a group of people may leave a place they call home. What problems might relocation cause for the group? Then make a list of the reasons people relocate and the problems that are caused by moving.

2. **ECONOMIC DEVELOPMENT** Make a list of major rivers found in the region and a list of major rivers found in the United States. How do the lists compare? What does this suggest about scarce resources in the region?

3. **RELIGIOUS CONFLICT** Study the cartoon on page 477. Who are the figures in the cartoon?

For more on these issues in Southwest Asia . . .

**CURRENT EVENTS**
CLASSZONE.COM

## POPULATION RELOCATION

### What kind of population movement is taking place in Southwest Asia?

This nomadic Kurdish family rests in the hills of eastern Turkey. The Kurds claim a homeland that crosses the boundaries of five countries: Turkey, Iraq, Iran, Syria, and Armenia.

## ECONOMIC DEVELOPMENT

### How can oil wealth help develop the region's economies?

Wealth from oil wells, like this one located at Al Ghawar in Saudi Arabia, may be used to develop economic activities that do not depend on oil.

## CASESTUDY

### Who should control Jerusalem?

In this cartoon, the dove symbolizes peace between Arabs and Israelis in Southwest Asia. Jerusalem plays a vital role in the peace process.

## RELIGIOUS CONFLICT

# Unit ATLAS

## Patterns of Physical Geography

Use the Unit Atlas to add to your knowledge of Southwest Asia. As you look at the maps and charts, notice geographic patterns and specific details about the region. For example, the chart gives details about the mountains and deserts of Southwest Asia.

After studying the graphics and physical map on these two pages, jot down answers to the following questions in your notebook.

### Making Comparisons

**1.** Which of Southwest Asia's deserts is about the same size as the Mojave Desert of the United States?

**2.** How do the tallest mountains of Southwest Asia compare to the tallest U.S. mountain?

**3.** Which mountain chains cut off Turkey and Iran from the rest of the region? How might isolation affect the way a country develops economically?

**For updated statistics on Southwest Asia . . .**

### ⓘ DATA UPDATE
CLASSZONE.COM

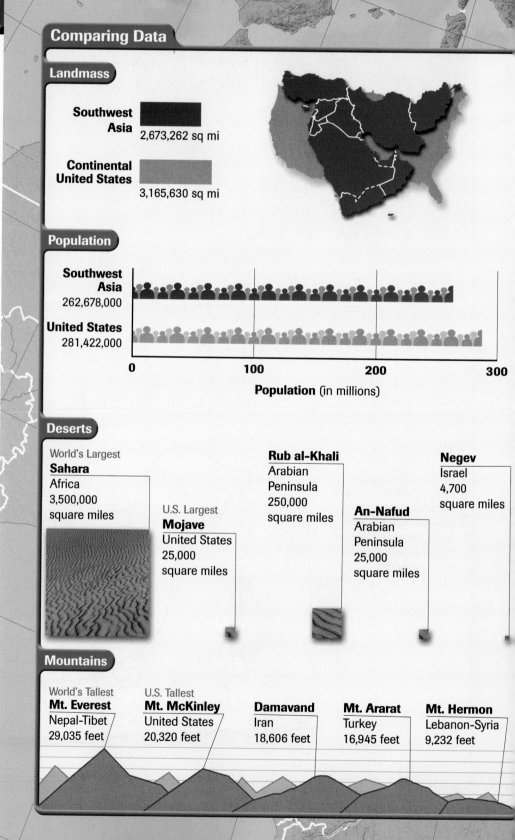

## Comparing Data

### Landmass

**Southwest Asia** 2,673,262 sq mi

**Continental United States** 3,165,630 sq mi

### Population

**Southwest Asia** 262,678,000

**United States** 281,422,000

**Population** (in millions)
0    100    200    300

### Deserts

World's Largest
**Sahara**
Africa
3,500,000
square miles

U.S. Largest
**Mojave**
United States
25,000
square miles

**Rub al-Khali**
Arabian
Peninsula
250,000
square miles

**An-Nafud**
Arabian
Peninsula
25,000
square miles

**Negev**
Israel
4,700
square miles

### Mountains

World's Tallest
**Mt. Everest**
Nepal-Tibet
29,035 feet

U.S. Tallest
**Mt. McKinley**
United States
20,320 feet

**Damavand**
Iran
18,606 feet

**Mt. Ararat**
Turkey
16,945 feet

**Mt. Hermon**
Lebanon-Syria
9,232 feet

**478** UNIT 7

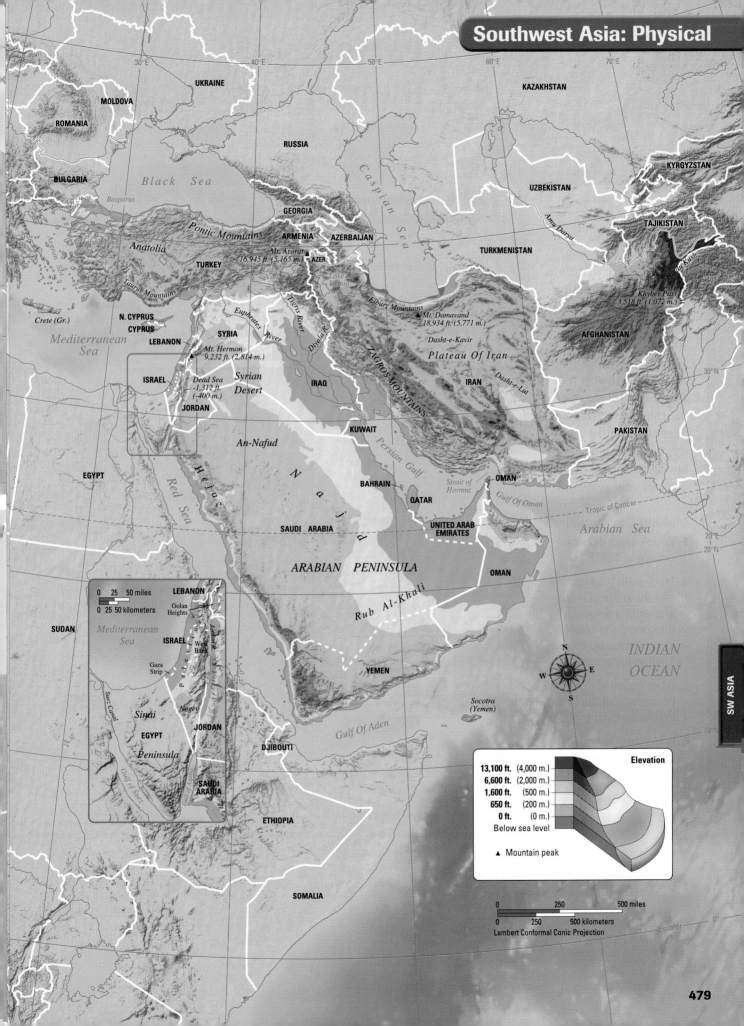

UKRAINE

MOLDOVA

ROMANIA

BULGARIA

*Black Sea*

RUSSIA

KAZAKHSTAN

KYRGYZSTAN

GEORGIA

ARMENIA AZERBAIJAN

*Caspian Sea*

UZBEKISTAN

TAJIKISTAN

*Pontic Mountains*

*Anatolia*

TURKEY

Mt. Ararat
16,945 ft. (5,165 m.) ▲ AZER.

*Lake Urmia*

TURKMENISTAN

*Amu Darya*

*Hindu Kush*

Khyber Pass
3,518 ft. (1,072 m.)

*Taurus Mountains*

N. CYPRUS
CYPRUS

*Crete (Gr.)*

*Mediterranean Sea*

LEBANON

SYRIA

*Euphrates River*

*Tigris River*

*Diyala R.*

*Elburz Mountains*

▲ Mt. Damavand
18,934 ft. (5,771 m.)

*Dasht-e Kavir*

AFGHANISTAN

Mt. Hermon
9,232 ft. (2,814 m.) ▲

*Plateau Of Iran*

*Syrian Desert*

ISRAEL

Dead Sea
-1,312 ft.
(-400 m.)

IRAQ

*ZAGROS MOUNTAINS*

IRAN

*Dasht-e Lut*

PAKISTAN

JORDAN

*An-Nafud*

KUWAIT

EGYPT

*Hejaz*

*N a j d*

*Red Sea*

BAHRAIN

*Persian Gulf*

*Strait of Hormuz*

OMAN

QATAR

*Gulf Of Oman*

Tropic of Cancer

UNITED ARAB
EMIRATES

SAUDI ARABIA

*Arabian Sea*

*ARABIAN PENINSULA*

OMAN

*Rub Al-Khali*

YEMEN

*INDIAN OCEAN*

N
W   E
S

SUDAN

LEBANON

Golan
Heights

ISRAEL

West
Bank

*Jordan R.*

Gaza
Strip

*Palestine*

*Dead Sea*

*Mediterranean Sea*

*Negev*

JORDAN

*Socotra (Yemen)*

*Gulf Of Aden*

SW ASIA

*Suez Canal*

*Sinai*

EGYPT

*Peninsula*

*Gulf of Suez*

SAUDI
ARABIA

DJIBOUTI

0   25   50 miles
0   25 50 kilometers

ETHIOPIA

### Elevation

13,100 ft.  (4,000 m.)
6,600 ft.  (2,000 m.)
1,600 ft.  (500 m.)
650 ft.  (200 m.)
0 ft.  (0 m.)
Below sea level

▲  Mountain peak

SOMALIA

0        250        500 miles
0     250    500 kilometers
Lambert Conformal Conic Projection

*Equator*

PHYSICAL GEOGRAPHY OF SOUTHWEST ASIA
# Harsh and Arid Lands

**Wind-shaped sand dunes
in Arabia's An-Nafud
Desert sometimes reach
a height of 600 feet.**

## GeoFocus

### Why does the physical geography make this a vital region?

**Taking Notes** Copy the graphic organizer below into your notebook. Use it to record information from the chapter about the physical geography of Southwest Asia.

| | |
|---|---|
| Landforms | |
| Resources | |
| Climate and Vegetation | |
| Human–Environment Interaction | |

# Landforms and Resources

## Main Ides

- The Southwest Asian landforms have had a major impact on movement in the region.
- The most valuable resources in Southwest Asia are oil and water.

## Places & Terms

**Golan Heights**

**wadi**

**Tigris River**

**Euphrates River**

**Jordan River**

**Dead Sea**

### CONNECT TO THE ISSUES

RESOURCES Enormous oil reserves have brought changes to the economic and political standing of this region.

**A HUMAN PERSPECTIVE** Artillery shells and sniper fire rained down on the lands below a small plateau in southwestern Syria. Airplanes bombed the military positions on the plateau itself. Families in nearby villages huddled in their homes, hoping for the shelling to stop. Israeli Army engineers struggled to build a road to enable tanks to reach the top. Thousands died in the 1967 war when Syria and Israel fought for control of the **Golan Heights,** also called Al Jawlan, a hilly plateau overlooking the Jordan River and the Sea of Galilee. This landform's strategic location has made it the site of conflict in Southwest Asia for decades. It is one of many landforms that divide the region.

## Landforms Divide the Region

People sometimes picture Southwest Asia as a region of rippling sand dunes and parched land occasionally interrupted with an oasis. But the lands of Southwest Asia actually range from green coastal plains to snow-peaked mountains. Southwest Asia forms a land bridge connecting Asia, Africa, and Europe. As you can see on the map on page 37, the region is situated at the edge of a huge tectonic plate. Parts of the Arabian Peninsula are pulling away from Africa, and parts of the Anatolian Peninsula are sliding past parts of Asia. Still other plates are pushing up mountains in other areas of the Asian continent.

**PENINSULAS AND WATERWAYS** The most distinctive landform in Southwest Asia is the Arabian Peninsula, which is separated from the continent of Africa by the Red Sea on the southwest and from the rest of Asia by the Persian Gulf on the east. The Red Sea covers a rift valley created by the movement of the Arabian plate. The Zagros, Elburz, and Taurus mountains at the north side of the plate cut off part of the region from the south. Another important landform in the region is the Anatolian Peninsula, which is occupied by the country of Turkey. It marks the beginning of the Asian continent. (See the map on page 479.)

Both peninsulas border on strategic waterways. On the southwest side of the Arabian Peninsula are the Red Sea and a strategic opening to the Mediterranean Sea—the Suez Canal. Goods from Asia flow through this canal to ports in Europe and North Africa.

PLACE The Golan Heights are a strategic location near the source of water in the region. **How will control of this area affect those who live on lands below the top of the plateau?**

SW ASIA

487

The Anatolian Peninsula is located between the Black Sea and the Mediterranean Sea. Two narrow waterways, the Bosporus Strait and the Dardenelles Strait, are situated at the west end of the peninsula. Both straits have always been highly desirable locations for controlling trade and transportation to Russia and the interior of Asia.

Farther south is a narrow passageway leading from the Arabian Sea to the Persian Gulf called the Straits of Hormuz. These straits are the only waterway to the huge oilfields of Kuwait, Saudi Arabia, and Iraq. Because access to oil is essential to the world-wide economy, this water-way is very important.

**BACKGROUND**
The Persian Gulf is also called the Arabian Gulf.

**PLAINS AND HIGHLANDS** Much of the Arabian Peninsula is covered by plains. Because of the dry, sandy, and windy conditions, few activities using the land take place here. Most of the land is barren with some low hills, ridges, and **wadis,** which are riverbeds that remain dry except during the rainy seasons. On the southwestern corner of the peninsula, a range of mountains—the Hejaz Mountains—pokes out of the land. People living on the Arabian Peninsula have adapted to the harsh conditions by living nomadic lives in search of water.

The heart of Iran is a plateau surrounded by mountains. Isolated and very high, the land is a stony, salty, and sandy desert. The foothills surrounding the plateau are able to produce some crops. Much of the Anatolian Peninsula is also a plateau. Some areas are productive for agriculture, while other areas support flocks of grazing animals such as sheep and goats. The Northern Plain of Afghanistan, a well-watered agricultural area, is surrounded by high mountains that isolate it from other parts of the region.

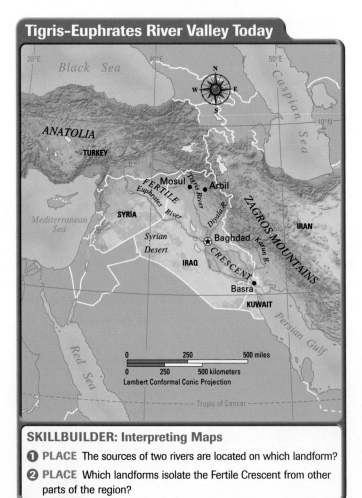

## Tigris-Euphrates River Valley Today

**SKILLBUILDER: Interpreting Maps**

❶ **PLACE** The sources of two rivers are located on which landform?

❷ **PLACE** Which landforms isolate the Fertile Crescent from other parts of the region?

**Geographic Thinking**

**Making Comparisons**
Ⓐ How are the plateaus of Iran and Anatolia different?

**MOUNTAINS** Rugged mountains divide the land and countries. As you study the map on page 479, you will see that the Hindu Kush Mountains of Afghanistan are linked with other ranges of mountains that frame southern Asia. Afghanistan is land-locked and mountainous, so contact with the outside world is difficult.

The Zagros Mountains on the western side of Iran help isolate that country from the rest of Southwest Asia. The Elburz Mountains south of the Caspian Sea cut off easy access to that body of water by Iran. Finally, the Taurus Mountains separate Turkey from the rest of Southwest Asia. In spite of these physical barriers, people, goods, and ideas move through the entire region. One of the ways they move is by water.

## 5 THEMES

### PLACE

#### The Dead Sea

The Dead Sea is a landlocked salt lake, so salty that almost nothing can live in the water. It has been described as the world's largest spa. (A spa is a place with healing waters.) For thousands of years, people have come to the edges of the landlocked sea to bathe in its mineral waters and soak in its black mineral mud.

Imagine floating in water so salty that you cannot sink. Salt concentration in the Dead Sea water is 31.5 percent, nine times higher than in the world's oceans. The evaporation rate of the water is about 55 inches per year, keeping the water very salty despite the flow of fresh water from the Jordan River.

**WATER BODIES** Southwest Asia is almost completely surrounded by bodies of water. They provide vital avenues for trade and access to other parts of the region and to the rest of the world. However, because much of the region is arid, there are few rivers that flow the entire year. As you can see on the map on page 488, two of the most important rivers—the **Tigris** and the **Euphrates**—supported several ancient river valley civilizations in an area called the Fertile Crescent. They included Sumerians, Assyrians, Babylonians, and Chaldeans.

Today, the Tigris and Euphrates flow through parts of Turkey, Syria, and Iraq. The valleys are fertile, well watered, and good for agriculture. The two rivers flow almost parallel to each other for hundreds of miles before joining at a place called Shatt al Arab. They spread out into slow moving water and swamps, finally emptying into the Persian Gulf. **B**

Tumbling down from the mountains of Lebanon near Mt. Hermon, the **Jordan River** provides one of the most precious resources in the entire region—water. Farther south, the river serves as a natural boundary between Israel and Jordan. The Jordan River flows into the salty waters of the **Dead Sea,** a landlocked salt lake. The Dead Sea is so salty that only bacteria can live in the waters. Thousands of years ago the earth was heaved up on the south end of the area now controlled by Israel. The outlet to the sea was blocked, creating the salt lake. The Dead Sea is 1,349 feet below sea level—the lowest place on the exposed crust of the earth. (See The Dead Sea, above.)

**CONNECT TO THE ISSUES**
**B** RESOURCES
Why is control of water resources important in this region?

## Resources for a Modern World

It is almost impossible to think about resources in Southwest Asia without including oil. It is the region's most abundant resource. Major oil

# Comparing Cultures

## Religious Architecture

Throughout the world and across time, people have created spaces in their communities for the worship of God. Sometimes the space is reserved for only a special few, such as priests. Other times the space is designed to bring many worshippers together to create a sense of community. Religious requirements, available building materials, and artistic expression come together in the "houses of god."

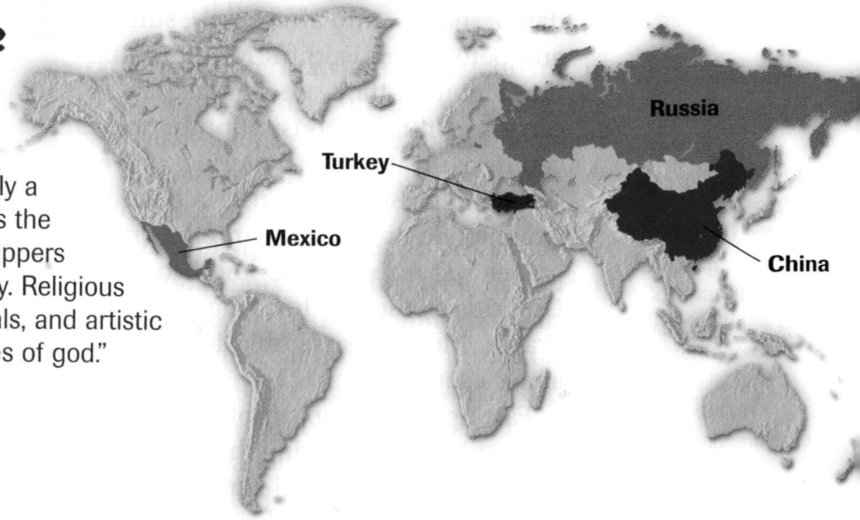

Russia

Turkey

Mexico

China

**A Buddhist temple, such as this one located in Chufu, China,** is sometimes called a pagoda. The temple itself usually is a wooden hall with several tiled roofs that curve up on the edges.

**The Sultan Ahmed Cami Mosque in Turkey is** considered one of the finest examples of Muslim religious architecture. Most mosques feature a minaret, a slender tower from which believers are called to prayer. This mosque is unusual because it has six minarets.

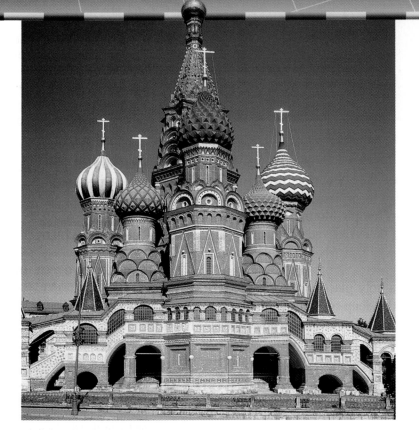

**St. Basil's Cathedral in Moscow, Russia,** is really eight smaller churches around a main one. The basic plan of the church forms a cross. The exterior was originally white. The colorful domes are covered with roof tiles that were added in the 17th century.

**The Pyramid of the Sun in Mexico** is the largest Meso-American religious structure. Its size was designed to inspire awe in the worshipper. A small temple on the top was usually visited only by priests.

## GeoActivity

### CREATING A MODEL

Choose one of the major religions of the world. With a small group, use the Internet to research more about the religious architecture of that religion.

- Create a model of a worship space showing the unique aspects of that religion's architecture.

- Create a brochure explaining your model.

**RESEARCH LINKS**
CLASSZONE.COM

## GeoData

### PLACES OF WORSHIP

**THE MOSQUE**

- Muslims are instructed to face toward Mecca when they pray. Inside the mosque, a special recess in the wall—*mihrab*—marks the direction of Mecca.

- The Sultan Ahmed Cami Mosque is also called the Blue Mosque because of the bluish haze given to the interior by 21,043 blue-glazed tiles on the walls.

**THE PYRAMID**

- Standing 216 feet high and 720 by 760 feet at the base, the Pyramid of the Sun is one of the largest structures of its type in the Western Hemisphere.

**ST. BASIL'S CATHEDRAL**

- St. Basil's was built by Ivan IV, also called Ivan the Terrible, as an offering to God for military victories over Tatar armies.

- Legend has it that the architect of St. Basil's was blinded so that he could never create anything similar to St. Basil's.

# Disasters!

## Earthquake in Turkey

As the Arabian Plate pushes northward, it squeezes the Anatolian Plate into the Eurasian Plate. Caught like a slippery seed squeezed between two fingers, the Anatolian Plate slips westward. This movement causes the earth to quake. At 3 A.M. on August 17, 1999, residents of Gölcük, a city near Izmit, Turkey, were thrown from their beds by 45 seconds of earth-shaking terror. When it was over, the quake—which measured 7.4 on the Richter Scale—had taken the lives of 17,000 people and caused billions of dollars of damage.

Izmit, Turkey, was at the epicenter of the quake. It is located on one of the world's most active fault lines—the North Anatolian Fault. Since 1939, 11 major quakes have hit along the Anatolian Fault Line.

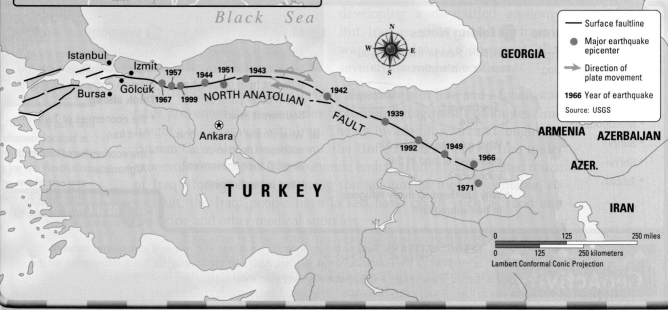

Surface faultline

Major earthquake epicenter

Direction of plate movement

**1966** Year of earthquake

Source: USGS

0   125   250 miles
0   125   250 kilometers
Lambert Conformal Conic Projection

The quake destroyed 85,000 buildings. Many of the buildings were poorly constructed with inferior building materials. Floors of buildings "pancaked" and crushed the residents.

About 40,000 families were made homeless by the quake. Survivors were housed in 168 tent cities. Unfortunately, few were winterized, and thousands of people shivered through Turkey's winter.

## GeoData

### THE MERCALLI INTENSITY SCALE
- The Mercalli Intensity Scale measures an earthquake's effect on people and buildings.
- Mercalli ranges from I to XII. Here are some examples.

| | |
|---|---|
| **I.** | No damage |
| **VI.** | Pictures fall off the wall |
| **VII.** | Slight damage to structures |
| **X.** | Most masonry structures destroyed; landslides; ground cracked |
| **XII.** | Total damage |

### RICHTER SCALE
- The Richter Scale measures the magnitude of energy released during an earthquake.
- Here are some examples of Richter Scale measurements:

| | |
|---|---|
| **2** | Just felt |
| **4.5** | Damage newsworthy |
| **7** | A major quake |
| **8** | Great damage |
| **8.9** | Largest quake ever recorded |

# South Asia

South Asia includes the Indian subcontinent and its nearby island It is a region of ancient cultures, spectacular landforms, and rapidl growing populations.

**PLACE** The Taj Mahal, at Agra, India, is said to be one of the world's most beautiful buildings. Constructed of marble, it was built in the 17th century by Emperor Shah Jahan as a tomb for his wife.

## GeoData

**LOCATION** South Asia is mainly a triangular peninsula that juts out from the Asian mainland into the Indian Ocean.

**REGION** The seven countries of South Asia have great cultural and religious diversity.

**HUMAN-ENVIRONMENT INTERACTION** Life in South Asia is greatly influenced by its varied landforms and its extreme weather, especially the seasonal monsoons.

**For more information on South Asia . . .**

**RESEARCH LINKS**
**CLASSZONE.COM**

**LOCATION** Elephants wearing richly decorated cloth coverings are central figures in the 14-night Esala Perahera festival in Kandy, Sri Lanka. It is one of many religious festivals held in South Asia.

**REGION** The world's highest mountains, the majestic snow-capped Himalayas, form the northern border of the Indian subcontinent. Mt. Everest, to the left, is the world's tallest peak at 29,035 feet.

SOUTH ASIA

# Today's Issues in South Asia

Today, South Asia faces the issues previewed here. As you read Chapters 24 and 25, you will learn helpful background information. You will study the issues themselves in Chapter 26.

In a small group, answer the questions below. Then have a class discussion of your answers.

## Exploring the Issues

1. **POPULATION** What might be some of the effects of rapid population growth on both humans and the environment?

2. **EXTREME WEATHER** Consider news stories that you have heard or read about that refer to extreme weather in various parts of South Asia. Make a list of the types of extreme weather that affect South Asians.

3. **TERRITORIAL DISPUTE** Search the Internet for the latest information about the dispute over Kashmir. What position does each side hold?

For more on these issues in South Asia . . .

**CURRENT EVENTS**
CLASSZONE.COM

**POPULATION EXPLOSION**

## How can South Asia's population growth be managed?

Many problems come with rapid population growth, including crowded cities. Kolkata, pictured here, had a population of more than 4 million in the 1990s, and a population density of more than 61,900 persons per square mile.

## EXTREME WEATHER

### How do people cope with extreme weather?

People find a way to continue with their lives despite the severe flooding that plagues South Asia during the summer monsoons. Residents of Dhaka, Bangladesh, shown here, navigate flooded streets as best they can.

## CaseStudy

### How can India and Pakistan resolve their dispute over Kashmir?

India and Pakistan have spent millions of dollars to develop nuclear weapons in their continuing dispute over Kashmir. This has left less money to spend on improving the lives of their citizens.

TERRITORIAL DISPUTE

As you saw on the map on page 543, natural barriers help to separate the South Asian subcontinent from the rest of Asia. The Himalayas and other mountain ranges form the northern border, while water surrounds the rest of the region. The South Asian peninsula, which extends south into the Indian Ocean, is bordered by the Arabian Sea to the west and the Bay of Bengal to the east.

**NORTHERN MOUNTAINS** Millions of years ago, the land that is now South Asia was actually part of East Africa. About 50 million years ago, it split off and drifted northward. As the illustration on page 551 shows, it collided with Central Asia. The gradual collision of these two large tectonic plates forced the land upward into enormous mountain ranges. These mountains, which are still rising, now form the northern edge of the South Asian subcontinent.

The magnificent Himalayas are a system of parallel mountain ranges. They contain the world's highest mountains, with nearly two dozen peaks rising to 24,000 feet or above. The Himalayas stretch for 1,500 miles and form a giant barrier between the Indian subcontinent and China. Mt. Everest, the world's tallest peak, sits at the heart of the Himalayas. Nestled high up within these mountains are the remote, landlocked kingdoms of Nepal and Bhutan. Ⓐ

The Hindu Kush are mountains that lie at the west end of the Himalayas. They form a rugged barrier separating Pakistan from Afghanistan to the north. For centuries, the Hindu Kush stood in the way of Central Asian tribes trying to invade India. Bloody battles have been fought over control of major land routes through these mountains, including the Khyber Pass. The mighty Karakoram Mountains rise in the northeastern portion of the chain. They are the home of the world's second highest peak, K2.

**SOUTHERN PLATEAUS** The collision of tectonic plates that pushed up the Himalayas also created several smaller mountain ranges in central India, including the Vindhya (VIHN·dyuh) Range. To the south lies the Deccan Plateau. This large tableland tilts east, toward the Bay of Bengal, and covers much of southern India. Two mountain ranges, the Western Ghats and the Eastern Ghats, flank the plateau, separating it from the coast. These mountains also block most moist winds and keep rain from reaching the interior. As a result, the Deccan is a largely arid region.

## Rivers, Deltas, and Plains

The Northern Indian Plain, or Indo-Gangetic Plain, lies between the Deccan Plateau and the northern mountain ranges. This large lowland region stretches across northern India and into Bangladesh. It is formed by three great river systems: the Indus, the Ganges, and the Brahmaputra.

**GREAT RIVERS** The three great rivers of South Asia have their origins among the snowcapped peaks of the high

As you saw on the map on page 543

As the illustration on page 551 shows

---

**Connect TO THE Issues**

**EXTREME WEATHER**

**THE GANGES DELTA**

Water, water, and more water! Three major rivers meet in Bangladesh to form the Ganges Delta at the Bay of Bengal, shown in the satellite photo below. They are the Brahmaputra, the Ganges, and the Meghna.

These rivers bring rich alluvial soil to the delta, a region covering 65,500 square miles. But above all, these rivers bring water. Every summer, melting snow and monsoon-driven rains force the rivers to burst their banks. In fact, so much water comes that central Bangladesh is turned into an inland sea before the land dries.

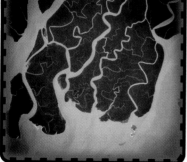

---

**Geographic Thinking**

**Seeing Patterns**

Ⓐ What role have the Himalayas played in the development of Nepal and Bhutan?

**BACKGROUND**
The name *Himalayas* is Sanskrit for "abode of snow."

Himalayas. The Indus flows west and then south through Pakistan to the Arabian Sea. The Ganges drops down from the central Himalayas and flows eastward across northern India. The Brahmaputra winds its way east, then west and south through Bangladesh. The Ganges and Brahmaputra eventually meet to form one huge river delta before entering the Bay of Bengal.

**FERTILE PLAINS** These rivers play a key role in supporting life in South Asia. Their waters provide crucial irrigation for agricultural lands. They also carry rich soil, called alluvial soil, on their journey down from the mountains. When the rivers overflow their banks, they deposit this soil on **alluvial plains,** lands that are rich farmlands. As a result, the Indo-Gangetic Plain is one of the most fertile farming regions in the world.

The Indo-Gangetic Plain is also the most heavily populated part of South Asia. In fact, the area contains about three-fifths of India's population. Many of the subcontinent's largest cities, including New Delhi and Kolkata in India, and Dakha in Bangladesh, are located there. Population densities at the eastern end of the plain, particularly in the Ganges-Brahmaputra delta, are especially high, as you can see on the map on page 547. To the west, in the area between the Indus and Ganges rivers, the plain becomes drier and requires more irrigation. To the south lies one of the world's most arid regions—the Thar, or Great Indian Desert. **B**

**Geographic Thinking**

**Using the Atlas**
**B** Use the map on page 543. Locate the Thar Desert. What two countries share its land?

## Offshore Islands

Two island groups are also countries of South Asia—Sri Lanka and the Maldives. Sri Lanka is located in the Indian Ocean just off India's southeastern tip. The Maldives island group is situated farther off the Indian coast to the southwest.

**SRI LANKA: THE SUBCONTINENT'S "TEAR DROP"** Sri Lanka (sree LAHNG·kuh) is a large, tear-shaped island country. It is a lush tropical land of great natural beauty. Dominating the center of the island is a range of high, rugged mountains that reach more than 8,000 feet in elevation. Many small rivers cascade from these mountains to the lowlands below. The northern side of the island consists of low hills and gently rolling farmland. Circling the island is a coastal plain that includes long, palm-fringed beaches.

**THE MALDIVES ARCHIPELAGO** The Maldives comprise an **archipelago,** or island group, of more than 1,200 small islands. These islands stretch north to south for almost 500 miles off the Indian coast near the equator. The islands (shown at right) are the low-lying tops of submerged volcanoes, surrounded by coral reefs and shallow lagoons. This type of island is called an **atoll.** The total land area of the Maldives is 115 square miles (roughly twice the size of Washington, D.C.). Only about 200 of the islands are inhabited.

**PLACE** Not one of the more than 1,200 small coral islands that make up the Maldives rises more than six feet above the Indian Ocean.
**How might global warming affect these islands?**

# Disasters!

## The Cyclone of 1970

On November 13, 1970, a violent tropical storm struck Bangladesh, bringing death and destruction in its wake. Hundreds of thousands of people and their homes, crops, and animals were swept away in the fury of the 20th century's worst tropical storm. The cyclone's winds, rains, and floods claimed an estimated 300,000 to 500,000 lives. Also, approximately one million were left homeless, roughly 80 percent of the rice crop was lost, and about 70 percent of the country's fishing boats were wrecked. More than any other South Asian country, Bangladesh—with its low-lying coastal plain—suffers from these frequently occurring storms.

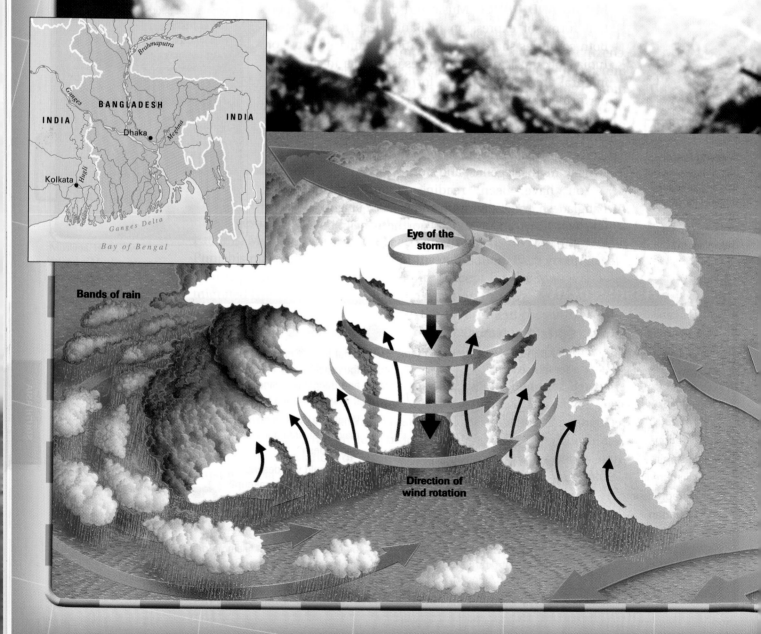

Eye of the storm

Bands of rain

Direction of wind rotation

The damage inflicted on this village in Bangladesh in 1991 is typical of the destructive force of a cyclone's winds and the torrential rains and floods that are a part of this weather system.

## GeoActivity

**ANNOUNCING THE DAMAGE**
Use the Internet to research the cyclone of November 1970. Read accounts of its destructive force. Gather data on the storm itself and the damage that it caused. Then prepare a **press release** about the storm.

- Begin with an overview of the storm.
- Provide a map and statistics.
- Present your press release to a group of student reporters.

**RESEARCH LINKS**
CLASSZONE.COM

## GeoData

**TROPICAL STORMS**
Violent tropical storms are called cyclones in the Indian Ocean, typhoons in the northwestern Pacific Ocean, and hurricanes in the Atlantic Ocean. These storms:

- develop over tropical waters in the late summer and fall when ocean temperatures are warmest
- usually begin as a cluster of thunderstorms that start to spiral and then form a single violent storm
- may be as wide as 675 miles
- have winds that range from 75 to 150 miles per hour
- generally last a week but some may take two or three weeks to die out
- produce heavy flooding that is the cause of most of the destruction and deaths
- inflict most of their damage along coastlines

**OTHER BANGLADESHI STORMS**
- May 28–29, 1963—22,000 deaths
- May 11–12, 1965—17,000 deaths
- June 1–12, 1965—30,000 deaths
- April 30, 1991—139,000 deaths

Concrete shelters constructed on stilts, as shown here, and reinforced school buildings are refuges from high floodwaters and winds that can knock down all but the strongest buildings.

# Comparing Cultures

## Musical Instruments

No one is exactly certain when or where music began to be made or what the first musical instrument was. But scholars believe that music has been part of all cultures, possibly even from earliest times. The first musical instrument may have been the human voice, which may have been used to mimic the sound of birds. Next, the human body was used to make rhythms, by clapping hands or stomping feet. When instruments began to be made, early musicians adapted available materials, such as wood and animal skins. Eventually, four basic types of instruments were developed: percussion, wind, string, and keyboard. Today, thousands of different instruments are played worldwide.

United Kingdom

India

Tanzania

Australia

**The bagpipe is a wind instrument that is associated with Scotland,** although it is played in other countries. It consists of an animal skin or rubberized cloth bag fitted with one or more pipes that produce a continuous flow of sound when blown.

**The drum is a percussion instrument from Africa** that probably was made first from wood or stone. It is played by striking with hands or other objects. These drums are made of skins stretched over a frame. Also shown is another percussion instrument—the xylophone.

**The didgeridoo is a wind instrument played by aboriginal people in Australia.** Made of bamboo or a hollow sapling, it can be as long as five feet. It is generally painted and used in ritual ceremonies.

**[Th]e sitar is a stringed instrument [fr]om India.** It has a wooden body [an]d is used mainly to play classical [m]usic. Anoushka Shankar, shown [he]re with her sitar, is the daughter [of] famed sitarist Ravi Shankar, who [br]ought the instrument to the world's [att]ention with his playing in the 1960s.

## GeoActivity

**FORMING A BAND**

With a small group, research other musical instruments. Plan a band that includes at least one of each of the four types of instruments. Then create **a multimedia presentation.**

• Provide visuals of each instrument.

• Write a description of each instrument's sound.

• Make an audiotape that has the sound of each instrument and play it in class.

**RESEARCH LINKS**
CLASSZONE.COM

## GeoData

**OTHER INSTRUMENTS**

**ASIA**
• Empty conch shells with broken tips give off a loud sound when blown and have been used in ceremonies for centuries in many regions, including the islands of Polynesia.

**EUROPE**
• The organ is the oldest keyboard instrument and was found in ancient Greece more than 2,000 years ago. It gave birth to other keyboard instruments such as the harpsichord, clavichord, and piano.

**THE AMERICAS**
• Native American cultures have strongly emphasized the voice in making music.

**AFRICA**
• Wall paintings in 4,000-year-old tombs in Egypt show musicians playing lutes.

• Some African cultures still use a stone gong—a hanging stone that gives off a sound when struck.

# CaseStudy

## How can India and Pakistan resolve their dispute over Kashmir?

Snowcapped mountains tower over a village in the valley of the Suru River in the disputed territory of Kashmir.

Kashmir is a territory of towering mountains, dense forests, and fertile river valleys. It is strategically located at the foot of the Himalayas and is surrounded by India, Pakistan, and China. Since 1947, India and Pakistan have fought to control this territory of 12 million people. The territorial dispute has caused three Indo-Pakistani wars and, in just the last decade alone, cost up to 75,000 lives. It poses a threat to the political stability of South Asia and the economic well-being of the countries involved. And, because both India and Pakistan have nuclear weapons, the Kashmir conflict has the potential to lead to nuclear war.

## A Controversy Over Territory

In 1947, the British government formally ended its colonial rule over the Indian subcontinent after 90 years. It partitioned, or divided, the subcontinent into two independent countries. India had a predominantly Hindu population. Pakistan was mostly Muslim. Britain gave each Indian state the choice of joining either country or remaining independent. Muslim states joined with Pakistan, while Hindu states remained part of India. Kashmir, however, had a unique problem.

**POLITICS AND RELIGION** Kashmir was mainly Muslim, but its leader, the Maharajah of Kashmir, was a Hindu. Faced with a difficult decision, the maharajah tried to keep Kashmir independent. But the plan failed. The maharajah then ceded Kashmir to India in 1947, but Pakistani soldiers invaded Kashmir. After a year's fighting, India still controlled much of the territory. Since then, India and Pakistan have fought two

**KASHMIR CONFLICT**

1940    1960    1970    1980    1990    2000

**1947**
India and Pakistan gain independence.

**1948**
Year-long **Indo-Pakistani war** over Kashmir ends.

**1965**
Second Indo-Pakistani war is fought.

**1971**
India and Pakistan fight again over Kashmir.

**1972**
Cease-fire agreement signed by India and Pakistan.

**1974**
India explodes its first nuclear device.

**1998**
**Pakistan** begins nuclear testing.

**1999**
Indian and Pakistani military clash at cease-fire line.

more wars, in 1965 and in 1971. Although a cease-fire was signed in 1972, the situation remains unresolved. As you can see on the map below, India and Pakistan each control part of the disputed territory. Even China controls a portion, having seized a remote northern mountain area in 1962.

**A QUESTION OF ECONOMICS** There's more to this conflict than just politics and religion. The Indus River flows through Kashmir, and many of its tributaries originate in the territory. The Indus is a critical source of drinking and irrigation water for all of Pakistan. As a result, the Pakistanis are unwilling to let India control such a vital resource. Kashmir has become a strategic prize that neither country is willing to give up.

# A Nuclear Nightmare

**SEE**
**PRIMARY SOURCE B**

In 1998, India and Pakistan each tested nuclear weapons. The rest of the world was horrified by the thought that the 50-year-old dispute over Kashmir might finally end with vast areas of South Asia destroyed by nuclear bombs. After the tests, both nations vowed to seek a political solution to the conflict. But the possibility of a nuclear war has made the dispute even more dangerous. Despite frequent cease-fires, the border clashes have continued. Also, Pakistan is supporting Muslims in Kashmir who have been fighting Indian rule since the late 1980s.

**SEE**
**PRIMARY SOURCE A**

**A QUESTION OF PRIORITIES** Both India and Pakistan have large populations and widespread poverty. The money that they have spent on troops, arms, and nuclear programs might have been used to educate millions of children and to address many social problems.

**SEE**
**PRIMARY SOURCE E**

Resolving the status of Kashmir would offer the people of India, Pakistan, and Kashmir the peace they need to begin improving the quality of their lives. It would also reduce political tensions in the region. The Case Study Project and primary sources that follow will help you to explore the Kashmir question.

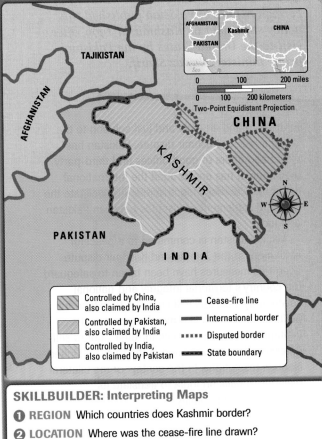

**Kashmir**

Controlled by China, also claimed by India

Controlled by Pakistan, also claimed by India

Controlled by India, also claimed by Pakistan

—— Cease-fire line

—— International border

····· Disputed border

▬▬▬ State boundary

Two-Point Equidistant Projection

**SKILLBUILDER: Interpreting Maps**

❶ **REGION** Which countries does Kashmir border?

❷ **LOCATION** Where was the cease-fire line drawn?

**SOUTH ASIA**

## VISUAL SUMMARY
### TODAY'S ISSUES IN SOUTH ASIA

### Economics

**Population Explosion**
- Though only about one-third the size of the United States, India has over three times as many people.
- India's government has taken steps to control population growth but has had only mixed success.
- Many parents continue to have large numbers of children because of India's high infant mortality rates, the extra income brought in by children, and the need for caregivers as parents age.

### Environment

**Living with Extreme Weather**
- The physical damage caused by extreme weather patterns in South Asia, such as cyclones, can be devastating to the region's people.
- The impact of extreme weather is not limited to physical damage. These forces can also disrupt the economy and cause serious political tensions.

### Government

**Case Study: Territorial Dispute**
- Kashmir is a strategically located territory, surrounded by Pakistan, India, and China.
- India and Pakistan have fought three wars over this territory since 1947.
- Money spent by India and Pakistan for armaments, including nuclear weapons, has not been available to help improve the lives of the people of these countries.

## Reviewing Places & Terms

**A. Briefly explain the importance of each of the following.**

1. basic necessities
2. illiteracy
3. summer monsoon
4. winter monsoon

**B. Answer the questions about vocabulary in complete sentences.**

5. Which winds stir up powerful storms in South Asia that release vast amounts of rain and cause severe flooding?

6. Which winds blow from the southwest across the Indian Ocean toward South Asia from June through September?

7. Food, shelter, and clothing are all examples of what?

8. Which winds blow from the northeast across the Himalayas from October through February?

9. What is the term for the inability to read or write?

10. What was the Indian government finding difficult to provide for its people?

## Main Ideas

### Population Growth (pp. 593–596)

1. Currently, about how many babies are born in India every day? Annually?

2. Why might the lack of basic necessities in a region concern demographers—people who study population?

3. Why might a high rate of infant mortality affect the size of families?

4. What percentage of the world's population is found in South Asia?

5. How would education play an important role in slowing population growth?

### Living with Extreme Weather (pp. 597–599)

6. What are South Asia's two monsoon seasons? How do they differ?

7. When do these wind seasons occur?

8. What are some of the precautions that people in South Asia have taken to lessen the damage caused by cyclones?

9. What type of international aid have the countries of South Asia received?

10. What political tensions have resulted from the effects of extreme weather?

### Case Study: Territorial Dispute over Kashmir (pp. 600–603)

11. Where is Kashmir located?

12. What countries have fought three wars over control of Kashmir?

13. When and why did the dispute over Kashmir begin?

14. Why are world leaders particularly concerned about the dispute?

15. What might happen if the dispute were resolved?

## Critical Thinking

### 1. Using Your Notes

Use your completed chart to answer these questions.

|  | Causes | Effects |
|---|---|---|
| Issue 1: Population |  |  |
| Issue 2: Extreme Weather |  |  |

a. Why might parents in India want a large family?

b. Why is Kashmir economically important to Pakistan?

### 2. Geographic Thinking

a. **REGION** How is the religious make-up of Kashmir related to conflict over the territory?

b. **MOVEMENT** Why might people in India and the other heavily populated countries in South Asia move to other parts of the world?

### 3. Identifying Themes

Why is Bangladesh especially vulnerable to the cyclones that occasionally devastate the region? Which of the five themes applies to this situation?

### 4. Making Comparisons

Why might India and Bangladesh fear the weather that can arrive during the summer?

### 5. Determining Cause and Effect

How might the dispute over Kashmir affect the social and educational programs in the region?

Additional Test Practice, pp. S1–S37

**TEST PRACTICE**
CLASSZONE.COM

## Geographic Skills: Interpreting Graphs

**Ethnic Indian Population Outside of India**

Use the graph at right to answer the following questions.

1. **PLACE** On what continent outside of South Asia do most Indians live?

2. **PLACE** About how many Indians live in South America?

3. **LOCATION** Why do you think most ethnic Indians living outside of India live in South Asian countries?

## GeoActivity

Carry out research on people from India who live in the United States. Create a table of the five cities with the largest populations of people from India.

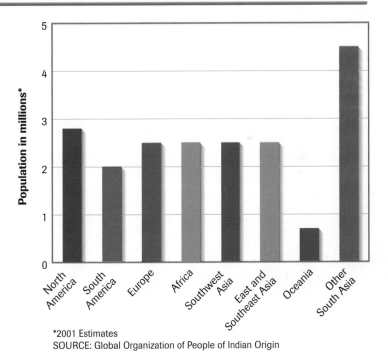

*2001 Estimates
SOURCE: Global Organization of People of Indian Origin

## INTERNET ACTIVITY

Use the links at **classzone.com** to continue research on population growth in India. Focus on how the limited availability of basic necessities has affected the daily life of the country's people.

**Creating a Multimedia Presentation** Use your research to create an electronic presentation. Combine charts, maps, images, objects, and written accounts to provide your audience with a picture of daily life in India.

SOUTH ASIA

East Asia is made up of a vast mainland area and a number of important islands off the eastern coast.

**PLACE** The Forbidden City is a walled enclosure in Beijing, China. Inside is a complex of palaces where 24 emperors ruled. Once closed to the public, it is now a museum and tourist attraction.

**PLACE** East Asia includes huge mountains and large deserts.

**LOCATION** The region is called "East Asia" because it is on the eastern edge of the Asian continent, bordered by the Pacific Ocean to the east, Russia to the north, and the countries of south and southeast Asia to the south.

**REGION** This area is bordered by a number of bodies of water, including the Pacific Ocean, the Sea of Japan, the East China Sea, and the South China Sea.

**For more information on East Asia . . .**

**RESEARCH LINKS** CLASSZONE.COM

**HUMAN–ENVIRONMENT INTERACTION**
The traditional pagoda, or temple, sits amidst the bustle of economic activity in the city center of Seoul, South Korea.

**LOCATION** Mount Fuji, the highest peak in Japan at 12,388 feet, is a volcano that last erupted in 1707. It is considered a sacred mountain.

# Today's Issues in East Asia

Today, East Asia faces the issues previewed here. As you read Chapters 27 and 28, you will learn helpful background information. You will study the issues themselves in Chapter 29.

In a small group, answer the questions below. Then participate in a class discussion of your answers.

## Exploring the Issues

**1. PHYSICAL FORCES** What might be some of the effects of earthquakes and volcanoes on daily life in the region? How might the effects be similar or different in an urban and a rural area?

**2. TRADE** What are some items you or your family have bought that were made in East Asia?

**3. POPULATION** Parts of East Asia are very crowded. What might be some of the advantages and challenges of living around so many people?

For more on these issues in East Asia . . .

**CURRENT EVENTS**
CLASSZONE.COM

**PHYSICAL FORCES**

## How might people in East Asia prepare for earthquakes and volcanoes?

A bus teeters on the edge of a highway torn apart by an earthquake in Kobe, Japan, in 1995.

## What are some benefits of global trade?

Hong Kong is a thriving center of trade and economic activity. Once a colony of Britain, it is now a part of China. Its wealth and trading expertise are helping China compete with leading industrial nations.

POPULATION

## CaseStudy

### What pressures does population put on the environment?

Subway attendants in Tokyo push people into crowded subway trains. Japan has a large number of people living on a small amount of land.

# Patterns of Physical Geography

Use the Unit Atlas to add to your knowledge of East Asia. As you look at the maps and charts, notice geographic patterns and specific details about the region. For example, the charts on pages 610–611 give details about the rivers and mountains of East Asia.

After studying the pictures, graphs, and physical map on these two pages, jot down in your notebook the answers to the following questions.

### Making Comparisons

1. What three main river systems run from west to east in China?

2. Which of the bodies of water surrounding Japan is the largest?

3. Compare East Asia's size and population to those of the United States. Based on that data, how might the population densities of the two compare?

For updated statistics on East Asia . . .

**DATA UPDATE**
CLASSZONE.COM

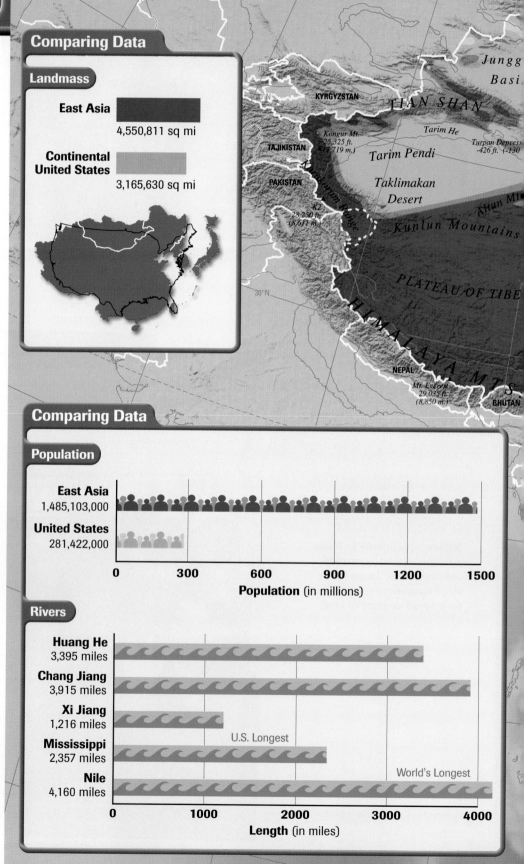

## Comparing Data

### Landmass

**East Asia**
4,550,811 sq mi

**Continental United States**
3,165,630 sq mi

## Comparing Data

### Population

**East Asia**
1,485,103,000

**United States**
281,422,000

0     300     600     900     1200     1500
**Population** (in millions)

### Rivers

**Huang He**
3,395 miles

**Chang Jiang**
3,915 miles

**Xi Jiang**
1,216 miles

**Mississippi**
2,357 miles
U.S. Longest

**Nile**
4,160 miles
World's Longest

0     1000     2000     3000     4000
**Length** (in miles)

RUSSIA

MONGOLIA

ALTAI MTS.

MONGOLIAN
PLATEAU

G O B I

Great Khingan Mountains

Amur R.

Songhua R.

Liao He

Manchurian
Plain

Sakhalin I.

Hokkaido

Sea of
Japan

Honshu

Mt. Fuji
12,388 ft.
(3,776 m.)

JAPAN

Huang He (Yellow R.)

Mu Us
Desert

Wei He

Qinling Shandi

CHINA

Huang He (Yellow R.)

Grand Canal

North
China
Plain

Yalu Jiang

NORTH
KOREA

Korea
Bay

Bo Hai

SOUTH
KOREA

Korea Strait

Yellow
Sea

Cheju I.

Shikoku

Kyushu

Gongga Shan
24,790 ft.
(7,556 m.)

Chang Jiang (Yangtze R.)

Dongting
L. Hu

Poyang
Hu

East China
Sea

Ryukyu Islands

PACIFIC
OCEAN

Mekong R.

Salween R.

MYANMAR

Xi Jiang (West R.)

VIETNAM

LAOS

THAILAND

Gulf of
Tonkin

Hainan

South China
Sea

Taiwan Strait

TAIWAN

Luzon
Strait

PHILIPPINES

### Elevation

| 13,100 ft. | (4,000 m.) |
| 6,600 ft. | (2,000 m.) |
| 1,600 ft. | (500 m.) |
| 650 ft. | (200 m.) |
| 0 ft. | (0 m.) |

Below sea level

▲ Mountain peak

0 · · · 250 · · · 500 miles
0 · · · 250 · · · 500 kilometers
Two-Point Equidistant Projection

## Comparing Data

### Mountains

| World's Tallest | U.S. Tallest | | | |
|---|---|---|---|---|
| **Mount Everest** | **Mount McKinley** | **Mount Kongur** | **Mount Paektu** | **Mount Fuji** |
| Nepal-Tibet | United States | China | Korea | Japan |
| 29,035 feet | 20,320 feet | 25,325 feet | 9,022 feet | 12,388 feet |

**611**

# Patterns of Human Geography

Over the course of centuries, the political map of East Asia has changed. The Chinese empire expanded over thousands of years, absorbing much of the region. Study the historical and political maps of East Asia on these two pages. In your notebook, answer these questions.

## Making Comparisons

1. What differences do you notice when you compare the historical map of the Chinese empire to the map of East Asia today?

2. What are some of the similarities between the historical map and the contemporary map of East Asia?

3. What countries in the region used to be a part of the Chinese empire but are now independent? Which country in the region was never a part of the empire?

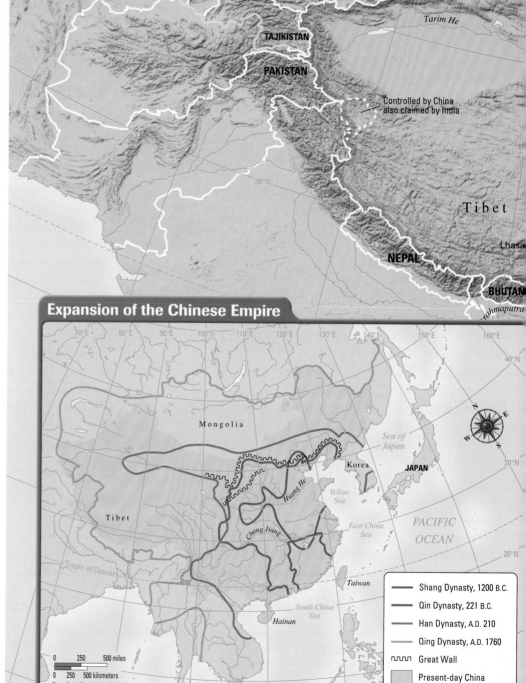

KAZAKHSTAN

KYRGYZSTAN

Ürümqi

Tarim He

TAJIKISTAN

PAKISTAN

Controlled by China also claimed by India

Tibet

Lhasa

NEPAL

BHUTAN

Brahmaputra

**Expansion of the Chinese Empire**

Mongolia

Sea of Japan

Korea

JAPAN

Tibet

Huang He

Yellow Sea

East China Sea

PACIFIC OCEAN

Chang Jiang

Tropic of Cancer

Taiwan

South China Sea

Hainan

| | |
|---|---|
| 0    250    500 miles | |
| 0    250    500 kilometers | |
| Two–Point Equidistant Projection | |

| | |
|---|---|
| —— | Shang Dynasty, 1200 B.C. |
| —— | Qin Dynasty, 221 B.C. |
| —— | Han Dynasty, A.D. 210 |
| —— | Qing Dynasty, A.D. 1760 |
| ⊓⊔⊓⊔ | Great Wall |
| ▓ | Present-day China |

# East Asia: Political

RUSSIA

*Amur R.*

*Manchuria*

*Songhua R.*

Harbin

Changchun

*Liao He*

Shenyang

*Yalu Jiang*

MONGOLIA

Ulaanbaatar ✪

*Huang He (Yellow R.)*    *Great Wall*

✪ Beijing

Tianjin

*Great Wall*

Lanzhou

*Wei He*    Xi'an

*Huang He (Yellow R.)*

*Grand Canal*

CHINA

Chengdu

*Chang Jiang (Yangtze R.)*

Nanjing

Wuhan    Hangzhou

Chongqing

Three
Gorges
Dam

*Dong*    *Poyang*

*Mekong R.*

Kunming

*Salween R.*

*Xi Jiang (West R.)*

Guangzhou

Hong Kong

Macao

MYANMAR

VIETNAM

THAILAND    LAOS

*Gulf of
Tonkin*

*Hainan*

*South China
Sea*

NORTH
KOREA

✪ Pyongyang

*Korea
Bay*

*Bo Hai*

✪ Seoul

SOUTH
KOREA

Pusan

*Yellow
Sea*

*Cheju I.*

Shanghai

Wenzhou

Taipei ★

TAIWAN

*Taiwan Strait*

*Luzon
Strait*

*Sea of
Japan*

*Hokkaido*

Sapporo

*Honshu*

JAPAN

Tokyo ✪

Nagoya    Yokohama

Kyoto

Osaka

Hiroshima

Fukuoka

*Shikoku*

*Kyushu*

*Korea Strait*

*East China
Sea*

*Ryukyu Islands*

*Philippine Sea*

PACIFIC
OCEAN

N
W    E
S

PHILIPPINES

*Sakhalin I.*

40°N

140°E

30°N

20°N

130°E

100°E

110°E

120°E

| ✪ | National capital |
|---|---|
| ● | Other city |
| ⋯ | Great Wall |

0 — 250 — 500 miles
0 — 250 — 500 kilometers
Two-Point Equidistant Projection

EAST ASIA

# Regional Patterns

These two pages contain a graph and three thematic maps. The graph shows the religions of East Asia. The maps show other important features of East Asia: its vegetation, languages, and population density. After studying these two pages, answer the questions below in your notebook.

## Making Comparisons

1. Where is most of the population located in China? Why might people have settled in these areas rather than in other areas?

2. Which is the smallest country in East Asia?

3. What is the vegetation in much of southern China, Taiwan, southern Korea, and southern Japan? How does it differ from the vegetation in Mongolia?

### Religions of East Asia

Other 3%

Christianity 6%

Atheist/
Nonreligious 58%

Buddhism 16%

Folk 17%

SOURCE: *Britannica Book of the Year 2000*

### Vegetation of East Asia

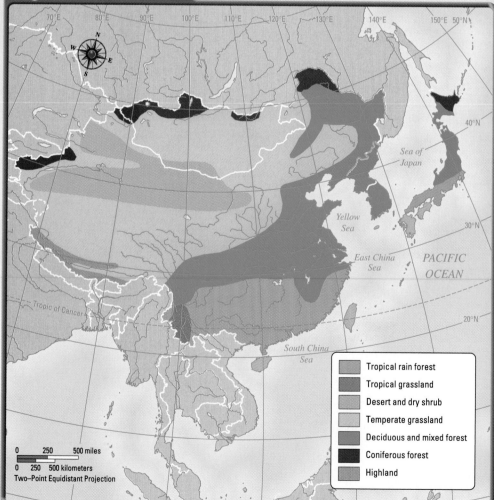

Sea of Japan

Yellow Sea

East China Sea

PACIFIC OCEAN

Tropic of Cancer

South China Sea

0    250    500 miles
0    250    500 kilometers
Two-Point Equidistant Projection

Tropical rain forest
Tropical grassland
Desert and dry shrub
Temperate grassland
Deciduous and mixed forest
Coniferous forest
Highland

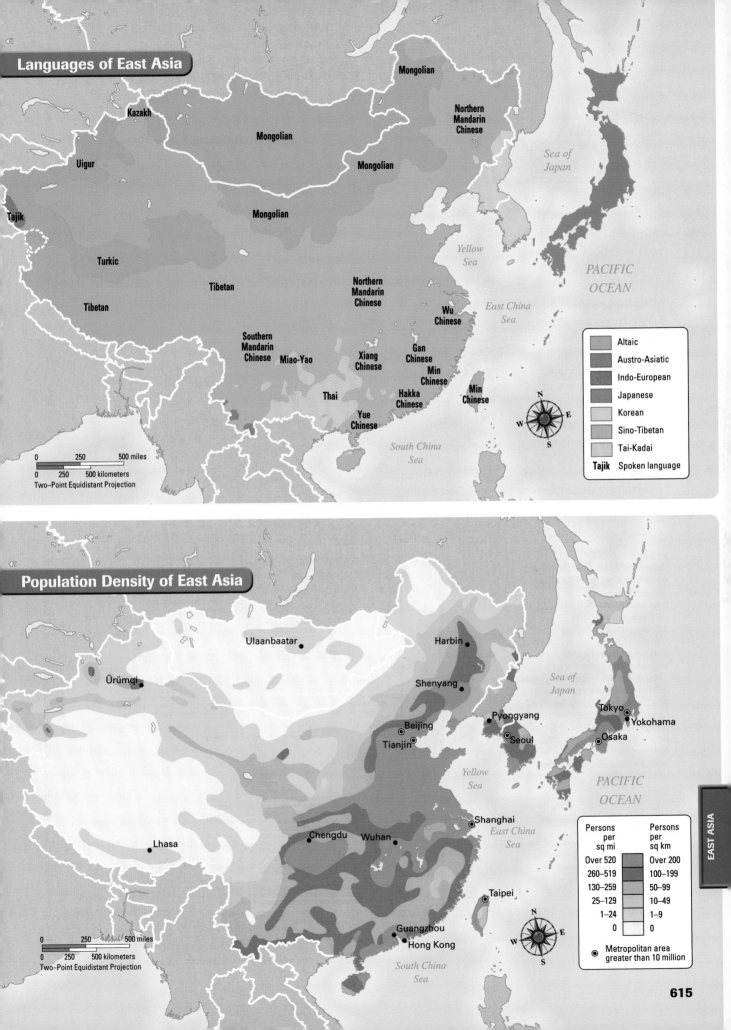

## Languages of East Asia

Mongolian

Kazakh

Northern
Mandarin
Chinese

Uigur

Mongolian

Mongolian

*Sea of
Japan*

Tajik

Mongolian

Turkic

*Yellow
Sea*

PACIFIC
OCEAN

Tibetan

Northern
Mandarin
Chinese

Tibetan

*East China
Sea*

Wu
Chinese

Southern
Mandarin
Chinese

Miao-Yao

Xiang
Chinese

Gan
Chinese

Min
Chinese

Thai

Hakka
Chinese

Min
Chinese

Yue
Chinese

*South China
Sea*

| | |
|---|---|
| | Altaic |
| | Austro-Asiatic |
| | Indo-European |
| | Japanese |
| | Korean |
| | Sino-Tibetan |
| | Tai-Kadai |
| **Tajik** | Spoken language |

0    250    500 miles
0    250    500 kilometers
Two–Point Equidistant Projection

## Population Density of East Asia

Ulaanbaatar •

Harbin •

Shenyang •

*Sea of
Japan*

Ürümqi •

Tokyo •
Yokohama •

Pyongyang •

Beijing •

Seoul •

Osaka •

Tianjin •

*Yellow
Sea*

PACIFIC
OCEAN

Lhasa •

Chengdu •

Wuhan •

Shanghai •

*East China
Sea*

Taipei •

Guangzhou •

Hong Kong •

*South China
Sea*

| Persons per sq mi | | Persons per sq km |
|---|---|---|
| Over 520 | | Over 200 |
| 260–519 | | 100–199 |
| 130–259 | | 50–99 |
| 25–129 | | 10–49 |
| 1–24 | | 1–9 |
| 0 | | 0 |
| ◉ | Metropolitan area greater than 10 million | |

0    250    500 miles
0    250    500 kilometers
Two–Point Equidistant Projection

EAST ASIA

# Regional Data File

Study the charts on the countries of East Asia. In your notebook, answer these questions.

## Making Comparisons

**1.** Which countries have the most people? Locate them on the map. Are they also the largest countries in terms of total area?

**2.** In which part of the region are the highest elevations located? What might this suggest about settlement patterns in the region?

| Country Flag | Country/ Capital | Population (2000) | Life Expectancy (years) (2000) | Birthrate (per 1,000 pop.) (2000) | Infant Mortality (per 1,000 live births) (2000) |
|---|---|---|---|---|---|
| | **China*** Beijing | 1,264,536,000 | 71 | 15 | 31.4 |
| | **Japan** Tokyo | 126,876,000 | 80 | 9 | 3.5 |
| | **Mongolia** Ulaanbaatar | 2,472,000 | 63 | 20 | 34.1 |
| | **North Korea** Pyongyang | 21,688,000 | 70 | 21 | 26.0 |
| | **South Korea** Seoul | 47,275,000 | 74 | 14 | 11.0 |
| | **Taiwan** Taipei | 22,256,000 | 75 | 13 | 6.6 |
| | **United States** Washington, D.C. | 281,422,000 | 77 | 15 | 7.0 |

**Sources:**
*Europa World Year Book 2000*
*Human Development Report 2000,* United Nations
*International Data Base,* 2000, U.S. Census Bureau online
*Merriam-Webster's Geographical Dictionary,* 1997
*Statesman's Yearbook 2001*
*2000 World Population Data Sheet,* Population Reference Bureau online
U.S. Census Bureau, 2000 Census
*WHO Estimates of Health Personnel,* World Health Organization online
*World Almanac and Book of Facts 2001*
*World Education Report 2000,* UNESCO online
*World Factbook 2000,* CIA online
N/A = not available

**Notes:**
* Figures do not include Hong Kong or Macao, both Special Administrative Regions.
ª A comparison of the prices of the same items in different countries is used to figure these data.
ᵇ Includes land and water, when figures are available.

**For updated statistics on East Asia . . .**

**DATA UPDATE**
CLASSZONE.COM

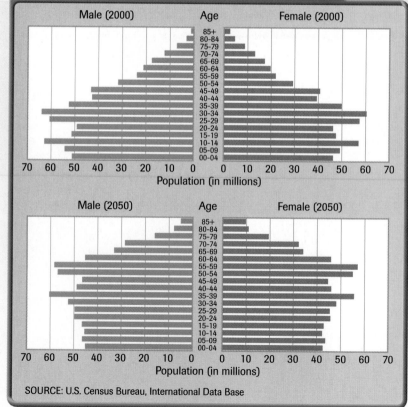

**China Population Pyramids, 2000 and 2050**

SOURCE: U.S. Census Bureau, International Data Base

| Doctors (per 100,000 pop.) (1995–1998) | GDP[a] (billions $US) (1998–1999) | Import/Export[a] (billions $US) (1998–1999) | Literacy Rate (percentage) (1998) | Televisions (per 1,000 pop.) (1998) | Passenger Cars (per 1,000 pop.) (1996–1997) | Total Area[b] (square miles) | |
|---|---|---|---|---|---|---|---|
| 162 | 4,800.0 | 165.8 / 194.9 | 82 | 205 | 4 | 3,704,427 | |
| 193 | 2,950.0 | 275.4 / 413.0 | 99 | 684 | 367 | 143,619 | |
| 243 | 6.1 | 0.472 / 0.317 | 83 | 45 | 8 | 604,247 | |
| N/A | 22.6 | 0.859 / 0.680 | 99 | 48 | N/A | 46,609 | |
| 127 | 625.7 | 104.4 / 144.0 | 98 | 334 | 165 | 38,022 | |
| N/A | 357.0 | 91.5 / 121.6 | 94 | 395 | 198 | 13,887 | |
| 251 | 9,255.0 | 820.8 / 663.0 | 97 | 847 | 489 | 3,787,319 | |

## Profile of East Asia

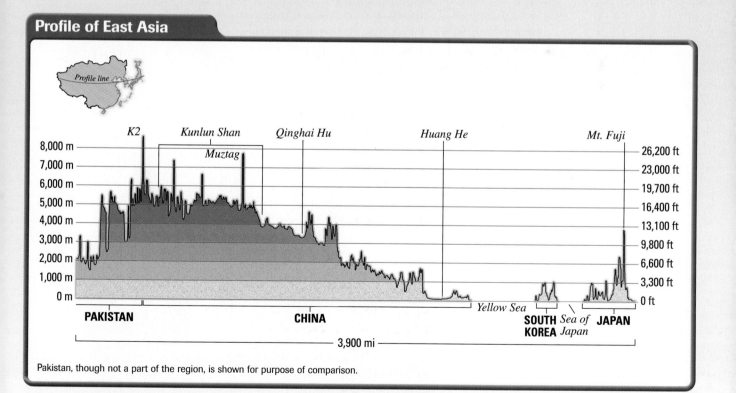

Pakistan, though not a part of the region, is shown for purpose of comparison.

# Chapter 27

# PHYSICAL GEOGRAPHY OF EAST ASIA
## A Rugged Terrain

**SECTION 1**
### Landforms and Resources

**SECTION 2**
### Climate and Vegetation

**SECTION 3**
### Human–Environment Interaction

The Great Wall is an ancient line of fortifications across northern China. Its oldest sections were built in the third century B.C. by hundreds of thousands of laborers. Over the years, it proved ineffective against invaders.

## GeoFocus

### How does physical geography influence the lives of East Asians?

**Taking Notes** Copy the graphic organizer below into your notebook. Use it to record information about the physical geography of East Asia.

| Landforms | |
|---|---|
| Resources | |
| Climate and Vegetation | |
| Human-Environment Interaction | |

# Landforms and Resources

## Main Ideas

- East Asia has a huge mainland area that includes rugged terrain.
- East Asia has a number of important islands off its eastern coast.

## Places & Terms

**Kunlun Mountains**

**Qinling Shandi Mountains**

**Huang He**

**Chang Jiang**

**Xi Jiang**

### CONNECT TO THE ISSUES

**PHYSICAL FORCES** East Asia's rough terrain and unevenly distributed resources have influenced settlement and ways of life in the region.

**A HUMAN PERSPECTIVE** Time and again in its early history, China was attacked by invaders from the steppes of Central Asia. The Chinese built and extended the Great Wall over many centuries in an attempt to keep out such invaders from Mongolia. From the Yellow Sea to the Gobi Desert, the wall twisted for thousands of miles across China. The wall was built by hundreds of thousands of peasant workers. Many died from the backbreaking labor or the severe weather. The Great Wall remains one of the largest building feats in history—partly because it had to cross mile after mile of China's difficult terrain.

## Landforms: Mountains and Plateaus

East Asia stretches from the western provinces of China to the eastern coast of Japan. Mongolia, Taiwan, North Korea, and South Korea are the other countries in the region. East Asia includes high mountains, vast deserts, cold climates, and Pacific waters. The mostly rugged terrain was formed by the collision of tectonic plates. One result of these natural barriers was to limit people's movement and increase their isolation.

**MOUNTAIN RANGES OF THE REGION** High mountains in the region limited contact between people living in China and in other parts of Asia. The world's highest mountains are located on the western edge of East Asia in southwestern and northwestern China and western Mongolia. The **Kunlun Mountains,** which are located in the west of China, are the source of two of China's great rivers, the Huang He (Yellow) and the Chang Jiang (Yangtze). In southeastern and east central China, the **Qinling Shandi Mountains** divide the northern part of China from the south.

**PLATEAUS AND PLAINS** The landscape of East Asia is among the roughest in the world. The mountain areas in the western part of the region restricted movement and were underpopulated. Although few flat surfaces exist, the region has some low basins and barren deserts. These include the Plateau of Tibet (also known as the Xizang Plateau), the Tarim Pendi Basin in western China, and the Taklimakan Desert in western China. All these areas are sparsely populated.

**PLACE** The Potala Palace in Lhasa, Tibet, has many floors and more than 1,000 rooms. It was once the residence of the Dalai Lama and other monks and is now a major pilgrimage site.

619

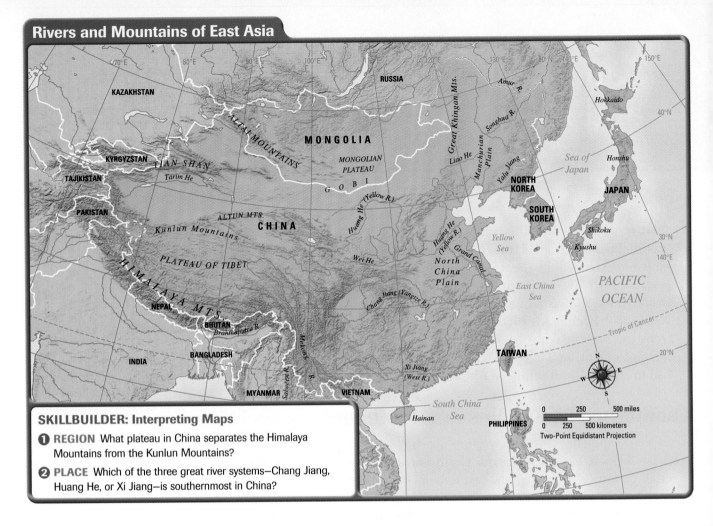

**SKILLBUILDER: Interpreting Maps**

❶ **REGION** What plateau in China separates the Himalaya Mountains from the Kunlun Mountains?

❷ **PLACE** Which of the three great river systems—Chang Jiang, Huang He, or Xi Jiang—is southernmost in China?

One of the largest deserts in the world—the Gobi—stretches from northwest China into Mongolia. It covers more than 500,000 square miles, which is larger than Texas and California combined. The Mongolian Plateau reaches into northeastern China. Northern China encompasses the Manchurian Plain and the North China Plain.

## Peninsulas and Islands

East Asia includes a number of important peninsulas. Most of these form a part of China, although one peninsula contains independent nations. In addition, a number of islands off the coast of China include possessions of China as well as independent nations.

**THE COAST OF CHINA** The eastern coast of China features several peninsulas. These include the Shandong Peninsula, the Leizhou Peninsula, and the Macao Peninsula. Macao was owned by Portugal until 1999, when it returned to Chinese control. Because of its peninsulas, China has a long coastline that has allowed several major port cities, such as Shanghai, to develop. Bordering China on the east is the Korean Peninsula, which contains the two independent nations of North Korea and South Korea.

**THE ISLANDS OF EAST ASIA** An important feature of East Asia is the continental shelf—the submerged border of the continent—that extends east from China. A number of islands stand above this continental shelf. The isolation of the islands has permitted them to develop in greater security and peace than parts of the mainland. Further, many of these islands have developed trading economies.

The islands off China include Hainan and part of Hong Kong. Long one of the major harbors in the world, Hong Kong (while originally a part of China) used to be a British colony. In 1997, Hong Kong once again came under the authority of mainland China.

The smaller nations of East Asia are located on islands and peninsulas. For example, Japan is an island nation with enormous economic power. Taiwan is a separate island that at one time belonged to mainland China—and is still claimed by China.

**BACKGROUND**
Japan is made up of four main islands and numerous smaller islands.

## River Systems

China has three great rivers, which have been critical to the development of China's civilization. The rivers have helped to feed hundreds of millions of people because of the fields and crops they irrigate.

**THE HUANG HE** The **Huang He** (or Yellow River) of northern China starts in the Kunlun Mountains in the west. It winds east for about 3,000 miles before emptying into the Yellow Sea. Both the sea and the river get their names from the yellow silt, or particles of soil, that the river carries to its delta. Another name for the river is "China's Sorrow" because of the terrible floods that it has caused.

**THE CHANG JIANG** The **Chang Jiang** (or Yangtze River) is the longest river in all of Asia. The name Chang Jiang means "long river." It flows about 3,900 miles from Xizang (Tibet) to the East China Sea. The river has been a major trade route since ancient times. Even today, the Chang Jiang carries most of the goods shipped on China's waterways. But this river, too, floods frequently, causing a great deal of damage to nearby villages, as well as to the surrounding countryside. ◄A

**CONNECT TO THE ISSUES**
A▶ How might rivers facilitate trade?

**THE XI JIANG** The **Xi Jiang** (or West River) runs its course in the south of China. It flows eastward through southeast China and joins up with

**MOVEMENT**
Workers pull a boat ashore along the Huang He (Yellow River).
**What are some of the uses that people might make of a river?**

621

# Interpreting a Contour Map

Suppose that you are vacationing on the Japanese island of Hokkaido. As part of your trip, you will be climbing Mount Asahi, the highest point on the island. The members of your group decide to study a contour map to understand the challenge that faces you. You can use a contour map to get a better idea of elevation and the steepness of the mountain.

**THE LANGUAGE OF MAPS** A **contour map** shows elevations and surface configuration by means of contour lines. Contour lines are lines on a map that show points of equal elevation. These lines are also called isolines. Numbers on the contour lines show the elevation in meters.

## Elevation on Hokkaido

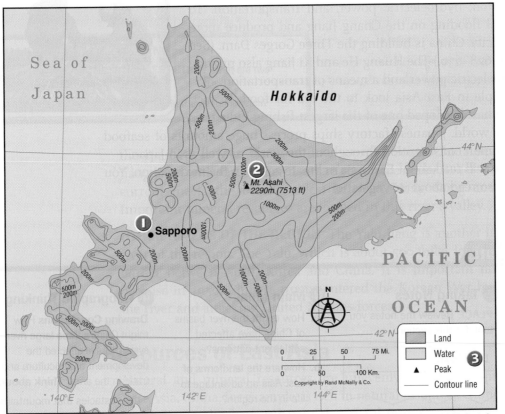

Copyright by Rand McNally & Co.

① Sapporo, the largest city on the island, is situated at a low elevation.

② Mount Asahi is the highest point on the island.

③ The key shows that Mount Asahi is a peak. The key shows that the red lines are contour lines. If you were to follow one contour line around its entire perimeter, you would remain at the same elevation throughout your walk.

## Map and Graph Skills Assessment

**1. Seeing Patterns**
How high, in meters, is Mount Asahi? What is the elevation of the last contour line on the map before the peak?

**2. Making Decisions**
From what direction of the compass would you approach Mount Asahi if you wanted to make the steepest climb?

**3. Drawing Conclusions**
Where on the island do the isolines converge most densely to show a very dramatic increase in elevation?

# Climate and Vegetation

## Main Ideas
- East Asia has a dry highland climate in the west.
- The region has a humid climate in the east.

## Places & Terms
**typhoon**

**Taklimakan Desert**

**Gobi Desert**

### CONNECT TO THE ISSUES
**POPULATION** To feed its population, East Asian countries have had to farm in highly productive ways.

**A HUMAN PERSPECTIVE** Kublai Khan was the ruler of the Mongol Empire (which included China) in the 13th century. In 1281, the Great Khan sent a huge fleet against Japan. A **typhoon**—a tropical storm that occurs in the western Pacific—swept across the Sea of Japan and sank the Mongol ships or dashed them against the rocky Japanese shore. The typhoon had changed the course of history. Typhoons occur in parts of East Asia, but in other ways the weather is similar to that of the United States. Both are at the same latitude, and both have similar climate zones.

## High Latitude Climate Zones

The climates in the highest latitudes present a serious challenge to all but the most hardy nomads and herders. These zones generally have severely cold climates. In addition, they tend to be very dry.

**SUBARCTIC** Subarctic climate zones occur in a small sliver along Mongolia's and China's northern borders with Russia. The summers in these areas range from cool to cold. The winters are brutally cold, testing the survival skills of the inhabitants. The climate is generally dry.

The typical vegetation of this region is the northern evergreen forest. Varieties of mosses and lichens also grow on rocks and tree trunks throughout subarctic zones.

**HIGHLAND** Highland climates are found mostly in western China. The temperature in highland zones varies with latitude and elevation. In general, the farther north the latitude and the higher the elevation, the colder the climate. The severe climate and topography of the western highlands are two of the reasons that the area is sparsely populated.

The vegetation in the highlands also varies with elevation. Forests and alpine tundra are the typical vegetation. Vast tundras reach as far as the eye can see. Tundras have no trees, and the soil a few feet below the surface is permanently frozen. In this environment, only mosses, lichens, and shrubs can grow. Because of the cold and the difficulty of growing crops, few people scratch out a living here.

**HUMAN-ENVIRONMENT INTERACTION** A 78-year-old woman tends sheep from the back of a camel in a semiarid zone typical of Mongolia. **What does the occupation of sheepherding and livestock grazing suggest about the vegetation in Mongolia?**

## VISUAL SUMMARY
### PHYSICAL GEOGRAPHY OF EAST ASIA

### Landforms

**Major Mountain Ranges:** Himalayas, Kunlun, Altun, Altay, Qinling Shandi

**Major Rivers:** Huang He, Chang Jiang, Xi Jiang

**Major Deserts:** Taklimakan, Gobi

**Major Plateaus and Plains:** Plateau of Tibet, Tarim Pendi Basin, Mongolian Plateau, Manchurian Plain, North China Plain

### Resources

- China, Mongolia, and North Korea have significant natural resources.
- Japan, South Korea, and Taiwan have limited natural resources.

### Climate and Vegetation

- East Asia has a dry continental climate in the west and a humid climate in the east.
- Its mid-latitude zones, both humid continental and humid subtropical, are the most densely populated areas.

### Human-Environment Interaction

- The Three Gorges Dam is being built along the Chang Jiang to control flooding.
- Urban Japan is very crowded, and people must adapt to space limitations.

## Reviewing Places & Terms

**A. Briefly explain the importance of each of the following.**

1. Kunlun Mountains
2. Huang He
3. Chang Jiang
4. Xi Jiang
5. typhoon
6. Taklimakan Desert
7. Gobi Desert
8. Three Gorges Dam
9. PCBs
10. landfill

**B. Answer the questions about vocabulary in complete sentences.**

11. On which river will the Three Gorges Dam attempt to control flooding?
12. What is another name for a tropical cyclone or hurricane?
13. What is the source of two of China's great rivers?
14. Which river joins with others to form an estuary between Hong Kong and Macao?
15. How have landfill sites been used in Tokyo?
16. Where in the region is there a rich supply of dinosaur fossils?
17. What has contributed to the poisoning and pollution of the environment in Japanese cities?
18. Which desert is located in western China near the Kunlun Mountains?
19. Which river is known as "China's Sorrow"?
20. What project is supposed to contain flooding?

## Main Ideas

### Landforms and Resources (pp. 619–624)

1. Why are the Kunlun Mountains especially important to China?
2. What is the approximate size of the Gobi Desert?
3. What are some of the important islands off the coast of China?
4. Why are China's three river systems so important to the country?

### Climate and Vegetation (pp. 625–627)

5. In which latitude and climate zones is most of China's productive agricultural land located?
6. What landforms make up the dry zones of the region?
7. What two factors affect vegetation and temperature in the highland climate?

### Human-Environment Interaction (pp. 628–631)

8. What will be some benefits of the Three Gorges Dam?
9. What will be some drawbacks of the dam?
10. What are some of the ways in which the Japanese have adapted to living in a crowded space?

# Critical Thinking

## 1. Using Your Notes

Use your completed chart to answer these questions.

| Landforms | |
|-----------|--|
| Resources | |

a. Where are the highest mountains in China located?

b. What are some energy resources found in abundance in China and Korea?

## 2. Geographic Themes

a. **LOCATION** Where is the largest desert found in East Asia?

b. **REGION** Write a sentence or two describing the settlement patterns of East Asia in terms of its mountains and coasts.

## 3. Identifying Themes

Based on landforms and climate, which areas of East Asia would be the least agriculturally productive? Which of the five themes are reflected in your answer?

## 4. Making Decisions

What factors must people in China consider when they are trying to decide what to do about flooding along one of their great rivers?

## 5. Drawing Conclusions

How does a typhoon create so much damage?

Additional Test Practice, pp. S1–S37

**TEST PRACTICE**
CLASSZONE.COM

# Geographic Skills: Interpreting Maps

## Precipitation in East Asia

Use the map at right to answer the following questions.

1. **REGION** Which parts of the region have the least precipitation?

2. **REGION** Which parts of the region have the most precipitation?

3. **MOVEMENT** How might precipitation patterns have affected settlement in the region?

### GeoActivity

Create a way to display the map information in graph form. Be sure to list the six countries of the region by name in your graph.

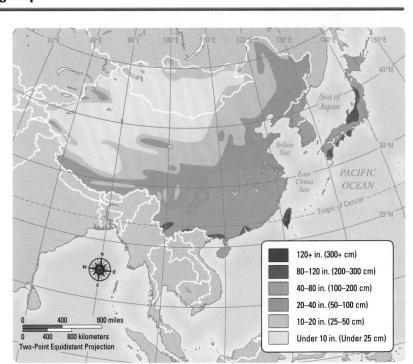

120+ in. (300+ cm)
80–120 in. (200–300 cm)
40–80 in. (100–200 cm)
20–40 in. (50–100 cm)
10–20 in. (25–50 cm)
Under 10 in. (Under 25 cm)

0    400    800 miles
0    400    800 kilometers
Two-Point Equidistant Projection

## INTERNET ACTIVITY

Use the links at **classzone.com** to do research on the most productive agricultural regions of East Asia. You might focus on the impact that precipitation has had on settlement patterns and crop growth.

**Creating Multimedia Presentations** Combine charts, maps, or other visual images in an electronic presentation that shows the most productive farming areas and the most common crops in the region.

# Chapter 28

## HUMAN GEOGRAPHY OF EAST ASIA
# Shared Cultural Traditions

**Four Subregions of East Asia**

China
Mongolia and Taiwan
North Korea and
South Korea
Japan

MONGOLIA

NORTH KOREA

SOUTH KOREA

JAPAN

Sea of Japan

Korea Bay

Bo Hai

Yellow Sea

Korea Strait

CHINA

East China Sea

PACIFIC OCEAN

Tropic of Cancer

TAIWAN

Taiwan Strait

Luzon Strait

Bay of Bengal

Gulf of Tonkin

Philippine Sea

South China Sea

Equator

0    250    500 miles
0    250    500 kilometers
Two-Point Equidistant Projection

## GeoFocus

### How has China influenced the cultures of East Asia?

**Taking Notes** In your notebook, copy a cluster diagram like the one below. For each subregion of East Asia, take notes about its history, economics, culture, and modern life.

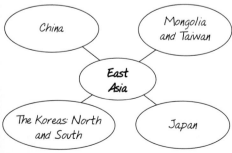

China

Mongolia and Taiwan

East Asia

The Koreas: North and South

Japan

# China

**Main Ideas**
- China is the world's most populous country.
- China has been the dominant culture of East Asia since ancient times.

**Places & Terms**
**dynasty**
**spheres of influence**
**Boxer Rebellion**
**Mao Zedong**
**Confucianism**
**Taoism**
**Buddhism**

**CONNECT TO THE ISSUES**
**POPULATION** China's huge population puts a great strain on the environment.

**A HUMAN PERSPECTIVE** In ancient times, China had been open to attack from nomadic horsemen who roamed the plains of northern China and Mongolia. Around 220 B.C., the emperor Shi Huangdi decided to build the Great Wall of China by closing the gaps between smaller walls built by earlier rulers. Hundreds of thousands of peasants were used as forced labor to build the Great Wall. The workers hauled and dumped millions of tons of rubble to fill the core of the wall. From the Yellow Sea in the east to the Gobi desert in the west, the Great Wall twisted and turned for thousands of miles, protecting and isolating China from the barbarian warriors beyond its borders.

## China's Early History

China is the world's oldest continuous civilization. The beginnings of that civilization extend back into the mists of prehistory. Because of China's geography—the long distances that separated it from Europe and other continents—it followed its own direction.

**EARLY CIVILIZATION AND THE DYNASTIES** China has been a settled society for more than 4,000 years. In its earliest days, China was made up of a number of Stone Age cultures. Then it was ruled by dynasties. A **dynasty** is a series of rulers from the same family. The first Chinese dynasty was the Shang. This dynasty arose during the 1700s B.C. It ruled a central area in China for about 600 years until it was overthrown by the Zhou Dynasty, which ruled part of northern China.

The next important dynasty, the Qin (chihn), gave its name to China. In 221 B.C., the Qin Dynasty united a number of smaller states under a strong central government and established an empire. The first Qin emperor was Shi Huangdi, the builder of the Great Wall. The Chinese empire, ruled by different dynasties, lasted for more than 2,000 years.

Another important Chinese dynasty was that of the Han. These rulers pushed the empire into central Asia, home to many nomadic tribes. Many other dynasties followed over the centuries.

In 1644, the Manchu people of Manchuria invaded China and established the Qing (chihng) Dynasty. In 1911, the Manchus were overthrown by revolutionaries, and this ended the dynasties and the Chinese empire.

**PLACE** Thousands of life-sized terra cotta (clay) soldiers have been unearthed by archaeologists near the tomb of the emperor Shi Huangdi near Xian, China.

has industrial centers in Guangzhou, Hangzhou, Suzhou, Wuhan, and Wuxi.

China has developed heavy industries, such as steel and machinery. It also produces consumer goods. For example, the country has a huge textile (cloth) industry that produces goods for the home market and export. Many textiles are exported to the United States. **B**

## A Rich and Complex Culture

As the world's oldest civilization, China has one of the world's richest cultures. The country has highly developed art, architecture, literature, painting, sculpture, pottery, printing, music, and theater. In all these areas, the Chinese have made influential contributions to the cultures of Korea, Japan, and other countries in the region.

**FROM POTTERY TO PAINTING** Some of the earliest Chinese works of art have been found in burial sites. Pottery, bronze vessels, and jade disks have been discovered in the excavation of old tombs. In addition, paintings have been found on tiles decorating the walls of tombs. Chinese artists created beautiful works using different materials, such as clay, bronze, jade, ivory, and lacquer.

**CHINESE INVENTIONS** The Chinese introduced many inventions to the world, such as paper, printing, and gunpowder. Other Chinese inventions include the compass, porcelain, and silk cloth.

**RELIGIOUS AND ETHICAL TRADITIONS** China has three major religions or ethical traditions. The beliefs of most people include elements of all three. Those traditions have influenced beliefs throughout the region.

Confucius was a Chinese philosopher who lived from 551 to 479 B.C. He believed in respect for the past and for one's ancestors. He thought that in an orderly society, children should obey their parents and parents should obey the government and emperor. He stressed the importance of education in a well-run society. His thinking about the importance of order, education, and hierarchy in a well-ordered society is called **Confucianism.**

**Taoism** gets its name from a book called the *Tao-te Ching,* based on the teaching of Lao-tzu, who lived in the sixth century B.C. He believed in the importance of preserving and restoring harmony in the individual and in the universe. He also thought the government should leave the people alone and do as little as possible. Another of his major beliefs was that the individual should seek harmony with nature.

**Buddhism** came to China from India and grew into an important religion in China by the 300s A.D. Confucianism and Taoism influenced Buddhism as it developed in China. Among ideas important in Buddhism are rebirth and the end of the rebirth cycle.

**CONNECT TO THE ISSUES**
TRADE
**B** Why might trade between the United States and China be important to both countries?

**BACKGROUND**
Other important Chinese art forms include calligraphy and brush painting.

**Chinese Artifacts**

An ancient Chinese coin *(above left)* is from about 450 B.C. The jade pendant *(above right)* is from about 250 B.C.

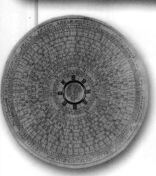

This printed book *(above)* from about A.D. 1000 contains a Buddhist prayer. This navigational compass *(left)* dates from the 18th century.

# The Most Populous Country

One out of every five people in the world lives in China. This makes it the most populous country in the world.

**POPULATION PATTERNS** China's estimated population in the year 2000 was about 1.3 billion. Somewhere between 30 and 40 Chinese cities have populations of more than one million people. Many of China's 22 provinces have more people than entire countries. In the year 2000, Henan province was estimated to have a population of about 93 million people—more than the population of Great Britain. ◀

Seventy percent of the people live in 12 provinces located in the east. (See map, page 615.) About 6 percent of the people live in the west on 55 percent of the land.

**HEALTH CARE** One of the great achievements of China since 1950 has been to provide health care for its enormous and far-flung population. The country has pursued a dual strategy in developing its health-care system.

On the one hand, people make use of traditional Chinese medicines, including herbal remedies. Acupuncture is another important part of Chinese medicine.

On the other hand, China's doctors also use Western medicine to treat disease. Western drugs and surgery have their place in the treatment of illness. Most Chinese cities have hospitals, and the villages have clinics staffed by trained medical workers called "barefoot doctors."

In the next section, you will read about two of China's neighbors, Mongolia and Taiwan. China has greatly influenced both places.

### Geographic Thinking

**Seeing Patterns**

▷ What does the immense size of China suggest about its future?

## SECTION 1 Assessment

### ❶ Places & Terms

Identify each of the following places and terms.

- dynasty
- spheres of influence
- Boxer Rebellion
- Mao Zedong
- Confucianism
- Taoism
- Buddhism

### ❷ Taking Notes

**REGION** Use your notes to answer the questions below.

- What are aspects of China's cultural legacy?
- What are some Chinese dynasties?

### ❸ Main Ideas

a. Why is China's rural economy still so important?

b. What are some of China's most important religious ideas?

c. Why is population such an important issue in China?

### ❹ Geographic Thinking

**Making Generalizations** How has China's rugged terrain affected its relations with other countries and civilizations? **Think about:**

- the mountains and deserts to the west
- the ocean to the east

🅢 **See Skillbuilder Handbook, page R6.**

**GeoActivity**

**SEEING PATTERNS** Pair with a partner and investigate an invention of the Chinese, such as printing or the compass. Then present your findings to the class in a brief **oral report** accompanied by an illustration of the invention.

**EAST ASIA**

# Disasters!

## Chang Jiang (Yangtze River) Flood of 1931

Throughout Chinese history, the flooding of the Chang Jiang has cost millions of lives. On average, the Chang Jiang has caused a major flood about every 50 years, although in the past century or so the floods have been more frequent. The floods of 1931 and 1954 were particularly devastating. The 1931 flood resulted from monsoon rains. In May and June of that year, six enormous waves poured down the river, demolishing dams and dikes. More than 35,000 square miles of land were flooded and many thousands of people died. Floods along the Chang Jiang continue to the present day. Bad floods occurred in both 1996 and 1998.

CHINA

Nanjing

Wuhan

Chang Jiang (Yangtze R.)

Nanjing was one of the cities in China that remained underwater for weeks because of the 1931 flood.

**Wu**chang, **Han**yang, and **Han**kou are three cities that make up one huge urban complex called Wuhan. Much of **Wuhan** remained underwater for more than four months in 1931. The water ranged from 6 feet to 20 feet in depth.

The Three Gorges Dam is currently under construction to control the flooding of the Chang Jiang.

In the city of Hankou during the flood, wealthy people traveled in boats while poor tradespeople waded up to their necks through the water.

This panoramic aerial view of one of the Chinese cities flooded in 1931 was taken by Charles Lindbergh. He was the American aviator who had made the first solo flight across the Atlantic Ocean in 1927.

Along the Chang Jiang, human labor is still essential for flood control. These laborers work with shovels and other tools to fortify the banks of the river with dirt to prevent flooding.

## GeoActivity

### UNDERSTANDING FLOODS

Working with a partner, use the Internet to research one of the floods listed below. Then create a **presentation** about it.

• Create a diagram showing the extent of the flood, the damage caused by it, and the number of lives lost.

• Add a map of the affected region.

• Write a paragraph explaining how the flood affected the people and life of the region.

**RESEARCH LINKS**
CLASSZONE.COM

## GeoData

### OTHER DEADLY RIVER FLOODS

**1887**
Huang He in northeastern China; possibly more than 1,000,000 people killed

**1889**
Johnstown, Pennsylvania, on May 31; about 2,200 deaths (more than any other river flood in U.S. history)

**1911**
Chang Jiang in China; 100,000 killed

**1937**
Mississippi and Ohio rivers; about 250 killed

**1988**
Three major rivers in Bangladesh; about 1,600 deaths

**1993**
Mississippi River; millions of acres flooded; about 50 dead

**1998**
Chang Jiang in China during July and August; about 4,000 dead

# Comparing Cultures

## Masks

Masks are coverings that disguise the face. Most cultures use masks for a variety of purposes. Followers sometimes wear ceremonial masks during religious celebrations. Actors wear theatrical masks during performances such as those in the classical drama of ancient Greece, China, and Japan. Mourners sometimes placed burial masks over the faces of the dead before they were buried. In ancient Egypt, they placed the mask directly on the mummy or else on the mummy case. Participants sometimes wear festival masks during celebrations such as Mardi Gras in New Orleans or Carnival in Rio de Janeiro.

United States

Japan

Angola    Indonesia

**A masked dancer in Bali, Indonesia,** performs a ritual dance. Balinese dancers move to the music of gongs and flutes. In their dances, each movement and gesture helps to tell the story.

**This mask from Angola** represents a female ancestor with an elaborate headdress. A member of the Chokwe culture in Africa created this mask out of wood and fibers in the 20th century.

**Native American ceremonial masks** were used to calm angry spirits. This mask is a product of the Iroquois culture of the northeast woodlands and was used in healing ceremonies.

**Japanese masks and costumes** are worn by a performer in a Noh drama, the classical drama of Japan. Masked performers create music and dance in a highly stylized manner.

## GeoActivity

### MAKING MASKS

Use the Internet to research how to make different kinds of masks. Choose materials that are easy to obtain. Then make a **mask** that you will show to the class.

• Use a technique about which you have found information.

• Write a description of the procedure you followed to make the mask.

• Display your mask in an area set aside in the classroom.

**RESEARCH LINKS**
CLASSZONE.COM

## GeoData

### ODD FACTS ABOUT MASKS

• In Europe, masks have been discovered that date back as early as 30,000 years ago to Paleolithic times.

• The solid gold death mask of the pharaoh Tutankhamen, which covered the head of his mummy, weighs 22.5 pounds.

• Masks were worn by the performers of tragedies and comedies in ancient Greece.

• The Senesi people of New Guinea use masks that include skirts that cover much of the body.

• The Aleuts of Alaska cover the faces of their dead with wooden masks.

• Death masks made of plaster are sometimes put on the face of the dead to preserve their features for posterity. Death masks exist for Napoleon Bonaparte and Ludwig van Beethoven.

• The mask worn by actor Clayton Moore in the television show *The Lone Ranger* was sold at auction for $33,000.

# Chapter 29

### SECTION 1
## The Ring of Fire

### SECTION 2
## Trade and Prosperity

**CASESTUDY**
## POPULATION AND THE QUALITY OF LIFE

For more on these issues in East Asia . . .

**CURRENT EVENTS**
CLASSZONE.COM

# TODAY'S ISSUES
# East Asia

A bus teeters on the edge of a highway torn apart by an earthquake in Kobe, Japan, in 1995.

## GeoFocus

### How do people in East Asia deal with issues of a rapidly changing society?

**Taking Notes** In your notebook, copy a cause-and-effect chart like the one below. Then take notes on causes and effects of some aspect of each issue.

|  | Causes | Effects |
|---|---|---|
| Issue 1: Ring of Fire |  |  |
| Issue 2: Trade |  |  |
| Case Study: Population |  |  |

# The Ring of Fire

**How might people in East Asia prepare for earthquakes and volcanoes?**

## Main Ideas

- The islands of Japan form part of a geologically active area called the Ring of Fire.
- Because of its location, Japan has faced disastrous earthquakes, volcanic eruptions, and tsunamis.

## Places & Terms

**Ring of Fire**

**Great Kanto earthquake**

**tsunami**

**A HUMAN PERSPECTIVE** On January 17, 1995, at 5:46 A.M., a severe earthquake rocked Kobe, Japan's sixth largest city. When the dust settled and the last of the fires burned out, about 6,000 people lay dead, and more than 40,000 suffered injuries. The government quickly began rebuilding the port city, but psychologists warned that reviving the spirit of Kobe's people would take time. Many lost family members. Entire neighborhoods vanished. A year after the quake, nearly 50,000 people were still living in temporary shelters, and anger grew against the government. Clearly, much more than glass, steel, bricks, and mortar would be needed to bring Kobe fully back to life.

## Physical Forces in the Ring of Fire

Like Kobe, many Japanese cities are threatened by earthquakes. This is because Japan is part of the **Ring of Fire**—a chain of volcanoes that line the Pacific Rim. (See the map on the next page.)

**SHIFTING PLATES** As you learned in Unit 1, the outer crust of the earth is made up of a number of shifting tectonic plates that continually bump and slide into each other. When a dense oceanic plate meets a less dense continental plate, the oceanic plate slides under the continental plate in a process called subduction. The area where the oceanic crust is subducted is called a trench.

In East Asia, the Pacific oceanic plate encounters the Eurasian continental plate. When the oceanic plate moves under the continental plate, it crumples the continental crust, building mountains and volcanoes such as those that form the Ring of Fire.

At the same time, tremendous stress builds up along the edges of the plates. The stress keeps building until eventually the plates move suddenly and violently. The result is an earthquake.

**HUMAN-ENVIRONMENT INTERACTION** An elderly woman is carried from a collapsing building during the earthquake in Kobe, Japan, in 1995.
**What damage is apparent in the photograph?**

*The Ring of Fire* **661**

# Interpreting a Proportional Circle Map

The earthquake that devastated Kobe, Japan, in 1995 measured 6.8 on the Richter scale, which is a scale for measuring the magnitude of earthquakes. About 6,000 people died and many thousands more were injured. Although the Kobe quake was the most destructive in recent years, there have been many others in Japan in the 1990s. Some of these were more powerful than the Kobe quake but they did not do as much damage.

**THE LANGUAGE OF MAPS** A **proportional circle map** shows the relative sizes of objects or events, such as earthquakes. This map shows major earthquakes in Japan during a ten-year period beginning in 1991. The larger the circle on the map, the greater the magnitude of the earthquake as measured by the scale.

## Major Earthquakes in Japan, 1991–2000

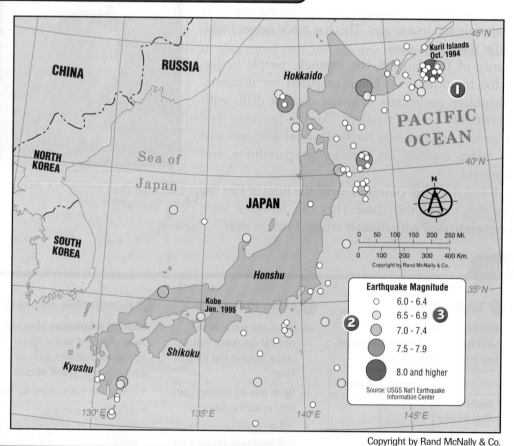

Copyright by Rand McNally & Co.

**①** A cluster of circles indicates that an area is prone to frequent quakes.

**②** The key explains that the bigger and darker a circle is on the map, the greater the size and intensity of the quake.

**③** Values on an earthquake magnitude scale are typically between 1 and 9. This map shows earthquakes with a magnitude of 6 and higher. Each increase of .5 represents an increase in released energy. Scales for measuring earthquakes include the Richter, the moment magnitude, and others.

## Map and Graph Skills Assessment

**1. Analyzing Data**

What was the intensity of the earthquake that struck Kobe?

**2. Making Comparisons**

On which islands did the most powerful quake occur in this period? In what range did it fall, as measured by the scale?

**3. Making Inferences**

Why do you think the quake you identified in question 2 was not as destructive as the Kobe quake?

# Trade and Prosperity

**What are some benefits of global trade?**

## Main Ideas

- East Asian economies became global powerhouses in the 1970s and 1980s.
- The decline of Asian economies in the 1990s created a crisis that spread around the globe.

## Places & Terms

**UNICEF**

**global economy**

**Jakota Triangle**

**recession**

**sweatshop**

**A HUMAN PERSPECTIVE** At the beginning of the 1990s, the economies of East Asia were growing very rapidly. Unfortunately, there was a dark side to this prosperity. In 1995, <u>**UNICEF (the United Nations Children's Fund)**</u> reported that more than half a million children in East Asia were working in factories or begging on the streets. UNICEF regional director Daniel Brooks noted that, due to fast-paced economic growth, "We are seeing the erosion of family values and that includes the exploitation of children." This is one of the important issues facing the region.

## Opening Doors

The process by which East Asia became an economic powerhouse took centuries. Until the 1500s, the nations of East Asia had been isolated from the rest of the world. As Western demand for Asian products grew, European traders used a variety of means—including force—to end East Asia's isolation.

Eventually, the economies of the region were to emerge as major players in the global economy. However, foreign intervention and world war lay ahead before East Asian nations achieved widespread prosperity.

**OPENING TO THE WEST** By the 1800s, the nations of Europe had signed treaties that gave them distinct spheres of influence in the East. These were areas where they could control trade without interference from other Western nations. In 1853, Commodore Matthew Perry set sail from the United States to Japan to persuade the Japanese to establish trade and diplomatic relations with the United States. The naval warships that accompanied Perry intimidated Japan into opening its doors to the United States and the West.

**MOVEMENT** Japan exports about 4½ million vehicles each year. Here, cars are about to be loaded onto a boat in the port of Nagoya.

EAST ASIA

# CaseStudy

## POPULATION AND THE QUALITY OF LIFE

### What pressures does population put on the environment?

Trams, buses, and people crowd the streets of Hong Kong.

**The Voyageur Experience in World Geography**
**China:** Food for a Billion Plus

**B**ecause East Asia has changed so much, it's hard to imagine how different the region looked 50 years ago. Today, some of the countries and cities of the region are among the most prosperous in the world. In Japan, South Korea, and Taiwan, the statistics on per capita income, length of life, and literacy are all high. Despite recent problems, the economies are generally prosperous, as can be seen in the glittering shopping districts and luxurious residential neighborhoods of Tokyo, Seoul, and Taipei. But it wasn't always that way. If the big problem of the past was industrializing, today it is managing population.

## Patterns of Population

Many of the countries of East Asia have been so successful in dealing with the basic problems of feeding their people and industrializing that they now face other problems. Several of these problems are caused by the expanding populations in the region.

**THE SITUATION AT MID-CENTURY**  At the middle of the 20th century, the nations of East Asia ranked among the least developed in the world. In fact, statistics on health, literacy, fertility, and economics in East Asia mirrored those of the poorest region of the world—sub-Saharan Africa. Widespread poverty was the norm. Life expectancy was short. Fertility rates were high, as were infant and maternal death rates. In 1950, East Asian women often married young and gave birth to six children on average during their lifetimes. Most economies remained rural.

## Addressing Population Problems

Policy makers in the region understood that population control was key to solving a wide range of social and economic woes. Among the successful programs were those that stressed education and family planning.

**ENVIRONMENTAL STRESS**  Unrestricted population growth put tremendous strain on the quality of life in the region and on the environment. Food production on existing farmland was barely adequate. The absence of basic sanitation fouled the region's water supplies. In some countries, such as China, the water tables were drained to dangerously low levels. Fortunately, the governments of East Asia recognized this catastrophe-in-the-making. They moved quickly to reverse course.

**PROBLEMS AND POLICIES** Aggressive family planning programs were begun in the region. Birth rates began leveling off and then dropping. By the year 2000, women were marrying much later and giving birth to an average of 2.5 children. In China alone, the birth rate dropped from 6.22 children per woman in 1950–1955 to just 1.82 in the year 2000.

**IMPRESSIVE RESULTS** This drop in birth rates, combined with industrialization, led to fast economic growth. By the 1990s, the economies of East Asia were booming, transforming social and economic conditions. In just over a generation, the region's quality of life has improved to the point where life expectancy and literacy rates are among the highest in the world.

## The Quality of Life

Although these changes in East Asia have been dramatic, they have not solved all of the region's problems. Some countries in the region, such as China and Japan, are among the most populous in the world. Furthermore, life expectancy in East Asia has increased from 41 years in the period 1950–1955 to 69 years in the year 2000.

**SOME ONGOING PROBLEMS** The huge populations of the region continue to put pressure on the

SEE PRIMARY SOURCE **A**

environment. Even if China were to maintain a modest growth rate of one percent a year, it would still add 13 million people to its population annually.

The growing populations are concentrated in the cities of the region, where they must be provided with housing, sanitation, and transportation. Pollution, overcrowding, and flooding are all problems that are made worse by an expanding population.

However, not all family planning programs were well received. Some citizens criticized China's one-child-per-family policy as harsh and an assault on their rights. In the face of such criticism, the region's family planning efforts were expanded.

Despite these difficulties, East Asia has shown the world that rapid social and economic progress are possible. This requires that people and their leaders join hands with the world community to make difficult deci-

SEE PRIMARY SOURCE **D**

sions and put in place sound policies.

A case study project on population follows on the next two pages.

---

**Population**

**Some Major Cities of East Asia, 1995–1999**

| City | Population (in millions) |
|---|---|
| Shanghai, China | 13.58 |
| Beijing, China | 11.30 |
| Seoul, South Korea | 10.29 |
| Tianjin, China | 9.42 |
| Tokyo, Japan | 7.85 |
| Hong Kong, China | 6.84 |
| Shenyang, China | 5.12 |
| Guangzhou, China | 4.49 |
| Wuhan, China | 4.25 |
| Pusan, South Korea | 3.87 |
| Chongqing, China | 3.47 |
| Xian, China | 2.97 |
| Nanjing, China | 2.96 |
| Taipei, Taiwan | 2.60 |
| Osaka, Japan | 2.48 |

SOURCE: The Statesman's Yearbook (2001)

**SKILLBUILDER:**
**Interpreting Charts**

❶ **HUMAN-ENVIRONMENT INTERACTION** What are the two largest cities in South Korea?

❷ **REGION** Which country on the chart has most of the largest cities?

## VISUAL SUMMARY
### TODAY'S ISSUES IN EAST ASIA

### Environment

**The Ring of Fire**
- Parts of East Asia are located along the northwestern edge of the Pacific Ocean's Ring of Fire.
- The heavily populated areas of East Asia (especially Japan) are endangered by the earthquakes, volcanic eruptions, and tsunamis along the Ring of Fire.

### Economics

**Trade and Prosperity**
- Most of the nations of East Asia have prospered from trade with each other and with other parts of the world.
- In the second half of the 20th century, many countries in East Asia developed powerful economies.
- In the 1990s, there was a decline in the economies of the region but they have begun to recover.

### Population

**Case Study: Population and the Quality of Life**
- East Asia has a huge population.
- Despite a reduced birth rate, the population in the region will continue to grow well into the 21st century.
- A growing population affects the quality of life in a nation.

## Reviewing Places & Terms

### A. Briefly explain the importance of each of the following.

1. Ring of Fire
2. Great Kanto earthquake
3. tsunami
4. UNICEF
5. global economy
6. Jakota Triangle
7. recession
8. sweatshop

### B. Answer the questions about vocabulary in complete sentences.

9. How many people were killed and how many homes destroyed in the Great Kanto earthquake?
10. What is the basic cause of the physical events that characterize the Ring of Fire?
11. Upon what is the prosperity of the Jakota Triangle primarily based?
12. Why are sweatshops profitable?
13. What sorts of natural disasters occur around the Ring of Fire?
14. How does Japan participate in the global economy?
15. How might economic reform in East Asia affect sweatshops?
16. What besides earthquake damage made the Great Kanto earthquake so destructive?
17. What are three causes of tsunamis?
18. Which countries in the region experienced a recession?
19. What sorts of economies make up the Jakota Triangle?
20. With what issues does UNICEF concern itself?

## Main Ideas

**The Ring of Fire (pp. 661–664)**

1. What causes an earthquake?
2. Why are the Japanese islands so unstable?
3. What are some Japanese organizations that help prepare for disasters?

**Trade and Prosperity (pp. 665–667)**

4. What effect did Western nations have on economic development in East Asia?
5. What is the connection between industrialization and globalization?
6. What are some of the things that went wrong in the economies of the region?

**Case Study: Population and the Quality of Life (pp. 668–671)**

7. What are some examples of the stress that population growth puts on the environment?
8. What are some effective ways to manage population growth?
9. How developed was East Asia in the middle of the 20th century?
10. How had East Asia changed by the beginning of the 21st century?

# Critical Thinking

## 1. Using Your Notes

Use your completed chart to answer these questions.

| | Causes | Effects |
|---|---|---|
| Issue 1: Ring of Fire | | |
| Issue 2: Trade | | |

a. What are some of the effects of the Ring of Fire?

b. What role did labor play in the booming economies of East Asia after World War II?

## 2. Geographic Themes

a. **REGION** What are some of the ways that people respond to the dangers of living in the Ring of Fire?

b. **HUMAN-ENVIRONMENT INTERACTION** How does a rising population put a strain on the environment?

## 3. Identifying Themes

What might be some of the advantages of reducing population growth in the region? Which of the five themes apply to this situation?

## 4. Determining Cause and Effect

What might be the connection between population and trade in some of the economies of the region?

## 5. Making Inferences

Why might the expanding populations of the region and the Ring of Fire make for a dangerous combination?

Additional Test Practice, pp. S1–S37

**TEST PRACTICE**
CLASSZONE.COM

# Geographic Skills: Interpreting Graphs

## World Population and Growth

Use the graph to answer the questions.

1. **ANALYZING DATA** What was the population of the world in the year 1?

2. **MAKING COMPARISONS** How long did it take for the world's population to double from the year 1?

3. **MAKING COMPARISONS** How many years might it take for the world's population to double after 1974? What is the total expected to be in 2028?

### GeoActivity

Do research to create a bar graph showing population growth and doubling time in one country in the region. Compare it with a bar graph showing the same information for the United States. Display the two bar graphs side by side.

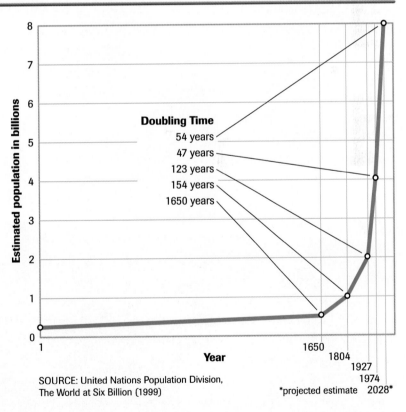

Doubling Time
54 years
47 years
123 years
154 years
1650 years

Estimated population in billions

Year

1650
1804
1927
1974
*projected estimate 2028*

SOURCE: United Nations Population Division, The World at Six Billion (1999)

## INTERNET ACTIVITY

Use the links at **classzone.com** to do research about the Ring of Fire. Focus on major eruptions, earthquakes, and tsunamis in the region.

**Creating Multimedia Presentations** Combine charts, maps, or other visual images in a presentation showing strategies to prepare for natural disasters along the Ring of Fire.

# Unit 10

# Southeast Asia, Oceania, and Antarctica

Ranging from flat plateaus to volcanic peaks, this region has diverse landforms. The vast Pacific Ocean links the scattered parts of this region together.

REGION Towering cliffs covered with snow and ice are a distinctive characteristic of the landscape of Antarctica.

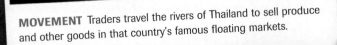

MOVEMENT Traders travel the rivers of Thailand to sell produce and other goods in that country's famous floating markets.

## GeoData

**REGION** Oceania includes the Pacific Islands not considered to be part of Southeast Asia. Some people include New Zealand and Australia, even though Australia is a continent, not an island.

**LOCATION** Australia is known as the "Land Down Under." It is the only inhabited continent to lie completely in the Southern Hemisphere.

**HUMAN–ENVIRONMENT INTERACTION** Farmers have adapted to the region's varied environments. They use terraced fields on steep Southeast Asian slopes and irrigate arid parts of Australia.

**For more information on Southeast Asia, Oceania, and Antarctica . . .**

**RESEARCH LINKS**
CLASSZONE.COM

# Today's Issues in Southeast Asia, Oceania, and Antarctica

Today, Southeast Asia, Oceania, and Antarctica face the issues previewed here. As you read Chapters 30 and 31, you will learn helpful background information. You will study the issues themselves in Chapter 32.

In a small group, answer the questions below. Then participate in a class discussion of your answers.

## Exploring the Issues

1. **LAND CLAIMS** Search the Internet for information about Aboriginal land claims in Australia. What are the different sides in the conflict?

2. **INDUSTRIALISM** Make a list of the possible results of industrial growth, both positive and negative. How might a country reduce the negative effects?

3. **ENVIRONMENTAL CHANGE** Consider news stories that you've heard about global warming and the ozone hole. What are some of the predicted effects? Make a list of all the effects you can remember.

For more on these issues in Southeast Asia, Oceania, and Antarctica . . .

**CURRENT EVENTS**
CLASSZONE.COM

**LAND CLAIMS**

## Should native people be given back their ancestors' land?

These two Aboriginal men are elders of the Wuthathi people. They have come to bury the skull of an ancestor in their homeland. Aboriginal people feel a strong spiritual connection to their land and do not want to be separated from it even in death.

## How does industrialization affect cities?

This slum in Jakarta, Indonesia, shows how difficult it is to provide adequate housing for the thousands of people who move to cities seeking factory jobs.

# CASESTUDY

## How have people changed the atmosphere?

The green and blue areas in these satellite images show where the ozone layer over Antarctica is thinnest. Ozone in the stratosphere, a layer of the atmosphere, protects the living things of earth from harmful ultraviolet radiation.

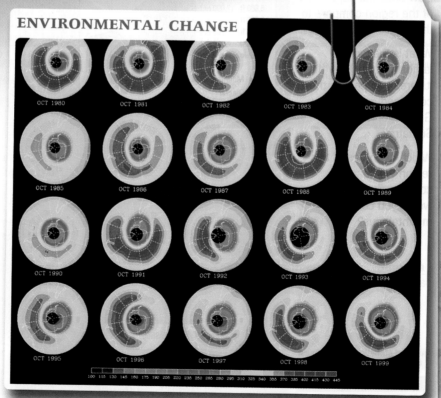

ENVIRONMENTAL CHANGE

OCT 1980   OCT 1981   OCT 1982   OCT 1983   OCT 1984

OCT 1985   OCT 1986   OCT 1987   OCT 1988   OCT 1989

OCT 1990   OCT 1991   OCT 1992   OCT 1993   OCT 1994

OCT 1995   OCT 1996   OCT 1997   OCT 1998   OCT 1999

100 115 130 145 160 175 190 205 220 235 250 265 280 295 310 325 340 355 370 385 400 415 430 445

# Patterns of Human Geography

Study the map on page 681 to learn about ancient kingdoms and empires of Southeast Asia and the map on both pages to learn about the present-day nations of the region. Then write in your notebook the answers to these questions.

## Making Comparisons

**1.** Which ancient kingdoms or empires have names similar to present-day countries in Southeast Asia? How do their locations compare?

**2.** Which are the largest countries in the region?

**3.** Which country includes part of the Asian mainland and part of a large island?

CHINA

N. KOREA

S. KOREA

JAPAN

INDIA

MYANMAR

LAOS

THAILAND

Hanoi

Vientiane

Yangon

Bangkok

VIETNAM

CAMBODIA

Phnom Penh

Ho Chi Minh City

TAIWAN

PACIFIC OCEAN

Tropic of Cancer

Luzon

Quezon City

Manila

Philippine Sea

NORTHERN MARIANA (U.S.)

GUAM (U.S.

Micronesia

Andaman Sea

Gulf of Thailand

South China Sea

PHILIPPINES

Sulu Sea

BRUNEI

Bandar Seri Begawan

Davao

Mindanao

Koror

FEDERATED STATE OF MICRONESIA

Pal

Kuala Lumpur

MALAYSIA

SINGAPORE

Singapore

Medan

Strait of Malacca

Sumatra

Borneo

Celebes Sea

PALAU

Melanesi

Equator

Palembang

Jakarta

Java Sea

Bandung

Semarang

Surabaya

Java

INDONESIA

Sulawesi

Flores Sea

Banda Sea

PAPUA NEW GUINEA

Port Moresby

E. Timor (UN Admin.)

Timor Sea

Arafura Sea

Darwin

Gulf of Carpentaria

Cora Sea

20°S

Tropic of Capricorn

AUSTRALIA

Brisba

Perth

Great Australian Bight

Adelaide

Sydney

Ca

Melbourne

40°S

INDIAN OCEAN

INDIAN OCEAN

Tasmania

⊛ National capital

• Other city

0    400    800 miles

0    400    800 kilometers

Miller Projection

100°E

120°E

140°E

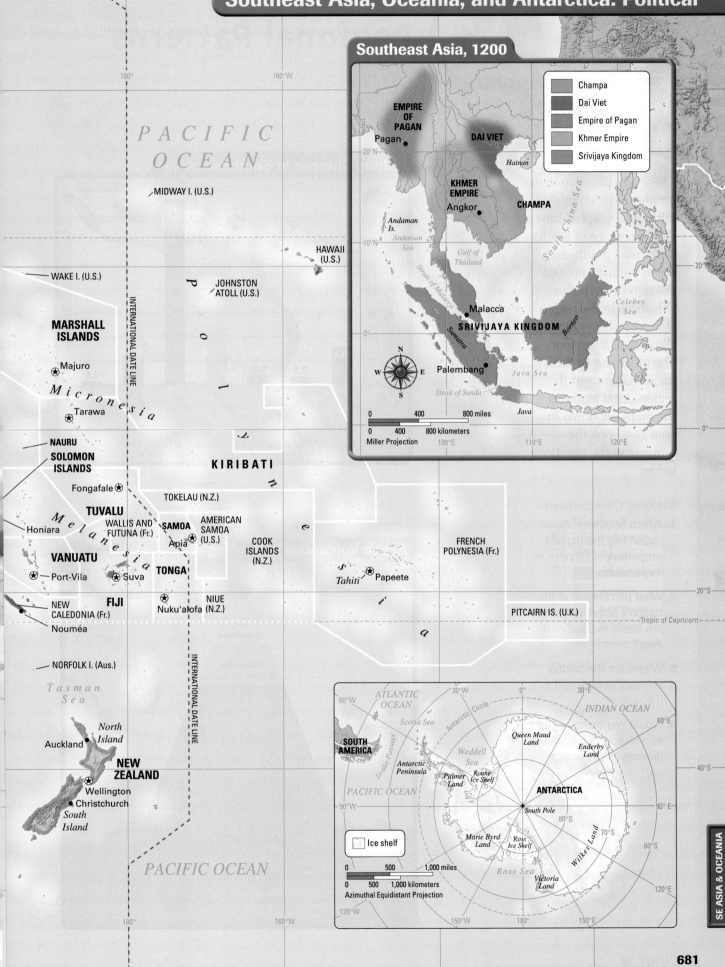

# Southeast Asia, Oceania, and Antarctica: Political

## Southeast Asia, 1200

| | |
|---|---|
| | Champa |
| | Dai Viet |
| | Empire of Pagan |
| | Khmer Empire |
| | Srivijaya Kingdom |

EMPIRE OF PAGAN

Pagan

DAI VIET

Hainan

KHMER EMPIRE

Angkor

CHAMPA

Andaman Is.

Andaman Sea

Gulf of Thailand

Strait of Malacca

Malacca

Sumatra

Borneo

South China Sea

Celebes Sea

SRIVIJAYA KINGDOM

Palembang

Java Sea

Strait of Sunda

Java

N W E S

0    400    800 miles
0    400    800 kilometers
Miller Projection

20°N

10°N

0°

100°E    110°E    120°E

PACIFIC OCEAN

MIDWAY I. (U.S.)

WAKE I. (U.S.)

MARSHALL ISLANDS

Majuro

Micronesia

Tarawa

NAURU

SOLOMON ISLANDS

Fongafale

TUVALU

Honiara

Melanesia

WALLIS AND FUTUNA (Fr.)

VANUATU

Port-Vila

Suva

NEW CALEDONIA (Fr.)

Nouméa

NORFOLK I. (Aus.)

Tasman Sea

North Island

Auckland

NEW ZEALAND

Wellington

Christchurch

South Island

PACIFIC OCEAN

JOHNSTON ATOLL (U.S.)

HAWAII (U.S.)

INTERNATIONAL DATE LINE

KIRIBATI

TOKELAU (N.Z.)

SAMOA

Apia

AMERICAN SAMOA (U.S.)

COOK ISLANDS (N.Z.)

TONGA

FIJI

Nuku'alofa

NIUE (N.Z.)

FRENCH POLYNESIA (Fr.)

Tahiti

Papeete

PITCAIRN IS. (U.K.)

Polynesia

INTERNATIONAL DATE LINE

Tropic of Capricorn

20°S

180°    160°W

## Antarctica

ATLANTIC OCEAN

SOUTH AMERICA

Scotia Sea

Antarctic Peninsula

Drake Passage

PACIFIC OCEAN

Palmer Land

Marie Byrd Land

Ross Ice Shelf

Ross Sea

Victoria Land

Weddell Sea

Ronne Ice Shelf

Queen Maud Land

ANTARCTICA

South Pole

Wilkes Land

Enderby Land

INDIAN OCEAN

Antarctic Circle

Ice shelf

0    500    1,000 miles
0    500    1,000 kilometers
Azimuthal Equidistant Projection

60°W    30°W    0°    30°E    60°E

90°W    80°S    70°S    90°E

120°W    150°W    180°    150°E    120°E

40°S

Chapter 30

SECTION 1
Landforms and Resources

SECTION 2
Climate and Vegetation

SECTION 3
Human–Environment Interaction

# PHYSICAL GEOGRAPHY OF SOUTHEAST ASIA, OCEANIA, AND ANTARCTICA

# A Region of Extremes

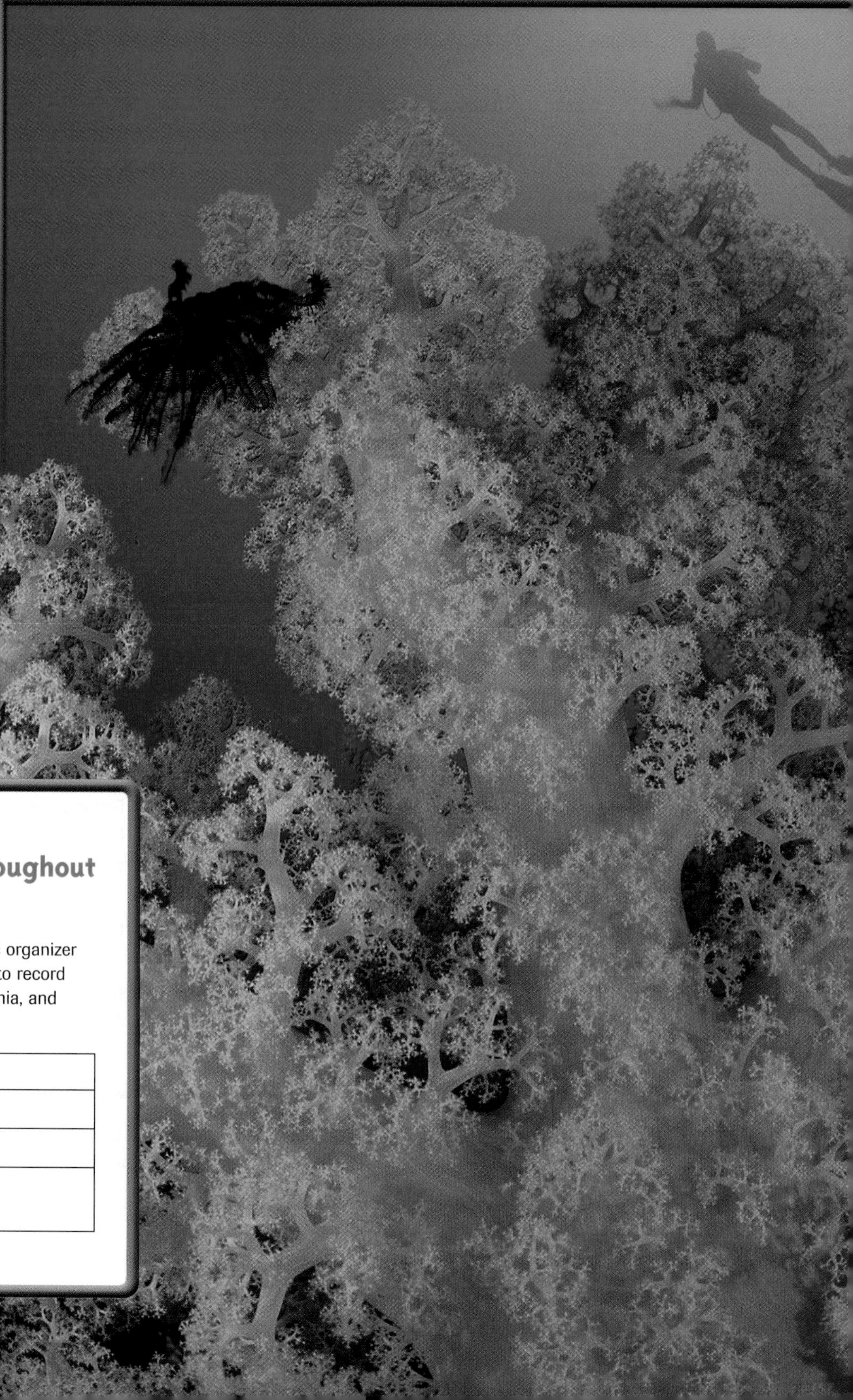

Scuba divers in Australia's Great Barrier Reef can observe some of its more than 1,500 species of fish and approximately 400 species of coral.

## GeoFocus

### How does physical geography vary throughout this vast region?

**Taking Notes** Copy the graphic organizer below into your notebook. Use it to record facts about Southeast Asia, Oceania, and Antarctica.

| | |
|---|---|
| *Landforms* | |
| *Resources* | |
| *Climate and Vegetation* | |
| *Human-Environment Interaction* | |

# Landforms and Resources

**Main Ideas**

- This region includes two peninsulas of Asia, two continents, and more than 20,000 islands.
- Its landforms include mountains, plateaus, and major river systems.

**Places & Terms**

| | |
|---|---|
| archipelago | low island |
| Oceania | Great Barrier |
| high island | Reef |

**CONNECT TO THE ISSUES**

**INDUSTRIALIZATION**
Some countries of this region have used their resources to develop industry, with mixed results.

**A HUMAN PERSPECTIVE** The Aeta (EE·duh) people of the Philippines lived on the volcano Mount Pinatubo for generations. They knew this volcano so well that they timed the planting and harvesting of their crops by the amount of steam rising from a vent on its slope. In 1991, the Aeta noticed changes in the mountain and concluded that it was about to erupt. Tens of thousands of Aeta fled their homes as did count- less other Filipinos. Pinatubo did erupt for the first time in 600 years, spewing ash for miles. Since then, many of the Aeta have formed new communities, but they still miss their homeland. As their story shows, the geologic processes that destroy landforms also disrupt human lives.

## Southeast Asia: Mainland and Islands

Southeast Asia has two distinct subregions: the southeastern corner of the Asian mainland and a great number of islands. Both the mainland and the islands have many high mountains.

**PENINSULAS AND ISLANDS** The most notice- able feature of mainland Southeast Asia is that it lies on two peninsulas. The Indochinese Peninsula, located south of China, has a rectangular shape. In contrast, the Malay Peninsula is a narrow strip of land about 700 miles long, stretching south from the mainland and then curving southeast. It serves as a bridge between the mainland and islands.

Most of the islands of Southeast Asia are found in archipelagoes. An **archipelago** is a set of closely grouped islands, which sometimes form a curved arc. The Philippines and the islands of Indonesia are part of the Malay Archipelago. (See the map on page 680.) A few Southeast Asian islands, such as Borneo, are actually the high points of a sub- merged section of the Eurasian plate.

**MOUNTAINS AND VOLCANOES** On the map at right, you can see that the mainland has several mountain ranges, such as the Annamese Cordillera, running roughly north and south. These ranges fan out from a mountainous area to the north.

**Southeast Asian Mountains and Rivers**

**SKILLBUILDER: Interpreting Maps**

❶ **PLACE** Which mountain chain lies east of the Mekong River?

❷ **LOCATION** How would you describe the relative location of the Chao Phraya?

SE ASIA & OCEANIA

# Disasters!

## Krakatoa

Imagine an explosion so destructive that it sends volcanic ash 50 miles into the air and so loud that people hear it about 3,000 miles away. In 1883, the Indonesian volcano Krakatoa (also spelled *Krakatau*) erupted in an explosion that created those effects. But the blast was only the beginning of the disaster. The eruption caused the volcano to collapse into the sea and triggered a series of deadly tsunamis, or giant waves. The greatest of those towered 120 feet high. The tsunami swept the coasts of Java and Sumatra, killing more than 36,000 people.

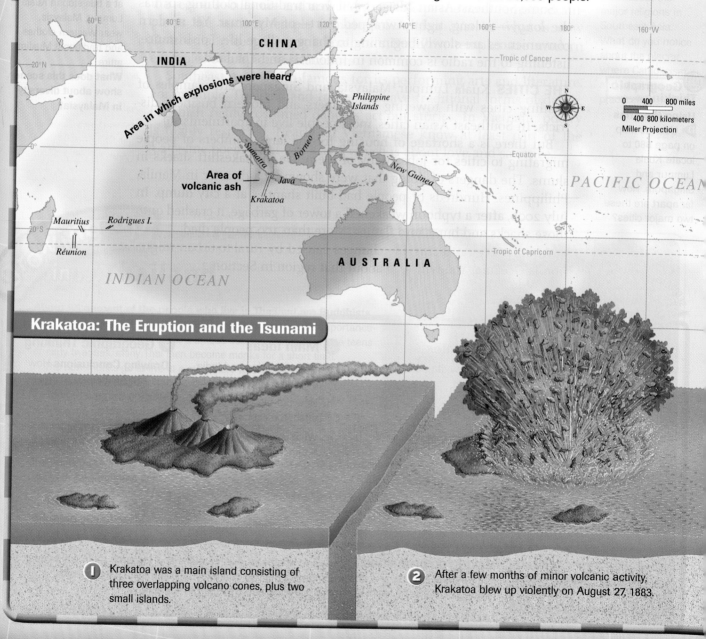

**Krakatoa: The Eruption and the Tsunami**

① Krakatoa was a main island consisting of three overlapping volcano cones, plus two small islands.

② After a few months of minor volcanic activity, Krakatoa blew up violently on August 27, 1883.

**In the Sunda Strait,** in 1927, lava began to flow through a crack in the sea floor beneath the site of the old island. By 1928, a new island was born and named Anak Krakatoa, which means "child of Krakatoa." The island is still volcanically active, but it is not considered dangerous.

③ All three cones disappeared, leaving only a small island. Massive amounts of sea water were displaced. The disturbance of the ocean created giant tsunamis. The tsunamis destroyed about 163 villages.

## GeoData

**DUST IN THE WIND**

- Krakatoa threw so much ash and dust into the air that temperatures dropped by about 0.9°F around the world.
- The dust filtered light and caused spectacular sunsets around the world for about a year.
- The dust in the atmosphere also made the moon look shades of green and blue.

**FIVE DEADLIEST VOLCANOES SINCE 1500**

**1792**
Unzen, Japan:
15,000 dead

**1815**
Tambora, Indonesia:
92,000 dead

**1883**
Krakatoa, Indonesia:
36,000 dead

**1902**
Mount Pelée, Martinique:
30,000 dead

**1985**
Nevado del Ruiz, Colombia:
25,000 dead

# Comparing Cultures

## Regional Costumes

Blue jeans have spread around the globe and become a popular item of clothing symbolizing U.S. culture. But traditional items of clothing remain important in many regions of the world. Regional costumes are unique not only because of their styles but also because of the materials from which they are made.

Japan

Fiji

India

Peru

**In India, the traditional garment of women for centuries has been the sari—** five to seven yards of unstitched cloth wrapped around the body. The most valuable saris are made of silk, but saris of cotton and synthetic fabrics are also common.

**In Fiji, traditional outfits are made from tapa cloth,** a nonwoven fabric made from the inner bark of trees. This woman is wearing a skirt of tapa cloth. Fijians often decorate the cloth with geometric designs painted in brown, black, or reddish bark dyes.

**Although colorful silk kimonos symbolize Japan,** neither the fabric nor the robe itself originated there. Silk was first developed in China, and kimonos are patterned after a wide-sleeved Chinese robe, the *p'ao*.

**These Indians of Peru wear traditional wool clothing woven from llama hair;** llamas are native to South America. Each village has it own set of traditional patterns that are woven into its cloth. Some of the designs indicate local landscapes; others depict animals or historical events.

## GeoData

**Tapa Cloth**
• Tapa cloth is also made in other Melanesian islands, New Guinea, and northern Australia.
• The most popular material for tapa is the inner bark of the mulberry.

**Silk**
• The Chinese began to produce silk in about 2700 B.C. and kept their methods a secret until about 140 B.C.
• The wide silk or satin sash worn with a kimono is called an obi. It is about 12 feet long.

**Cotton**
• South Asia was one of the first regions of the world where cotton was cultivated—starting in about 3000 B.C.
• Indian men also wear a type of wrapped garment called a dhoti. Mohandas Gandhi wore a dhoti to show his allegiance to the common Indian man.

**Wool**
• Wool is the fiber forming the coats of such hairy mammals as sheep, goats, camels, and llamas.
• Intricate textiles have been produced in Peru since about 1000 B.C.

AFGHANISTAN— I entered Afghanistan from the north on an aging ferry boat at dusk on October 22. All I could see in the encroaching darkness were silhouettes of Northern Alliance fighters with Kalishnikov weapons slung loosely on their shoulders. My passport was stamped in a small mud hut under a dim lantern, then I was off to the village of Hoja Baddahuin, where the Northern Alliance had set up headquarters after the Taliban had taken over most of the country.

The United States had entered the war in Afghanistan after the terrorist attacks on September 11, 2001. Covering the war in Afghanistan has been the single most challenging experience of my career as a reporter at USA TODAY.

The most dangerous part of the experience was traveling through the front lines as I made my way to Kabul. My jeep had to cross minefields and the most narrow mountain roads imaginable. At Taloqan, the first city to be restored to the Northern Alliance, I wrote my stories while gunfire erupted outside my walled compound. I paid two men to stay inside with their machine guns and to answer the door should someone come knocking. Taliban fighters were still hiding out in houses just down the street. Through it all, I learned to stay calm by doing the best I could to ensure both my safety and the safety of my team, and to leave the rest to a healthy dose of faith.

## Selected Terrorist Attacks Around the World Since 1972

**United States 2001**
Arab terrorists crash hijacked airliners into the World Trade Center in New York City and the Pentagon in Arlington, VA, September 11.

**Peru 1999**
Peruvian soldiers hunt for Shining Path terrorists near Lima, July 13.

# Hunting for the Terrorists

Terrorism is not new. Reporters like Tim Friend have been covering terrorist attacks across the globe for the last three decades. Throughout history, individuals, small groups, and governments have used terror tactics to try to achieve political or social goals—whether it be to bring down a government, eliminate opponents, or promote a cause.

In recent times, however, terrorism has become an international problem. Since the late 1960s, more than 14,000 terrorist attacks have occurred worldwide. International terrorist groups have carried out increasingly destructive, high-profile attacks to attract global attention. Many countries also face domestic terrorists who oppose their governments' policies or have special interests to promote.

The reasons for modern terrorism are many. The traditional motives, such as gaining independence, expelling foreigners, or changing society, still drive various terrorist groups around the world. These terrorists use violence to force concessions from their enemies, usually the governments in power. But other kinds of terrorists, driven by radical religious motives, began to emerge in the late 20th century.

The goal of these terrorists is the destruction of what they consider the forces of evil. This evil might be located in their own countries or in other parts of the world. These terrorists often threaten to use weapons of mass destruction, such as chemical, biological, or nuclear weapons, to kill their enemies.

**West Germany 1972**
Israeli athletes are killed after being taken hostage by Arab terrorists at the Summer Olympics in Munich, September 5.

**Japan 1995**
The Tokyo subway system is attacked with deadly nerve gas by the Aum Shinrikyo cult, March 20.

**Northern Ireland 1979**
Irish Republican Army assassinates Lord Mountbatten, a member of the British royal family, by blowing up his boat off the Irish coast, August 30.

**Israel 2001**
Suicide bombings by Hamas terrorists in Jerusalem and Haifa kill and wound many civilians, December.

**India 2001**
Kashmiri terrorists attack the Indian Parliament Building in New Delhi, with guns and grenades, December 13.

**Kenya 1998**
U.S. Embassy personnel in Nairobi, Kenya, evacuate area after Arab terrorists detonate truck bombs at embassy buildings there, and in Tanzania, August 7.

## TERRORISM AROUND THE WORLD

The problem of international terrorism first came to world attention in a shocking way during the 1972 Summer Olympic Games in Munich, Germany (then West Germany). Eight members of a Palestinian terrorist group called Black September killed two Israeli athletes and took nine others hostage. Five of the terrorists, all the hostages, and a police officer were later killed in a bloody gun battle. The attack became known as the Munich Massacre. Since then, few regions of the world have been spared from terrorist attacks.

**The Middle East** Like Black September, many terrorist organizations have their roots in the Israeli-Palestinian conflict over land in the Middle East.

("Middle East" is the political term for the geographic region of Southwest Asia.) Arab terrorist groups such as the Palestine Islamic Jihad, Hamas, and Hizballah have sought to prevent a peace settlement between Israel and the Palestinians. They want a homeland for the Palestinians on their own terms, with the most extreme among them denying Israel's right to exist. In a continual cycle of violence, the Israelis retaliate after each terrorist attack, and the terrorists attack again.

Among Muslims in the Middle East, the Israeli-Palestinian violence has bred widespread Arab anger at Israel—and at the United States for supporting Israel. For example, the Lebanese-based group Hizballah seeks to eliminate all non-Islamic influences in Muslim countries. It is thought to have been

# World Geography

## Reference Section

# Contents

## CRITICAL THINKING AND GEOGRAPHY SKILLS

## USING TECHNOLOGY SOURCES

**Indus Valley civilization** *n.* the largest of the world's first civilizations in what is now Pakistan; this was a highly developed urban civilization, lasting from 2500 B.C. to about 1500 B.C. (p. 573)

**infant mortality rate** *n.* the number of deaths among infants under age one as measured per thousand live births. (p. 79)

**infrastructure** *n.* the basic support systems needed to keep an economy going, including power, communications, transportation, water, sanitation, and education systems. (pp. 94, 177, 212)

**innovation** *n.* taking existing elements of society and creating something new to meet a need. (p. 72)

**Institutional Revolutionary Party (PRI)** *n.* the political party introduced in 1929 in Mexico that helped to introduce democracy and maintain political stability for much of the 20th century. (p. 218)

**Islam** *n.* a monotheistic religion based on the teachings of the prophet Muhammad, and the biggest cultural and religious influence in North Africa. (pp. 439, 503)

### J

**Jakota Triangle** *n.* a zone of prosperity during the 1980s and early 1990s—Japan, South Korea, and Taiwan. (p. 666)

**Jordan River** *n.* a river that serves as a natural boundary between Israel and Jordan, flowing from the mountains of Lebanon with no outlet to the Mediterranean Sea. (p. 489)

**junta** (HOON•tah) *n.* a government run by generals after a military takeover. (p. 249)

### K

**Kashmir** *n.* a region of northern India and Pakistan over which several destructive wars have been fought. (p. 574)

**Khmer Empire** *n.* a powerful empire that lasted roughly from the 9th to the 15th centuries in what is now Cambodia. (p. 706)

**King Leopold II** *n.* the Belgian king who opened up the African interior to European trade along the Congo River and by 1884 controlled the area known as the Congo Free State. (p. 449)

**KLA (Kosovo Liberation Army)** *n.* a group that fought against Serbian attempts to control the region of Kosovo in the 1990s. (p. 321)

**Kunlun Mountains** *n.* mountains located in the west of China that are the source of two of China's great rivers, the Huang He (Yellow) and the Chang Jiang (Yangtze). (p. 619)

**Kurds** *n.* an ethnic group in Southwestern Asia that has occupied Kurdistan, located in Turkey, Iraq, and Iran, for about a thousand years, and who have been involved in clashes with these three countries over land claims for most of the 20th century. (p. 516)

### L

**landfill** *n.* a method of solid waste disposal in which refuse is buried between layers of dirt in order to fill in or reclaim low-lying ground. (p. 631)

**landform** *n.* a naturally formed feature on the surface of the earth. (p. 33)

**landlocked** *adj.* having no outlet to the sea. (p. 84)

**land reform** *n.* the process of breaking up large landholdings to attain a more balanced land distribution among farmers. (pp. 250, 569)

**Land Rights Act of 1976** *n.* a special law passed for Aboriginal rights in Australia giving Aboriginal people the right to claim land in the Northern Territory. (p. 728)

**Landsat** *n.* a series of satellites that orbit more than 100 miles above the earth. Each satellite picks up data in an area 115 miles wide. (p. 12)

**latitude (lines)** *n.* a set of imaginary lines that run parallel to the equator, and that are used in locating places north or south. The equator is labeled the zero-degree line for latitude. (p. 6)

**lava** *n.* magma that has reached the earth's surface. (p. 40)

**lithosphere** *n.* the solid rock portion of the earth's surface. (p. 28)

**llanos** (LAH•nohs) *n.* a large, grassy, treeless area in South America, used for grazing and farming. (p. 202)

**lock** *n.* a section of a waterway with closed gates where water levels are raised or lowered, through which ships pass. (p. 129)

**loess** (LOH•uhs) *n.* wind-blown silt and clay sediment that produces very fertile soil. (p. 44)

**longitude (lines)** *n.* a set of imaginary lines that go around the earth over the poles, dividing it east and west. The prime meridian is labeled the zero-degree line for longitude. (p. 6)

**Louisiana Purchase** *n.* the territory, including the region between the Mississippi River and the Rocky Mountains, that the United States purchased from France in 1803. (p. 136)

**low islands** *n.* Pacific islands made of coral reefs. (p. 691)

### M

**Mabo Case** *n.* in Australia, the law case that upheld Aboriginal Eddie Mabo's land claim by which the Court recognized that Aboriginal people had owned land before the British arrived. (p. 728)

**Mackenzie River** *n.* Canada's longest river, which is part of a river system that flows across the Northwest Territories to the Arctic Ocean. (p. 121)

**magma** *n.* the molten rock material formed when solid rock in the earth's mantle or crust melts. (p. 28)

**malaria** *n.* an infectious disease of the red blood cells, carried by mosquitoes, that is characterized by chills, fever, and sweating. (p. 466)

**mandala** *n.* in Tibetan Buddhism, a geometric design that symbolizes the universe and aids in meditation. (p. 583)

**mandala** *n.* a state organized as a ring of power around a central court, which often changed in size over time, and which was used instead of borders in early Southeast Asian states. (p. 705)

**mantle** *n.* a rock layer about 1,800 miles thick that is between the earth's crust and the earth's core. (p. 28)

**Maori** *n.* the first settlers of New Zealand, who had migrated from Polynesia more than 1,000 years ago. (p. 719)

**Mao Zedong** *n.* the leader of the Communists in China who defeated the Nationalists in 1949; he died in 1976. (p. 636)

**map projection** *n.* a way of mapping the earth's surface that reduces distortion caused by converting three dimensions into two dimensions. (p. 10)

**map** *n.* a two-dimensional graphic representation of selected parts of the earth's surface. (p. 10)

**maquiladora** *n.* a factory in Mexico that assembles imported materials into finished goods for export. (p. 220)

**market economy** *n.* a type of economic system in which production of goods and services is determined by the demand from consumers. Also called a demand economy or capitalism. (pp. 91, 313)

**Massif Central** (ma•SEEF sahn•TRAHL) *n.* the uplands of France, which account for about one-sixth of French lands. (p. 275)

**Mecca** *n.* the holiest city of Islam, located in Saudi Arabia, where people make pilgrimages to fulfill Islamic religious duty. (p. 503)

**mechanical weathering** *n.* natural processes that break rock into smaller pieces. (p. 42)

**megalopolis** *n.* a region in which several large cities and surrounding areas grow together. (p. 146)

**Melanesia** *n.* a region in Oceania meaning "black islands." (p. 713)

**Meseta** (meh•SEH•tah) *n.* the central plateau of Spain. (p. 275)

**Mesopotamia** *n.* a region in Southwest Asia between the Tigris and the Euphrates rivers, which was the location of some of the earliest civilizations in the world; part of the cultural hearth known as the Fertile Crescent. (p. 516)

**métis** (may•TEES) *n.* a person of mixed French-Canadian and Native American ancestry. (p. 161)

**metropolitan area** *n.* a functional area including a city and its surrounding suburbs and exurbs, linked economically. (pp. 87, 148)

**microcredit** *n.* a small loan available to poor entrepreneurs, to help small businesses grow and raise living standards. (p. 575)

**Micronesia** *n.* one of three regions in Oceania, meaning "tiny islands." (p. 713)

**Midwest** *n.* the region that contains the 12 states of the north-central United States. (p. 147)

**migration** *n.* the movement of peoples within a country or region. (p. 135)

**Mississippi River** *n.* a major river that runs north-south almost the length of the United States, from Minnesota to the Gulf of Mexico, and is part of the longest river system on the continent. (p. 121)

**mistral** (MIHS•truhl) *n.* a cold, dry wind from the north. (p. 279)

**Mobutu Sese Seko** *n.* the leader of Zaire, which is now the Democratic Republic of the Congo, from its independence in the 1960s until 1997. He brought the country's businesses under national control, profited from the reorganization, and used the army to hold power. (p. 450)

**monarchy** *n.* a type of government in which a ruling family headed by a king or queen holds political power and may or may not share the power with citizen bodies. (p. 83)

**monsoon** *n.* a seasonal wind, especially in South Asia. (p. 558)

**moraine** *n.* a ridge or hill of rock carried and finally deposited by a glacier. (p. 44)

**mortality rate** *n.* the number of deaths per thousand. (p. 79)

**mosque** *n.* an Islamic place of worship, where Muslims pray facing toward the holy city of Mecca. (p. 504)

**Mount Kilimanjaro** *n.* a volcano in Tanzania in Africa, also Africa's highest peak. (p. 417)

**Mughal Empire** *n.* the Muslim empire established by the early 1500s over much of India, which brought with it new customs that sometimes conflicted with those of native Hindus. (p. 568)

**Muhammad** *n.* the founder and a prophet of Islam, who lived part of his life in the city of Mecca. (p. 503)

**multinational** *n.* a corporation that engages in business worldwide. (p. 142)

**Mutapa Empire** *n.* a state founded in the 15th century by a man named Mutota and that extended throughout all of present-day Zimbabwe except the eastern part. (p. 453)

## N

**Nagorno-Karabakh** *n.* the mountainous area of Azerbaijan, fought over by Armenia and Azerbaijan. (p. 386)

**nation** *n.* a group of people with a common culture living in a territory and having a strong sense of unity. (p. 83)

**nationalism** *n.* the belief that people should be loyal to their nation, the people with whom they share land, culture, and history. (p. 297)

**nation-state** *n.* the name of a territory when a nation and a state occupy the same territory. (p. 83)

**natural resource** *n.* a material on or in the earth, such as a tree, fish, or coal, that has economic value. (p. 93)

**needleleaf** *adj.* characteristic of trees like pine, fir, and cedar, found in northern regions of North America. (p. 66)

**Nelson Mandela** *n.* one of the leaders of the African National Congress who led a struggle to end apartheid and was elected president in 1994 in the first all-race election in South Africa. (p. 454)

**New England** *n.* the six northern states in the Northeast United States—Maine, Vermont, New Hampshire, Massachusetts, Rhode Island, and Connecticut. (p. 145)

**Niger delta** *n.* delta of the Niger River and an area of Nigeria with rich oil deposits. (p. 424)

**Nile River** *n.* the world's longest river, flowing over 4,000 miles through the Sudan Basin into Uganda, Sudan, and Egypt. (p. 416)

**nomad** *n.* a person with no permanent home who moves according to the seasons from place to place in search of food, water, and grazing land. (pp. 127, 378)

**nonviolent resistance** *n.* a movement that uses all means of protest except violence. (p. 568)

**Nordic countries** *n.* countries of northern Europe, including Denmark, Finland, Iceland, Norway, and Sweden. (p. 302)

**NAFTA (North American Free Trade Agreement)** *n.* an important trade agreement creating a huge zone of cooperation on trade and economic issues in North America. (p. 220)

**North Atlantic Drift** *n.* a current of warm water from the Tropics. (p. 278)

**Nunavut** *n.* one of Canada's territories and home to many of Canada's Inuit; it was carved out of the eastern half of the Northwest Territories in 1999. (p. 169)

## O

**oasis** *n.* a place where water from an aquifer has reached the surface; it supports vegetation and wildlife. (pp. 421, 492)

**Oceania** *n.* the group of islands in the Pacific, including Melanesia, Micronesia, and Polynesia. (p. 690)

**Olduvai Gorge** *n.* a site of fossil beds in northern Tanzania, containing the most continuous known record of humanity over the past 2 million years, including fossils from 65 hominids. (p. 431)

**oligarchy** (AHL•ih•GAHR•kee) *n.* a government run by a few persons or a small group. (p. 249)

**"one-commodity" country** *n.* a country that relies on one principal export for much of its earnings. (p. 462)

**Ontario** *n.* one of Canada's Core Provinces. (p. 167)

**OPEC** *n.* the Organization of Petroleum Exporting Countries, a group established in 1960 by some oil-producing nations to coordinate policies on selling petroleum products. (p. 505)

**Orinoco River** *n.* a river mainly in Venezuela and part of South America's northernmost river system. (p. 202)

**outback** *n.* the dry, unpopulated inland region of Australia. (p. 697)

**outrigger canoe** *n.* a small ship used in the lagoons of islands where Pacific Islanders settled. (p. 699)

**ozone** *n.* a chemical created when burning fossil fuels react with sunlight; a form of oxygen. (p. 325)

### P

**Pacific Rim** *n.* an economic and social region including the countries surrounding the Pacific Ocean, extending clockwise from New Zealand in the western Pacific to Chile in the eastern Pacific and including the west coast of the United States. (p. 645)

*pakehas n.* a Maori term for white people, for the New Zealanders of European descent. (p. 722)

**Palestine Liberation Organization (PLO)** *n.* a group formed in the 1960s to regain the Arab land in Israel for Palestinian Arabs. (p. 513)

**Palestinians** *n.* a displaced group of Arabs who lived or still live in the area formerly called Palestine and now called Israel. (p. 527)

**pampas** (PAHM•puhs) *n.* a vast area of grassland and rich soil in south-central South America. (p. 202)

**Panama Canal** *n.* a ship canal cut through Panama connecting the Caribbean Sea with the Pacific Ocean. (p. 226)

**pandemic** *n.* a disease affecting a large population over a wide geographic area. (p. 435)

**Paraná River** *n.* a river in central South America and one of its three major river systems, originating in the highlands of southern Brazil, travelling about 3,000 miles south and west. (p. 203)

**parliament** *n.* a representative lawmaking body whose members are elected or appointed and in which legislative and executive functions are combined. (pp. 158, 303)

**parliamentary government** *n.* a system where legislative and executive functions are combined in a legislature called a parliament. (p. 158)

**particulate** *n.* a very small particle of liquid or solid matter. (p. 324)

**partition** *n.* separation; division into two or more territorial units having separate political status. (p. 574)

**pastoral lease** *n.* in Australia, a huge chunk of land still owned by the government; ranchers take out leases, renting the land from the government. (p. 729)

**PCB** *n.* an industrial compound that accumulates in animal tissue and can cause harmful effects and birth defects; PCBs were banned in the United States in 1977. (p. 631)

**peat** *n.* partially decayed plant matter found in bogs. (p. 277)

**penal colony** *n.* a place to send prisoners. (p. 718)

**per capita income** *n.* the average amount of money earned by each person in a political unit. (p. 94)

**permafrost** *n.* permanently frozen ground. (pp. 63, 123)

**polder** *n.* land that is reclaimed from the sea or other body of water by diking and drainage. (p. 282)

**Polynesia** *n.* one of three regions in Oceania, meaning "many islands." (p. 713)

**population density** *n.* the average number of people who live in a measurable area, reached by dividing the number of inhabitants in an area by the amount of land they occupy. (p. 81)

**population pyramid** *n.* a graphic device that shows gender and age distribution of a population. (p. 79)

**postindustrial economy** *n.* an economic phase in which manufacturing no longer plays a dominant role. (p. 142)

**Prairie Provinces** *n.* in Canada, the provinces west of Ontario and Quebec—Manitoba, Saskatchewan, and Alberta. (p. 168)

**precipitation** *n.* falling water droplets in the form of rain, sleet, snow, or hail. (p. 50)

**prevailing westerlies** *n.* winds that blow from west to east. (p. 124)

**prime meridian** *n.* the imaginary line at zero meridian used to measure longitude east to west, and dividing the earth's east and west halves; also called the Greenwich Meridian because it passes through Greenwich, England. (p. 6)

**prime minister** *n.* the head of a government; the majority party's leader in parliament. (p. 158)

**privatization** *n.* the selling of government-owned business to private citizens. (p. 388)

**province** *n.* a political unit. (p. 156)

**pull factor** *n.* a factor that draws or attracts people to another location. (pp. 81, 211)

**push factor** *n.* a factor that causes people to leave their homelands and migrate to another region. (pp. 81, 211, 730)

**Pyongyang** *n.* the largest city in North Korea, with more than 2.5 million people. (p. 650)

### Q

**Qin Ling Mountains** *n.* mountains in southeastern and east-central China; they divide the northern part of China from the southern part. (p. 619)

**Quebec** *n.* one of Canada's Core Provinces. (p. 167)

**Quechua** (KEHCH•wuh) *n.* the language of the Inca Empire, now spoken in the Andes highlands. (p. 231)

### R

*rai n.* a kind of popular Algerian music developed in the 1920s by poor urban children that is fast-paced with danceable rhythms; was sometimes used as a form of rebellion to expose political unhappiness. (p. 440)

**rain forest** *n.* a forest region located in the Tropical Zone with a heavy concentration of different species of broadleaf trees. (pp. 66, 207)

**rain shadow** *n.* the land on the leeward side of hills or mountains that gets little rain from the descending dry air. (p. 51)

*raj n.* the period of British rule in India, which lasted for nearly 200 years, from 1857 to 1947. (p. 568)

**Ramadan** *n.* an Islamic practice of month-long fasting from sunup to sundown. (p. 576)

**rate of natural increase** *n.* also called population growth rate—the rate at which population is growing, found by subtracting the mortality rate from the birthrate. (p. 79)

**recession** *n.* an extended period of decline in general business activity. (p. 667)

**Red Army** *n.* the name of the Soviet Union's military. (p. 371)

**refinery** *n.* a place where crude oil is converted into useful products. (p. 497)

**Reformation** *n.* a movement in Western Europe beginning in 1517, when many Christians broke away from the Catholic Church and started Protestant churches; this led to mutual hostility and religious wars that tore apart Europe. (p. 297)

**reggae** *n.* a style of music that developed in Jamaica in the 1960s and is rooted in African, Caribbean, and American music, often dealing with social problems and religion. (p. 227)

**relative location** *n.* describes a place in relation to other places around it. (p. 6)

**relief** *n.* the difference in elevation of a landform from the lowest point to the highest point. (p. 36)

**religion** *n.* the belief in a supernatural power or powers that are regarded as the creators and maintainers of the universe, as well as the system of beliefs itself. (p. 75)

**Renaissance** *n.* a time of renewed interest in learning and the arts that lasted from the 14th through 16th centuries; it began in the Italian city-states and spread north to all of Europe. (p. 291)

**representative democracy** *n.* a government in which the people rule through elected representatives. (p. 139)

**republic** *n.* a government in which citizens elect representatives to rule on their behalf. (p. 290)

**reserve** *n.* public land set aside for native peoples by the government. (p. 162)

**Richter scale** *n.* a way to measure information collected by seismographs to determine the relative strength of an earthquake. (p. 40)

**rift valley** *n.* a long, thin valley created by the moving apart of the continental plates, present in East Africa, stretching over 4,000 miles from Jordan in Southwest Asia to Mozambique in Southern Africa. (p. 416)

**Ring of Fire** *n.* the chain of volcanoes that lines the Pacific Rim. (pp. 41, 661)

**Rocky Mountains** *n.* a major mountain system of the United States and Canada, extending 3,000 miles from Alaska south to New Mexico. (p. 119)

**Rub al Khali** *n.* also known as the Empty Quarter; one of the largest sandy deserts in the world, covering about 250,000 square miles; located on the Arabian Peninsula. (p. 491)

**Russian Revolution** *n.* the revolt of 1917, in which the Russian Communist Party, led by V. I. Lenin, took control of the government from the czars. (p. 363)

**runoff** *n.* rainfall not absorbed by soil, which can carry pesticides and fertilizers from fields into rivers, endangering the food chain. (p. 353)

**S**

**Sahara** *n.* the largest desert in the world, stretching 3,000 miles across the African continent, from the Atlantic Ocean to the Red Sea, and measuring 1,200 miles from north to south. (p. 420)

**Sahel** *n.* a narrow band of dry grassland, running east to west on the southern edge of the Sahara, that is used for farming and herding. (p. 424)

**St. Lawrence Seaway** *n.* North America's most important deepwater ship route, connecting the Great Lakes to the Atlantic Ocean by way of the St. Lawrence River. (p. 129)

**St. Petersburg** *n.* the old capital of Russia, established by Peter the Great, who moved it there from Moscow because St. Petersburg provided direct access by sea to Western Europe. (p. 362)

**salt flat** *n.* flat land made of chemical salts that remain after winds evaporate the moisture in the soil. (p. 492)

**samba** *n.* a Brazilian dance with African influences. (p. 239)

**samurai** *n.* a professional soldier in Japan who served the interests of landowners and clan chiefs. (p. 651)

**satellite nation** *n.* a nation dominated by another country. (p. 312)

**savanna** *n.* the term for the flat, grassy, mostly treeless plains in the tropical grassland region. (p. 66)

**seawork** *n.* a structure used to control the sea's destructive impact on human life. (p. 283)

**sectionalism** *n.* when people place their loyalty to their region, or section, above loyalty to the nation. (p. 136)

**sediment** *n.* small pieces of rock produced by weathering processes. (p. 42)

**seismograph** (SYZ•muh•GRAF) *n.* a device that measures the size of the waves created by an earthquake. (p. 39)

**Seoul** *n.* the largest city in South Korea, with a population of more than ten million people. (p. 650)

**Serengeti** *n.* an area of East Africa, containing some of the best grasslands in the world and many grazing animals. (p. 422)

**service industry** *n.* any kind of economic activity that produces a service rather than a product. (p. 142)

**Sherpa** *n.* a person of Tibetan ancestry in Nepal, who serves as the traditional mountain guide of the Mount Everest region. (p. 582)

**Shi'ite** *n.* one of the two main branches of Islam including most Iranians and some populations of Iraq and Afghanistan. (p. 517)

**shogun** *n.* the general of the emperor's army with the powers of a military dictator, a position created by the Japanese emperor in 1192 after a struggle between two powerful clans. (p. 651)

**Siberia** *n.* a region of central and eastern Russia, stretching from the Ural Mountains to the Pacific Ocean, known for its mineral resources and for being a place of political exile. (p. 349)

**Siddhartha Gautama** *n.* the founder of Buddhism and known as the Buddha, born in southern Nepal in the sixth century B.C. (p. 582)

**Silicon Glen** *n.* the section of Scotland between Glasgow and Edinburgh, named for its high concentration of high-tech companies. (p. 305)

**Silk Road** *n.* the 4,000-mile route between China and the Mediterranean Sea, named for the costly silk acquired in China. (p. 375)

**silt** *n.* loose sedimentary material containing very small rock particles, formed by river deposits and very fertile. (p. 426)

**Sinhalese** *n.* an Indo-Aryan people who crossed the strait separating India and Sri Lanka in the sixth century B.C. and who created an advanced civilization there, adopting Buddhism. (p. 584)

Bucharest (44°26'N/26°06'E) The capital of Romania, 268

Budapest (47°30'N/19°05'E) The capital of Hungary, 266

Buenos Aires (34°35'S/58°40'W) The capital of Argentina, 211

Bujumbura (3°23'S/29°22'E) The capital of Burundi, 408

Bulgaria (43°00'N/25°00'E) A country in Eastern Europe, 308

Burkina Faso (13°00'N/2°00'W) A country in West Africa, 442

Burundi (3°00'S/29°30'E) A country in East Africa, 431

Cairo (30°03'N/31°15'E) The capital of Egypt, 408

California (37°15'N/119°45'W) A state in the western United States, 149

Cambodia (13°00'N/105°00'E) A country in Southeast Asia, 705

Cameroon (6°00'N/12°00'E) A country in Central Africa, 448, m450

Cameroon, Mount (4°12'N/9°11'E) A mountain in Cameroon, 417

Canada (60°00'N/96°00'W) A country in northern North America that consists of ten provinces and three territories, 117

Canadian Shield (55°00'N/90°00'W) A rocky, flat region that encircles Hudson Bay, m118, 119

Canberra (35°17'S/149°13'E) The capital of Australia, 684

Cape Verde (16°00'N/24°00'W) A country formed by a group of islands in West Africa, 442

Caracas (10°30'N/66°55'W) The capital of Venezuela, 198

Caribbean Islands Three major groups of islands: the Bahamas (in the Atlantic Ocean near southeastern Florida) and the Greater Antilles and the Lesser Antilles (in the Caribbean Sea), 203

Caribbean Sea (15°00'N/75°00'W) A body of water bounded by South America, Central America, the Gulf of Mexico, and the Greater Antilles, 191

Carson City (39°10'N/119°43'W) The capital of Nevada, 110

Carthage (36°51'N/10°20'E) A city located in northeastern Tunisia; in ancient times, the center of the Carthaginian Empire, 438

Cascade Range (44°43'N/122°03'W) A North American mountain range that runs parallel to the Pacific coastline from California to British Columbia, Canada, 120

Caspian Sea (42°00'N/50°00'E) A lake that lies between southeast Europe and western Asia, 348

Castries (14°00'N/61°00'W) The capital of Saint Lucia, 198

Catskill Mountains (42°15'N/74°15'W) A North American mountain range located in the northern part of the Appalachian system, 119

Caucasus (42°00'N/45°00'E) A region that includes the Caucasus Mountains, which stretch between the Black and Caspian seas, 385, m385

Caucasus Mountains (42°30'N/45°00'E) A mountain range that stretches across the isthmus that separates the Black and Caspian seas, 346

Central Africa A region of Africa that includes Cameroon, Central African Republic, Democratic Republic of the Congo, Republic of the Congo, Equatorial Guinea, Gabon, and São Tomé & Príncipe, 448, m450

Central African Republic (7°00'N/21°00'E) A country in Central Africa, 448, m450

Central America A Latin American subregion bounded by Mexico, the Caribbean Sea, the Pacific Ocean, and South America, 223

Central Asia A region that includes Kazakhstan, Kyrgyzstan, Tajikistan, Turkmenistan, and Uzbekistan, 375

Central Siberian Plateau (66°00'N/106°00'E) A plateau in central Russia, 345

Chad (15°00'N/19°00'E) A country in West Africa, 442

Chad, Lake (13°20'N/14°00'E) A lake in western Chad; on the borders of Nigeria, Niger, and Chad, 425

Chang Jiang (also called Yangtze River) (31°47'N/121°08'E) The longest river in Asia; flows from Xizang (Tibet) across China to the East China Sea, m620, 621

Charleston (38°21'N/81°38'W) The capital of West Virginia, 112

Charlotte Amalie The capital of the U.S. Virgin Islands, 112

Charlottetown (46°14'N/63°08'W) The capital of Prince Edward Island, Canada, 114

Chechnya (43°18'N/45°42'E) A Russian republic in the Caucasus, 385, m385

Chennai (also called Madras) (13°05'N/80°17'E) A city in southern India, m569, 570

Chernobyl (51°16'N/30°14'E) A city in north-central Ukraine, 392

Cheyenne (41°08'N/104°49'W) The capital of Wyoming, 112

Chicago (41°50'N/87°41'W) Located in northeastern Illinois; the largest city in the Midwest, 137

Chile (30°00'S/71°00'W) A country that runs along the southern Pacific coast of South America, 230, m234

China (35°00'N/105°00'E) A country in East Asia, 635

Chisinau (47°00'N/28°51'E) The capital of Moldova, 342

Chittagong A city in Bangladesh, 573

Chittagong Hills (23°00'N/92°15'E) A hilly region in southeastern Bangladesh, 576

Chota Nagpur Plateau (23°00'N/85°00'E) A plateau in India that is northeast of the Deccan Plateau, 552

Cincinnati (39°09'N/84°31'W) A city in southwestern Ohio, 147

Cleveland (41°29'N/81°40'W) A city in northern Ohio, 137

Colombo (6°56'N/79°51'E) The capital of Sri Lanka, 585

Colorado (39°00'N/105°30'W) A state in the western United States, 108

Colorado River (31°54'N/114°57'W) A river that rises in the Rocky Mountains, flow through the southwestern United States, and empties into the Gulf of California in northwest Mexico, 149, m149

Colombia (4°00'N/72°00'W) A country in northern South America, 230, m234

Columbia (34°00'N/81°02'W) The capital of South Carolina, 112

Columbus (39°59'N/82°59'W) The capital of Ohio, 110

Comoros (12°10'S/44°15'E) A country formed by a group of islands in Southern Africa, 453, m454

Conakry (9°31'N/13°43'W) The capital of Guinea, 410

Concord (43°14'N/71°34'W) The capital of New Hampshire, 110

Congo River (6°04'S/12°24'E) A river in Central Africa that flows through the Democratic Republic of the Congo and empties into the Atlantic Ocean, 416

Congo, Democratic Republic of the (0°00'N/25°00'E) A country in Central Africa, 448, m450

Congo, Republic of the (1°00'S/15°00'E) A country in Central Africa, 408

Connecticut (41°40'N/72°40'W) A state in New England in the northeastern United States, 145

Continental Divide The line of highest points in the Rockies that marks the separation between rivers flowing eastward and westward, 120

Copenhagen (55°40'N/12°35'E) The capital of Denmark, 266

**Core Provinces** An area located in east central Canada that includes Quebec and Ontario, 167

**Corsica** (42°00′N/9°00′E) An French-owned island in the western Mediterranean Sea, 272

**Costa Rica** (10°00′N/84°00′W) A country in Central America, 223

**Côte d'Ivoire** (8°00′N/5°00′W) A country in West Africa, 442

**Crete** (35°15′N/24°45′E) A Greek-owned island in the eastern Mediterranean Sea, 272

**Croatia** (45°10′N/15°30′E) A country in Eastern Europe, 308

**Cuba** (21°30′N/80°00′W) An island country in the Caribbean Sea, 226

**Cyprus** (35°00′N/33°00′E) A Southwest Asian island country in the Mediterranean Sea, south of Turkey, 513

**Czech Republic** (49°45′N/15°00′E) A country in Eastern Europe, 308

**Dagestan** (43°00′N/47°00′E) A Russian republic in the Caucasus, 385, *m385*

**Dakar** (14°40′N/17°26′W) The capital of Senegal, 412

**Dallas–Fort Worth** A metropolitan area in east central Texas formed by the rapid growth of Dallas (32°47′N/96°48′W) and Ft. Worth (32°44′N/97°19′W), 148

**Damascus** (33°30′N/36°18′E) The capital of Syria, 484

**Damavand, Mount** (35°57′N/52°07′E) A mountain in Iran, 478

**Danube River** (45°20′N/29°40′E) A European river that flows from southwest Germany, across southeast Europe, and into the Black Sea, 273, *m273*

**Dardenelles Strait** A narrow waterway in northwest Turkey that joins the Sea of Marmara and the Aegean Sea, 488

**Dasht-e Kavir Desert** A salt flat desert in central Iran, 492

**Dasht-e Lut Desert** A salt flat desert in eastern Iran, 492

**Dead Sea** (31°30′N/35°30′E) A landlocked salt lake that lies between Israel and Jordan, 489

**Deccan Plateau** (14°00′N/77°00′E) A large plateau in central India, 552

**Delaware** (39°00′N/75°30′W) A state in the southern United States (sometimes included with the Middle Atlantic states), 108

**Denali** (also called Mount McKinley) (63°04′N/151°00′W) North America's highest mountain; located in Alaska, 120

**Denmark** (56°00′N/10°00′E) A Northern European country located on the Jutland Peninsula, 300

**Denver** (39°44′N/104°59′W) The capital of Colorado, 108

**Des Moines** (41°36′N/93°37′W) The capital of Iowa, 108

**Detroit** (42°20′N/83°03′W) A city in southeastern Michigan, 137

**Dhaka** (23°43′N/90°25′′E) The capital of Bangladesh, 548

**District of Columbia** (38°54′N/77°02′W) A federal district in the eastern United States; occupied by the city of Washington, 108

**Djibouti** (11°30′N/42°30′E) A country in East Africa, 463

**Djibouti, the city of** (11°36′N/43°09′E) The capital of Djibouti, 408

**Dnieper River** (46°30′N/32°18′E) A river that flows from west-central Russia through Belarus and Ukraine to the Black Sea, 361

**Dodoma** (6°10′S/35°45′E) The capital of Tanzania, 412

**Doha** (25°17′N/51°32′E) The capital of Qatar, 484

**Dom** (46°06′N/7°51′E) A mountain in Switzerland, 260

**Dominica** (15°30′N/61°20′W) An island country in the eastern Caribbean Sea, 196

**Dominican Republic** (19°00′N/70°40′W) A country that occupies the eastern two-thirds of the island of Hispaniola in the Caribbean Sea, 196

**Dover** (39°09′N/75°31′W) The capital of Delaware, 108

**Dublin** (53°20′N/6°15′W) The capital of Ireland, 266

**Durham** (36°00′N/78°54′W) A city in North Carolina, 178

**Dushanbe** (38°34′N/68°46′E) The capital of Tajikistan, 342

**East Africa** A region in Africa that includes Burundi, Djibouti, Eritrea, Ethiopia, Kenya, Rwanda, Seychelles, Somalia, Tanzania, and Uganda, 431

**East Antarctica** (80°00′S/80°00′E) A major region in Antarctica lying on the Indian Ocean side of the Transantarctic Mountains, 692

**East Asia** A region that includes China, Japan, Mongolia, Taiwan, North Korea, and South Korea, 619

**Eastern Europe** A region that includes Albania, Bosnia and Herzegovina, Bulgaria, Croatia, the Czech Republic, Hungary, Macedonia, Poland, Romania, Slovakia, and Yugoslavia, 308

**Eastern Ghats** (14°00′N/78°50′E) A mountain range that runs along the east coast of India, 552

**Eastern Mediterranean Region** A region that includes Lebanon, Syria, Jordan, and Israel, 510

**Ecuador** (2°00′S/77°30′W) A country in northwestern South America, 230, *m234*

**Edinburgh** (55°57′N/3°12′W) A city in Scotland, 303

**Edmonton** (53°33′N/113°30′W) The capital of Alberta, Canada, 114

**Egypt** (27°00′N/30°00′E) A country in North Africa, 438

**El Salvador** (13°50′N/88°55′W) A country in Central America, 223

**Elbe River** (53°50′N/9°00′E) A European river that runs north from the Czech Republic, across Germany, and into the North Sea, 260

**Elburz Mountains** (36°00′N/53°00′E) A mountain range in northern Iran, 488

**Ellesmere** (79°00′N/82°00′W) A large island in northern Canada, 121

**Equatorial Guinea** (2°00′N/10°00′E) A country in Central Africa, 448, *m450*

**Erie Canal** Opened in 1825; crosses upstate New York and is used as a water link between the Atlantic Ocean and the Great Lakes; now part of the New York State Barge Canal System, 129

**Erie, Lake** (42°15′N/81°25′W) One of the Great Lakes of North America, *m118*, 121

**Eritrea** (15°00′N/39°00′E) A country in East Africa, 431

**Estonia** (59°00′N/26°00′E) A country west of Russia; one of the Baltic Republics, 361

**Ethiopia** (8°00′N/38°00′E) A country in East Africa, 431

**Ethiopian Highlands** A mountainous area in Ethiopia, 417

**Euphrates River** (31°00′N/47°25′E) A river that rises in central Turkey, flows southeast through Syria and Iraq, and joins the Tigris River; together they form the Shatt al Arab, which flows into the Persian Gulf, *m488*, 489

**Eurasia** The combination of Europe and Asia; some consider it to be a single continent, 346

**Europe** A peninsula of the Eurasian land mass; a continent bounded by Asia, the Mediterranean Sea, the Atlantic Ocean, and the Arctic Ocean, 28, *m29*

**Everest, Mount** (27°59′N/86°56′E) The world's tallest mountain; located on the border of Nepal and China, 551

**Everglades** (26°05′N/80°46′W) A huge swampland in southern Florida that covers about 4,000 square miles, 126

**Farakka dam** (24°49′N/87°56′E) A dam that crosses the Ganges River at a point just before it enters Bangladesh, 599

**Feni River** (22°46′N/91°26′E) A river in Bangladesh, 562

Fiji (18°00′S/178°00′E) A country that consists of an island group of Oceania in the Pacific Ocean, 712, *m713*

Finland (64°00′N/26°00′E) A country in Northern Europe, 300

Florence (43°46′N/11°15′E) A city in north-central Italy, 291

Florida (28°45′N/82°30′W) A state in the southern United States, 108

Fongafale (8°31′S/179°13′E) The capital of Tuvalu, 686

Foraker, Mount (62°58′N/151°24′E) A mountain in Alaska in the United States, 102

France (46°00′N/2°00′E) A country in Western Europe, 294

Frankfort (38°12′N/84°52′W) The capital of Kentucky, 108

Fredericton (45°57′N/66°38′W) The capital of New Brunswick, Canada, 114

Freetown (8°29′N/13°14′W) The capital of Sierra Leone, 412

French Guiana (4°20′N/53°00′W) A French overseas department in northern South America, 230, *m234*

Fuji, Mount (35°22′N/138°43′E) A volcanic mountain in Japan, 662

Gaborone (24°39′S/25°55′E) The capital of Botswana, 408

Gabon (1°00′S/11°45′E) A country in Central Africa, 448, *m450*

Galilee, Sea of (also called Lake Kinneret) (32°48′N/35°35′E) A freshwater lake in northeastern Israel, 495

Gambia (13°30′N/15°30′W) A country in West Africa, 442

Ganges River (23°22′N/90°32′E) A river that rises in the central Himalayas, flows eastward across northern India, and joins the Brahmaputra river; together they form a huge delta before entering the Bay of Bengal, 553

Ganges-Brahmaputra River delta (23°00′N/89°00′E) A triangular area of land formed by the mouth of the combined Ganges and Brahmaputra rivers, 553

Gaza Strip (31°25′N/34°20′E) A territory along the Mediterranean Sea just northeast of the Sinai Peninsula, 527

Georgetown (6°48′N/58°10′W) The capital of Guyana, 198

Georgia (42°00′N/43°30′E) A country in Transcaucasia, 370, *m370*

Georgia, the U.S. state of (32°45′N/83°30′W) A state in the southern United States, 108

Germany (51°30′N/10°30′E) A country in Western Europe, 294

Ghana (8°00′N/2°00′W) A country in West Africa, 442

Glasgow (55°50′N/4°15′W) A city in Scotland, 303

Gobi Desert (44°00′N/105°00′E) A large desert that stretches from northern China into Mongolia, 627

Godwin Austen, Mount (also called K2) (35°52′N/76°34′E) The world's second tallest mountain; located in northern Pakistan, 552

Golan Heights (also called Al Jawlan) (33°00′N/35°45′E) Located in Syria; a hilly plateau overlooking the Jordan River and the Sea of Galilee, 487

Gorèe Island (14°40′N/17°24′W) An island off the coast of Senegal; served as one of the busiest departure points for slaves during the slave trade from the mid-1500s to the mid-1800s, 442

Granada (37°11′N/3°36′W) A city in southern Spain, 291

Great Barrier Reef (18°00′S/146°50′E) A chain of more than 2,500 reefs and islands; located off the northeast coast of Australia, 692

Great Britain (54°00′N/2°00′W) An island consisting of England, Scotland, and Wales and located north of France, 272

Great Dividing Range (25°00′S/147°00′E) A mountain range near the eastern coast of Australia, 692

Great Drakensberg An escarpment in Southern Africa, 417

Great Lakes (45°41′N/84°26′W) A chain of five large lakes—Huron, Ontario, Michigan, Erie, and Superior—located in central North America, *m118,* 121

Great Plains (39°25′N/101°18′W) A largely treeless area that extends from the Interior Plains to the Rocky Mountains, *m118,* 119

Great Smoky Mountains (35°35′N/83°31′W) A North American mountain range located in the southern part of the Appalachian system, 119

Greater Antilles (20°00′N/74°00′W) A group of islands in the Caribbean Sea; includes Cuba, Jamaica, Hispaniola, and Puerto Rico, 203

Greece (39°00′N/22°00′E) A Mediterranean country of Europe, 287

Green Mountains (42°34′N/72°36′W) A North American mountain range located in the northern part of the Appalachian system, 119

Greenland (72°00′N/40°00′W) The largest island in the world; bounded by the northern Atlantic Ocean and the Arctic Ocean and owned by Denmark, 272

Greenwich (51°28′N/0°00′E) A town in England and site of the Royal Observatory, through which the prime meridian, or longitude 0°, passes, 6

Grenada (12°07′N/61°40′W) A country consisting of the island of Grenada and the southern Grenadines in the Caribbean Sea, 196

Grozny (43°18′N/45°42′E) The capital of Chechnya, *m385,* 386

Guam (13°27′N/144°44′E) A U.S. territory and island in the Pacific, 112

Guangzhou (23°07′N/113°15′E) A city in China, 637

Guatemala (15°30′N/90°15′W) A country in Central America, 223

Guatemala City (14°38′N/90°31′W) The capital of Guatemala, 196

Guiana Highlands (4°00′N/60°00′W) A mountain range in northeast South America, 202, *m203*

Guinea (11°00′N/10°00′W) A country in West Africa, 442

Guinea-Bissau (12°00′N/15°00′W) A country in West Africa, 442

Gulf Coastal Plain A broad plain that stretches along the Gulf of Mexico from Florida into Texas, 119

Gulf of Mexico (26°00′N/91°00′W) An arm of the Atlantic Ocean bordering on eastern Mexico, the southeastern United States, and Cuba, *m118,* 121

Guyana (5°00′N/59°00′W) A country in northern South America, 230, *m234*

Hagatna (13°28′N/144°45′E) The capital of Guam, 112

Hainan (19°00′N/109°30′E) An island off the coast of southern China, *m620,* 621

Haiti (19°00′N/72°25′W) A country that occupies the western one-third of the island of Hispaniola in the Caribbean Sea, 198

Halabja (35°21′N/45°54′E) A city in Iraq, 516

Halifax (44°39′N/63°36′W) The capital of Nova Scotia, Canada, 166

Hangzhou (30°15′N/120°10′E) A city in China, 637

Hanoi (21°02′N/105°51′E) The capital of Vietnam, 686

Harare (17°50′S/31°03′E) The capital of Zimbabwe, 412

Harrisburg (40°16′N/76°53′W) The capital of Pennsylvania, 112

Hartford (41°46′N/72°41′W) The capital of Connecticut, 108

Havana (23°08′N/82°22′W) The capital of Cuba, 196

**Hawaii** (20°45′N/156°30′W) A state in the western United States that consists of several islands in the central Pacific, 108

**Hawaiian Islands** (20°45′N/156°30′W) A chain of islands in the central Pacific Ocean that make up the state of Hawaii, 121

**Hejaz Mountains** A mountain range on the southwest corner of the Arabian Peninsula; part of the western region of Saudi Arabia, 488

**Helena** (46°36′N/112°02′W) The capital of Montana, 110

**Helsinki** (60°11′N/24°56′E) The capital of Finland, 266

**Hermon, Mount** (33°25′N/35°51′E) A mountain on the border between Lebanon and Syria, 478

**Himalaya Mountains** (28°00′N/84°00′E) The world's highest mountain range; located in Nepal, Bhutan, northern India, and southwestern China, 551

**Hindu Kush** (35°00′N/71°00′E) A mountain range in eastern Afghanistan and northern Pakistan, 488

**Holland** (52°30′N/5°45′E) Another name for the Netherlands, a country in Northern Europe, 280

**Hollywood** (34°06′N/118°20′W) A district of Los Angeles, California; the center of the motion picture industry in the United States, 143

**Honduras** (15°00′N/86°30′W) A country in Central America, 223

**Hong Kong** (22°15′N/114°10′E) A region on the coast of southeastern China; includes Hong Kong Island and nearby areas, 621

**Honiara** (9°26′S/159°57′E) The capital of the Solomon Islands, 684

**Honolulu** (21°18′N/157°52′W) The capital of Hawaii, 108

**Honshu** (36°00′N/138°00′E) The largest island of Japan, 653

**Houston** (31°20′N/95°25′W) A city in southeastern Texas, 148

**Huang He** (also called Yellow River) (37°45′N/119°05′E) A Chinese river that rises in the Kunlun Mountains, flows east for about 3,000 miles, and empties into the Yellow Sea, *m620,* 621

**Hudson Bay** (52°52′N/102°25′W) An extended bay located in Canada, 119

**Hungary** (47°00′N/20°00′E) A country in Eastern Europe, 308

**Huron, Lake** (44°30′N/82°00′W) The second largest of the Great Lakes of North America, *m118,* 121

**Iberian Peninsula** (40°00′N/5°00′W) A southwestern peninsula of Europe bounded by France, the Mediterranean Sea, and the Atlantic Ocean and occupied by Spain and Portugal, *m271,* 272

**Iceland** (65°00′N/18°00′W) An island country in the North Atlantic, northwest of Great Britain, 300

**Idaho** (44°30′N/114°15′W) A state in the western United States, 108

**Ijsselmeer** (52°49′N/5°15′E) A freshwater lake in the Netherlands, 281

**Illinois** (40°00′N/89°15′W) A state in the Midwest of the United States, 108

**India** (20°00′N/77°00′E) A country in South Asia, 567

**Indian Ocean** (10°00′S/70°00′E) The world's third largest ocean; extends from southern Asia to Antarctica and from western Australia to eastern Africa, 32

**Indiana** (40°00′N/86°15′W) A state in the Midwest of the United States, 108

**Indo-Gangetic Plain** (also called the Northern Indian Plain) (27°00′N/80°00′E) A plain in northern India and Bangladesh that lies between the Deccan Plateau and the northern mountains, 552

**Indochina** A peninsula located south of China; includes Myanmar, Thailand, Laos, Cambodia, Vietnam, and West Malaysia, 689

**Indonesia** (5°00′S/120°00′E) A Southeast Asian country that consists of several islands between the Asian mainland and Australia, 705

**Indus River** (24°20′N/67°47′E) A river that flows west and then south through Pakistan to the Arabian Sea, 553

**Indus Valley** (29°00′N/71°00′E) A valley formed by the Indus River in Pakistan, 567

**Ingushetia** (43°13′N/44°47′E) A Russian republic in the Caucasus, 385, *m385*

**Interior Plains** A lowland area that extends from the Appalachians to about 300 miles west of the Mississippi River, *m118,* 119

**Iowa** (42°00′N/93°30′W) A state in the Midwest of the United States, 108

**Iqaluit** (63°44′N/68°30′W) The capital of Nunavut, Canada, 114

**Iran** (32°00′N/53°00′E) A country in the northeast region of Southwest Asia, 516, *m516*

**Iraq** (33°00′N/44°00′E) A country in the northeast region of Southwest Asia, 516, *m516*

**Ireland** (53°00′N/8°00′W) A country occupying most of the island of Ireland, which is west of Great Britain, 272

**Islamabad** (33°42′N/73°10′E) The capital of Pakistan, 548

**Israel** (31°30′N/34°45′E) A country in the Eastern Mediterranean in Southwest Asia, 512, *m512*

**Issyk-Kul, Lake** (42°25′N/77°15′E) A lake in Kyrgyzstan, 336

**Italian Peninsula** A southern peninsula of Europe bounded by the Mediterranean Sea, the Adriatic Sea, France, Switzerland, Austria, and Slovenia and occupied by Italy, *m271,* 272

**Italy** (42°50′N/12°50′E) A Mediterranean country of Europe, 266

**Jackson** (32°18′N/90°11′W) The capital of Mississippi, 110

**Jaffna Peninsula** (9°45′N/80°10′E) A peninsula on the northern tip of the island of Sri Lanka, 585

**Jakarta** (6°10′S/106°49′E) The capital of Indonesia, 684

**Jamaica** (18°15′N/77°30′W) An island country in the Caribbean Sea, 198

**Jamestown** (37°19′N/78°18′W) Founded in 1607; the first permanent English settlement in the United States, 136

**Japan** (36°00′N/138°00′E) An East Asian country consisting of several islands in the western Pacific Ocean, 651, *m652*

**Jefferson City** (38°35′N/92°10′W) The capital of Missouri, 110

**Jerusalem** (31°47′N/35°13′E) A holy city for Jews, Muslims, and Christians; also the capital of Israel, 510, *m512*

**Johannesburg** (26°12′S/28°05′E) The largest city in South Africa, 457

**Jordan** (31°00′N/36°00′E) A country in the Eastern Mediterranean in Southwest Asia, 511, *m512*

**Jordan River** A river that flows south from Syria through the Sea of Galilee to the Dead Sea, 489

**Juneau** (58°18′N/134°25′W) The capital of Alaska, 108

**Jutland Peninsula** A Northern European peninsula that consists of Denmark and northern Germany, 271, *m271*

**K2** (also called Mount Godwin Austen) (35°52′N/76°34E) The world's second tallest mountain; located in northern Pakistan, 552

**Kabul** (34°31′N/69°11′E) The capital of Afghanistan, 484

**Kalahari** (23°00′S/22°00′E) A desert in Southern Africa, 420

**Kaliningrad** (54°43′N/20°30′E) A city in western Russia, 345

**Kamchatka** (56°00′N/160°00′E) A peninsula of northeastern Russia bounded by Sea of Okhotsk and the Bering Sea, 346

**Kampala** (0°19′N/32°35′E) The capital of Uganda, 412

**Kanchenjunga** (27°42′N/88°08′E) A mountain on the border of India and Nepal, 542

**Kansas** (38°30′N/98°30′W) A state in the Midwest of the United States, 108

**Kansas City (Kansas)** (39°07′N/94°44′W) A city in northeastern Kansas, 147

**Kansas City (Missouri)** (39°05′N/94°35′W) A city in western Missouri, 147

**Kara Kum** (39°00′N/60°00′E) A large, black sand desert in Central Asia, 352

**Karakoram Mountain Range** (34°00′N/78°00′E) A mountain range in northern Pakistan, northern India, and southwestern China, 552

**Karnataka Plateau** A plateau in Karnataka, a state in southwestern India, 552

**Kashmir** A territory located at the foot of the Himalayas in northern Pakistan, northern India, and southwestern China, 600, *m601*

**Kathmandu** (27°43′N/85°19′E) The capital of Nepal, 581

**Kathmandu Valley** (27°40′N/85°21′E) A valley in Nepal, 582

**Kazakhstan** (48°00′N/68°00′E) A country in Central Asia, 375

**Kentucky** (37°30′N/85°15′W) A state in the southern United States, 108

**Kenya** (1°00′N/38°00′E) A country in East Africa, 431

**Kenya, Mount** (0°10′S/37°20′E) A volcanic mountain in East Africa, 417

**Khartoum** (15°45′N/32°30′E) The capital of Sudan, 425

**Khyber Pass** (34°04′N/71°13′E) A major land route through the Safed Koh Mountains, 552

**Kiev** (50°26′N/30°31′E) The capital of the Ukraine, 345

**Kigali** (1°57′S/30°04′E) The capital of Rwanda, 412

**Kilimanjaro, Mount** (3°04′S/37°22′E) Africa's highest peak; a volcanic mountain in Tanzania in East Africa, 417

**Kingston** (18°00′N/76°48′W) The capital of Jamaica, 198

**Kingstown** (13°08′N/61°13′W) The capital of Saint Vincent and the Grenadines, 198

**Kinneret, Lake** (also called the Sea of Galilee) (32°48′N/35°35′E) A freshwater lake in northeastern Israel, 495

**Kinshasha** (4°20′S/15°19′E) The capital of the Democratic Republic of the Congo, 408

**Kiribati** (5°00′S/170°00′W) A country that consists of an island group of Oceania in the Pacific Ocean, 712, *m713*

**Kjolen Mountains** (65°00′N/14°00′E) An upland area of Scandinavia, 273

**Kobe** (34°41′N/135°10′E) A city in Japan, 661

**Kolkata (Calcutta)** (22°34′N/88°22′E) A city in eastern India, *m569*, 570, 599

**Kongur, Mount** (38°40′N/75°21′E) A mountain in China, 611

**Korea Strait** (34°00′N/129°00′E) A waterway between southern South Korea and southwestern Japan that connects the Sea of Japan with the East China Sea, 647

**Korean Peninsula** A peninsula bounded by the Yellow Sea and the Sea of Japan and occupied by North Korea and South Korea, 620

**Koror** (7°20′N/134°28′E) The capital of Palau, 684

**Kosovo** (42°35′N/21°00′E) A province of southern Yugoslavia, 319

**Kuala Lumpur** (3°10′N/101°42′E) The capital of Malaysia, 709

**Kunlun Mountains** (36°00′N/84°00′E) A mountain range in western China, 619, *m620*

**Kuril Islands** (46°10′N/152°00′E) A chain of Russian-owned islands that extend off the southern tip of Kamchatka Peninsula; Japan claims ownership of some of the islands, 346

**Kuwait** (29°30′N/47°45′E) A country in the Arabian Peninsula of Southwest Asia, 503

**Kuwait City** (29°22′N/47°59′E) The capital of Kuwait, 484

**Kyoto** (35°00′N/135°45′E) A city in Japan, 654

**Kyrgyzstan** (41°00′N/75°00′E) A country in Central Asia, 375

**Kyzyl Kum** (42°30′N/64°30′E) A large red sand desert in Central Asia, 352

**La Paz** (16°30′S/68°09′W) The administrative capital of Bolivia, 196

**Labrador** A section of Newfoundland, Canada, 167

**Lansing** (42°44′N/84°33′W) The capital of Michigan, 110

**Laos** (18°00′N/105°00′E) A country in Southeast Asia, 705

**Las Vegas** (36°11′N/115°08′W) A city in southern Nevada, 149, *m149*

**Latin America** A region that includes Mexico, Central America, the Caribbean, and South America, 201, *m203*

**Latvia** (57°00′N/25°00′E) A country west of Russia; one of the Baltic Republics, 361

**Lebanon** (33°50′N/35°50′E) A country in the Eastern Mediterranean in Southwest Asia, 511, *m512*

**Leizhou Peninsula** (20°40′N/110°05′E) A peninsula in southern China between the South China Sea and the Gulf of Tonkin, 620

**Lena** (72°20′N/126°37′E) A river that flows through east-central Russia and empties into the Laptev Sea, 347

**Lesotho** (29°30′S/28°15′E) A country in Southern Africa, 453, *m454*

**Lesser Antilles** (15°00′N/61°00′W) A group of islands southeast of Puerto Rico; divided into the Leeward Islands and Windward Islands, 203

**Liberia** (6°30′N/9°30′W) A country in West Africa, 442

**Libreville** (0°23′N/9°27′E) The capital of Gabon, 410

**Libya** (25°00′W/17°00′E) A country in North Africa, 438

**Libyan Desert** (24°00′N/25°00′E) A desert in northeast Africa; the northeast section of the Sahara, 420

**Liechtenstein** (47°10′N/9°32′E) A country in Western Europe, 294

**Lilongwe** (13°59′S/33°47′E) The capital of Malawi, 410

**Lima** (12°03′S/77°03′W) The capital of Peru, 211

**Lincoln** (40°48′N/96°40′W) The capital of Nebraska, 110

**Lisbon** (38°43′N/9°08′W) The capital of Portugal, 268

**Lithuania** (56°00′N/24°00′E) One of the Baltic Republics, 361

**Little Rock** (35°45′N/92°17′W) The capital of Arkansas, 108

**Ljubljana** (46°03′N/14°31′E) The capital of Slovenia, 268

**Llanos** (5°00′N/70°00′W) Vast plains located in Colombia and Venezuela, 202, *m203*

**Logan, Mount** (60°34′N/140°25′W) A mountain in Canada, 102

**Lombardy** (45°40′N/9°30′E) A region in northern Italy, 273

**Lomè** (6°08N/1°13′E) The capital of Togo, 412

**London** (51°30′N/0°08′W) The capital of the United Kingdom, 304

**Los Angeles** (34°03′N/118°15′W) A major seaport city in southwestern California, 128, *m149*

**Louisiana** (31°00′N/92°00′W) A state in the southern United States, 148

**Lowell** (42°39′N/71°19′W) A city in Massachusetts that became a textile center by the 1840s, 136

**Luanda** (8°50′S/13°14′E) The capital of Angola, 408

**Lusaka** (15°25′S/28°17′E) The capital of Zambia, 412

**Luxembourg** (49°45′N/6°10′E) A country in Western Europe, 294

**Luxembourg City** (49°37′N/6°08′E) The capital of Luxembourg, 266

**Macao Peninsula** A peninsula in southeast China just west of Hong Kong, 620

**Macedonia** (41°50′N/22°00′E) A country in Eastern Europe, 308

**MacKenzie River** (69°20′N/134°00′W) The largest river in Canada; flows across the Northwest Territories to the Arctic Ocean, 121

**Madagascar** A country in Southern Africa, 453, *m454*

**Madison** (43°05′N/89°23′W) The capital of Wisconsin, 112

**Madras** (also called Chennai) (13°05′N/80°17′E) A city in southern India, *m569,* 570

**Madrid** (40°24′N/3°41′W) The capital of Spain, 268

**Maine** (45°30′N/69°15′W) A state in New England in the northeastern United States, 145

**Majuro** (7°06′S/171°23′E) The capital of the Marshall Islands, 684

**Makalu** (27°55′N/87°08′E) A mountain on the border of China and Nepal, 542

**Malabo** The capital of Equatorial Guinea, 408

**Malawi** (3°21′N/8°40′E) A country in Southern Africa, 453, *m454*

**Malay Archipelago** (0°00′N/120°00′E) An island group of Southeast Asia; separates the Pacific and Indian oceans and includes the Philippines, Malaysia, and the islands of Indonesia, 689

**Malay Peninsula** (6°00′N/102°00′E) A narrow strip of land about 700 miles long that stretches south from the Indochinese Peninsula and then curves southeast, 689

**Malaysia** (2°30′N/112°30′E) A Southeast Asian country that occupies part of the island of Borneo and the southern end of the Malay Peninsula, 705

**Maldives** (3°12′N/73°00′E) A South Asian country that occupies a chain of islands in the Indian Ocean off the southwest coast of India, 584

**Male** (4°10′N/73°30′E) The capital of the Maldives, 548

**Mali** (17°00′N/4°00′W) A country in West Africa, 442

**Malta** (35°55′N/14°26′E) An island country in the Mediterranean Sea, off the southern coast of Sicily, 268

**Managua** (12°09′N/86°25′W) The capital of Nicaragua, 198

**Manama** (26°14′N/50°35′E) The capital of Bahrain, 484

**Manchurian Plain** (44°00′N/124°00′E) A plain in northeastern China, 620, *m620*

**Manila** (14°35′N/121°00′E) The capital of the Philippines, 684

**Manitoba** (55°00′N/97°00′W) A Prairie Province of Canada, 168

**Maputo** (25°58′S/32°35′E) The capital of Mozambique, 410

**Marrakesh** (31°38′N/8°00′W) A city in Morocco, *m439,* 440

**Marshall Islands** (10°00′N/167°00′E) A country that consists of an island group of Oceania in the Pacific Ocean, 712, *m713*

**Maryland** (39°00′N/76°45′W) A state in the southern United States (sometimes included with the Middle Atlantic states), 110

**Maseru** (29°19′S/27°29′E) The capital of Lesotho, 410

**Massachusetts** (42°15′N/71°30′W) A state in New England in the northeastern United States, 145

**Massif Central** Uplands located in central France, 273

**Mauritania** (20°00′N/12°00′W) A country in West Africa, 442

**Mauritius** (20°18′S/57°35′E) An island country in Southern Africa, 453, *m454*

**Mbabane** (26°19′S/31°08′E) The capital of Swaziland, 412

**McKinley, Mount** (also called Denali) (63°04′N/151°00′W) North America's highest mountain; located in Alaska, 120

**Mecca** (21°26′N/39°50′E) The holiest city of Islam; located in western Saudi Arabia, 503

**Mediterranean Europe** A region that includes Spain, Italy, and Greece, 287

**Mediterranean Sea** (35°00′N/20°00′E) An inland sea bounded by southern Europe, northern Africa, and southwestern Asia, 277

**Mekong River** (10°15′N/105°55′E) A river that begins in China and crosses several Southeast Asian nations before becoming a wide delta on Vietnam's coast, *m689,* 690

**Melanesia** (12°00′S/160°00′E) A region in southwestern Oceania that consists of numerous Pacific islands, 713, *m713*

**Meseta** (41°00′N/4°00′W) A central plateau of Spain, 273

**Mexico** (23°00′N/102°00′W) A Latin American country bounded by the United States, the Gulf of Mexico, the Pacific Ocean, and Central America, 217

**Mexico City** (19°26′N/99°08′W) The largest city in Latin America and the capital of Mexico, 211

**Miami** (25°46′N/80°12′W) A city in southern Florida, 148

**Michigan** (44°15′N/85°30′W) A state in the Midwest of the United States, 110

**Michigan, Lake** (43°20′N/87°10′W) The third largest of the Great Lakes of North America, *m118,* 121

**Micronesia** (9°00′N/155°00′E) A region in northwestern Oceania that consists of numerous Pacific islands, 713, *m713*

**Micronesia, Federated States of** (5°00′N/152°00′E) A country that consists of an island group of Oceania in the Pacific Ocean, 712, *m713*

**Mid-Atlantic Ridge** (0°00′N/20°00′W) The mountain range on the ocean floor; extends for thousands of miles north to south through the middle of the Atlantic Ocean, 36

**Middle Atlantic States** The states of Pennsylvania, New York, and New Jersey (sometimes Maryland and Delaware are included in this group), 145

**Midwest** An area of the north-central United States that includes Michigan, Ohio, Indiana, Illinois, Wisconsin, Minnesota, Iowa, Missouri, Kansas, Nebraska, North Dakota, and South Dakota, 147

**Milwaukee** (43°04′N/87°58′W) A city in southeastern Wisconsin, 147

**Minneapolis** (44°58′N/93°16′W) A city in eastern Minnesota, 147

**Minnesota** (46°15′N/94°15′W) A state in the Midwest of the United States, 110

**Minsk** (53°54′N/27°34′E) The capital of Belarus, 342

**Mississippi** (32°45′N/89°45′W) A state in the southern United States, 110

**Mississippi River** (29°09′N/89°15′W) A North American river that runs from Minnesota to the Gulf of Mexico, *m118,* 121

**Missouri** (38°15′N/92°30′W) A state in the Midwest of the United States, 110

**Missouri River** (38°49′N/90°07′W) A North American river that runs from the Rocky Mountains in southwest Montana into the Mississippi River, *m118,* 121

**Mogadishu** (2°04′N/45°22′E) The capital of Somalia, 412

**Mojave Desert** (35°25′N/115°35′W) A desert in southern California, 124

**Moldova** (47°00′N/29°00′E) A country that lies between the Ukraine and Romania, 361

**Monaco** (43°44′N/7°24′E) A principality bounded by France and the Mediterranean Sea, 268

**Monaco, the village of** (43°44′N/7°25′E) The capital of Monaco, 268

**Mongolia** (46°00′N/105°00′E) A country in East Asia, 642

**Mongolian Plateau** A plateau in Mongolia and northeastern China, 620, *m620*

**Monrovia** (6°19′N/10°48′W) The capital of Liberia, 421

**Montana** (47°00′N/109°45′W) A state in the western United States, 110

**Montevideo** (34°51′S/56°10′W) The capital of Uruguay, 198

**Montgomery** (32°22′N/86°18′W) The capital of Alabama, 108

**Montpelier** (44°16′N/72°34′W) The capital of Vermont, 112

**Montreal** (45°30′N/73°35′W) Located in Quebec, Canada; the second largest metropolitan area in the country, 168

**Morocco** (32°00′N/5°00′W) A country in North Africa, 438

**Moroni** (11°42′S/43°14′E) The capital of Comoros, 408

**Moscow** (55°45′N/37°37′E) The capital of Russia, 366

**Mozambique** (18°15′S/35°00′E) A country in Southern Africa, 453, *m454*

**Mumbai** (also called Bombay) (18°59′N/72°50′W) A city in western India, *m569, 570*

**Murray River** (35°22′S/139°22′E) The largest river of Australia; flows into an arm of the Indian Ocean, 692

**Muscat** (23°37′N/58°36′E) The capital of Oman, 484

**Myanmar** (22°00′N/98°00′E) A country in Southeast Asia, 705

**N'Djamena** (12°07′N/15°03′E) The capital of Chad, 408

**Nagorno-Karabakh** (40°00′N/46°35′E) A mountainous republic of Azerbaijan, 386

**Nagoya** (35°10′N/136°55′E) A city in Japan, 630

**Nairobi** (1°17′S/36°49′E) The capital of Kenya, 410

**Namib** (23°00′S/15°00′E) A desert in southwest Africa, 420

**Namibia** (22°00′S/17°00′E) A country in Southern Africa, 453, *m454*

**Nashville** (36°10′N/86°47′W) The capital of Tennessee, 112

**Nassau** (25°05′N/77°21′W) The capital of the Bahamas, 196

**Nasser, Lake** (22°50′N/32°30′E) A lake created by the Aswan High Dam; lies in southern Egypt and northern Sudan, 426, *m427*

**Nauru** (0°32′S/166°55′E) An island country of Oceania in the Pacific Ocean, 712, *m713*

**Nebraska** (41°30′N/99°45′W) A state in the Midwest of the United States, 110

**Negev** (30°34′N/34°43′E) A desert area that occupies southern parts of Israel, 492

**Nepal** (28°00′N/84°00′E) A country in South Asia, 580

**Netherlands** (52°30′N/5°45′E) A country in Western Europe, 294

**Nevada** (39°15′N/116°45′W) A state in the western United States, 110

**New Brunswick** (46°30′N/66°45′W) An Atlantic Province of Canada, 166

**New Caledonia** (21°30′S/165°30′E) A French overseas territory that consists of an island group of Oceania in the Pacific Ocean, 691

**New Delhi** (28°36′N/77°12′E) The capital of India, 548

**New England** An area of the northeastern United States that includes Maine, Vermont, New Hampshire, Massachusetts, Rhode Island, and Connecticut, 145

**New Guinea** (5°00′S/140°00′E) An island north of Australia; occupied by the countries of Indonesia (west half) and Papua New Guinea (east half), 679

**New Hampshire** (43°40′N/71°30′W) A state in New England in the northeastern United States, 145

**New Jersey** (40°10′N/74°30′W) A Middle Atlantic state of the eastern United States, 145

**New Mexico** (34°30′N/106°00′W) A state in the western United States, 110

**New Orleans** (29°58′N/90°04′W) A city in southeastern Louisiana, 148

**New York** (43°00′N/75°30′W) A Middle Atlantic state in the eastern United States, 145

**New York City** (40°41′N/73°59′W) A major seaport city located in southeastern New York State, *m145, 147*

**New Zealand** (42°00′S/174°00′E) A country that consists of several islands (including North Island and South Island) in the Pacific Ocean off the southeast coast of Australia; part of Oceania, 691

**Newfoundland** (52°00′N/56°00′W) An Atlantic Province of Canada, 166

**Newfoundland Island** (49°00′N/56°00′W) An island that makes up part of Newfoundland, Canada, 167

**Niamey** (13°31′N/2°07′E) The capital of Niger, 412

**Nicaragua** (13°00′N/85°00′W) A country in Central America, 223

**Nicosia** (35°10′N/33°22′E) The capital of Cyprus, 484

**Niger** (16°00′N/8°00′E) A country in West Africa, 442

**Niger River** (5°33′N/6°33′E) A river that begins in Guinea and flows toward the Sahara (northeast); it then cuts through Nigeria and empties into the Gulf of Guinea, 416

**Niger River Delta** (4°50′N/6°00′E) A triangular area of land formed by the mouth of the Niger River, 425

**Nigeria** (10°00′N/8°00′E) A country in West Africa, 442

**Nile River Delta** (31°00′N/31°00′E) A triangular area of land formed by the mouth of the Nile River, 416

**Nile River** (l30°10′N/31°06′E) The world's longest river; flows through Uganda, Sudan, and Egypt and empties into the Mediterranean Sea, 416

**Nordic countries** The Northern European countries of Denmark, Finland, Iceland, Norway, and Sweden, 300

**Norilsk** (69°20′N/88°06′E) A Siberian mining center in Russia, 354

**North Africa** A region of Africa that includes Algeria, Egypt, Libya, Morocco, Sudan, and Tunisia, 438

**North America** The northern continent of the Western Hemisphere; bounded by the Arctic Ocean, the Atlantic Ocean, the Pacific Ocean, and the Caribbean Sea, 28, *m29*

**North Carolina** (35°30′N/80°00′W) A state in the southern United States, 110

**North China Plain** (34°00′N/116°00′E) A plain in northern China, 620, *m620*

**North Dakota** (47°30′N/100°00′W) A state in the Midwest of the United States, 110

**North Island** (37°20′S/173°30′E) The northern of the two main islands that make up New Zealand, 691

**North Korea** (40°00′N/127°00′E) A country in East Asia, 648, *m648*

**North Ossetia** (43°00′N/44°15′E) A Russian republic in the Caucasus, 385, *m385*

**North Pole** (90°00′N) The northern end of the earth's axis of rotation; a point located in the Arctic Ocean, 56

**North Sea** (55°20′N/3°00′E) An arm of the Atlantic Ocean bounded by Norway, Denmark, Germany, the Netherlands, England, and Scotland, 271, *m271*

**Northeast Region of Southwest Asia** A region that includes Turkey, Iran, Iraq, and Afghanistan, 516

**Northern Europe** A region that includes the United Kingdom, Ireland, Denmark, Finland, Iceland, Norway, and Sweden, 300

**Northern European Plain** A fertile plain that stretches across parts of France, Belgium, the Netherlands, Denmark, Germany, and Poland, 273

**Northern Indian Plain** (also called the Indo-Gangetic Plain) (27°00′N/80°00′E) A plain in northern India that lies between the Deccan Plateau and the northern mountains, 552

**Northern Plains of Afghanistan** A plain in northern Afghanistan, 488

**Northwest Territories** (65°00′N/118°00′W) A territory in north-central Canada, 169

**Norway** (62°00′N/10°00′E) A Northern European country that occupies the western part of the Scandinavian Peninsula, 300

**Norwegian Sea** (70°00′N/5°00′E) An extension of the Atlantic Ocean off the northwest coast of Norway, 271, *m271*

**Nouakchott** (18°06′N/15°57′W) The capital of Mauritania, 410

**Nova Scotia** (45°00′N/63°00′W) An Atlantic Province of Canada, 166

**Nuku'alofa** (21°08′S/125°12′W) The capital of Tonga, 686

**Nunavut** (70°00′N/90°00′W) A territory in north-central Canada; home to many of Canada's Inuit, 169

**Ob River** (66°45′N/69°30′E) A river in central Russia that flows into the Gulf of Ob, 347

**Oceania** A region that includes Australia, New Zealand, and the Pacific Islands (but not the Philippines, Indonesia, and other islands near Asia), 690

**Ogallala Aquifer** The largest aquifer in the United States; stretches from South Dakota to Texas, 33

**Ohio** (40°15′N/83°00′W) A state in the Midwest of the United States, 110

**Ohio River** (36°59′N/89°08′W) A North American river that runs from the Allegheny Mountains into the Mississippi River, *m118*, 121

**Oklahoma** (35°30′N/97°30′W) A state in the south-central United States, 110

**Oklahoma City** (35°28′N/97°31′W) The capital of Oklahoma, 110

**Olduvai Gorge** (2°58′S/35°22′E) A ravine in northern Tanzania that contains archeological sites rich in fossils, 431

**Olympia** (47°02′N/122°54′W) The capital of Washington, 112

**Omaha** (41°16′N/95°56′W) A city in eastern Nebraska, 147

**Oman** (21°00′N/57°00′E) A country in the Arabian Peninsula of Southwest Asia, 503

**Ontario** (50°00′N/86°00′W) A Core Province of Canada, 167

**Ontario, Lake** (43°40′N/78°00′W) The smallest of the Great Lakes of North America, *m118*, 121

**Oregon** (44°00′N/120°03′W) A state in the western United States, 148

**Orinoco River** (41°12′S/68°15′W) A river that flows through the northern part of South America, mainly in Venezuela, 202

**Osaka** (35°57′N/137°16′E) A city in Japan, 630

**Oslo** (59°55′N/10°45′E) The capital of Norway, 268

**Ouagadougou** (12°22′N/1°31′W) The capital of Burkina Faso, 408

**outback** The dry, interior region of Australia, 697

**Pacific Ocean** (0°00′N/180°00′E) The world's largest ocean; extends from the Arctic Circle and northeastern Asia to Antarctica and from the western Americas to eastern Asia and Australia, 32

**Paektu, Mount** (41°59′N/128°05′E) A mountain in Korea, 611

**Pago Pago** (14°17′S/170°42′W) The capital of American Samoa, 112

**Pakistan** (30°00′N/70°00′E) A country in South Asia, 573

**Palau** (7°30′N/134°27′E) A country that consists of an island group of Oceania in the Pacific Ocean, 712, *m713*

**Palestine** (18°30′N/73°45′W) A historical region of Southwest Asia located between the Mediterranean Sea and the Jordan River, 511

**Palikir** (6°55′N/158°09′E) The capital of the Federated States of Micronesia, 684

**pampas** (35°00′S/63°00′W) Vast plains located in Uruguay and south-central Argentina, 202 *m203*

**Panama** (9°00′N/80°00′W) A country in Central America, 223

**Panama Canal** (9°20′N/79°55′W) A canal that cuts through Panama and connects the Caribbean Sea and Pacific Ocean, 226, *m226*

**Panama City** (8°58′N/79°32′W) The capital of Panama, 198

**Papua New Guinea** (6°00′S/147°00′E) A country that consists of an island group of Oceania in the Pacific Ocean, 712, *m713*

**Paraguay** (22°60′S/57°60′W) A country in south-central South America, 230, *m234*

**Paramaribo** (5°52′N/55°10′W) The capital of Suriname, 198

**Paraná River** (33°43′S/59°15′W) A river that begins in the highlands of Brazil and runs south and west through Paraguay and Argentina. It then turns eastward and empties into the Atlantic, 203, *m203*

**Paris** (48°52′N/2°20′E) The capital of France, 266

**Patagonia** (44°00′S/68°00′W) A region of South America, mostly in Argentina, 209

**Pearl River** (also called Zhu Jiang) (22°46′N/113°38′E) A river in southeastern China that joins the Xi Jiang (or West River) and empties into the South China Sea, 622

**Pennsylvania** (40°45′N/77°45′W) A Middle Atlantic state of the eastern United States, 145

**Persian Gulf** (27°00′N/51°00′E) An extension of the Arabian Sea situated between the Arabian Peninsula and Iran, 487, *m488*

**Peru** (10°00′S/76°00′W) A country in western South America, 230, *m234*

**Philadelphia** (39°57′N/75°10′W) A city in southeastern Pennsylvania, 146, *m145*

**Philippines, the** (13°00′N/122°00′E) A Southeast Asian country that occupies about 7,100 islands east of the Asian mainland and northeast of Borneo, 712, *m713*

**Phnom Penh** (11°33′N/104°55′E) The capital of Cambodia, 684

**Phoenix** (33°27′N/112°4′W) The capital of Arizona, 149, *m149*

**Pierre** (44°22′N/100°21′W) The capital of South Dakota, 112

**Pinatubo, Mount** (15°08′N/120°21′E) A volcanic mountain in the Philippines, 689

**Pittsburgh** (40°26′N/79°60′W) A city in southwestern Pennsylvania, 137

**Plateau of Tibet** (33°00′N/92°00′E) A vast tableland in south-central Asia; mostly in Tibet, but extends into China, 619, *m620*

**Poland** (52°00′N/20°00′E) A country in Eastern Europe, 308

**Polynesia** (10°0′S/150°00′W) A region in central Oceania that consists of numerous Pacific islands, 713, *m713*

**Port Louis** (20°10′S/57°30′E) The capital of Mauritius, 410

**Port Moresby** (9°28′S/147°12′E) The capital of Papua New Guinea, 684

**Port-of-Spain** (10°39′N/61°31′W) The capital of Trinidad and Tobago, 198

**Port-au-Prince** (18°32′N/72°20′W) The capital of Haiti, 198

**Port-Vila** (17°44′S/168°19′E) The capital of Vanuatu, 686

**Porto-Novo** (6°29′N/2°37′E) The capital of Benin, 408

**Portugal** (39°04′N/8°14′W) A country located on the Iberian Peninsula; bounded by the Atlantic Ocean and Spain, 268

**Prague** (50°5′N/14°28′E) The capital of the Czech Republic, 312

**Praia** (14°55′N/23°31′W) The capital of Cape Verde Island, 408

**Prairie Provinces** An area located in west-central Canada that includes Manitoba, Saskatchewan, and Alberta, 168

**Pretoria** (25°42′S/28°14′E), **Cape Town** (33°55′S/18°25′E), **Bloemfontein** (20°08′S/26°12′E) The capital towns of South Africa, 412

**Prince Edward Island** (46°20′N/63°30′W) An Atlantic Province of Canada, 166

**Providence** (41°49′N/71°25′W) The capital of Rhode Island, 112

**Puerto Rico** (18°15′N/66°30′W) An island in the Caribbean Sea that is a self-governing commonwealth in union with the United States, 112

**Puerto Vallarta** (20°37′N/105°15′W) A city in Mexico, 213

**Pyongyang** (39°1′N/125°45′E) The capital of North Korea, 616

**Pyrenees** (42°40′N/1°00′E) A European mountain range that forms a border between France and Spain, *m271, 272*

**Qatar** (25°30′/51°15′E) A country in the Arabian Peninsula of Southwest Asia, 503

**Qinling Shandi Mountains** (33°30′N/108°36′E) A mountain range that divides the northern part of China from the southern part, 619

**Quebec** (54°00′N/72°00′W) A Core Province of Canada, 167

**Quebec City** (46°49′N/71°15′W) The capital of Quebec, Canada, 167

**Quito** (0°13′S/78°30′W) The capital of Ecuador, 196

**Rabat** (34°02′N/6°50′W) The capital of Morocco, 410

**Raleigh** (35°46′N/78°38′W) The capital of North Carolina, 110

**Red Sea** (19°00′N/39°30′E) A long, narrow sea situated between northeast Africa and the Arabian Peninsula, 487, *m488*

**Regina** (50°27′N/104°37′W) The capital of Saskatchewan, Canada, 114

**Reykjavik** (64°09′N/21°57′W) The capital of Iceland, 266

**Rhine River** (51°58′N/4°05′E) A European river that flows from the interior of Europe north to the North Sea, 273, *m273*

**Rhode Island** (41°45′N/71°30′W) A state in New England in the northeastern United States, 145

**Richmond** (37°33′N/77°28′W) The capital of Virginia, 112

**Riga** (56°57′N/24°06′E) The capital of Latvia, 342

**Ring of Fire** A chain of volcanoes that line the Pacific Rim, *m37*, 41, 661, *m662*

**Rio de Janeiro** (22°54′S/43°14′W) A city in Brazil, 239

**Rìo de la Plata** The name for the last stretch of the Paraná River before it empties into the Atlantic Ocean between Argentina and Uruguay, 203

**Rio Grande** (23°51′N/102°59′W) A river that forms part of the Mexican-U.S. border, 102

**Riyadh** (24°38′N/46°46′E) The capital of Saudi Arabia, 484

**Rocky Mountains** (43°22′N/110°55′W) A mountain system in the western United States and Canada that extends about 3,000 miles from the Arctic to the Mexican frontier, 119

**Romania** (46°00′N/25°00′E) A country in Eastern Europe, 308

**Rome** (41°54′N/12°29′E) The capital of Italy, 266

**Rosa, Monte** (45°55′N/7°53′E) A mountain on the border of Switzerland and Italy, 260

**Roseau** (15°18′N/61°24′W) The capital of Dominica, 196

**Rub al-Khali** (21°00′N/51°00′E) A large desert in the southern part of the Arabian Peninsula, 491

**Russia** An empire that extended from eastern Europe across north-central Asia to the Pacific Ocean, 361, *m362*

**Russia and the Republics** A region that stretches across much of eastern Europe and north-central Asia to the Pacific; consists of Russia and 14 other countries (republics), 345

**Russian Far East** The area of eastern Russia, 345

**Rwanda, Republic of** (2°00′S/30°00′E) A country in East Africa, 431

**Sacramento** (38°35′N/121°30′W) The capital of California, 108

**Sahara** (26°00′N/13°00′E) The largest desert in the world; stretches across northern Africa, from the Atlantic Ocean to the Red Sea, 420

**Saint Augustine** (29°54′N/81°19′W) Founded in 1565; the oldest permanent European settlement in the United States, 135

**Saint Elias, Mount** (60°18′N/140°56′W) A mountain located on the U.S.-Canada border, 102

**Saint George's** (12°03′N/61°45′W) The capital of Grenada, 196

**Saint John** (45°16′N/66°04′W) A city in New Brunswick, Canada, 166

**Saint John's** (17°07′N/61°51′W) The capital of Antigua and Barbuda, 196

**Saint John's, Canada** (47°28′N/52°18′W) The capital of Newfoundland, Canada, 114

**Saint Kitts and Nevis, Federation of** (17°20′N/62°45′W) A country consisting of the islands of Saint Kitts, Nevis, and Sombrero in the Caribbean Sea, 198

**Saint Lawrence River** (49°30′N/65°00′W) A Canadian river that flows from Lake Ontario to the Gulf of Saint Lawrence, *m118*, 129

**Saint Lawrence Seaway** (45°20′N/74°50′W) A waterway that connects the Great Lakes to the Atlantic Ocean by way of the Saint Lawrence River, 129

**Saint Louis** (38°38′N/90°12′W) A city in eastern Missouri, 147

**Saint Lucia** (13°53′N/60°58′W) An island country in the Caribbean Sea, 198

**Saint Paul** (44°57′N/93°06′W) The capital of Minnesota, 147

**Saint Petersburg** (59°54′N/30°16′E) A city in western Russia, 362

**Saint Vincent and the Grenadines** (13°05′N/61°12′W) A country consisting of Saint Vincent Island and the northern islets of the Grenadines in the Caribbean Sea, 198

**Sakhalin Island** An island, governed by a Russian Federation, off the east coast of Russia, 346

**Salem** (44°57′N/123°02′W) The capital of Oregon, 110

**Salt Lake City** (40°46′N/111°53′W) The capital of Utah, 112

**Samoa, Independent State of** (13°35′S/172°20′W) A country that consists of an island group of Oceania in the Pacific Ocean, 712

**San Antonio** (29°25′N/98°30′W) A city in southern Texas, 148

**San Diego** (34°43′N/117°09′W) A city in southwestern California, m149, 150

**San Francisco** (37°47′N/122°25′W) A city in western California, 150

**San José** (9°56′N/84°05′W) The capital of Costa Rica, 196

**San Juan** (18°28′N/66°06′W) The capital of Puerto Rico, 112

**San Marino, Republic of** (43°56′N/12°25′E) A tiny country surrounded by Italy, 268

**San Marino, the city of** (43°55′N/12°28′E) The capital of San Marino, 268

**San Salvador** (13°42′N/89°12′W) The capital of El Salvador, 196

**Sanaa** (15°21′N/44°12′E) The capital of Yemen, 484

**Santa Fe** (35°41′N/105°56′W) The capital of New Mexico, 110

**Santiago** (33°27′S/70°40′W) The capital of Chile, 211

**Santo Domingo** (18°28′N/69°54′W) The capital of the Dominican Republic, 196

**São Paulo** (23°32′S/46°37′W) A city in Brazil, 239

**São Tomé** (00°20′N/6°44′E) The capital of São Tomé and Príncipe, 412

**São Tomé and Príncipe** (1°00′N/7°00′E) An island country off the coast of Gabon in Central Africa, 448, m450

**Sapporo** (43°03′N/141°21′E) A city in Japan, 630

**Sarajevo** (43°51′N/18°23′E) The capital of Bosnia and Herzegovina, 266

**Sardinia** (40°00′N/9°00′E) An autonomous region of Italy; an island in the central Mediterranean Sea, 272

**Saskatchewan** (54°00′N/106°00′W) A Prairie Province of Canada, 168

**Saudi Arabia** (25°00′N/45°00′E) A country that occupies most of the Arabian Peninsula of Southwest Asia, 503

**Scandinavian Peninsula** (65°00′N/16°00′E) A European peninsula bounded by the Norwegian Sea, the North Sea, and the Baltic Sea; occupied by Norway, Sweden, and Denmark, 271, m271

**Sea of Japan** (43°30′N/135°45′E) An enclosed arm of the Pacific Ocean; bounded by Japan, North Korea, South Korea, and Russia, 647

**Seattle** (47°36′N/122°20′W) A city in northwestern Washington, 150

**Senegal** (14°00′N/14°00′W) A country in West Africa, 442

**Seoul** (37°34′N/126°60′E) The capital of South Korea, 616

**Serengeti Plains** (3°25′S/38°00′E) A tropical grassland in East Africa, 422

**Seychelles** (4°35′S/55°40′E) A country formed by a group of islands off the east coast of Africa; part of East Africa, 431

**Shandong Peninsula** (37°00′N/121°00′E) A peninsula in northeastern China bounded by the Bo Hai and the Yellow seas, 620

**Shanghai** (31°14′N/121°28′E) A city in China, 637

**Siberia** (60°00′N/100°00′E) A region, largely in Russia, that lies on the continent of north-central Asia, 349

**Sicily** (37°45′N/14°15′E) An autonomous region of Italy; an island located off the coast of southern Italy, 272

**Sierra Leone** (8°30′N/11°30′W) A country in West Africa, 442

**Sierra Madre** A mountain range that runs down Mexico, 201, m203

**Sierra Nevada Mountains** (37°42′N/119°19′W) A North American mountain range that runs parallel to the Pacific coastline from California to British Columbia in Canada, 120

**Silicon Glen** An area in Scotland that has many high-tech companies, 303

**Silicon Valley** An area in western California known for high-technology industries, 141

**Sinai Peninsula** (29°30′N/34°00′E) A peninsula at the north end of the Red Sea; situated between the Gulf of Suez on the west and the Gulf of Aqaba on the east, 527

**Singapore** (1°22′N/103°48′E) A Southeast Asian country that occupies Singapore Island and nearby smaller islands, 705

**Singapore City** (1°18′N/103°51′E) The capital of Singapore, 709

**Skopje** (42°00′N/21°26′E) The capital of Macedonia, 268

**Slovak Republic** (48°40′N/19°30′E) A country in Eastern Europe, 308

**Slovenia, Republic of** (46°15′N/15°10′E) A country in Eastern Europe, 308

**Sofia** (42°41′N/23°19′E) The capital of Bulgaria, 266

**Solomon Islands** (8°00′S/159°00′E) A country that consists of an island group of Oceania in the Pacific Ocean, 712, m713

**Somalia** (6°00′N/48°00′E) A country in East Africa, 431

**Sonoran Desert** An arid region in west North America, 124

**South, the** The south-central and southeastern area of the United States that includes the states of Maryland, Delaware, West Virginia, Virginia, North Carolina, South Carolina, Kentucky, Tennessee, Georgia, Florida, Alabama, Mississippi, Louisiana, Arkansas, Texas, and Oklahoma, 148

**South Africa, Republic of** (30°00′S/26°00′E) A country in Southern Africa, 453, m454

**South America** The southern continent of the Western Hemisphere bounded by the Caribbean Sea, the Atlantic Ocean, and the Pacific Ocean, 28, m29

**South Asia** A region that includes Afghanistan, India, Pakistan, Bangladesh, Bhutan, Nepal, Sri Lanka, and the Maldives, 551

**South Carolina** (34°00′N/81°00′W) A state in the southern United States, 112

**South China Sea** (15°00′N/115°00E) An arm of the Pacific Ocean bounded by southeastern China, Taiwan, Borneo, the Philippines, and Indochina, m620, 622

**South Dakota** (44°30′N/100°15′W) A state in the Midwest of the United States, 112

**South Island** (43°00′S/171°00′E) The southern of the two islands that make up New Zealand, 691

**South Korea, Republic of** (37°00′N/127°30′E) A country in East Asia, 648, m648

**South Pole** (9°S) The southern end of the earth's axis of rotation; a point located in Antarctica, 56

**Southeast Asia** A region that includes the countries of Brunei, Cambodia, Indonesia, Laos, Malaysia, Myanmar, the Philippines, Singapore, Thailand, and Vietnam, 705

**Southern Africa** A region of Africa that includes Angola, Botswana, Comoros, Lesotho, Madagascar, Malawi, Mauritius, Mozambique, Namibia, South Africa, Swaziland, Zambia, and Zimbabwe, 453, m454

**Southern Alps** (43°30′S/170°30′E) A mountain range on South Island, New Zealand, 691

**Southwest Asia** A region that includes Bahrain, Iran, Iraq, Israel, Jordan Kuwait, Lebanon, Oman, Qatar, Saudi Arabia, Syria, Turkey, United Arab Emirates, and Yemen, 487

**Spain** (40°00′N/4°00′W) A Mediterranean country in Europe, 268

**Springfield** (39°48′N/89°39′W) The capital of Illinois, 108

**Sri Lanka, Democratic Socialistic Republic of** (7°00′N/81°00′E) A South Asian island country off the southeast coast of India, 584

**steppe** A grassland that extends from southern Ukraine through northern Kazakhstan to the Altai Mountains, 352

**Stockholm** (59°20′N/18°03′E) The capital of Sweden, 268

**Straits of Hormuz** (26°37′N/56°30′E) A narrow waterway between Oman and southern Iran that connects the Persian Gulf with the Gulf of Oman, 488

**Sucre** (19°03′S/65°16′W) The constitutional capital of Bolivia, 196

**Sudan** (15°00′N/30°00′E) A country in North Africa, 438

**Suez Canal** (29°55′N/32°33′E) A canal connecting the Mediterranean Sea with the Red Sea, 487

**Sumatra** (0°00′N/102°00′E) An island southwest of the Malay Peninsula; part of Indonesia, 678

**Superior, Lake** (47°38′N/89°20′W) The largest of the Great Lakes of North America, *m118,* 121

**Suriname** (4°00′N/56°00′W) A country in northern South America, 230, *m234*

**Suva** (18°08′S/178°25′E) The capital of Fiji, 684

**Suzhou** (33°38′N/116°59′E) A city in China, 637

**Swaziland** (26°30′S/31°30′E) A country in Southern Africa, 453, *m454*

**Sweden** (62°00′N/15°00′E) A Northern European country that occupies the eastern part of the Scandinavian Peninsula, 300

**Switzerland** (47°00′N/8°00′E) A country in Western Europe, 294

**Syria** (35°00′N/38°00′E) A country in the Eastern Mediterranean region of Southwest Asia, 511, *m512*

**Syrian Desert** (32°00′N/40°00′E) A desert that extends north from the An-Nafud Desert and separates the coastal regions of Lebanon, Israel, and Syria from the Tigris and Euphrates valleys, *m488,* 492

**taiga** (56°04′N/85°05′E) A large forest holding the world's largest timber reserve; located south of the tundra in Russia, 352

**Taipei** (25°01′N/121°27′E) The capital of Taiwan, 616

**Taiwan** (24°00′N/121°00′E) An island country off the coast of southeastern China, 642

**Tajikistan** (39°00′N/71°00′E) A country in Central Asia, 375

**Taklimakan** (39°00′N/83°00′E) A desert in western China, 627

**Tallahassee** (30°26′N/84°17′W) The capital of Florida, 108

**Tallinn** (59°26′N/24°44′E) The capital of Estonia, 342

**Tampa-Saint Petersburg** A metropolitan area in western Florida formed by the growth of two cities, Tampa (27°57′N/82°28′W) and Saint Petersburg (27°46′N/82°41′W), 148

**Tanganyika, Lake** (6°00′S/29°30′E) The longest freshwater lake in the world; forms the border between The Democratic Republic of the Congo and Tanzania, 417

**Tanzania** (6°00′S/35°00′E) A country in East Africa, 431

**Tarim Basin** (41°00′N/84°00′E) A lowland area in western China, 619

**Tashkent** (41°19′N/69°15′E) The capital of Uzbekistan, 342

**Taurus Mountains** (37°00′N/33°00′E) A mountain range in southern Turkey, 488

**Tbilisi** (41°43′N/44°47′E) The capital of Georgia, 342

**Tegucigalpa** (14°06′N/87°13′W) The capital of Honduras, 198

**Tehran** (35°40′N/51°25′E) The capital of Iran, 484

**Tennessee** (35°45′N/86°15′W) A state in the southern United States, 112

**Texas** (31°15′N/99°15′W) A state in the south-central United States, 148

**Thailand** (15°00′N/100°00′E) A country in Southeast Asia, 705

**Thar Desert** (27°00′N/71°00′E) A desert in southeastern Pakistan and northwestern India, 558

**Thimphu** (27°29′N/89°36′E) The capital of Bhutan, 548

**Three Gorges Dam** A dam under construction in 2001 by China; eventually it will span a valley more than one mile wide, 629

**Tian Shan** (42°00′N/80°00′E) A mountain range in Central Asia, 346

**Tianjin** (39°09′N/117°11′E) A city in China, 637

**Tibesti Mountains** (21°30′N/17°30′E) A mountain range in the Sahara, 417

**Tierra del Fuego** (54°00′S/70°00′W) The southernmost tip of South America, 201

**Tigris River** (31°00′N/47°25′E) A river that rises in eastern Turkey, flows southeast through Iraq, and joins the Euphrates River; together they form the Shatt al Arab, which flows into the Persian Gulf, *m488,* 489

**Timor** (10°08′S/125°00′E) An island of southeast Indonesia, 705

**Tiranë** (41°20′N/19°49′E) The capital of Albania, 266

**Togo** (8°00′N/1°10′E) A country in West Africa, 442

**Tokyo** (35°41′N/139°45′E) One of the largest cities of the world; the capital of Japan, 630

**Tonga** (20°00′S/175°00′W) A country that consists of an island group of Oceania in the Pacific Ocean, 712, *m713*

**Topeka** (39°03′N/95°41′W) The capital of Kansas, 108

**Toronto** (43°40′N/79°25′W) The capital of Ontario, Canada; the most populous city in the country, 168

**Transantarctic Mountains** (85°00′S/175°00′W) Mountain ranges in Antarctica, 692

**Transcaucasia** (42°00′N/45°00′E) A region bounded by Russia, the Caspian Sea, the Black Sea, Turkey, and Iran and consisting of Armenia, Azerbaijan, and Georgia, 346

**Trenton** (40°13′N/74°45′W) The capital of New Jersey, 110

**Trinidad and Tobago** (11°00′N/61°00′W) A country consisting of the islands of Trinidad and Tobago in the Atlantic Ocean near northeast Venezuela, 198

**Tripoli** (32°54′N/13°11′E) The capital of Libya, 410

**Tucson** (32°13′N/110°56′W) A city in southern Arizona, 149, *m149*

**Tunis** (36°48′N/10°11′E) The capital of Tunisia, 412

**Tunis, Gulf of** (36°58′N/10°46′E) An inlet of the Mediterranean Sea near the city of Tunis, 438

**Tunisia** (34°00′N/9°00′E) A country in North Africa, 438

**Turkey** (39°00′N/35°00′E) A country in the northwest region of Southwest Asia, 516, *m516*

**Turkmenistan** (40°00′N/60°00′E) A country in Central Asia, 375

**Tuvalu** (8°00′S/178°00′E) A country that consists of an island group of Oceania in the Pacific Ocean, 712, *m713*

**U.S. Virgin Islands** A U.S. territory that consists of the southwest group of the Virgin Islands, 112

**Uganda** (2°00′N/33°00′E) A country in East Africa, 431

**Ukraine** (49°00′N/32°00′E) A country that is west of Russia, 361

**Ulaanbaatar** (47°55′N/106°55′E) The capital of Mongolia, 616

**United Arab Emirates** (24°00′N/54°00′E) A country in the Arabian Peninsula of Southwest Asia, 503

**United Kingdom** (54°00′N/4°00′W) A Northern European nation consisting of England, Wales, Scotland, and Northern Ireland, 300

**United States** (38°00′N/110°00′W) A country in North America that consists of 50 states, the District of Columbia, and four territories, 117

**Ural Mountains** (60°00′N/60°00′E) A mountain range that runs north and south in western Russia; some consider it as the border between Europe and Asia, 345

**Uruguay** (33°00′S/56°00′W) A country in southern South America, 230, *m234*

**Utah** (39°15′N/111°45′W) A state in the western United States, 112

**Uzbekistan** (41°00′N/64°00′E) A country in Central Asia, 375

**Vaduz** (47°08′N/9°31′E) The capital of Liechtenstein, 266

**Valletta** (35°54′N/14°31′E) The capital of Malta, 268

**Vancouver** (49°15′N/123°08′W) A city in British Columbia, 169

**Vanuatu** (16°00′S/167°00′E) A country that consists of an island group of Oceania in the Pacific Ocean, 712, *m713*

**Vatican City** (41°54′N/12°27′E) An independent papal state located near Rome, Italy, 268

**Venezuela** (8°00′N/66°00′W) A country in northern South America, 230, *m234*

**Venice** (45°26′N/12°20′E) A city in northeastern Italy, 281

**Verkhoyansk** (67°35′N/133°27′E) A city in Siberia in Russia, 354

**Vermont** (44°00′N/72°45′W) A state in New England in the northeastern United States, 145

**Victoria** (48°26′N/123°21′W) The capital of British Columbia, Canada, 169

**Victoria** (4°37′S/55°27′E) The capital of Seychelles, 412

**Victoria Island** (71°00′N/110°00′W) A large island in northern Canada, 121

**Victoria, Lake** (1°00′S/33°00′E) The second largest freshwater lake in the world; lies in East Africa, 417

**Vienna** (48°12′N/16°22′E) The capital of Austria, 266

**Vientiane** (17°58′N/102°36′E) The capital of Laos, 684

**Vietnam** (16°00′N/106°00′E) A country in Southeast Asia, 705

**Vilnius** (54°41′N/25°19′E) The capital of Lithuania, 342

**Vindhya Mountains** (24°37′N/82°00′E) A mountain range in central India, 552

**Virginia** (37°30′N/78°30′W) A state in the southern United States, 148

**Volga River** (45°51′N/47°58′E) The longest river in Europe; rises near Moscow, flows east and then south, and empties into the Caspian Sea, 347

**Warsaw** (52°15′N/21°00′E) The capital of Poland, 268

**Washington** (47°30′N/120°30′W) A state in the northwestern United States, 148

**Washington, D.C.** (38°54′N/77°02′W) The capitol of the United States, *m145*, 147

**Wellington** (41°18′S/174°47′E) The capital of New Zealand, 684

**West, the** An area of the United States that stretches from the Great Plains to the Pacific Ocean and includes Alaska and Hawaii. Other states in this area are Montana, Wyoming, Colorado, New Mexico, Arizona, Utah, Idaho, Washington, Oregon, Nevada, and California, 148

**West Africa** A region of Africa that includes Benin, Burkina Faso, Cape Verde, Chad, Côte d'Ivoire, Gambia, Ghana, Guinea, Guinea-Bissau, Liberia, Mali, Mauritania, Niger, Nigeria, Senegal, Sierra Leone, and Togo, 442

**West Antarctica** A region of Antarctica; a group of islands of Antarctica linked by the ice that covers them, 692

**West Bank** (31°40′N/35°15′E) A strip of land on the west side of the Jordan River, 527

**West Siberian Plain** (60°00′N/75°00′E) A plain in west central Russia, 345

**West Virginia** (38°30′N/80°30′W) A state in the southern United States, 112

**Western Europe** A region that includes France, Germany, Austria, Liechtenstein, Switzerland, Belgium, the Netherlands, and Luxembourg, 294

**Western Ghats** (14°00′N/75°00′E) A mountain range that runs along the west coast of India, 552

**Western Republics** Countries located west of Russia; they include Ukraine, Belarus, Moldova, Latvia, Lithuania, and Estonia, 361

**Whitehorse** (60°43′N/135°03′W) The capital of the Yukon Territory of Canada, 114

**Windhoek** (22°34′S/17°05′E) The capital of Namibia, 410

**Winnipeg** (49°53′N/97°10′W) The capital of Manitoba, Canada, 114

**Wisconsin** (44°30′N/90°00′W) A state in the Midwest of the United States, 112

**Wuhan** (30°35′N/114°16′E) A city in China, 637

**Wuxi** (31°36′N/120°17′E) A city in China, 637

**Wyoming** (43°00′N/107°30′W) A state in the western United States, 112

**Xi Jiang** (also called West River) (22°48′N/113°03′E) A river that flows through southeast China, joins the Pearl River (Zhu Jiang) and empties into the South China Sea, 621, *m620*

**Yalu River** (39°56′N/124°19′E) A river that forms the border between North Korea and China, 622, *m620*

**Yamoussoukro** (6°49′N/5°17′W) The capital of Côte d'Ivoire, 408

**Yangon** (16°47′N/96°10′E) The capital of Myanmar, 684

**Yangtze River** (also called Chang Jiang) (31°47′N/121°08′E) The longest river in Asia; flows from Xizang (Tibet) across China to the East China Sea, *m620*, 621

**Yaoundé** (3°52′N/11°31′E) The capital of Cameroon, 408

**Yellow River** (also called Huang He) (37°45′N/119°05′E) A Chinese river that rises in the Kunlun Mountains, flows east for about 3,000 miles, and empties into the Yellow Sea, *m620*, 621

**Yellow Sea** (36°00′N/124°00′E) An arm of the Pacific Ocean between the Korean Peninsula and northeastern China, *m620*, 621

**Yellowknife** (62°27′N/114°21′W) The capital of the Northwest Territories of Canada, 114

**Yemen** (15°16′N/42°35′E) A country in the Arabian Peninsula of Southwest Asia, 503

**Yenisey River** (71°50′N/82°40′E) A river that flows through central Russia and empties into the Kara Sea, 347

**Yerevan** (40°11′N/44°30′E) The capital of Armenia, *m370*, 371

**Yugoslavia** (43°45′N/20°45′E) A country in Eastern Europe, 308

**Yukon Territory** (63°00′N/136°00′W) A territory in northwestern Canada, 169

**Zagreb** (45°48′N/16°00′E) The capital of Croatia, 266

**Zagros Mountains** (33°40′N/47°00′E) A mountain range in western Iran, 488, *m488*

**Zambia** (15°00′S/30°00′E) A country in Southern Africa, 453, *m454*

**Zimbabwe** (19°00′S/29°00′E) A country in Southern Africa, 453, *m454*

INDEX

# Acknowledgments

## TEXT ACKNOWLEDGMENTS

**Unit 1,** Adapted "Figure 9.51," from *Physical Geography, Second Edition.* Copyright © 1989, 1992 by West Publishing Company. Reprinted by permission of Thomson Learning.

Excerpt from "Flight of a Lifetime" by James Irwin, from *The Greatest Adventure.* Copyright © 1994 by the Association of Space Explorers.

Excerpt from "To Really See It, Leave It" by Sally Ride, from *The Greatest Adventure.* Copyright © 1994 by the Association of Space Explorers.

**Unit 3,** Excerpt from "Brazilian police go on trial for murder of street children" by Marina Mirabella, from CNN World News, April 26, 1996. Copyright © 1996 by Cable News Network, Inc. Reprinted by permission of Cable News Network, Inc.

Excerpt from "Hope for the no-hopers," from the *Economist,* December 23, 2000. Copyright © 2000 by the *Economist.* Reprinted by permission of the *Economist.*

Excerpt from "Rich-poor gap as wide as ever in Latin America" by Steve Gutkin, from *The Times of India Online,* September 5, 2000. Copyright © 2000 by Times Internet Limited. Reprinted by permission of Times Internet Limited. All rights reserved.

**Unit 4,** Excerpt from "Poland Opens Door to West, and Chills Blow Both Ways" by Edmund L. Andrews, from the *New York Times,* June 21, 1999. Copyright © 1999 by the *New York Times.* Reprinted by permission of the *New York Times.*

Excerpt from "Britain and the Single Currency," from Global Britain Briefing Note, No. 1, January 25, 1999. Copyright © 1999 by Global Britain. Reprinted by permission of Global Britain.

**Unit 5,** Excerpt from "Workers Bid Ill-Fated Chernobyl a Bitter Farewell" by Michael Wines, from the *New York Times,* December 15, 2000. Copyright © 2000 by the *New York Times.* Reprinted by permission of the *New York Times.*

Excerpt from "Reducing Russian Dangers," from the *New York Times,* January 21, 1999. Copyright © 1999 by the *New York Times.* Reprinted by permission of the *New York Times.*

**Unit 6,** Excerpt from "Cash Strapped African Leaders Beg To Be Re-Colonized" by Ron Daniels, from the *Black World Today,* August 1, 1999. Copyright © 1999 by the *Black World Today.* Reprinted by permission of the *Black World Today.*

Excerpt from "An African Success Story," from the *New York Times,* January 8, 2001. Copyright © 2001 by the *New York Times.* Reprinted by permission of the *New York Times.*

**Unit 7,** Excerpt from "All Sides Resist Plan by Clinton For the Mideast" by John Kifner, from the *New York Times,* December 31, 2000. Copyright © 2000 by the *New York Times.* Reprinted by permission of the *New York Times.*

Excerpt from "The Price of Peace Will Be Paid in Dreams" by John F. Kifner, from the *New York Times,* December 31, 2000. Copyright © 2000 by the *New York Times.* Reprinted by permission of the *New York Times.*

Excerpt from "A City That Echoes Eternity" by Kenneth L. Woodward, from *Newsweek,* July 24, 2000. Copyright © 2000 by Newsweek, Inc. Reprinted by permission of Newsweek, Inc. All rights reserved.

Excerpts from "City of Jerusalem," from *United Nations: General Assembly Resolution 181,* November 29, 1947. Copyright © 1947 by the United Nations. Reprinted by permission of the United Nations.

**Unit 8,** Excerpt from President K. R. Narayanan's state dinner toast, March 21, 2000. Copyright © 2001 by the Embassy of India, Press and Information. Reprinted by permission of the Embassy of India.

**Unit 9,** Excerpt from "Clinton in Hong Kong, prods China on environment," from CNN.com, July 2, 1998. Copyright © 1998 by Cable News Network, Inc. Reprinted by permission of Cable News Network, Inc.

Excerpt from "Six Billion People," from *Asiaweek.com,* October 29, 1999, Vol. 25, No. 43. Copyright © 1999 by Asiaweek. Reprinted by permission of Asiaweek.

**Unit 10,** Excerpt from "Record Ozone Hole Refuels Debate on Climate" by Andrew C. Revkin, from the *New York Times,* October 10, 2000. Copyright © 2000 by the *New York Times.* Reprinted by permission of the *New York Times.*

Excerpts from *Dear America, Letters Home from Vietnam* edited by Bernard Edelman. Copyright © 1985 by The New York Vietnam Veterans Memorial Commission. Reprinted by permission of Simon & Schuster.

Excerpt from "Heroes for the Planet" by Terry McCarthy, from *Time,* Apr-May 2000. Copyright © 2000 by Time, Inc. Reprinted by permission of Time, Inc.

Excerpt from "There is No Global Warming," from the American Policy Center. Copyright © 2001 by the American Policy Center. Reprinted by permission of the American Policy Center.

The editors have made every effort to trace the ownership of all copyrighted material found in this book and to make full acknowledgment for its use. Omissions brought to our attention will be corrected in a subsequent edition.

## ART CREDITS

**Cover front** *background* Copyright © Orbital Imaging Corporation and processing by NASA Goddard Space Flight Center. Image provided by ORBIMAGE; *insets, top to bottom* Copyright © Hugh Sitton/Stone; Copyright © George Hunter/H. Armstrong Roberts; Copyright © James Martin/Stone; Copyright © Michael Dunning/Image Bank.

**Front Matter ii–iii** *background* Copyright © Orbital Imaging Corporation and processing by NASA Goddard Space Flight Center. Image provided by ORBIMAGE; **ii** *top, left to right* Copyright © Hugh Sitton/Tony Stone Images; Copyright © George Hunter/ H. Armstrong Roberts; Copyright © James Martin/Tony Stone Images; **iii** *right* Copyright © Michael Dunning/Image Bank; **v, vi–vii** *background* Earth from space; **viii** *top* Copyright © Schafer & Hill/Tony Stone Images; *bottom* Copyright © 1994 Jeffrey Aaronson/Network Aspen. All rights reserved; **ix** *top* SuperStock; *bottom* Copyright © Kevin Miller/Tony Stone Images; **x** *top* Copyright © Loren McIntyre; *bottom* Copyright © Ary Diesendruck/Tony Stone Images; **xi** *top* Copyright © Eye Ubiquitous/Corbis; *bottom* Ric Ergenbright Photography; **xii** *top* Sovfoto/Eastfoto; *bottom* Copyright © David Sutherland/Tony Stone Images; **xiii** *top* Copyright © Daryl Balfour/Tony Stone Images; *center* Copyright © Mitch Reardon/Tony Stone Images; *bottom* Copyright © M. Thonig/H. Armstrong Roberts; **xiv** *top* Copyright © Ali Kazuyoshi Namachi/Pacific Press; *bottom* Copyright © John Egan/Hutchison Picture Library; **xv** *top* Copyright © Paul Harris/Tony Stone Images; *bottom* Copyright © Martin Puddy/Tony Stone Images; **xvi** *top* Copyright © David Ball/Tony Stone Images; *center* Copyright © Tony Stone Images; *bottom* Copyright © John Lamb/Tony Stone Images; **xvii** *top* Copyright © Roger Near/Tony Stone Images; *center* Copyright © Nicholas DeVore/Tony Stone Images; *bottom* Copyright © David Austen/Tony Stone Images. **xxiv** Copyright © Dani/Jeske/Animals Animals; Copyright © Patti Murray/Earth Scenes; Copyright © J. Carnemolla/Australian Picture Library; Copyright © John Cancalosi/Peter Arnold Inc.; Copyright © Norman Owen Tomalin/Bruce Coleman; Copyright © Tim Flach/Tony Stone Images; **xxv** *top* The Granger Collection, New York; *bottom* Copyright © 2001 The New Yorker Collection from cartoonbank.com. All rights reserved.

**Maps pp. A1–A25,** 64, 102–115, 131, 179, 190–199, 206, 248, 262–271, 281, 322, 336–343, 357, 391, 402–413, 419, 464, 478–485, 494, 528, 542–549, 559, 596, 610–617, 624, 664, 678–687, **© Rand McNally & Company. All rights reserved.**

**Units Unit 1, 2–3** *background* Copyright © Earth Imaging/Tony Stone Images; **2** *foreground* Copyright © Schafer & Hill/Tony Stone Images; **3** *foreground* Copyright © Damir Sagolj/Reuters/Archive Photos; **4** *background, left* MapQuest.com; **7** Copyright © Eduardo Garcia/FPG International/PictureQuest; **8** Copyright © Alan Weiner/Liaison; **10** Globe (c. 1492), Martin Benham. Bibliotheque Nationale, Paris/Giraudon/Art Resource, New York; **11** *background* Copyright © Paul Morrell/Tony Stone Images; *top left* National Oceanic and Atmospheric Administration/Department of Commerce; **12** *top left* Copyright © Bob Krist/ eStock Photography/PictureQuest; *top center* Copyright © PhotoDisc/Getty Images; **13** Copyright © Erwin and Peggy Bauer/Bruce Coleman Inc.; **14** *background* National Oceanic and Atmospheric Administration/Department of Commerce; *top* AP/Wide World Photos; *bottom left* Science Museum/Science & Society Picture Library, London; *bottom right* Copyright © Owen Franken/Stock Boston/PictureQuest; **26** Copyright © Paul Morrell/Tony Stone Images; **30–31** *background,* **31** Illustrations by Roberta Polfus; **32** Copyright © SuperStock; **33** Illustration by Stephen R. Wagner; **34–35** Illustration by Ken Goldammer; **36** Copyright © Earth Satellite Corporation/Science Photo Library/Photo Researchers Inc.; **38–39** Illustration by Roberta Polfus; **40** Copyright © Chip Hires/Liaison; **41** Copyright © HO/Reuters/Archive Photos; **42** Copyright © David Muench/Corbis; **43** AP/Wide World Photos; **44** Copyright © Jerryl Hout/ Bruce Coleman Inc.; **48** Copyright © SuperStock; **50** Illustration by Stephen R. Wagner; **51** National Oceanic and Atmospheric Administration/Department of Commerce; **52** *inset* Copyright © Chris Johns/Tony Stone Images; **53** Getty News Services; **59** Copyright © Vladpans/eStock Photography/PictureQuest; **60** *top* Copyright © SuperStock; *bottom* Copyright © 1994 Michael Fogden/Bruce Coleman Inc./PictureQuest; **61** *top insert* Copyright © 1999 Picture Finders Ltd./ eStock Photography/PictureQuest; *bottom insert* Copyright © Daniel J. Cox/ Liaison; **62** Copyright © Charlie Waite/Tony Stone Images; **63** Copyright 1993 © Richard Olsenius/Black Star/PictureQuest; **67** *left* Used by permission, Utah State Historical Society. All rights reserved; *right* Copyright © Tom Till Photography; **70** Copyright © 1994 David Hiser/Photographers/Aspen/PictureQuest; **72** Copyright © Adrian Arbib/Corbis; **73** Courtesy Medmaster, Inc. Miami, Florida; **77** Copyright © Werner Forman/Corbis; **81** Copyright © 1994 Jeffrey Aaronson/Network Aspen. All rights reserved; **83** Copyright © 1960 Sergio Larrain/Magnum Photos; **85** Copyright © D. E. Cox/Tony Stone Images; **87** Copyright © SuperStock; **88** Copyright © Earth Imaging/Tony Stone Images; **91** Copyright © SuperStock; **92** Photograph by Sharon Hoogstraten; **94** *top row, pots* Copyright © 1999 Stockbyte/PictureQuest; *bicycles* Copyright © Image Club/EyeWire; *middle row, kettles and sieves* Copyright © 1999 Stockbyte/PictureQuest; *televisions* Copyright © Digital Stock/Corbis; *stereos* Copyright © Jeffrey Coolidge/Image Bank; *bottom row, bicycle* Copyright © Image Club/EyeWire; *radios* Copyright © Digital Stock/Corbis; *VCR* Copyright © 1999–2001 PhotoDisc/Getty Images; **95** *top row, bicycles* Copyright © Image Club/EyeWire; *radios and telephone* Copyright

© Digital Stock/Corbis; *bottom row, television* Copyright © Digital Stock/Corbis; *microwave* Copyright © 1999 Stockbyte/PictureQuest; *car, computer, and VCR* Copyright © 1999–2001 PhotoDisc/Getty Images.

**Unit 2, 98** *top, bottom* Copyright © SuperStock; **98–99** Copyright © WorldSat International/Science Source/Photo Researchers Inc.; **99** Copyright © Joseph Sohm/ChromoSohm Inc./Corbis; **100** Copyright © Gary Braasch/Corbis; **101** *top* Copyright 1999 © Pictor International/Pictor International Ltd./PictureQuest; *bottom* Copyright © Gilles Mingasson/Liaison; **108–115** MapQuest.com; **116** Copyright © SuperStock; **117** Copyright © Mark E. Gibson; **118** *top right inset* Copyright © 1994 Jim Schwabel/Southern Stock/PictureQuest; *bottom left inset* Copyright © 2000 Jake Rajs/Tony Stone Images; *bottom right inset* Copyright © Eric Carle/Stock Boston/PictureQuest; **118–119** Copyright © SuperStock; **122** Copyright © 1998 Jim Pickerell/Stock Connection/PictureQuest; **123** Copyright © Bryan and Cherry Alexander Photography; **126** AP/Wide World Photos; **127** Copyright © Mark Wagner/Tony Stone Images; **128** Copyright © Roger Ressmeyer/Corbis; **135** Copyright © SuperStock; **137** *top, Lewis and Clark at Three Forks* (date unknown), E. S. Paxson. Mural in the Montana State Capitol. Courtesy of the Montana Historical Society. Photograph by John Reddy. Montana Historical Society #952-803; *middle* Copyright © 1999 Ewing Galloway/Index Stock Imagery/PictureQuest; *bottom, The Last Spike* (1869). William T. Garrett Foundry, San Francisco. 17 6/10" carat gold, alloyed with copper. 5 9/16" × 7/16" × 1/2" (shaft including head), 1/2" × 1 3/8" × 1 1/4". Iris & B. Gerald Cantor Center for Visual Arts at Stanford University. Gift of David Hewes, 1998.115; **138** *top* AP/Wide World Photos; *middle* Copyright © 1994 Dan McCoy/Rainbow/PictureQuest; *bottom* Copyright © 1999–2000 PhotoDisc/Getty Images. All rights reserved; **143** Copyright © Terry Cryer/Corbis; **144** Copyright © Mark Gibson/Corbis; **147** Copyright © Mike Magnuson/Stock Connection/PictureQuest; **148, 150–151** *background* AP/Wide World Photos; **151** *top inset, bottom inset* Library of Congress; **155** Copyright © SuperStock; **156** *left* Copyright © James P. Blair/ Corbis; *right, Fathers of Confederation* (1969), Rex Woods (after Robert Harris). Oil on canvas, 61" × 36". Courtesy Rogers Communications Inc., Toronto, Canada; **158** Copyright © Kevin Miller/Tony Stone Images; **161** *left* Copyright © Allen McInnis/Liaison; *right* Copyright © 2001 Corbis; **162** Copyright © Vern McGrath/ Valan Photos; **163** Copyright © David Hiser/Photographers/Aspen/PictureQuest; **164–165** *background* Copyright © Brian Sytnyk/Masterfile; **164** *left inset* Copyright © SuperStock; *right inset* Copyright © AFP/Corbis; **165** *bottom inset* Copyright © 1997 John Madere/The Stock Market; **168** Copyright © SuperStock; **169** AP/Wide World Photos; **172** Copyright © Gary Braasch/Corbis; **174** Copyright © 1999 Ann and Carl Purcell/Words & Pictures/PictureQuest; **175** Copyright © 1993 Jose Azel/Aurora; **177** *left* AP/Wide World Photos; *right* Copyright © 1999 Pictor International/Pictor International Ltd./PictureQuest; **180** Copyright © Gilles Mingasson/Liaison.

**Unit 3, 186–187** *background* MapQuest.com; **186** *left* The Granger Collection, New York; *right* Copyright © Loren McIntyre; **187** Copyright © Ary Diesendruck/Tony Stone Images; **188** Copyright © Luiz C. Marigo/Peter Arnold Inc.; **189** *top* AP/Wide World Photos; *bottom* Copyright © G. Boutin/Explorer/Photo Researchers Inc.; **200** Copyright © Robert Madden/NGS Image Collection; **201** Copyright © Jerry Alexander/Tony Stone Images; **202** Copyright © 1989 M. Sutton/FPG International; **205** Copyright © 1998 Robert Caputo/Aurora; **210, 211** Copyright © Erick C. M. Fernandes/Department of Crop and Soil Sciences, Cornell University, ecf3@cornell.edu; **212** *background* Copyright © Nicholas DeVore III/Photographers/Aspen; **213** Copyright © 1999 Don Hebert/FPG International; **217** Copyright © Nigel Atherton/Tony Stone Images; **218** *top, middle* The Granger Collection, New York; *bottom* Copyright © Wesley Bocxe/ Liaison; **219** *The Cry of Dolores,* Juan O'Gorman. Mural. The Granger Collection, New York; **221** Copyright © Joel Sartore/NGS Image Collection; **222** *bottom right* Courtesy of El Museo del Barrio, New York; **223** Copyright © Gordon Gahan/NGS Image Collection; **225** Copyright © Glyn Genin/Glyfada; **226** *background* Copyright © IFA Bilderteam/Leo de Wys; **227** Archive Photos; **228–229** *background* Copyright © Alain Buu/Liaison; **229** *top* Copyright © Robert Linstrom; **230** *left* The Granger Collection, New York; *right* National Museum of the American Indian; **231** *bottom left* The Granger Collection, New York; *bottom right* AP/Wide World Photos; **232** University of Chile; **233** *left* Copyright © 1996 Michele Burgess/Stock Market; *middle* Copyright © R. Giling/Lineair/Peter Arnold Inc.; *right* Copyright © Jeff Greenberg/Peter Arnold Inc.; **235** Gustau Nacarino/Reuters/Archive Photos; **237** Copyright © Martin Wendler/Peter Arnold Inc.; **239** Copyright © Herb Zulpier/Masterfile; **240** *left* Copyright © Tim Holt/ Photo Researchers Inc.; *right* Copyright © SuperStock; **241** *top* Copyright © Trip/Dinodia; *bottom* Copyright © Steve Vidler/Leo de Wys; **243** The Newberry Library, Chicago; **244** Copyright © Luiz C. Marigo/Peter Arnold Inc.; **246** Copyright © Steve Winter/NGS Image Collection; **249** Copyright © 2001 The New Yorker Collection from cartoonbank.com. All rights reserved; **250** AP/Wide World Photos; **251** Copyright © Ary Diesendruck/Tony Stone Images; *bottom inset* AP/Wide World Photos; **252** Copyright © Robert Frerck/Tony Stone Images; **253** Copyright © G. Boutin/Explorer/Photo Researchers Inc.

**Unit 4, 258** Ric Ergenbright Photography; **258–259** *background* Copyright © ESA/K. Horgan/Tony Stone Images; **259** *left* Copyright © Eye Ubiquitous/Corbis; *right* Copyright © C. Liewig/Tempsport Newsport Photography; **260** Copyright © Reuters NewMedia/Corbis; **261** *top* Copyright © Ferenczy/Liaison; *bottom inset* Copyright © Edmund Nägele/International Stock; *bottom* Copyright © *Oliphant*/Universal Press Syndicate. Reprinted with permission. All rights reserved; **272** Copyright © Pal Hermansen/Tony Stone Images; **274** Ric Ergenbright Photography; **277** Copyright © Peter Vandermark/Stock Boston/PictureQuest; **279** Copyright © Michael Busselle/Corbis; **280** Copyright © Chad Ehlers/Tony Stone Images; **282** *top* Illustration by Stephen R. Wagner; *bottom left* Copyright © Paul Almasy/Corbis; **284** Copyright © Guido Alberto Rossi; **285** Copyright © C. T. K./Liaison; **289** Copyright © SuperStock; **291** *top, La Vierge et l'enfant entoures de cinq anges* [The Virgin and child surrounded by five angels], Sandro Botticelli. Musée du Louvre, Paris/Giraudon, Paris/SuperStock; *bottom* Copyright © Ruggero Vanni/Corbis; **293** AP/Wide World Photos; **295** Illustrations by Stephen R. Wagner; **296** *left, Idealbildnis Kaiser Karls des Großen* [Ideal portrait of Emperor Charlemagne] (1511), Albrecht Dürer. Copyright © Germanisches Nationalmuseum, Nuremberg, Germany/Lauros-Giraudon, Paris/SuperStock; *top right* Self-portrait, Leonardo da Vinci. Biblioteca Reale, Turin, Italy/Scala/Art Resource, New York; *bottom right* Detail of *Portrait of Martin Luther* (1529), Lucas Cranach the Elder. Museo Poldi Pezzoli, Milan, Italy/Bridgeman Art Library, London; **297** *left* The Granger Collection, New York; *center, Napoleon on His Imperial Throne* (1806), Jean August Dominique Ingres. Musée de l'Armée, Paris/Giraudon/Art Resource, New York; *right* Photograph by Margaret Bourke White/*Life* Magazine. Copyright © Time Inc.; **298** Copyright © SuperStock; **300** Copyright © Eddy Posthuma de Boer; **302** The Granger Collection, New York; **306** Copyright © SuperStock; **307** Copyright © 1995 Culver Pictures/PictureQuest; **308–309** *background* Copyright © 1983 Duomo; **308** Copyright © Delangue Christian/Liaison; **309** *top* Copyright © Ron Levy/Liaison; *bottom* Copyright © 1990 Anchorage Daily News/Liaison; **310** *center* Copyright © Ali Meyer/Corbis; *right* Copyright © Archivo Iconografico, S.A./Corbis; **311** *left* The Granger Collection, New York; *right* Copyright © Reuters NewMedia/Corbis; **312** AP/Wide World Photos; **314** *left, right* Photographs by Sharon Hoogstraten; **315** Copyright © Grant V. Faint/The Image Bank; **318** Copyright © Reuters NewMedia/Corbis; **319** *The Kosovo Maiden* (1917), Uros Predic. National Museum of Belgrade (Yugoslavia); **320** AP/Wide World Photos; **321** Copyright © AFP/Corbis; **323** Copyright © Ferenczy/Liaison; **324** Copyright © 1994 Sovfoto/Eastfoto/PictureQuest; **326** *top* Copyright © Reuters NewMedia/Corbis; *bottom* Copyright © Edmund Nägele/International Stock; **329** Copyright © *Oliphant*/Universal Press Syndicate. Reprinted with permission. All rights reserved.

**Unit 5, 332–333** *background* Copyright © Tom Van Sant/Geosphere Project/Planetary Visions/Science Photo Library/Photo Researchers, Inc.; **332** Copyright © Fritz Dressler; **333** *left* Estate of Fitzroy Maclean; *right* Copyright © Vadim Gippenreiter; **334** Copyright © Laurent van der Stockt/Liaison; **335** *top* Cartoon by Pat Bagley/Salt Lake Tribune; *bottom* Copyright © Gerd Ludwig/NGS Image Collection; **344** Copyright © 2000 Sarah Leen/Matrix; **345** Copyright © Dean Conger/NGS Image Collection; **346** Copyright © James Strachen/Getty Images; **347** *top left, right,* **348** Copyright © Dean Conger/NGS Image Collection; **349** Copyright © Steve Ravmar/NGS Image Collection; **350** Sovfoto/ Eastfoto; **352** Copyright © Dean Conger/NGS Image Collection; **353** *left, right* Copyright © WorldSat International, Inc.; **354** Copyright © Gerd Ludwig/NGS Image Collection; **356** Copyright © 1998 Gerd Ludwig/Visum/Saba; **361** Photograph copyright © Andy Crawford/State Historical Musuem, Moscow; **362** *left* Copyright © David Sutherland/Tony Stone Images; *background right* Copyright © K. Scholz/H. Armstrong Roberts; *right inset* The Granger Collection, New York; **363** *left* Napoleon's retreat from Moscow (19th century), Adolf Northen. Sotheby's Picture Library, London; *center* Sovfoto/Eastfoto; *right* AP/Wide World Photos; **364** Copyright © 2001 Henri Cartier-Bresson/Magnum Photos; **365** Copyright © Dean Conger/NGS Image Collection; **366** *top* The Granger Collection, New York; *bottom* The Hoover Archives, RU/SU1748; **367** Copyright © Dean Conger/NGS Image Collection; **368** *background* Reuters/Archive Photos; *top right* RIA-Novosti/Sovfoto/Eastfoto; **369** *background* Stringer/Reuters/Archive Photos; *top* Copyright © Gerd Ludwig/NGS Image Collection; *bottom* Gleb Garnich/Reuters/Archive Photos; **371** Borromeo/Art Resource, New York; **372** Sovfoto/Eastfoto; **374** Copyright © Dean Conger/NGS Image Collection; **376** *clockwise from top left* Copyright © David M. Schleser/Nature's Images, Inc./Photo Researchers, Inc.; Copyright © Joyce Photographics/Photo Researchers, Inc.; Copyright © O. S. F./Animals Animals; Copyright © Catherine Karnow/Corbis; Sovfoto/Eastfoto; Sovfoto/Eastfoto; **378** Copyright © Ergun Cagatay/Tetragon; **379** Estate of Fitzroy Maclean; **380–381** *background* Copyright © James Strachan/Tony Stone Images; **380** *left* Copyright © David Rosenberg/Tony Stone Images; **381** *top* Copyright © 1997 George Steinmetz/NGS Image Collection; *bottom* Copyright © M. Thonig/H. Armstrong Roberts; **383** Map by Alex Verbitsky; **386** Reuters TV/Reuters/Archive Photos; **387** Copyright © Laurent van der Stockt/Liaison; **388** Copyright © Steven Weinberg/Tony Stone Images; **390** Copyright © Mark H. Millstein/ANS/Liaison; **392** *top* Copyright © Gerd Ludwig/ NGS Image Collection; **393** AP/Wide World Photos; **394** Copyright © 2000 Nick Anderson, The Washington Post Writers Group. Reprinted with permission.

**Unit 6, 398–399** *background* Copyright © European Space Agency/Science Photo Library/Photo Researchers, Inc.; **398** *top* Copyright © Hugh Sitton/Tony Stone Images; *bottom* R. G. V. Wendel de Joode; **399** *bottom* Copyright © Daryl Balfour/Tony Stone Images; **400** Copyright © 1968 Rene Burri/Magnum Photos; **401** *top* Copyright © Wendy Stone/Liaison; *bottom* Copyright © 1996 Alan King. National Archives of Canada, Ottawa, ref. no. R2905-116; **414** SuperStock; **416** Copyright © Christophe Ratier/NHPA/Photo Researchers, Inc.; **418** Copyright © 1988 Christopher Pillitz/Weststock; **420** Copyright © M. Thonig/H. Armstrong Roberts; **422** Copyright © Wendy Stone/Odyssey/Chicago; **423** Copyright © Bruce Davidson/Animals Animals; **424** *background* Copyright © PhotoDisc/Getty Images; **424** *foreground* Illustrations by Stephen R. Wagner; **425** *background* Copyright © PhotoDisc/Getty Images; **425** *foreground* Illustrations by Stephen R. Wagner; **426** *bottom* Copyright © Lloyd Cluff/Corbis; **432** Copyright © Werner Forman/Art Resource, New York; **433** *top left* The Granger Collection, New York; *top right* Copyright © 2001 John Moss/Black Star; **434** Copyright © Mitch Reardon/Tony Stone Images; **436** Copyright © Raffaele Ciriello; **437** *top left* Greg Marinovich; *top right, bottom* AP/Wide World Photos; **438** Copyright © Guido

Alberto Rossi/The Image Bank; **440** Copyright © Rohan/Tony Stone Images; **441** Copyright © Wolfgang Kaehler; **444** *bottom, bottom inset* Copyright © Robert Frerck/Odyssey/Chicago; **445** Copyright © Deborah Feingold/Archive Photos; **446** *clockwise from top right* Copyright © Trip/Dinodia; Copyright © 1996 Christopher Liu/ChinaStock; Copyright © Trip/H. Rogers; **447** *top* SuperStock; *bottom* Copyright © Robert Frerck/Odyssey/Chicago; **449** Cartoon by Linley Sambourne (1906). Mary Evans Picture Library, London; **451** *When There is Work, the Village Expands,* Mode Muntu. Collection of Guy de Plaen; **452** Copyright © 1995 Malcolm Linton/Liaison; **453** Robert Aberman/Art Resource, New York; **455** *from top to bottom* The Granger Collection, New York; Copyright © Hulton/Archive Swimming Pool Database-Big Picture; The Royal Collection copyright © 2001 Her Majesty Queen Elizabeth II; Copyright © Mark Peters/Sipa Press; **456** Copyright © Robert Frerck/Odyssey/Chicago; **460** Copyright © 1968 Rene Burri/Magnum Photos; **461** Photograph by Bjorn Klingwall; **463** Copyright © Piotr Jaxa/The Rolex Awards for Enterprise; **465** Copyright © Malcolm Linton/Liaison; **467** *top right* Copyright © Wendy Stone/Liaison; **468** Corbis-Bettmann; **469** *bottom* AP/Wide World Photos; **471** Copyright © 1996 Alan King. National Archives of Canada, Ottawa, ref. No. R2905-116.

**Unit 7, 474–475** *background* Copyright © 1995 WorldSat International and J. Knighton/Photo Researchers, Inc.; **474** *left* Copyright © Sylvain Grandadam/Tony Stone Images; *right* Copyright © Bernard Gerard/Hutchison Picture Library; **475** Copyright © Ali Kazuyoshi Nomachi/Pacific Press Service; **476** Copyright © John Egan/Hutchison Picture Library; **477** *top* Copyright © Robert Azzi/Woodfin Camp; *bottom* Mark Fiore. San Francisco, California. www.markfiore.com; **484–485** MapQuest.com; **486** Copyright © Peter Sanders; **487** Copyright © Richard T. Nowitz/Corbis; **489** Copyright © Roger Antrobus/Corbis; **490** AP/Wide World Photos; **491** Copyright © Alistair Duncan/DK Images; **493** Copyright © Nik Wheeler/Corbis; **495** Copyright © Alan Puzey/Tony Stone Images; **496** *background* Copyright © PhotoDisc/Getty Images; *clockwise from top left* Copyright © Richard T. Nowitz/NGS Image Collection; Copyright © Trip/H. Rogers; Copyright © Peter J. Ochs II; Copyright © Christopher Rennie/Robert Harding Picture Library; **497** Getty News Services, #372147_06; **503** Copyright © Nabeel Turner/Tony Stone Images; **504** Scala/Art Resource, New York; **506** Copyright © 1985 Robert Azzi/Woodfin Camp; **507** Copyright © 2001 Stern Magazine/Black Star; **508–509** *background* Copyright © Hugh Sitton/Tony Stone Images; **508** SEF/Art Resource, New York; **509** *top* SuperStock; *bottom* Copyright © 1995 David Hiser/Photographers/Aspen/PictureQuest; **510** AP/Wide World Photos; **511** Copyright © Ilene Perlman/Stock Boston/PictureQuest; **513, 514** AP/Wide World Photos; **515** Copyright © Trip/H. Rogers; **517** Copyright © Peter Jordan/Liaison; **518** Copyright © Leo Touchet/Woodfin Camp; **519** Copyright © R. Ashworth/Robert Harding Picture Library; **521** *top* Copyright © ABC Basin Ajansi/Liaison; *bottom* AP/Wide World Photos; **524** Copyright © John Egan/Hutchison Picture Library; **525** Copyright © Thomas Hartwell/TimePix; **527** Copyright © Will Yurman/Liaison; **530** *top* Copyright © Ali Kazuyoshi Nomachi/Pacific Press Service; *bottom* Copyright © Baron Wolman; **531** Copyright © David & Peter Turnley/Corbis; **532** *top* AP/Wide World Photos; *bottom left* Corbis-Bettmann; *bottom right* Copyright © Dirck Halstead/Liaison; **535** Mark Fiore. San Francisco, California. www.markfiore.com.

**Unit 8, 538–539** *background* Copyright © Earth Imaging/Tony Stone Images; **538** Copyright © Paul Harris/Tony Stone Images; **539** *left* Copyright © 1997 Neal Beidleman/Network Aspen; *right* Copyright © Dominic Sansoni; **540** Copyright © James Strachan/Robert Harding Picture Library; **541** *top* Copyright © Chip Hires/Liaison; *bottom* Copyright © 1998 Carlson/Milwaukee Journal Sentinel; **550** Copyright © Jon Sparks/Corbis; **551** Illustration by Stephen R. Wagner; **552** Digital image copyright © 1996 Corbis. Original image courtesy of NASA/Corbis; **553** Copyright © E. Valentin/Photo Researchers, Inc.; **554** *inset* Copyright © Dominic Sansoni; **555** Copyright © Takeshi Takahara/Photo Researchers, Inc.; **556** Copyright © Brian Vikander/Corbis; **558** Copyright © E. Hanumantha Rao/Photo Researchers, Inc.; **560–561** Copyright © David Sutherland/Tony Stone Images; **562** Copyright © Pablo Bartholomew/Liaison; *inset right* Copyright © St. Franklin/Magnum Photos; **568** *top* Corbis-Bettmann; *bottom left* The Granger Collection, New York; *bottom right* Copyright © Roderick Johnson/Images of India; **570** Copyright © 1978 Dilip Mehta/Contact Press Images/PictureQuest; **571** Copyright © Anthony Cassidy/Tony Stone Images; **572** The Art Archive/Victoria & Albert Museum, London/Eileen Tweedy. Ref. no. AA328654; **573** Copyright © Photobank Photo Library; **575** *left* Copyright © David Sanger/Network Aspen; *right* Copyright © Brecel/J. Hodalic/Liaison; **576** Copyright © Robert Nickelsberg/TimePix; **577** Copyright © Beatrice Kiener/Liaison; **578–579** *background* National Oceanic and Atmospheric Administration/Department of Commerce; **578** *bottom* Illustration by Stephen R. Wagner; **579** *top* Copyright © Topham Picturepoint; *bottom* Jim Holmes/Eye Ubiquitous; **580** Thrikheb or "throne cover." Wool, silk, and cotton, 152 cm x 70 cm. Private collection, Oltromare, Geneva, Switzerland. Photograph copyright © Erich Lessing/ Art Resource; **581** Copyright © John Callahan/Tony Stone Images; **582** *background* Illustration by Stephen R. Wagner; *top inset* Copyright © Alison Wright/ Stock Boston/PictureQuest; **583** Copyright © Barbara Bussell/Network Aspen; **584** Copyright © Nokelsberg/Liaison; **585** Copyright © Hugh Sitton/Tony Stone Images; **586** Copyright © Martin Puddy/Tony Stone Images; **587** Copyright © Pete Seaward/Tony Stone Images; **588** *left* Copyright © Greig Cranna/Stock Boston/PictureQuest; *right* Copyright © Wolfgang Kaehler/Corbis; **589** *top* Copyright © 1999 Pictor International/Pictor International, Ltd./PictureQuest *bottom* AP/Wide World Photos; **592** Copyright © James Strachan/Robert Harding Picture Library; **593** Copyright © Bruno Barbey/ Magnum Photos; **595** Copyright © Jeroen Snjdera/Images of India; **598** Illustrations by Stephen R. Wagner; **599** *top* Courtesy David Cumming/ Hodder Wayland Picture Library; *bottom* Copyright © Trip/H. Rogers; **600** *top* Copyright © Ric Ergenbright/Corbis *bottom left* Corbis-Bettmann; *bottom right* Reuters/Archive Photos; **603** Copyright © 1998 Carlson/Milwaukee Journal Sentinel.

**Unit 9, 606–607** *background* Copyright © Tom Van Sant/Geosphere Project/Planetary Visions/Science Photo Library/Photo Researchers, Inc.; **606** SuperStock; **607** *left* Copyright © David Ball/Tony Stone Images; *right* SuperStock; **608** John Pryke/Reuters/Archive Photos; **609** *top* Copyright © Hugh Sitton/Tony Stone Images; *bottom* SuperStock; **618** SuperStock; **619** Copyright © Tony Stone Images; **621** Copyright © Keren Su/Corbis; **623** Copyright © Michael S. Yamashita/Corbis; **625** Copyright © Cynthia M. Beall/NGS Image Collection; **627** Digital image copyright © 1996 Corbis. Original image courtesy of NASA/Corbis; **628** *right* Copyright © 1997 Bob Sacha; **629** *left* NG Maps/NGS Image Collection; **630** *top to bottom* Copyright © Luo Wenfa/ChinaStock; Copyright © 1995 Wang Xinlin/ChinaStock; Copyright © ChinaStock; **631** Copyright © M. Bertinetti/White Star; **635** Copyright © Julian Calder/Tony Stone Images; **636** *left* Bibliothéque Nationale, Paris/Bridgeman Art Library, London/SuperStock; *center* By permission of The British Library, London; *right* The Granger Collection, New York; **637** *left* Copyright © ChinaStock; *right* The Granger Collection, New York; **638** *top left* Copyright © 1995 Christopher Liu/ChinaStock; *top right* The Metropolitan Museum of Art, New York. Gift of Ernest Erickson Foundation, Inc., 1985 (1985.214.99). Photograph copyright © 1986 the Metropolitan Museum of Art; *center* By permission of The British Library, London; *bottom* The Granger Collection, New York; **639** Copyright © Alain le Caromeu/Panos Pictures; **640–641** *background,* **641** *top* UPI/Corbis-Bettmann; **641** *bottom* Copyright © Tom Nebbia/Corbis; **642** Illustration by Patrick Whalen; **644** Copyright © Cynthia M. Beall & Melvyn C. Goldstein/NGS Image Collection; **646** AP/Wide World Photos; **647** Copyright © Bob Thomas/Tony Stone Images; **649** Copyright © Jean-Léo Dugast/Panos Pictures; **651** Copyright © Japan Archive/TimePix; **652** *left* The Granger Collection, New York; *right* Portrait of Kisegawa of Matsubaya (c. 1796), Kitagaw Utamoro. Fitzwilliam Museum, University of Cambridge, UK/The Bridgeman Art Library, London; **653** *bottom left* The Granger Collection, New York; *bottom right* Corbis-Bettmann; **654** Copyright © 1976 Kenneth Love; **655** SuperStock; **656** *left* Manu Sassoonian/Art Resource, New York; *right* SuperStock; **657** *top* Werner Forman Archive/Private collection, New York/Art Resource, New York; *bottom* SuperStock; **660** John Pryke/Reuters/Archive Photos; **661** AP/Wide World Photos; **663** Copyright © Bzad/ChinaStock; **665** Photograph by Manabu Watabe; **668** Copyright © John Lamb/Tony Stone Images; **671** Copyright © 2000 Nick Anderson, The Washington Post Writers Group. Reprinted with permission.

**Unit 10, 674** *left* Copyright © Tony Stone Images: *right* Copyright © Roger Near/Tony Stone Images; **676** Copyright © Thad Samuels/NGS Image Collection; **677** *top* Copyright © Sergio Dorantes/Sygma; *bottom* National Oceanic and Atmospheric Administration/Department of Commerce; **687** The Granger Collection, New York; **688** Copyright © David Doubilet; **690** Illustrations by Stephen R. Wagner; **691** Copyright © David Moore/Black Star; **694** Copyright © Dani/Jeske/Earth Scenes; **695** Copyright © Denis Waugh/ Tony Stone Images; **696** Copyright © Dani/Jeske/Animals Animals; Copyright © Patti Murray/Earth Scenes; Copyright © J. Carnemolla/Australian Picture Library; Copyright © John Cancalosi/Peter Arnold Inc.; Copyright © Norman Owen Tomalin/Bruce Coleman; Copyright © Tim Flach/Tony Stone Images; **698** Copyright © Walter Edwards/NGS Image Collection; **699** Copyright © Greg Taylor; **700** Australian Picture Library; **701** Copyright © U.S. Government Air Force/NGS Image Collection; **705** Copyright © Glen Allison/Tony Stone Images; **708** Copyright © W. Robert Moore/NGS Image Collection; **709** Copyright © 1984 Jonathan Kirn/Liaison; **710–711** *bottom background* Illustration by Stephen R. Wagner; **711** *top* Copyright © Georg Gerster/Photo Researchers Inc.; **712** G. Burenhult Productions, Tjörnarp, Sweden; **714** *top* Copyright © Peter Stone/Pacific Stock; *center* Copyright © Joe Carini/Pacific Stock; *bottom* Copyright © Nicholas DeVore/Tony Stone Images; **716** *left* Copyright © Robert Frerck/Odyssey; *right* Copyright © 1991 Buddy Mays/FPG International; **717** *top* Copyright © Orion Press/Pacific Stock; *bottom* Copyright © 1988 Lee Kuhn/FPG International; **718** *left* Copyright © D. Johanson/Institute of Human Origins; *center* Detail of James Cook (1776), John Webber. Oil on canvas. The Granger Collection, New York; *right* Copyright © Douglass Bagli/Australian Picture Library; **719** *top* Australian Picture Library; *bottom* Copyright © Christopher Arnesen/Tony Stone Images; **720** Copyright © George F. Mobley/NGS Image Collection; **721** SuperStock; **722** Australian Picture Library/NZPL; **723** AP/Wide World Photos; **726** Copyright © Thad Samuels/NGS Image Collection; **727** credit to come; **729** Copyright © David Austen/Tony Stone Images; **730** Darren Whiteside/Reuters/Archive Photos; **731** Copyright © Sergio Dorantes/Sygma; **734** Copyright © Wolfgang Kaehler; **737** *top* National Climatic Data Center/NESDIS/NOAA; *bottom* National Oceanic and Atmosphere Administration/Department of Commerce.

**The War on Terrorism US2** Copyright © AFP/Corbis; *inset* Copyright © John Annerino/TimePix; **US3** *top* MapQuest.com; *bottom* Susan Walsh/AP/Wide World Photos; **US4** *left* AP/Wide World Photos; *right* MapQuest.com; **US5** USA TODAY®; **US6–US7** MapQuest.com; **US6** *inset* Copyright © Reuters NewMedia Inc./Corbis; **US7** *top inset* Katsumi Ksashara/AP/Wide World Photos; *bottom inset* Sayyid Azim/AP/Wide World Photos; **US9** *left* AP/Wide World Photos; **US10** USA TODAY®; *top inset* AP/Wide World Photos; *middle inset* Al-Jazeera/AP/Wide World Photos; *bottom inset* AP/Wide World Photos; **US11** *top* Copyright © David Hume Kennerly/Corbis Sygma; *bottom* MapQuest.com; **US12** Copyright © Jeff Christensen/Reuters/TimePix; *inset* Copyright © Greg Mathieson/MAI/TimePix; **US13** USA TODAY®; **US14** *left* Copyright © Digital Stock/Corbis; *top inset* Copyright © Kent Wood/Photo Researchers; *bottom* FBI/AP/Wide World Photos; *bottom inset* Justice Department/AP/Wide World Photos; **US15** Copyright © Eric Draper/The White House/TimePix.